1990

# TOURISM POLICY AND INTERNATIONAL TOURISM

## IN OECD MEMBER COUNTRIES

ORGANISATION FOR ECONOMIC CO-OPERATION AND DEVELOPMENT

Pursuant to article 1 of the Convention signed in Paris on 14th December 1960, and which came into force on 30th September 1961, the Organisation for Economic Co-operation and Development (OECD) shall promote policies designed:

- to achieve the highest sustainable economic growth and employment and a rising standard of living in Member countries, while maintaining financial stability, and thus to contribute to the development of the world economy;
- to contribute to sound economic expansion in Member as well as non-member countries in the process of economic development; and
- to contribute to the expansion of world trade on a multilateral, non-discriminatory basis in accordance with international obligations.

The original Member countries of the OECD are Austria, Belgium, Canada, Denmark, France, the Federal Republic of Germany, Greece, Iceland, Ireland, Italy, Luxembourg, the Netherlands, Norway, Portugal, Spain, Sweden, Switzerland, Turkey, the United Kingdom and the United States. The following countries became Members subsequently through accession at the dates indicated hereafter: Japan (28th April 1964), Finland (28th January 1969), Australia (7th June 1971) and New Zealand (29th May 1973).

The Socialist Federal Republic of Yugoslavia takes part in some of the work of the OECD (agreement of 28th October 1961).

Publié en français sous le titre :

**POLITIQUE DU TOURISME
ET TOURISME INTERNATIONAL
DANS LES PAYS MEMBRES DE L'OCDE**

The Tourism Commitee has published information for more than twenty-five years, on government policies in the field of tourism. This has been accompanied by statistics on recent trends observed in the development of international tourism in the OECD area.

The first Chapter of this year's Report deals with areas of common interest and Member countries' concern, relating to recent trends in markets and policies and their implications for tourism. From now on, this Chapter will alternate, in the Report, with the traditional analysis of the development of national tourism policies in Member countries.

The present edition discusses the future of tourism in the context of the development of transport policies. This theme was developed during a Seminar held by the Tourism Committee at its bi-annual meeting held in Estoril (Portugal) in April 1990. A synthesis of the discussion is presented in Chapter I; it is supplemented by contributions made by participants to this Seminar.

Chapters II and III and the Statistical Annex study the evolution of international tourism demand and supply in the OECD Member countries. This year, on the statistical side, new retrospective tables covering 1978-1989 have been added. There is also more extensive analysis of the main generating countries for the OECD area.

Chapter IV presents information concerning the development of transport policies – air, rail, road and sea – where these affect tourism movements.

This work has been carried out using information provided by national delegations and by the delegates to both the Tourism Committee and its Statistical Working Party.

This Report was adopted by the Tourism Committee, which transmitted it to the Secretary-General with a request that he recommend its derestriction to the Council. The Council agreed on 23rd October 1990 to make it publicly available.

## Also available

NATIONAL AND INTERNATIONAL TOURISM STATISTICS — 1974–1985/STATISTIQUES DU TOURISME NATIONAL ET INTERNATIONAL — 1974–1985 (1989) Bilingual
(78 89 01 3) ISBN 92–64–03221–5                                    FF380      £45.00   US$80.00      DM155

DEREGULATION AND AIRLINE COMPETITION (1988)
(24 88 02 1) ISBN 92–64–13101–9                                    FF100      £12.00   US$22.00      DM43

TRANSPORT AND THE ENVIRONMENT (1988)
(97 88 01 1) ISBN 92–64–13045–4                                    FF95       £11.20   US$21.00      DM41

ENVIRONMENTAL IMPACT OF TOURISM (1980)
Out of print. Available on microfiche.
Price per microfiche:                                              FF20       £2.50    US$4.50       DM8

*Prices charged at the OECD Bookshop.*

*The OECD CATALOGUE OF PUBLICATIONS and supplements will be sent free of charge
on request addressed either to OECD Publications Service,
2, rue André–Pascal, 75775 PARIS CEDEX 16,
or to the OECD Distributor in your country.*

# TABLE OF CONTENTS

# INTRODUCTION

## SALIENT FEATURES OF THE RECENT DEVELOPMENT OF INTERNATIONAL TOURISM IN THE OECD AREA

International tourism has continued to expand in the OECD area, as revealed by the figures available for 1989 which all show a consistently positive trend:

- Arrivals at frontiers: + 5 per cent (+ 6 per cent in 1988);
- Nights spent in means of accommodation: + 3 per cent (+ 2 per cent);
- Receipts in real terms: + 5 per cent (+ 9 per cent);
- Receipts in current dollars: + 5 per cent (+ 14 per cent) totalling $148.2 billion in 1989.

Overall, 1989 was a good year for most countries and trends by region were also satisfactory, despite great diversity at individual country level.

Thus, all the OECD regions saw an increase in the number of tourist visits in 1989 over the previous year:

- Europe: Nights spent in all forms of accommodation, + 5 per cent; in hotels, + 3 per cent [1];
- North America: Arrivals at frontiers, + 7 per cent, and
- Australasia-Japan: Frontier movements, + 6 per cent

Once again, the trend was towards a general levelling off or shortening of foreign tourists' length of stay [2].

In a period of buoyant demand growth, this points up a relatively new development, namely a greater subdivision of holidays.

In Europe, the moderate pace of growth may be explained by a pendulum effect. The 20 million fall in nights spent in the Mediterranean region (Greece, Italy, Spain and Yugoslavia) was in large measure offset by an exceptional year in France, an increase in the British Isles (with a trend reversal in the case of the United Kingdom), a pick-up in the Scandinavian countries as a group and in Switzerland, and an acceleration in Austria.

This reorientation of tourist destinations is evidence of the shift on the international tourism scene that has

been evident for some years in Europe. It is the tip of an iceberg that goes much deeper and reflects how tourists' attitudes and expectations are changing as a result of the differing aspirations of an ever more demanding clientele that is taking advantage of the keener competition among tourist destinations.

Indeed, for the third year running, bed occupancy rates continued to fall in the Southern European countries as a group, with a 7 per cent decline in nights spent between 1987 and 1989. In 1989, despite continuing growth in Portugal and Turkey, differing rates of decline were recorded for Spain (- 11 per cent) [3], Italy (- 6 per cent), Yugoslavia (- 6 per cent) and Greece (-2 per cent). Portugal, for its part, continued to post an increase (+ 3 per cent, after the + 4 per cent and + 3 per cent respectively recorded in the previous two years), while growth was only modest in Turkey (+ 2 per cent), after the steep surges of past years, with rates running at over 35 per cent since the mid-1980s.

Recognising the impact of fluctuations in demand from Germany and the United Kingdom addressed to these six European countries, it is noted that in 1989 German tourists generally stayed away from the region (Greece and Turkey apart) and that the British did likewise (Italy and Yugoslavia apart). Clearly, aside from environmental considerations which perhaps diverted a proportion of the German clientele to other destinations, unfavourable economic conditions in the United Kingdom (notably, mounting inflation and mortgage interest rates and a weak effective exchange rate) inhibited the demand for foreign tourism coming from this country in 1989.

For France, with 43 million arrivals and 51 million nights spent in hotels (up 12 per cent and 26 per cent respectively), 1989 was an exceptional year, as a result of both good weather and a strong promotional drive, centering on the Bicentennial of the French Revolution.

Very significant headway was also made in Ireland (arrivals up 17 per cent and nights spent up 20 per

## Trend of international tourism in the OECD area
### Per cent change over previous year

| | Arrivals at frontiers[1] | | Nights spent in means of accommodation[2] | | Receipts in national currency | | Receipts in real terms[3] | |
|---|---|---|---|---|---|---|---|---|
| | % 88/87 | % 89/88 | % 88/87 | % 89/88 | % 88/87 | % 89/88 | % 88/87 | % 89/88 |
| Austria | | | 2.2 | 8.4 | 11.2 | −1.1 | 9.0 | −3.6 |
| Belgium[4] | | | 5.1 | 1.9 | 12.6 | −4.4 | 11.2 | −7.3 |
| Denmark | | | −2.3 | 13.4 | 7.4 | 3.6 | 2.5 | −1.0 |
| Finland | | | 4.1 | 9.5 | 13.1 | 5.4 | 7.5 | −1.1 |
| France | 3.6 | 12.3 | 10.9 | 26.2 | 15.1 | 28.2 | 12.1 | 23.9 |
| Germany | | | 3.5 | 11.5 | 7.7 | 9.3 | 6.3 | 6.4 |
| Greece | 2.7 | 3.9 | −2.7 | −2.0 | 9.7 | −4.4 | −3.4 | −16.0 |
| Iceland | −0.4 | 1.3 | | | 42.0 | 32.7 | 13.8 | 9.9 |
| Ireland | 15.0 | 16.5 | 15.8 | 19.9 | 16.1 | 15.3 | 13.6 | 10.8 |
| Italy | 1.6 | −0.8 | 0.3 | −6.3 | 2.3 | 1.9 | −2.6 | −4.4 |
| Luxembourg[4] | | | 2.9 | 5.0 | 12.6 | −4.4 | 11.2 | −7.3 |
| Netherlands | | | −4.0 | 6.2 | 3.8 | 12.8 | 3.0 | 11.6 |
| Norway | | | −1.3 | 2.8 | 13.1 | −4.1 | 6.3 | −8.3 |
| Portugal | 8.6 | 7.4 | 4.0 | 2.5 | 15.4 | 16.4 | 5.9 | 3.4 |
| Spain | 7.2 | −0.2 | −4.4 | −11.4 | 6.5 | −1.0 | 1.6 | −7.3 |
| Sweden | | | 0.3 | 6.6 | 11.6 | 14.0 | 5.3 | 7.1 |
| Switzerland | 0.0 | 7.7 | −0.4 | 4.4 | 4.7 | 9.5 | 2.6 | 6.1 |
| Turkey | 46.1 | 6.9 | 40.0 | 1.8 | 127.3 | 62.1 | 29.9 | −4.4 |
| United Kingdom | 1.5 | 8.9 | −3.0 | 7.0 | −1.2 | 11.2 | −5.6 | 3.2 |
| **EUROPE**[5] | 5.0 | 4.9 | 0.6 | 4.0 | | | 4.1 | 2.2 |
| Canada | 3.4 | −2.3 | 8.3 | −2.0 | 8.0 | 4.8 | 4.5 | −0.2 |
| United States[6] | 9.7 | 11.7 | | | 23.8 | 19.0 | 18.9 | 13.5 |
| **NORTH AMERICA**[5] | 7.5 | 7.1 | | | | | 16.8 | 11.7 |
| Australia | 26.0 | −7.5 | 26.0 | | 37.7 | 0.9 | 29.0 | −6.2 |
| New Zealand | 2.4 | 4.2 | 2.0 | 1.8 | −2.5 | 8.5 | −7.9 | 2.5 |
| Japan | 9.3 | 20.4 | | | 23.2 | 17.4 | 23.2 | 14.8 |
| **AUSTRALASIA-JAPAN**[5] | 14.3 | 6.3 | | | | | 20.7 | 1.4 |
| **OECD**[5] | 5.7 | 5.4 | 1.5 | 3.2 | | | 8.6 | 5.1 |
| Yugoslavia | 13.3 | 15.1 | 0.1 | −6.1 | 330.6 | 1154.7 | 46.2 | −7.2 |

1. Arrivals of tourists except in Australia, Ireland, Japan, Spain, Turkey, United kingdom and Yugoslavia where arrivals concern visitors.
2. Nights spent in all means of accommodation except in Finland, France, Luxembourg, the Netherlands and Spain where nights spent concern hotels and similar establishments.
3. After correcting for the effects of inflation. For the regional and OECD totals, the receipts of the individual countries are weighted in proportion to their share in the total expressed in dollars.
4. Receipts apply to both Belgium and Luxembourg.
5. Overall trends for countries with data available from 1987 to 1989.
6. New series for receipts and expenditure from 1984 affecting regional as well as overall OECD volumes and trends.

cent) and the United Kingdom (+ 9 per cent and + 7 per cent respectively for arrivals and nights spent). In the case of Ireland, the synergy between the new policy allying the interests of the transport and tourisms sectors (with one Ministry responsible for both since 1987) and the promotional campaign pursued to this end for some years past would seem to be paying off, particularly as regards Ireland's two main markets, the United States and the United Kingdom; in addition, since the country is often associated with so-called "green" destinations, it has exploited some major niches, notably the German market which grew by 26 per cent in 1989 (in terms of nights spent). In the case of the United Kingdom, one of the main factors explaining the 1989 trend reversal was the shift in

exchange rates to the benefit of the Americans, Irish and French, with tourist flows (in terms of nights spent) up 8 per cent, 5 per cent and 16 per cent respectively.

Despite uncertain snow conditions over the winter season which is one of the peak tourist periods for the Alpine region, the alpine countries, in particular Austria and Switzerland, still managed to attract foreign tourists who spent more nights in 1989 than the year before. The number of nights spent, virtually flat since the middle of the decade, picked up in 1989 by 8 per cent in Austria and 4 per cent in Switzerland, accounting for over one-fifth of nights spent in OECD-Europe. The number of nights spent in Germany too rose by 12 per cent over the same period.

The Scandinavian countries, for their part, totalled 25 million nights spent in 1989, up 8 per cent year on year. Major contributory factors were an increase in intra-nordic flows and in the number of German tourists. In the first case, the only exceptions were tourist flows between Sweden and Norway (with the number of Swedes visiting Norway down 10 per cent and Norwegian flows to Sweden stagnant). The number of German tourists increased to all Nordic countries and the growth ranged from + 8 per cent in Norway to + 14 per cent in Denmark; this market now accounts for over one-fifth of nights spent in this region.

In North America, the number of frontier arrivals was again up by around 7 per cent. This performance was achieved despite the 2 per cent decline recorded by Canada, mainly due to the strength of its currency and hence less competitive tourist prices.

In the Pacific region, growth continued, up 6 per cent in 1989 against 14 per cent in 1988. The deceleration was primarily due to turnaround in Australia whose performance was affected by the return to normal of tourist flows after the Australian Bicentennial celebrations and the World Expo'88 in Brisbane, as well as by the airline pilots' strike.

International tourist receipts – excluding transport – accounted for 27 per cent of services exports by the OECD area, totalling $148.2 billion in 1989 or over 71 per cent of world tourist receipts. At the same time Member country residents spent an unprecedented $164.7 billion on travel abroad. In 1989 receipts and expenditure were thus 5 per cent and 4 per cent up on the previous year, giving a negative overall tourism balance of some $16.5 billion. There was further evidence of the economic impact of tourist expenditure by several generating countries on international tourism, with the steepest real growth being recorded by Japan, the United States, Canada, Italy and Spain in descending order; Turkey, for its part, increased its spending by 58 per cent.

Tourism's foreign exchange contribution is generally expressed in dollars, the common unit of account used in the Balance of Payments. But it is also enlightening to look at receipts in real terms, i.e. excluding the impact of inflation and exchange-rate variations. These increased by 2 per cent in Europe, by 12 per cent in North America and by 1 per cent in the Pacific region, against an OECD average of 5 per cent. The countries that showed the steepest rises were France (+ 24 per cent), Japan (+ 15 per cent), the United States (+ 14 per cent), the Netherlands (+ 12 per cent) and Ireland (+ 11 per cent).

Other evidence of the growth of international tourist demand is the growth of demand for passenger transport. In the case of air traffic, the provisional figures show that, worldwide, almost 1.1 billion passengers travelled on scheduled air services in 1987, up 2 per cent on the previous year; at the same time passenger-kilometres rose 4 per cent, with passenger load factors remaining at 68 per cent; on international non-scheduled air services, which accounted for 18 per cent of the total, traffic was up by 6 per cent on the previous year. As regards passenger rail services in Europe, the most recent figures show a 4 per cent increase in traffic in 1988, the largest annual rise over the period 1970-1988. Demand for cruises is mounting at an annual rate of over 15 per cent[4].

In the 1980s, and particularly in recent years, tourism growth has placed heavy demands on passenger transport and it is therefore logical to presume that the further expansion, expected by most forecasters, will continue to have a significant impact on the transport sector. The pressure on transport is such that it has created problems that in the long run have an adverse effect on tourism. The saturation of infrastructure, congestion on the ground and in the air and the safety and security risks associated with it, as well as the impact on the environment which cannot but harm the development of tourism, have been particularly severe. This must be taken into account, locally, regionally and nationally, by the OECD countries for whom tourism constitutes a major economic activity.

It was to address these problems and related issues that the Tourism Committee organised a seminar in April 1990 on "Tourism and Transport Policy Developments; What future?". The objective of the seminar, among others, was to consider alternatives offered to Member country governments, examining opportunities and constraints and drawing from the experience gained over the last years by OECD countries in this domain. A summary of the deliberations along with a supporting analysis is given in Chapter I.

This approach is part of a wider reflection on the topic "Tourism Policy Issues to the Millennium: Keys to Successful Strategies". These discussions are fully in line with OECD objectives, namely to enable Member country policymakers to follow policy developments designed to promote economic growth by exchanging information and views, and thereby foster closer co-operation in designing and framing solutions to problems of mutual concern. This is particularly relevant for the OECD Member countries which account for the major part of world tourist activity. Subsequent reports in this series will demonstrate this.

# NOTES

1. These figures cover groups of countries of differing composition and it would be wrong to infer that demand for non-hotel accommodation has risen more than that for hotel accommodation. On analysing the situation for countries for which the two types of data are available, this assumption is found to be borne out only for the Netherlands and Sweden and the opposite is the case in Denmark, Switzerland and Turkey.

2. See Statistical Annex, Table 9.

3. Since figures on the number of nights spent in all forms of accommodation were not available, this analysis is based on the number of nights spent in hotels.

4. For more ample information on transport policy developments affecting tourism, see Chapter IV.

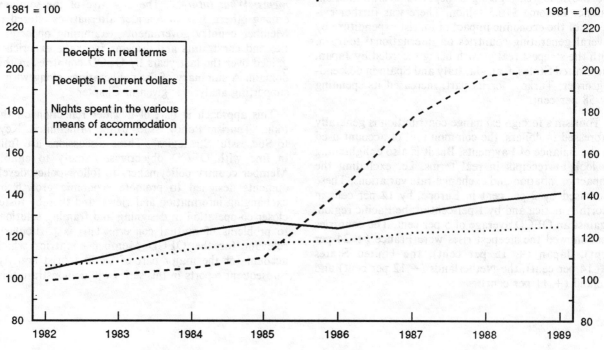

**Trends of international tourism in Europe**

Receipts in real terms

Receipts in current dollars

Nights spent in the various means of accommodation

Source: OECD.

# Trends of international tourism in North America

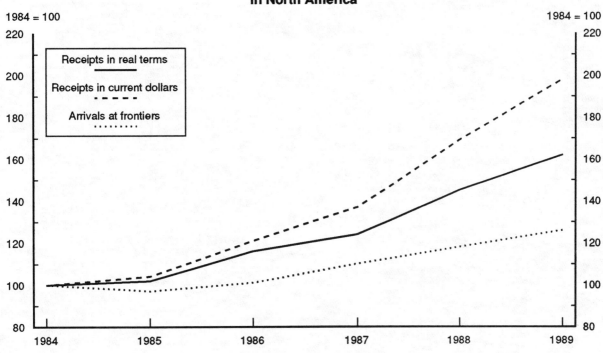

1984 = 100

Receipts in real terms
Receipts in current dollars
Arrivals at frontiers

Source: OECD.

# Trends of international tourism in Australasia-Japan

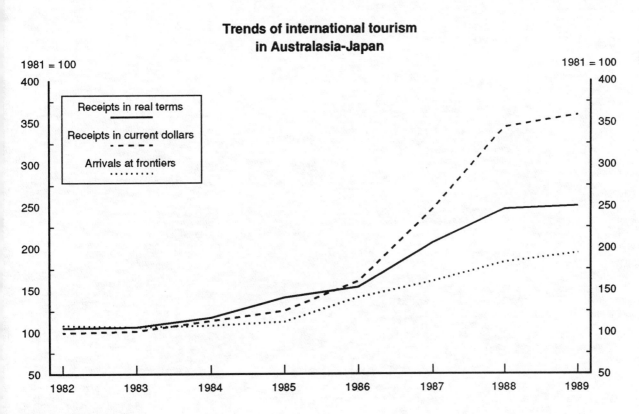

1981 = 100

Receipts in real terms
Receipts in current dollars
Arrivals at frontiers

Source: OECD.

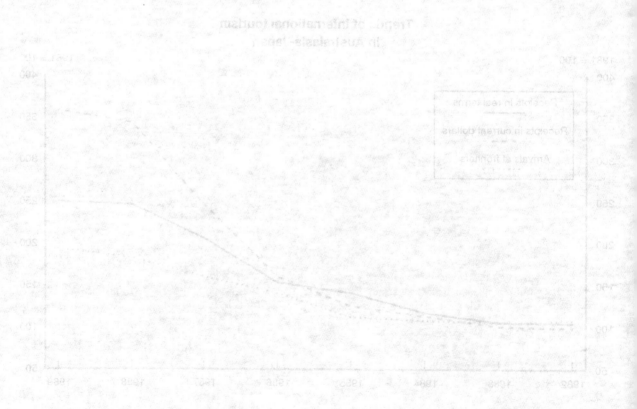

# I

# TOURISM AND TRANSPORT POLICY DEVELOPMENTS: WHAT FUTURE?

As its 57th Session, in October 1989, the Tourism Committee decided to organise a series of discussions or Seminars on "TOURISM POLICY ISSUES TO THE MILLENIUM: KEYS TO SUCCESSFUL STRATEGIES".

The objective of these Seminars is to give policy-makers in the countries responsible for most of the world's tourism trade a chance to exchange views and possibly co-ordinate their action in areas of common concern in the light of recent market and policy developments and their consequences for the future of tourism.

The first Seminar took place during the 58th Session of the Tourism Committee held in Estoril (Portugal) in April 1990 and was entitled *"Tourism and Transport Policy Developments: What future?"*.

This choice of subject resulted from a statement by the Austrian Delegate to the Tourism Committee, as follows:

"Recent developments indicate the necessity of reviewing tourism policy. Three factors in particular call for a new orientation – an international concept for tourism:

1. *The risk of a breakdown of air traffic in Europe and North America, and in some parts of East Asia, and of road traffic in Europe*: On the basis of existing forecasts, efforts to improve air traffic control and to reduce the air space blocked for military purposes will bring relief for a limited period only. Whether and to what extent the use of larger aircraft might remedy the situation has as yet to be assessed. Air space congestion during the summer season does not affect Europe, North America and East Asia alone but is a matter of concern for all countries anxious to attract tourists from these regions, since the distances to be covered make flying a must. Safety standards are deteriorating, flight plans are no longer respected, long hours of waiting and excessive delays exhaust passengers and air personnel physically and mentally.

Road traffic in Europe, and particularly on the North-South routes, has reached alarming density. Breakdowns in the traffic flow, jams on motorways and gruesome delays at frontier crossing points are ever more frequent. The resulting strain and discomfort for motorists and passengers negate the purpose of a vacation. Attention should also be paid to the growing nuisance suffered by those living close to motorways. No marked improvement is to be expected in this area either.

2. *Extensive damage to the Mediterranean, North and Baltic Sea coasts:* For many years, the threat posed by uncontrolled exploitation of coastal areas by industry – as well as tourism – has not been given sufficient attention. In the summer of 1988, and to an increasing extent in 1989, disastrous consequences came to light, with ensuing ecological breakdowns.

The attitudes of the affected countries indicate that the crux of the matter has not yet been fully recognised.

3. *The unco-ordinated tourism policies followed by some countries*: The desire to increase capacity leads to planning and constructing new infrastructures and superstructures without due attention to their effects on the environment and on traffic. Though some efforts are being made to bring this development under control, they are very uneven, both in Europe and elsewhere.

If the present situation is allowed to continue, it is likely to cause lasting damage and bring long-term recession in the tourism industry in the areas concerned. It is to be feared, for example, that potential tourists will prefer – on not always objective grounds – not to travel during their holidays. Countries offering a wide range of tourist attractions and counting on income from tourism would be faced with heavy losses and attendant negative economic consequences. OECD Member countries, as the major senders and receivers of international tourists, would suffer most.

It is imperative that the OECD Tourism Committee should discuss these problems and work out a new strategy on the ways and means to promote action by the competent bodies and organisations."

The objective of the Seminar was to address these problems and related issues and to consider alternatives offered to policy-makers of Member governments, examining opportunities and constraints, and drawing on the experience gained in recent years by OECD countries. It should be noted that the approach adopted deliberately disregards the side issues (such as the staggering of holidays) relating to congestion on departure and saturation of tourist areas on arrival.

# A. INTRODUCTION

## Background

Tourism is an important economic activity in the OECD area. It represents 26 per cent of the total export of services of Member countries, creates and maintains a number of direct, indirect and induced jobs, employing up to 14 per cent of the workforce in the service sector of certain countries, and it contributes to sustaining the economic development of many parts and regions of the OECD.

Over the last few decades, tourist spending has risen faster than general consumer expenditure, and all forecasts suggest that this trend, encouraged by the rise in purchasing power and increased leisure, will continue.

In the 1980s, the expansion of tourism put considerable pressure on demand for passenger transport and it may be inferred that further expansion of tourism will continue to have a significant impact on the transportation sector.

Yet the pressure on transport has been such that the resulting problems have in the end had adverse effects on tourism. The saturation of the infrastructure, the congestion on the ground and in the air, and the attendant safety and security risks, as well as the impact on the environment have been particularly severe and have created unfavourable conditions for the development of tourism. They will have to be taken into account at local, regional and national level in the OECD countries where tourism is an important economic activity.

## Description of the situation

The field of travel and tourism is one of the largest industries in the world, accounting for nearly $2 billion in sales in 1987, providing jobs for one out of every 16 workers world-wide, generating substantial tax revenues, creating demand for the purchase of $1 billion in goods and services from other industries, and giving rise to investments which exceed those of many key manufacturing industries[1]. Tourism is also a vital force for peace in the international community and can make a constructive contribution to policies for the protection of the physical, sociological and cultural environment. It is estimated that over three-quarters of tourism activity takes place in the OECD area, in which the main sending and receiving countries are found.

After a flattening of demand at the beginning of the 1980s, world tourism flows expanded again at an annual average growth rate of around 6 per cent. Within the OECD area, the evolution of international demand over the period 1981-1989 was characterised by well above average growth rates in the Pacific basin (with tourist flow, up 94 per cent and receipts in real terms up 148 per cent), and more modest though sizeable increases in North America (respectively 38 per cent and 37 per cent) and in Europe (25 per cent and 41 per cent). Patently tourism and tourism-related activities have flourished over the past decades.

Even if most forecasters are optimistic, predicting continuing growth of about 5 per cent a year in demand, including business travel as well as leisure tourism, the future is still uncertain, for this growth depends on certain conditions. These include a favourable economic and political climate, an integrated management approach covering all the sectors concerned, and greater government determination to anticipate events rather than simply react to them. The latter point applies particularly to developments in the transport sector.

In this context, some facts might be worth mentioning concerning the place occupied by the different modes of passenger transportation. First, travel by private car is far and away the most popular means of travel for most domestic and a great deal of regional international tourism. Second, rail travel plays a much more limited role than in the past, but could win back lost market shares. Third, air transport dominates long-distance and, increasingly middle-distance tourism. And, finally, other modes of travel (e.g. coach tours and cruises) are becoming popular, even if they are quantitatively less important.

The forecast future pattern of world travel suggests more long-haul travel, but relatively fewer visits to neighbouring countries[2]. This has already been observed in the OECD area over the period 1981-1989, "unusual" destinations, i.e. less well-known or perceived as more exotic and often outside Europe, having become more attractive, especially to well-travelled tourists. Typical of markets with a high level of departure rates are German, French and British tourism to North America (up 44 per cent) and to Australasia-Japan (up 74 per cent).

Forecasts also predict: that intra-European travel will continue to expand, as will travel within the Asia-Pacific region and between Europe and Asia (though this does not mean that their relative world shares may not decline); that there will be rapid growth in flows from Europe over the North Atlantic; that more people will take their holidays in two instalments as well as taking more short breaks and week-end excursions and trips[3].

These trends are bound to affect the travel trade in general and passenger transport in particular. Since the latter is essential to tourism, it calls for special attention from policy-makers.

## Main problems

An increase in traffic due to tourism growth puts pressure on transport and can eventually have adverse effects on tourism. And although situations in the OECD area vary widely – depending on whether regional, inter- or intra-continental movements of travellers are concerned – it seems that the problems encountered or emerging are basically of the same nature.

### Seasonality

Seasonal patterns of certain tourist flows entail overcrowding at certain times of the year, but low occupancy rates at others. At peak times, problems of congestion, safety, security and environment become markedly more severe.

### Congestion

Serious congestion problems affect most passenger transportation modes (especially road and air) at peak tourist periods, between the points of departure and arrival and at destination (resorts or cities). This often means long delays that are a waste of time and energy.

### Safety and security risks

Ensuring safety and security in transport services is a basic requirement for tourism. However, a considerable number of accidents still occur as a result of heavy traffic conditions.

### Impact on the environment

An increase in traffic may harm the environment in both quantitative and qualitative terms; it may have serious consequences unless there is integrated management taking economic, social and cultural costs into account. It may also cause different types of physical pollution (air, noise, etc.) and it often causes irreparable damage to the landscape.

All the above-mentioned problems have had and will have a considerable unfavourable impact on the perception travellers have of a holiday. This in turn might have damaging consequences on tourist destinations, particularly by spoiling their image.

# B. POLICY ISSUES

The purpose of the Seminar was to examine possible solutions to the transport problems that will face OECD member countries in the 1990s, in the light of the increasing growth forecast to occur in this segment of economic activity. In view of the widely different problems arising, this section considers separately the three main transport modes: air, road, and rail. (Little reference was made at the Seminar to sea transport, which suggests that this sector is confronted with fewer problems than the others.) The section ends with some considerations on overall policy problems relating to all means of transport. Different countries obviously face different problems but, broadly speaking, there does appear to exist ample scope for more integrated planning of transport. Although efforts in this direction have been made in individual countries and by regional

groups (e.g. by ECAC and Eurocontrol), more may need to be done in the near future.

## Travel by air

Air transport has undoubtedly benefited from the increase in tourist demand in recent decades. Air transport capacity has thus been modified – in terms of both quality and quantity – further evidence, if any were needed, that the relationship between these two sectors will always be a close one.

The industry now faces new and changing problems, partly resulting from past growth. In response to these new developments, certain member governments have adopted new policies in their civil air regulations which merit attention as a possible approach which other countries may wish to adopt, or at least consider as pointers for their overall strategies for the future.

In Australia, the government has handed over airport management to an independent body – the Federal Airports Corporation. This move has led to greater efficiency, profitability, and more timely decisions on the provision of additional infrastructure. In domestic aviation, three years' notice was given at the end of 1987 that deregulation of domestic operations would become effective in November 1990. As of April 1990, 16 carriers had stated their intention of providing domestic services. Although it is anticipated that few of these will be in a position to commence operations by November, the opening-up of the domestic market gives a prospect of keener competition, better passenger service and lower fares. As to the international network, the government announced in June 1989 that it would be adopting a new and more liberal approach in bilateral negotiations in order to encourage competition. Under this approach, tourism and trade interests as well as the interests of the national flag carriers are taken into account in formulating negotiating strategies.

In Canada, airlines have been developing the hub-and-spoke principle, whereby an airline concentrates its routes on one major airport, linking domestic and international flights. (This principle has already been applied in the United States, and certain European airlines are also adopting it.) New rules for passenger clearance have been implemented. The density of traffic to and from the US has in the past caused delays and irritation to passengers. Pre-clearance of passengers travelling from the US has therefore been introduced. This enables the American passenger to pass through immigration controls at the airport of departure in the US, thereby speeding passenger arrivals on entry at Canadian airports.

The spread of modern technology should ease the process of booking for the individual passenger during the 1990s. Airlines are developing new booking procedures. In due course, computer booking terminals will be able to take bookings not only for flights but also for accommodation, car hire, and other facilities which the passenger may wish to use during a holiday. Ultimately, this booking system could be extended into a "home service", enabling travel facilities to be booked through one's own personal TV set.

In the US, a study has recently been undertaken by the government to assess the effect – ten years after it was introduced – of the deregulation of the US domestic airline industry. Although fierce competition has resulted in some airlines being forced out of business, the study concludes that, on balance, the net result has been of benefit to consumers, by reducing fares and improving in-flight service. Internationally, the US Government has decided to allow overseas airlines to be licensed to operate new routes into secondary airports within the US. It is recognised that, by doing this, local economies around these secondary airports will benefit through the creation of new jobs.

There are three main problems which governments will particularly wish to continue to tackle in the years ahead: congestion; noise; and pollution.

Congestion has arisen as a result of the success in developing air transport. Too many aircraft are having to move around in limited space on the ground and in the air. The latest figures indicate that about a quarter of all flights depart at least 15 minutes late. The problem can be eradicated, since there is still plenty of airspace over Europe to accommodate additional flights. The infrastructure available and the need to connect different systems are the crux of the air traffic control problem. It is becoming increasingly difficult to cope with traffic growth and a country-by-country approach is still largely taken. Governments have been aware for some time of this problem and Ministers from European Civil Aviation Conference (ECAC) countries recently adopted a strategy and action programme to harmonize and integrate the operations of their air traffic control systems in the 1990s. Other OECD Member countries, because of their geographical location, do not face such a problem, with the notable exception of certain areas of the US.

Continuing growth of air traffic will require the construction of new airports. This creates problems in those countries where land space is at a premium. But efforts are being made to alleviate congestion at airports; for example, the construction of secondary runways and a reduction in night curfews have been considered.

Strong growth in leisure air traffic in the 1990s must not be taken for granted. Nor must it be forgotten that there are other modes of transport such as road and rail which could well take a greater share of the total traffic, if airline flying becomes too overburdened. Admittedly, roads too are congested, but the car is still the family favourite because it is so convenient. Rail, however, can offer a viable alternative where distances allow high-speed trains to compete effectively with air travel, particularly when it offers city-centre connections.

By their actions in recent years, governments have shown that they are aware of the increasing importance of air traffic to their economies. The problems that lie ahead are also being addressed. It is to be hoped that government departments responsible for tourist development will co-operate more closely with their counterparts responsible for air transport development. This is already the case in some Member countries, but it is essential that the problems confronting both sectors, should be clearly identified and understood by all concerned, including international organisations.

## Road transport

There can be little doubt that the share of car and coach travel will remain just as high in the future. This is particularly true in Europe and North America. For intercontinental travel, air travel will continue to predominate.

Although governments are continuing to invest significant sums in building new roads, countries with relatively small land masses are increasingly concerned about the effect of road development on the environment. The increasing level of pollution demands more attention by governments as each year passes, and solutions – even partial ones – will be sought which are bound to affect the growth of holiday traffic on the roads. Again, as with air transport, problems – and possible solutions – can be more easily identified if adjacent countries work together more closely. This is particularly important in European Member countries, which, in due course, will need to take into account the needs and concerns of Central and East European countries. Much can still be done, for instance by staggering holidays (and also travel during the week) and working with hotels and other forms of accommodation to make attractive offers.

## Rail transport

The effect of technological changes will be strongest in Europe, where shorter distances between capital cities open up great possibilities for the development of high-speed trains, as France has so convincingly shown. Until now, rail has been losing market shares to air and road. Although heavy investment will be necessary – in building new tracks and new locomotives and rolling stock – the nineties should see the railways winning back some of their lost share. Certain practical matters will need to be addressed if the full potential is to be realised, particularly on the facilities side. At present, except for the Paris-Geneva link, there are no high-speed train services between European countries. Moreover, some trains still have to stop at borders for immigration and customs clearance. Fortunately, however, in a majority of cases, governments have agreed to resolve these problems. Their initiative particularly concerns the European high-speed train system now being set up.

Traffic between the UK and nearby continental Europe should expand considerably when the Channel Tunnel opens for traffic in 1993. Although some air traffic, particularly business, may well transfer to rail, the opening of this new transport mode is expected to generate new traffic, in both directions, and the opening of a high-speed line between the tunnel and London should help even more in this regard.

## Policy considerations for the future

Tourism is expected to be the largest economic sector of the world's economy by the year 2000. Its importance therefore requires that governments give careful consideration to their overall policy for the tourism sector. Naturally the degree to which they do this will vary from one OECD Member country to another, but growth cannot be assured unless certain policy issues are addressed. The following points may deserve further consideration:

1. Since transport is fundamental in both business and leisure traffic, there should be continuing liaison between transport and tourist interests, both at governmental level and in the private sector. In many countries, this is already the case, but the importance of co-ordination cannot be stressed enough – and this also applies to intergovernmental bodies such as OECD and ECMT;

2. Because of this importance, governments, where this is not already the case, may wish to consider whether it would be appropriate for government departments responsible for transport and tourism to work more closely together:

3. Because of the rapidly changing face of tourism, where markets can quite rapidly be lost or regained, decisions on new investment need to be taken bearing in mind the relation of tourism to other sectors of the market. For example, there is little point in constructing a new airport if accommodation facilities are inadequate to cope with the increased traffic. (This does not apply to the new "hub-and-spoke" strategy);

4. Close liaison between adjoining countries is necessary if new motorways or railways are planned. Their main use might well stem from tourist demand;

5. Closer co-ordination between Member countries would be helpful when planning for future flows of traffic. Peak periods in certain member countries aggravate congestion. Much remains to be done to spread traffic across the months of the year and the days of the week;

6. Proper consideration should be given to the costs consumers should be expected to bear for transport services. For example, more work needs to be done on assessing the degree to which governments might be expected to pay (e.g. for airport development) and how much the consumer should pay. One possibility would be for governments to consider devoting more of their total expenditure to transport, in view of the above-average rate of return they could expect from such investment;

7. With increasing liberalization of air transport in Member countries, attention will need to be paid

to the benefits for the consumer. Some regulation will be necessary to ensure that conditions for fair and equal competition are preserved, without harming tourism;

8. Concern over the environment will increase during the 1990s. Tourist bodies should ensure that their voice is heard, and all the more so in that tourism can contribute to protecting and enhancing the environment, which is, after all, its basic asset.

Many of these points have already been addressed actively by Member governments. But the outcome of the discussion suggested that these issues were uppermost in the minds of countries' representatives and warrant particular attention in future discussions by the OECD Tourism Committee.

# C. CONCLUSIONS

The Tourism Committee's seminar on tourism and transport policy developments provided an opportunity for a dialogue between specialists in transport and tourism policy.

Participants noted that infrastructure and transport congestion during the tourism high season denotes a critical situation which could worsen with the exponential growth in demand forecast for all passenger transport modes up to the year 2000. Patently, too, this state of affairs could have serious effects on tourism growth. It is, for example, one of the factors that have contributed to the decline in tourist travel to some major Mediterranean countries in recent years.

To meet future needs, the following steps can be considered:

- To develop integrated policy management with the capacity to foresee and forestall these developments, rather than simply react to them;
- To promote the use of certain modes of transport (e.g. public services, rail, waterways) and discourage the use of others (e.g. highways and private cars): this might require a multimodal approach in a regional/international strategic programme, as tourists tend to use a combination of modes of transport from departure to destination country;
- To improve tourist traffic management;
- To provide a wide range of information to enable tourists to plan their journeys better;
- To extend the season(s) through appropriate incentives on both supply and demand sides;
- In the short term: to make better use of existing infrastructure (serving both transport and tourism), rather than planning to expand it when demand increases;
- In the long term: to plan infrastructure development on the basis of long-term demand projections;
- To promote and regulate multimodal services;
- To enhance international co-operation, in particular between generating and receiving countries.

It seems that a number of these possible measures to relieve congestion and remove other obstacles to growth in tourism depend on action by the authorities via resource allocation or regulatory provisions. The view could also be taken that policies designed to improve the functioning of markets are most likely to produce lasting solutions. Government intervention, whether by regulation or fiscal measures, to promote the use of certain transport modes and discourage others could create distortions elsewhere in the economy and thus only transfer problems from one area to another. Rather competition among transport services should be encouraged and pricing mechanisms which reflect the full economic costs for providing such services preferred. This might still, however, require some government involvement to ensure that effective economy-wide mechanisms were set up (e.g. trade practices commissions and environmental guidelines for operators in various industries) to protect the consumers and the social, cultural and physical environment.

It is also common knowledge that tourism competes with other sectors of activity and that, unless an efficient way can be found to allocate scarce resources (labour, capital and physical environment) among various economic activities, the benefits from tourism growth will be fewer. For countries which operate as market economies this requires first and foremost the removal of barriers to the effective operation of market forces. The reduction of protective and regulatory barriers which inhibit the capacity of tourism to compete for resources on an equal basis with other sectors of the economy is important in this regard. There is, in particular, a need to find ways of ensuring that price mechanisms operate to the maximum extent possible in decisions affecting infrastructure and that they also reflect diseconomies, for example environmental and social costs.

During the discussion a number of these proposals attracted particular attention. First, striking a new balance between the constantly growing demand for passenger transport and the available supply of capacity was seen as a priority target for the year 2000. This will necessitate co-ordinating transport and tourism policies before planning major transport infrastructures. The foreseeable growth in tourism will not come about without, at the very least, some adjustment to existing infrastructures so as to cope with peak period requirements. Such improvements, e.g. widening a motorway, extending an airport, or even building a bypass or link road, can represent solutions over the shorter term. In the longer run new infrastructures, like Europe's high-speed train system or the Channel tunnel, will be required.

But growing demand for tourism, in fact, can help to make the new infrastructures profitable, and even prompt their development. In these circumstances private capital can be attracted to fund the infrastructures and users can be charged, thus helping to speed up investment and reduce the financial burden on governments, as exemplified by Australia's new commercial organisation of airports and the motorway tolls now common in OECD Member countries.

In that context, tourism organisations and the tourism industry also have something to contribute to more effective utilisation of the existing infrastructures, in the form of a marketing policy designed to redirect tourism flows towards less overcrowded resorts, encourage off-peak tourism and inform the public more fully about the transport situation and the availability of tourism capacity via the new data transmission systems.

Another point is that the tourism boom since 1945 has been due in part to technological innovation in transport, particularly with the mass use of private cars and the introduction of the jet airliner. Tourism growth has been fostered by falling transport costs and offers of preferential fares. Airlines and railways have encouraged the public to travel as a way of earning a higher return on their ordinary infrastructure capacities. The combined effect of slower technological advance, rising energy and new infrastructure costs and the added dimension of environmental protection may be to make tourist travel more expensive and so

curb its growth. Tourism enterprises, with their high investment and staff costs, the seasonal factor which cramps profitability, and only limited scope for rationalisation, will not be in a position to offset the effects of higher transport charges. Travel and tourism may therefore become more expensive, encouraging qualitative growth while sharpening competition for an increasingly demanding clientele.

At the same time, other factors are boosting tourism and travel. Holidays are seen, above all, as the assertion of the right to free time. In addition, the economies of many peripheral regions rely on tourist demand. So care will be needed to see that infrastructure and fare policies do not discourage particular forms of tourist travel. The private car will remain the preferred transport mode for many holiday groups, especially families. Many an outlying region with little prospect of development other than through tourism is accessible only by individual road transport.

Another prerequisite for tourism to develop is an unspoilt environment. It follows that tourism itself must not be allowed to degrade the environment, which is a resource and a factor of production in its own right. Time is not a constraint for people on holiday. Large-scale links are of course necessary between urban centres and outlying tourism areas, but it would be a mistake to provide facilities that encourage hypermobility in resorts whose chief attractions are fresh air, peace and scenic views.

Lastly, the tourist/traveller will be prepared to allocate a larger proportion of his holiday budget to its transport component if the service is of high quality. This suggests that in future, to give the tourist full value for money, mass transport will need to provide a more comfortable journey.

## NOTES

1. Edwards, Anthony, "International Tourism Forecasts to 1999", The Economic Intelligence Unit, London, July 1988, 174 pages.
2. "The contribution of the World Travel & Tourism Industry to the Global Economy", The WEFA Group, prepared for the American Express Travel Related Services Company, Inc., New York, 1989, 35 pages.
3. *Ibid* note 2.

## SOURCES AND REFERENCES

EUROPEAN CONFERENCE OF MINISTERS OF TRANSPORT, Council of Ministers on "Transport and Environment", Press Communiqué after the Session, November 1989.

WHEATCROFT, Stephen, "Current trends in aviation", in Tourism Management, September 1989, pages 213-217.

HESLOP, Andrew, "Meeting the Channel Tunnel Challenge", in Tourism Management, September 1989, pages 218-220.

KORMOSS, I. B. F., "Future developments in North-West European tourism – Impact of transport trends", in Tourism Management, December 1989, pages 301-309.

ECAC, "The Future of European Leisure Air Transport", ECAC Symposium, Hamburg, 23rd-25th October 1989, 62 pages.

EDWARDS, Anthony, "Changes in real air fares and their impact on travel", in EIU Travel and Tourism Analyst, No 2, 1990, pages 76-85.

WILLIAMS, David, "European Rail Travel", in EIU Travel and Tourism Analyst, No 5, 1988, pages 5-18.

COCKERELL, Nancy, "Car Tourism in Europe", in EIU Travel and Tourism Analyst, October 1987, pages 31-42.

# D. SUPPLEMENTARY STUDIES

## AIR TRANSPORTATION AND TOURISM: COMPETING AND COMPLEMENTARY NEEDS

### Contribution of Canada

### Introduction

Canada's tourism industry is the ninth largest in the world in terms of gross receipts. The international sector is showing particularly strong growth, spurred by increasing numbers of visitors from Japan and West Germany. Canada's experience parallels that of many OECD nations. Like other members, Canada finds that tourism receipts account for a growing portion of its gross domestic product and an increasing share of final consumption. By 1987, 2.9 per cent of national consumption was spent on tourism. As a fraction of its exports, tourism is also increasing in importance. In 1987, the industry accounted for 4.2 per cent of Canada's exports. Canada's experience closely parallels that for other OECD members. It is experiencing many of the trends observed in other nations. These include an increase in international visitors, a tendency toward shorter vacations and a growing specialization and fragmentation of the market. While Canada's experience is not necessarily typical, it faces many of the same challenges and opportunities as its competitors.

Probably no industry is more essential to international tourism than aviation. The massive expansion in international travel both in and out of Canada over the last two decades is to a large extent the result of high quality and attractively priced air transport. Scheduled air services are rapidly evolving. The continuing industry restructuring, new approaches to network design, mounting congestion, new infusions of technology, the growing importance of computer reservations systems and emerging regulatory philosophies promise to accelerate this rapid transformation.

Tourism and commercial transportation have both complementary and competing needs. Both require continued economic expansion, a sensible development of supporting infrastructure and a liberal regulatory regime. However, there are areas for conflict. Policies to promote tourism are often at variance with the perceived needs of individual carriers or the industry. This paper focuses on the requirements of the aviation and tourist sectors. It highlights the important airline industry trends and how they may affect the evolution of international tourism. Although the interdependence of both industries will continue, the paper highlights areas of potential conflict.

### Airline networks

One of the most important changes in commercial aviation has been the restructuring of airline networks. Airlines are developing their systems along new approaches such as the hub-and-spoke principle. Other elements, including airport facilities, technologies, computer reservations systems and bilateral agreements become increasingly important opportunities or constraints. This section summarizes the evolution of airline networks and how it affects both the aviation and tourism industries.

#### Evolution in North America

Before 1978, the major US carriers operated long distance linear systems. At key gateways, they connected to local airlines which served specific regions. Different carriers worked together to enable a passenger to complete his or her journey. Since deregulation, the industry has transformed itself radically. Through internal growth and mergers, the surviving airlines have evolved into a set of parallel systems, each providing everywhere-to-everywhere connections. To retain as much of the revenues as is possible, the airlines discourage en route changes of airlines. Tactics include cancelling through fares, scheduling to optimize internal feed and frequent flyer plans. All of these measures have major implications for international tourism.

The hub-and-spoke system makes development of integrated, self-feeding systems possible. Most airlines operate several hubs. The principle of traffic consolidation is simple. The results are increased frequencies, enhanced connection opportunities, and the ability to serve routes on which point-to-point traffic is modest. The wave of mergers, route expansions, airline alliances and fare tactics are all designed to enhance the traffic consolidation power of the hub-and-spoke system.

The finely tuned hub-and-spoke systems emerging in the United States are unique. Other nations with different markets or a different geography have developed differently. In Canada, a programme for regulatory reform began in 1967. Creeping liberalization was the norm until 1988, when the National Transportation Act allowed a fully competitive market on intercity routes. The system remains essentially linear, with hubs located along a central axis. The hubs are mostly regional in scope. No airport, with the possible exception of Toronto, receives the frequent nationwide services typical of major US hubs.

## Requirements for a hub-and-spoke system

The hub-and-spoke system works best when there are no artificial restraints. The airline would prefer to be allowed to solicit traffic between any two cities on its system. For example, a Boston-San Francisco passenger might wish to be able to fly entirely by a Canadian carrier operating through a hub at Toronto or Montreal. A Lille-Nice passenger might also prefer a routing by a Swiss airline through a Geneva hub. This requirement of a hub system is in direct and immediate opposition to rules that reserve a nation's domestic traffic to its own carriers.

The hub-and-spoke system also requires large, uncongested air terminals and airports. Flights at a hub arrive and depart in several large clusters distributed through the day. To function as a hub, the airport must allow carriers to schedule large numbers of flights over very narrow time intervals. It is not sufficient to be able to squeeze a few extra flights in at one time or another.

## Airline alliances

Carriers are making an increasing number of interline alliances. These have always been common on international markets. Two carriers would often conclude ad hoc traffic exchange, joint fare and revenue sharing agreements. These were often part of the route exchange process. The new arrangements are different in that they are highly selective and often involve equity. They often are part of a global multi-carrier network strategy. Thus American Airlines, Qantas and Japan Airlines hold stakes in Air New Zealand, while Scandinavian and Continental also have a comprehensive agreement. There are many other examples.

Many observers suggest that the new alliances are precursors of a new international system. The new networks, it has been suggested, will operate under similar principles as the US hub-and-spoke system prototype. This, however seems unlikely. Congestion at European airports severely limits application of the hub-and-spoke system along US lines. Although many European airports play traffic consolidation roles, none have the capacity to support the highly synchronized connecting banks of flights. Nationality rules will probably continue to constrain the development of a pan-European airline network, notwithstanding the post-1992 regulatory changes.

The impact of these alliances is entirely open to speculation. Airlines are clearly posturing for a large, multinational industry and no company wants to be left out. As long as nations jealously protect the autonomy of their own airlines and limit foreign equity, the impact of the alliances is questionable. While they provide preferred feed, they are far from offering smooth, seamless connections across different airlines. They do not allow an alliance to exercise control of traffic over a global network or to develop the strong self-feeding network of a mega-carrier. The interline connections will not receive as favourable displays as itineraries requiring a single carrier. Unless the carriers already have mutually complementary networks and traffic flows, there is little point in developing an equity alliance. If the synergies are already there, an equity alliance may enhance an already strong relationship. The new alliances challenge current ownership rules, especially the association between an airline and its home nation. They may render the process for negotiating bilateral agreements, in which a political entity negotiates on behalf of its flag carriers, less relevant. But without these structural changes, the direct impact on competitive balance, traffic flows and tourism will be minor.

The modern hub-and-spoke systems can encourage traffic. They allow several carriers to offer competing routings between low density city pairs. Competition should remain strong as long as there is abundant capacity to allow entry of new competitors. Thus the needs of the tourist sector and the airlines for a liberal regulatory regime and for abundant system capacity are complementary.

## Air transport infrastructure

Throughout the world, the aviation industry faces increasingly onerous facility constraints. The lack of airport and airspace capacity has emerged as the leading constraint on the industry throughout the world. Between 1980 and 1987 international traffic has grown by 4.6 per cent annually according to the International Civil Aviation Organization. Some airports have grown rapidly, others have seen spectacular expansion. Between 1983 and 1988, total traffic at the Cairns, Australia airport has expanded by a factor of 2.6. This includes a 17-fold increase in international travel, buoyed by the growing popularity of sunny northern Queensland.

## Congestion problems worldwide

The Frankfurt, Chicago, Hong Kong, Sydney and Tokyo airports, to name only a few, have insufficient runway capacity. Others such as London and New York suffer from a shortage of ground facilities; gates, counter space, customs and immigration and security. Airspace itself is in critically short supply at major terminals throughout the world. It is particularly severe in western Europe, where a fragmented system of over 40 control centres prevents 50 per cent of all flights from operating at an efficient altitude. Today, almost one quarter of all European flights experience a delay of more than 15 minutes. A recent report estimates that congestion in Europe alone raises travel costs by $5 billion yearly. Except for a few notable standouts; Munich, Denver, Osaka, and Austin-airport construction activity worldwide is minimal. The time lag between a recognized need and new capacity is usually very long. Chicago is now planning for a new airport to open early in the next century.

Canada has significant congestion at two of its three major international gateways, Toronto and Vancouver. Delays are mounting rapidly. Canadian carriers alone lose $100 million per year in congestion at the two airports. This inevitably causes higher fares. To the tourist sector, the effects are compounded. These facilities, often the first experience a person has of Canada are crowded and often frustrating. Canada is making major new investments in additional terminal and runway capacity. These will alleviate congestion considerably but the problem will remain. Congestion, always a nuisance to the traveller, becomes a critical problem when working with well travelled, affluent, and increasingly discriminating tourists.

### Living with facility constraints

Some congestion will always be with us. Airports and air services generate a value that cannot be held in inventory. If an airline seat on a flight is unsold, it cannot be stockpiled for use later. An airport gate sitting for one hour idle represents an opportunity irrevocably lost. Airlines and airports must continually monitor their level of output, offering a prudent level of over-capacity at certain times but unable to accommodate all demands at others. An efficient air transportation system will by definition suffer from a shortage of gates at certain times, perceptible congestion and sometimes vexing delays. However, there is only a misallocation of resources if these problems become too frequent or too infrequent. Obtaining the correct balance will always be contentious.

Airport and airway congestion has become a factor that the tourist industry must learn to live with. Capacity cannot and will not be expanded quickly. Solutions might include promoting off-peak tourism. Preclearance could be used for flights bound to especially crowded facilities. A Boston-London passenger could be cleared for entry to Great Britain at Logan Airport. The passenger could then bypass the queues after arriving the next morning at Heathrow. Similar procedures are in use for Canada-United States traffic. Passengers travelling to the United States from Canada now pass US entry formalities at six Canadian airports. This system introduces legal, economic and facilities problems of its own. The airports to which these processes are shifted must have slack capacity of their own. Otherwise, the aviation industry has merely exported the congestion problem. Confining charter services to specific airports is another possibility. If, as

is expected, scheduled services continue to support the greater part of the industry, this solution will have only limited areas of usefulness.

Canada is now completing development of a third terminal for Toronto Airport. This facility, developed entirely by the private sector, has cost over half a billion dollars. It highlights the difficulties airlines and passengers will encounter in paying for the massive expansion of facilities needed worldwide. In most nations, the government traditionally has borne the larger portion of the expenses. However, the rapid increase in capital requirements will likely force much of the burden onto the private sector. Passengers will ultimately pay. How the industry attempts to optimize infrastructure needs and allocates expenses to its customers will have an important bearing on industry evolution. Peak-load pricing might be used to shift traffic away from especially critical times or seasons. Airlines might also be attracted to facilities having surplus capacity.

Both the tourist industry and the airlines have a vested interest in easing facility constraints. However, the question of how improvements are to be financed remains an important issue.

## Technology

Technological advances in aviation have drastically lowered the cost of travel. The declining costs of air transportation have allowed lower ticket prices. This has been among the most significant forces in developing international tourism. But the tourism and aviation industries must now learn to cope with a mature technology, in which drastic advances are not likely. They therefore cannot rely on steadily decreasing transportation costs but must look elsewhere for factors to drive tourism growth.

### Static technology and operating costs

Technology will remain very much as it now is. Growth will be evolutionary and use existing hardware as a base. Such time-honoured aircraft as the DC-9 and 737 are still under production, in a greatly enhanced form, a quarter-century after the first designs appeared.

Advanced materials, glass cockpits and a two-person crew have become industry standards. While widespread adoption will reduce operating costs, it will become increasingly difficult to squeeze any additional efficiency improvements from existing technology. The one possible exception is the propfan engine, a hybrid of the jet and turboprop engines. It provides potential fuel savings of up to 20 per cent, but technical problems have so far proven daunting. Much of the recent growth in recreational travel is the result of declining costs in the airline industry. The tourism industry can no longer count on continued decreases in the cost of air transportation to give cheap and effortless growth. It must examine other areas of the industry in order to find productivity increases and a lower cost structure.

### Overwater twinjets

When long-distance commercial air services first started, all aircraft used piston engines. These were unreliable and often had to be shut down in the middle of flight. Basic safety considerations required that overwater aircraft have at least four engines. When the first DC-8s and 707s entered the market, they too had four engines. Since then, improvements in engine performance and reliability make it possible for only two engines to power even wide body aircraft. In the early 1980s large, twin-engined aircraft in the 200-250 seat range started long-distance transcontinental services. Because of their reliability and operating economies, these aircraft, after lengthy study, were licensed for long-distance overwater services.

These "overwater twins" are smaller than the 300-450 passenger DC-10s and 747s that prevailed on most international routes. The twins, such as the A310, 767 and recently announced 777 have twin-engine fuel efficiencies but provide the level of comfort needed for long flights. They are well adapted to serve "long and thin" routes which have insufficient traffic to support the larger widebodies. Many citypairs e.g. Chicago-Dusseldorf, Ottawa-London, St. Louis-Paris, Pittsburgh-Frankfurt, Toronto-Copenhagen and others now receive direct services by the overwater twins. They have promoted a more fragmented Atlantic market in which interior airports challenge the established gateways of New York, Montreal and Boston. These services in turn cause fragmentation in the tourist industry. The new destinations receive greater prominence among foreign tourists and can solicit traffic more successfully than ever before. The new services greatly expand the number of businesses and public organizations having a large stake in international tourism. Cities will specialize in specific segments. Where Montreal or Toronto were once the gateways for all Canada, now the visitor seeking wilderness or scenic beauty might use Calgary, Winnipeg or Vancouver.

While common on the Atlantic, overwater twins see almost no application on the Pacific. As airlines gain operating experience, new gateways in both North America and the Orient will likely emerge; Edmonton, Fukuoka, Pusan, Sapporo and Penang. This will cause greater fragmentation, more specialization, and greater participation by interior points in Pacific tourism.

### Large widebody aircraft

The large 747s to appear in the mid and late 1990s may partially offset the decentralizing influence of the overwater twins. The new aircraft will reinforce routes now in operation and serve well established and high density citypairs. The very low costs per seat-mile will help keep fares low. Traditional high volume gateways will continue to receive the lowest fares. The low volume gateways, served by more expensive capacity, will continue to experience a disadvantage in serving the very lowest fare market segments.

### Technological lags

Although commercial aviation is a very dynamic sector, there is a lag of ten years or more in the development of new approaches to aircraft design. In 1973 the world first recognized that the era of cheap petroleum was over. New, fuel-efficient aircraft; the 757 and 767 did not enter service until the early 1980s.

Airport congestion has now become the leading industry constraint. Will airport congestion become a guiding force in aircraft design? Additional passenger exits, improved baggage and cargo aircraft: ground interfaces or improvements in on-ground servicing times could all contribute to increased gate throughput. There has already been some progress. Hinged winglets have been proposed for new widebodies so that existing lateral clearances remain valid for the latest long-winged aircraft. Airport constraints will likely become an important driving factor in aircraft design.

## Financing airline growth

The tourism industry relies on incentive fares. It has a strong interest in keeping fares low. Airlines have been able to offer attractive fares to tourists because of their premium traffic. Large numbers of full-fare business travellers provide sufficient revenues to support year-round scheduled services. Any residual seats remaining can then be sold at low cost to highly price-elastic discretionary travellers. The future will test the symbiosis between the two segments. Business passengers are becoming increasingly sensitive to fares. They are called to support a growing proportion of pleasure travellers. Airlines may be less able to market discounted seats in the future. The leisure traveller may be required to pay an increasing proportion of total operating costs. This will test the tourism industry's long reliance on low airfares to stimulate the market.

### Business and leisure travel needs

The most important feature of air tourism is the close linkage between discretionary and business travellers. Despite their completely different needs, both groups use the same aircraft and airports. There is some specialization. London's Stanstead Airport is an important charter facility. Some airlines specialize entirely in charter services and offer a distinctly different product from scheduled operators. However, most tourists share scheduled aircraft and facilities with business travellers. Scheduled operators fly to a wider range of destinations than do charter flights. They need not rely on securing a large number of leisure passengers all going to the same place at the same time. The scheduled carriers can also compete on price. They use sophisticated "yield management" techniques to estimate the number of unsold seats on any flight. They can sell any remaining inventories to leisure passengers at very low fares, effectively undercutting the charter operators. Charter flights do not have the revenue advantage of premium-fare passengers on board as well.

This will continue. As the market becomes increasingly fragmented and specialized, there will be a greater reliance on scheduled services. Large bulk charter services will lack the flexibility needed to service many small market niches. They will, of course continue to serve several large volume but seasonal markets such as Great Britain-Spain and Canada-Florida. However, it is expected that scheduled services will continue to dominate the market. While the mix of business and discretionary travellers will vary by route and season, both will continue as joint and closely-related products.

Scheduled services best meet the tourist's need for flexibility and choice of destination. But the relationship between tourist and business travel will be tested in the future. Fixed costs account for a high ratio of total expenses. Once an airline is committed to a schedule, most of its costs are already determined. The costs of serving an additional passenger are very low and only a small fraction of even the lowest priced ticket. This gives scheduled carriers a powerful incentive to reduce fares in order to fill their aircraft. Much of the past development of international tourism results from this process. Business travellers are showing increased sophistication and greater price sensitivity. Many now travel on excursion fares.

### Tourism development and declining yields

As a result, effective fares are falling in many markets. Between 1984 and 1988, the yield (revenue per passenger-mile) of US domestic carriers fell by 6.2 per cent before inflation. The decline in yields is especially troublesome for the tourist industry. Traditionally, the high priced full fare segment has supported leisure travel. Business travellers have provided the steady, year-round source of lucrative traffic that allows the airlines to stay in business. Any additional seats can then be sold at incentive rates to leisure travellers at pure profit. If the airline can prevent business passengers from travelling at the low fares paid by tourists, it can offer a quality service to both groups at a profit.

This is when continued growth in tourism poses a problem. As the proportion of people using incentive fares increases, yields will continue to decline. Price-sensitive business travellers will only exacerbate the problem. As average yields fall, carriers will have increasing problems remaining profitable and financing expansion. If the airline industry hopes to expand, leisure travellers must pay a larger share of the costs. They can no longer rely on cross-subsidization by full fare segments. Unless full fare travel receives a major stimulus, the scope for reduced airfares for discretionary segments will be modest.

### Yield management

Yield management may postpone the problem of declining yields. Yield management systems allow an airline to allocate the capacity of individual flights to specific fare classes. It maximizes the system-wide revenue through price discrimination. An airline can offer, and control, a larger number of individual fares. The ideal is to sell every seat on a flight, with each seat priced at the maximum the passenger is willing to pay. Although yield management is a potent force in increasing revenues, it does not protect an airline against erosion in the highest fare levels. If the return on the highest priced segments experiences dilution, discretionary travel will suffer, with or without yield management.

### Frequent flyer programmes - an opportunity?

Many airlines, especially in North America, have frequent flyer programmes. They are an important part of a strategy to attract and keep a loyal customer base. The spread of FFPs to other parts of the world is still a matter of speculation. If one carrier launches a programme, its rivals will likely introduce competing plans of their own. Whatever the degree of its adoption elsewhere, the frequent flyer programmes offer intriguing opportunities for tourism development.

Many passengers have accumulated a large supply of points and can travel with their families almost anywhere for free on their next vacation. With accumulated points, distance is no obstacle. Many people who otherwise could not or would not consider vacations to very distant destinations can now plan much more ambitious travels. Some destinations once too distant to compete effectively for certain market segments have seen this disadvantage lowered greatly by the FFPs. FFP members are mostly professionals and have above-average incomes. They are a large, prosperous and very attractive tourist market.

But there is a downside. As people who already spend a lot of time in the air, they may have an inclination not to fly unless absolutely essential. Frequent flyers are very demanding and less tolerant of missed connections, airport congestion and other familiar problems. They require a much higher level of service than persons who travel less often. A second problem occurs when tourism marketers try to develop tour packages with the airlines. The airlines are unlikely to encourage passengers who pay no fares to fly. Unless they can be convinced that reduced FFP liabilities are in their best interests, they will not help. Perhaps certain seasonal or low-yield markets may offer a place to reduce FFP accounts. The FFP does offer a new and very lucrative segment, and tourism promoters should find a creative way to develop it.

## Airline computer reservations systems

The computer reservations system (CRS) has grown in importance and complexity. Once merely an in-house tool that allowed airlines to control seat inventories, they have now become the premier channel of distribution for air services. Without a listing on the major CRS an airline cannot obtain a high profile for its products.

### Reservations systems bias

The computer reservations systems used by airlines have assumed a great strategic importance. The carrier that operates the system can manipulate flight displays to the detriment of its competitors. Controlling bias and safeguarding competition have absorbed considerable energy throughout the world. The key to a biased, or unbiased display is the "algorithm" that prioritizes connections. The computer surveys all routings between any city-pair and displays them on the travel agent's screen in the order specified by the algorithm. The algorithm considers time of departure, on-time performance, whether an option uses a nonstop or connecting flight and other factors. An "unbiased" display uses an algorithm that examines objective factors and whose ranking is independent of the airlines offering the flights.

A connection that requires a change of airline en route usually receives a much lower display than an online routing. The computer projects a primary display of connections to the workstation of the travel agent. This screen may show only online connections. A very high percentage of all bookings are made from the primary screen. If the travel agent wants to consider interline connections, he or she must enter extra keystrokes to call up additional displays. Travel agents often do not call up secondary screens and as their commissions are based on total sales they have little incentive to search for lower passenger fares.

The online/offline distinction is of greatest concern to international tourism. An en route change of carriers is still essential for many long haul passengers. A passenger travelling from Germany to a point in the interior of the United States can travel all the way on a US carrier and connect at a large American hub. He or she could also travel by Lufthansa to a US gateway, and change carriers. The computer will give a poorer display to the second alternative because it requires a change of airline en route. Even if Lufthansa and its connector offer an attractive joint fare, design their schedules to connect smoothly, and provide an efficient connection, they will face a daunting competitive hindrance. The travel agent's screen will not give the carriers the prominence they have worked for and will invariably favour the American carrier. Visitors may pay more than they need to and competition will suffer.

### Displays for interline connections

Many nations are addressing the issue of CRS bias. Although the International Civil Aviation Organization and the European Community are developing standards, a consensus on these issues remains far off. The way the algorithm treats interline connections in particular should be reviewed. A smooth, rapid and co-ordinated connection with attractive joint fares should have a more favourable display than one between hostile carriers who do everything they can to make it impossible. There is thus a great need to revise the CRS algorithms so that high quality connections, albeit with a change of airline receive a prominence commensurate with the convenience they offer the public. Another possibility is to provide improved displays of connections over which joint fares are available. This will encourage competition to non-gateway points.

A final possibility is to display connections according to fares. Although the fare is a critically important criterion in selecting a flight, the CRS do not rank competing routings on the primary screen in this manner. Systems will soon be available that can display the lowest priced ticket available on each flight.

The large US airlines have a strong incentive in retaining the present system of algorithms. Only an American carrier can offer online services from an overseas city to anywhere in the United States. Since the United States is a large and geographically fragmented market, its carriers have a vested interest in the status quo. Foreign carriers, and the tourist industry, could benefit from a better display of quality interline connections.

### Tourist information systems and the CRS

Tourists have different needs from business travellers. They require a much wider range of information; nearby recreational facilities, local attractions, climate data so that they can select the best time of the year to visit, etc. The need for even more extensive information will result as the market becomes increasingly specialized and fragmented. A visitor to the Northwest Territories might want information on the spectacular Nahanni Valley and how to get there. This will include data on tour outfitters, the required level of canoeing proficiency, conditions for joining a tour group, a description of wildlife encountered and almost anything else. An airline CRS, with links to travel agents everywhere, is one of the best means to distribute this information around the world.

The current CRS networks now play this role only to a limited extent. Costs of listing services on an airline CRS may be prohibitively high for smaller tourist operators. The structure of queries also needs modification. A CRS booking a flight assumes that the passenger already knows where he or she wishes to go; it tells the person how to get there. What happens if the potential tourist wants to view wildlife but does not care where? An African safari thus competes with a visit to India's game reserves, or a trip to Canada's Arctic to see polar bears.

The airlines may have difficulty in upgrading their systems into the comprehensive tourist information data bases the industry requires. However, a way should be found to exploit the trends in the CRS. One approach is to develop data bases and software which can be accessed by an airline CRS. Several nations have developed systems to promote their own industries. A common, unbiased international data base and set of computer protocols would permit any organization of any nation to have its services listed in a single transnational tourism data base. Besides allowing opportunities for all to participate, it may be more acceptable to the owners of the CRS networks. They may wish to provide general services, useful for all their flights, rather than information favouring a specific nation.

There is no reason why the airlines could not host a comprehensive CRS and tourist information system. However, these companies may have an inappropriate focus or corporate culture to develop the CRS fully. A firm dedicated to the CRS as its primary business might be better qualified and faster to spot new opportunities. This would be a strong argument for the airlines to divest of their CRS.

## Bilateral air agreements

The system of bilateral agreements continues to constrain the natural evolution of the industry. It was developed to reconcile many competing goals including safety, national autonomy, solvency of the flag carrier and economic development. A major objective was to protect an infant industry from excessive competition. It reflected the desire of most nations to have a national airline making a presence throughout the world. Through ensuring a rigorous balance of benefits, it protected fragile route networks from economic realities.

Today's airlines are hardly an infant industry, yet many operators continue to be protected by bilateral agreements. The tourist industry and the airlines often cannot attain a consensus on bilaterals. Different airlines have entirely different strategies and commercial interests. Aggressive airlines of the United States and

southeast Asia, supported by strong networks or a favourable cost structure, may favour liberalization. Others, more poorly positioned, wish continued barriers to entry. Many persons, however liberal, might not wish to see the end of their national airlines. This would be a consequence of any fundamental and global liberalization.

### The trade-offs

Consider a nation attempting to develop its tourism industry while promoting the interests of its national airline. While allowing foreign entrants to boost its tourism industry meets the first objective, it harms the second. Opportunities for it under the liberalized agreement may be insufficient to compensate it for the loss of traffic. The national carrier has a large vested interest against the new entrant and can usually calculate the loss it would incur. This, expressed in revenue now being received, may be substantial. It must lobby hard against the change. The national tourist industry might benefit more than the national airline loses. However, its benefits will be spread thinly over many businesses. No one entity may have a strong incentive to lobby in favour of the change. Any benefits can be expressed only as future revenues or opportunities rather than today's cash flow. Thus a beneficial change may be defeated by, in Milton Friedman's words, "the tyranny of the status quo."

### Fifth freedom rights

One major problem with bilaterals is just that; they are bilateral. An airline seeking to operate a new route faces all manner of problems because of the existing structure. For example, it may seek so-called fifth freedom rights; the ability to carry traffic between third countries. Many international services are dependent on this traffic. A Canadian carrier might, for example attempt to operate a Canada-Middle East-South East Asia route. The airline would like to carry traffic between the Middle East and South East Asian countries. To do so, it must negotiate rights with both third nations. If the Middle East nation grants it rights, but the South East Asian nation refuses, the airline is simply out of luck. Often, one nation will grant another blanket fifths to an entire continent, carefully excluding all nations which might have any inclination to grant fifth freedom rights. Once again, the needs of the tourism industry are subordinated to protecting small and vulnerable national carriers. A multilateral system of negotiations seems preferable on the surface. A group of nations could, for example, establish a common policy for granting fifth freedom rights to outsiders. This is what Europe is attempting to do. However, nations have such disparate needs and objectives that they will likely be unable to agree. Canada and the United States, for example, have been unable to revise substantially their bilateral for over fifteen years because of fundamental differences. While some form of multilateral negotiation seems superficially appealing, it is often unrealistic in practice.

### Cabotage

Cabotage is another contentious area. Cabotage is the right of a foreign carrier to carry the domestic traffic of another nation. A passenger flying from Frankfurt to Hamburg on Air New Zealand would be an example of cabotage. Cabotage is a major element of the new European regime and has also been discussed between Canada and the United States. Here, however, the legal and political obstacles are enormous. A cabotage policy is the cornerstone of a single, unified airline market within any group of states. It is only consistent with a removal of foreign ownership and control restrictions. It also ends the close legal and political association between an airline and its respective nation of establishment.

The difficulties of negotiating a cabotage agreement are enormous. Some nations, like the United States, Canada, India and Australia have large domestic markets. Others, the extreme example being Singapore, have no domestic services whatsoever. They can only trade additional fifths for cabotage, with the pitfalls mentioned above. The balance of benefits arguments becomes especially bewildering. The opportunities for operating a route profitably depend not only on the traffic base but on the strength of incumbent operators. This is hard to measure and trade off in negotiations. The high density New York-Los Angeles route is, on the surface, very attractive to a foreign operator. However, it must compete against domestic carriers having a formidable capacity and frequency advantage. The value of this opportunity may be zero. However, a much smaller route which lacks strongly entrenched carriers could be very profitable.

As Europe moves to a single market, cabotage will be a complicated and high profile issue. The degree to which nations cede a degree of control over domestic routes remains to be tested. A particularly complicated, and possibly acrimonious issue is how intra-Europe traffic rights of non-EC carriers are to be accommodated in the new order. Whatever the outcome of post-1992 Europe, the chance for a widespread move to exchanging cabotage rights is remote. It is opposed by powerful vested interests. Cabotage is unlikely unless preceded by a comprehensive integration of other sectors. Control of transportation continues to be a crucial element of a nation's perceived autonomy. As economic integration progresses, air transport will probably be one of the last sectors included.

While some carriers would support a liberalization, many others would oppose it. Each nation must therefore reconcile the needs of its airlines with local development and tourism imperatives. There is no simple solution; a nation-by-nation examination is essential.

## Summary

In summary, one can see the following trends:

### Networks

- The extension of the airline hub-and-spoke system to countries outside the United States will be moderated by geography, bilateral agreements and infrastructure constraints.
- The new set of international airline operating and equity alliances will have only a moderate impact on growth of multinational hub-and-spoke systems. The alliances will not promote global self-feeding networks without other major legal and regulatory changes in the nations involved.

### Air transportation infrastructure

- Airport congestion is inevitable. The optimal level of congestion will remain contentious.
- Because of the long lag in developing aviation infrastructure, tourism planners must assume increasing facility constraints.

### Technology

- The airline industry has a relatively mature technology. The tourism industry must rely on non-aviation components for any reduction in operating costs.
- A one-time decrease in airline operating costs may be possible as propfan aircraft begin operations.
- Overwater twin-engined widebody aircraft will allow the development of new international gateways and routes.

### Financing airline growth

- The growing volume of leisure travellers and greater price sensitivity of business passengers will make it more difficult for carriers to attain profitability and may limit further discretionary fare reductions.
- Yield management systems will only postpone the problems of a declining business passenger yield.

### Frequent flyer programmes

- Frequent flyer plans offer opportunities for high yield tourism. The industry should develop strategies to appeal to this segment.

### Computer reservations systems

- New methods are needed for ranking competing services on CRS displays, so that high quality interline connections can be presented fairly.
- Fare information can and should be a factor in ordering flights on a computer display.

*Regulatory*
- The regime of bilateral agreements often results in a conflict between the needs of airlines and the health of the national tourist industry.
- Widespread cabotage rights are unlikely through the next decade because of complex legal, economic and balance-of-benefits issues. Cabotage will likely be preceded by close economic integration in other sectors.

- Multilateral agreements, while attractive in principle, will be difficult to achieve in practice because of diverse interests.

How these trends will finally evolve and shape international tourism remains a subject for speculation. However, the issues highlighted in this paper will be important driving forces through the next decade. They will provide a challenge to everyone concerned.

# REMOVING THE BARRIERS - A MARKET APPROACH TO THE PROVISION OF AVIATION SERVICES

## Contribution of Australia

### Introduction

Over the last decade, the Australian Government has recognised that if industries are to be competitive in the world marketplace, they need to be freed from regulatory restraints and protective barriers which have characterized their operations to a greater or lesser degree for decades.

While it is not possible to remove all constraints instantly, the government has in recent years made considerable progress in this direction. It has developed an agenda for microeconomic reform of a number of major industries ranging from banking to motor vehicle manufacture; from iron and steel to shipping and the waterfront; and from telecommunications to aviation.

Of particular interest to the Seminar held by the Tourism Committee is the changes that have been made in the aviation industry. Recognising the importance of aviation to the tourism industry and the economy generally, the government has introduced several separate but integrated reforms in the aviation area. These have involved reforms to international aviation, to domestic aviation, and to the operation of major airports, including the provision of airport infrastructure.

The broad approach in each case has been to minimise the degree of government intervention.

This paper briefly outlines developments in each of the three subject areas, having regard to the benefits of the chosen approach from a tourism perspective, as well as an overall national economic perspective.

### Airports

In 1984 the Federal Government decided to move towards the establishment of a body to run Australia's major airports. In June 1986, the Federal Airports Corporation (FAC) came into being and on 1st January 1988, the FAC took over responsibility for running 17 of Australia's major airports, including most of our international gateways.

The FAC is not a private organisation – it remains government owned – but its charter is to act in a manner as if it were a fully commercial operation. Government powers over the FAC are relatively limited for all practical purposes, and are rarely exercised in a manner so as to impinge upon the day-to-day operations of the FAC.

The government's stated objective in establishing the fac was "to enhance the efficiency of airport operations, to encourage innovative and commercial use of airport terminals by airlines, and to put in place the most efficient possible regulatory regime".

Clearly, the previous arrangements where airports were run as part of the government bureaucracy through the Department of Transport/Aviation, was not considered to be an "efficient regime".

In addition to its stated objective in establishing the FAC, it can be assumed that the government saw benefits in removing airport funding and in particular the funding of additional infrastructure developments from its own budget process, and from the political arena.

In this context it is worth noting that over the twelve years from 1974/75 to 1985/86, the percentage of total attributable costs in the aviation industry which were actually recovered from users was as little as 55 per cent and never rose above 68 per cent. By way of comparison, in the first full year of operations (1988/89) the FAC made an operating profit of A$44 million, paying a dividend to government of A$13 million.

There can be little doubt that the requirement to fund major infrastructure developments through the budget process under successive governments had led to an inadequate allocation of resources to developments at some airports. Another effect of the previous arrangements, and it must be acknowledged a far less common one, was that in seeking to gain political advantage in a particular region, a government might allocate an excessive level of resources to airport infrastructure, leading to an overdevelopment of facilities. In both of these situations, the level of development had little if anything to do with the actual requirements of the marketplace and the demand for airport services.

By way of illustrating the extent to which airport development had suffered as a result of the processes described above, the FAC has within twelve months of taking over its initial 17 airports (six more have now been placed under its control) developed a capital expenditure programme for the years 1988/89 to 1997/98 totalling over A$2.6 billion. This level of proposed expenditure compares with a total asset base in December 1987 for the FAC of only A$1.1 billion. It is arguable that it is most unlikely that such a level of works could have been contemplated had funding been carried out through the government's own budget process.

Not only has the FAC planned for future development in response to anticipated growth in demand, but it has rigorously sought to obtain improvements in the efficient use of existing infrastructure. In some cases, such as Sydney's Kingsford Smith Airport, these measures have effectively been forced on the FAC because of increasing congestion resulting from the inadequacy of the existing facility. One of the chief measures being contemplated is the introduction of a variable pricing regime for landings/take offs, with prices related to the level of demand at peak and off-peak periods, to help ensure optimum utilization of available runway capacity.

## Domestic aviation

In October 1987, the government announced that 35 years of detailed economic regulation of Australia's interstate (domestic) aviation industry was to come to an end.

Under a long-standing agreement with the two major domestic airlines, three years' notice of termination was required before the so-called "two airlines policy" could be brought to an end. Deregulation of domestic aviation in Australia will therefore take effect from 1st November 1990.

The government's stated objective in ending the duopoly in the provision of domestic trunk air services is to create an environment which will foster:

- Increased responsiveness by airlines to consumer needs;
- A wider range of fares and types of services to provide enhanced travel opportunities;
- Increased competition and pricing flexibility leading to greater economic efficiency in the industry; and
- A continuation of Australia's world-renowned aviation safety record.

Ironically, the regulatory framework which had been put in place 35 years previously had been established to foster the development and growth of the "infant" aviation industry in an orderly manner, and to promote "fair and workable" competition between the airlines and discourage monopolization or uncompetitive practices within the industry.

While it may have served its purpose originally, the regulatory framework had, by the 1980s, not only failed to encourage "fair and workable" competition, but had in fact made it extremely difficult for any competition at all to take place.

Announcing the termination of the old agreement the government stated:

"The government is well aware that unlimited benefits do not always flow from the operation of market forces. However, it is clearly the case that the existing economic regulatory environment does not actively encourage industry efficiency, and is not an appropriate basis for the further development of the industry through the 1990s."

Under the old two airlines agreement, only the two major domestic carriers, Ansett and Australian Airlines (the latter of which was and still is government-owned), were permitted to operate on the major trunk routes. This restriction was backed up with prohibitions on the importation of large, jet aircraft. There were controls exercised over the number of seats each airline could operate vis-à-vis its "competitor" and fares were regulated. In this latter case, this was via an independent committee, which based its determinations on the cost structures of the two airlines, leaving little incentive for either to pursue efficiency gains, as extra costs could invariably be passed on to consumers through fare increases.

As a result of all these factors, the two airlines offered identical fares, (almost) identical timetables and route schedules, and competed only in terms of the level of service provided.

In addition, there was little incentive for either airline to actively chase the leisure travel market as, with seat numbers effectively limited, it made more sense to pursue the higher yield business travel market. As a result, the leisure air travel market in Australia remains relatively untapped.

Clearly, such a situation in an industry as vital to tourism and the economy generally (particularly in a country as large and sparsely populated as Australia) was not acceptable, and was inconsistent with the government's overall approach to industry reform.

It is difficult to predict the likely outcome of the deregulation of domestic aviation in the Australian market. Overseas experience, particularly that of the US, suggests that a possible scenario is a relatively short-lived period of intense initial competition, characterised by deep discounting and other fare initiatives, followed by a period of consolidation. If the US model is followed, this period could see many of the new entrants absorbed by the longer-established, bigger and more financially secure carriers who have been able to ride out the competitive storm.

Whether or not this eventuates is problematical, and whether or not at the end of such a process there are once again only two domestic carriers in Australia in a sense does not matter. What is important is that there is the opportunity for new entrants to come into the industry, to challenge existing operators. At the very least, domestic aviation deregulation in Australia will provide airlines with that opportunity.

### International aviation

Also as part of the government's agenda of microeconomic reform, the Minister for Transport and Communications announced in June 1989 a new, more liberal approach by Australia to international aviation arrangements.

His statement to Parliament entitled "International Aviation: Maximising the Benefits" outlined a new approach to the negotiation of air services within the existing framework of bilateral agreements which characterise international aviation.

The objective in adopting a new, more liberal approach was stated as seeking to secure "the best balance of overall benefits for Australia, including a bigger slice of the world's tourism and trade".

In making this statement, the government acknowledged that historically, and in common with many other countries, the interests of the national carrier had tended to dominate when the government was considering entering into new air services agreements or amending existing ones. Implicitly, a degree of protection had been afforded to the carrier (Qantas) by limiting the degree and scope of competition on many routes.

Often, little consideration had been given to the other benefits which can flow from an expansion of aviation services, such as increased volumes of inbound tourism and improved trade links.

The new approach does not mean the adoption of an "open skies" policy, whereby any foreign airline could fly to Australia even if their government denied the Australian carrier a fair chance to compete on an equal basis. Neither does it mean the abandonment of all controls over capacity and route entitlements within specific agreements.

What it does mean is demonstrating a readiness to encourage new services by foreign carriers where these will lead to improved tourism and trade opportunities for Australia; giving airlines greater commercial freedom to introduce new services and respond more quickly to market demand; adopting a more forward-looking approach to capacity, with services agreed to up to one or two years in advance of current requirements; maintaining a liberal international passenger charter policy; approving supplementary services promptly and, where required, well in advance; and exercising minimal control over air fares.

Under such a policy, Australia might well grant new services to a foreign carrier where Australia can win realisable longer term benefits of increased tourism, or flights for the foreign carrier might be traded for access to new destinations for the Australian carrier, even where Qantas may not plan to use those rights for some time. In short, there is likely to be a greater receptiveness on the part of the government to requests by foreign carriers to fly to Australia.

In giving effect to this policy, the government will include a wider range of views than had previously been taken into account in determining its negotiating strategies, particularly the views of tourism and trade, as well as those of Qantas.

In addition to the liberalization announced in June 1989, the government is currently reviewing its international charter policy to see whether there is scope for further liberalization of this aspect of its international aviation policy, with a particular view to encouraging greater flows of inbound tourism. The government will also be considering the recommendations of the recent Industries Commission report on Travel and Tourism which could lead to further liberalization in the regulation of international aviation.

While it is perhaps too early to assess the effectiveness of the new approach, since its adoption there have been new Air Services Agreements negotiated with Switzerland and Korea, and talks are scheduled with a number of countries for the introduction of new or additional services. The benefits to tourism and to the broader economy are difficult to measure, but there is every indication that the new approach will encourage greater inbound tourism flows and result in broad economic benefits.

### Conclusion

During the last five or six years, the Australian government has taken a number of major decisions in the aviation sphere, all of which can be broadly described as aimed at encouraging a more market-oriented approach by participants within the industry.

There have been three distinct but closely related elements to this strategy: the creation of a private enterprise style organization to run major airports on a fully commercial basis, the deregulation of domestic aviation and the adoption of a new, more liberal approach to international aviation arrangements.

With the possible exception of the running of airports which already seems to be demonstrating significant efficiency gains and more rational decisions on resource allocations to this sector, it is too early to assess the benefits of this new direction in aviation, and indeed in the case of domestic aviation, the announced reforms have yet to take effect.

Experience in Australia and overseas has shown, however, that government economic regulation of, or intervention in, most industries can create inefficiencies and lead to distortions in resource allocation.

Tourism as an industry is vitally dependent on the transport chain. In the case of a geographically isolated island country such as Australia, which also has vast distances between tourism attractions and major population centres, an efficient aviation sector is critical. If tourism is to prosper and to optimize its contribution to the national economy, it is essential that the correct decisions be made in providing resources to the aviation sector and that those resources are then utilised efficiently.

It is believed that the changes which have been put in train in recent years will now enable this to take place.

# AIR TRANSPORT: LIBERALIZATION VERSUS GROWTH CONSTRAINTS

Contribution of
International Air Transport Association – IATA

International air transport is enjoying a modest but steady boom. The year 1987 marked the first for which International Civial Aviation Organisation (ICAO) reported over one billion scheduled passenger journeys annually. In 1988, that figure was already surpassed by 5 per cent or, more impressively, by an additional 50 million scheduled passenger journeys. By the end of this century, it is expected that the annual schedule passenger journey figure will have reached two billion, twice the 1987 figure. While the airlines intend to buy or lease several hundred new aircraft to cope with this doubling of traffic over the coming decade, it seemed until recently that the infrastructure in which these aircraft would operate would largely be expected to cope as it presently stands.

The most recent IATA forecasts cover the period 1989-93 and reveal that passenger and freight traffic on international scheduled services are expected to show, worldwide, an average annual growth rate of about 7 per cent. In line with past trends, the forecasts show that Asia and the Pacific will remain the fastest growing region during the period with growth forecast to average 9 per cent to 11 per cent annually. This compares with growth forecast to an average of 6 per cent for Europe and North America and 3 to 4 per cent for traffic from Europe to Africa.

There is a common perception that liberalization will increase the level of traffic growth, though historically this is not always proven. For example the growth rate in the United States in the nine years following domestic deregulation was at 6.4 per cent, not dramatically higher than the 5.8 per cent experienced in the previous nine years. Similar comments could be made in comparing the seven European country pairs with which the UK made liberal bilateral agreements compared to the rest of Europe. There have been some striking developments however. Between the UK and Ireland, a relaxing of market entry and tariff controls in 1986 and of capacity control in early 1987 was followed by a 29.3 per cent increase in scheduled passenger traffic in the following year. In any event, in the absence of growth constraints, one can certainly expect traffic growth to at least match the IATA predictions for 1989-93 and probably surpass them as the historic growth trends would suggest.

What are the constraints which could hinder this growth? To this end, it is appropriate to concentrate on the situation from a European perspective, as it is the area where the largest number of variables is at work. On the assumption that the economic and political situation remains stable, the main constraints to growth are twofold: environmental and infrastructural, though they are interlinked.

At the moment, the chief environmental constraint is that of aircraft noise. The first noisy generation of jet transports such as the Boeing 707, DC8 and Caravelle have all but disappeared from the OECD area in their original form. Even the second generation jets, such as the Boeing 727 and DC9, have ceased production since 1988 and account for a quite rapidly declining percentage of airline fleets. In many airlines, these so-called

Chapter 2 aircraft have already disappeared altogether. Nevertheless, in most airlines, they will form a substantial though reducing part of fleets for the next five to ten years.

Growing air traffic in recent years and greater environmental awareness have led to increasingly vociferous campaigns by communities around airports to cut back on aircraft noise. Notwithstanding the fact that some of these communities owe their existence to the airport itself, the political fact is that a geographically coherent group of people can exercise more political clout locally than a vastly larger number of passengers who are drawn from a much wider area. This is not to say that airlines should not recognise the need to be sensitive to the problems of aircraft noise. They should be and they do, but there is a need to balance environmental benefits against the requirement to maintain sufficient growth and stability to fuel economic advancement. Responding to pressures for early action, both European Civil Aviation Conference (ECAC) and the European Community (EC) introduced rules which will prevent airlines in Europe from buying additional Chapter 2 aircraft into the region. These rules take effect late in 1990. While they will not have any immediate effect on the noise climate, they may have an adverse effect by reducing the saleability and therefore asset value of a large part of some fleets and oblige airlines to hold on to the older aircraft longer. The affected airlines will also need to fund large sums of money when it comes to buying new. While this may increase costs and therefore fares, it should not directly increase operational limitations until operating bans are introduced forcing a cut back in Chapter 2 operations which will redirect the additional aircraft use from traffic growth to capacity replacement. ICAO was unable to reach a consensus at its 1989 General Assembly on the question of an implementation date for a Chapter 2 operating ban. It will hold a special meeting in October 1990 to readdress the issue but the EC and some non-EC countries have indicated that environmental pressures may force them to pre-empt the ICAO Special Assembly.

Another environmental issue which is rapidly coming to the forefront is that of exhaust emissions. For the car industry, there is an admirable, if costly, remedy: the catalytic converter or "catalyser". Unfortunately, this technology is not applicable to jet engines. Though the latest generation of jet engines use considerably less fuel than their predecessors, they also emit far less hydrocarbons and carbon monoxides, two important pollutants. Unfortunately, because of their higher operating temperatures, the new engines produce about the same quantities of nitrous oxides (nox) as the older ones. because nox is a contributor to acid rain and to human health problems, steps have been taken in some countries to freeze nox emission levels. even though aircraft are responsible for only a very small proportion of nox emissions (roughly 1 to 2 per cent of the total), they are going to be caught by this freeze without having any timely technological solution available. if broadly applied, the freeze could have extremely far reaching consequences for traffic development by capping flight frequencies at present day levels.

The most immediate constraint on growth, one which is already making itself felt, is that of airport and airspace congestion particularly in Europe where the proportion of flights delayed by more than 15 minutes doubled between 1986 and 1989 to approximately 24 per cent. The cause is twofold: firstly, the inability of the air traffic control system to handle the traffic flow, and secondly, the inability of certain airports to handle the traffic volumes. At present, the public focus has been on the costly delays that so particularly affect the peak tourist traffic. In IATA, however it was realised that the congestion would soon reach the point where traffic expansion would be strangled. Recognising the gravity of the situation, IATA commissioned a special study from consultants SRI International to draw up a European planning strategy for air traffic to the year 2000.

In their detailed analysis, SRI identified a series of actions which could begin to remove these constraints to air transport and economic growth. They confirmed the view that the system for handling air traffic in Europe is over-complicated, fragmented and not efficient. Despite some efforts to improve flow management, it is forecast that the system as it stands will be unable to cope with traffic growth after 1995. Similarly, without enhancements at least ten major airports will be seriously constrained by insufficient capacity between 1995 and 2000. The report includes a capacity/demand evaluation of not just the air traffic control system over the next 20 years, but a similar analysis for 26 key European airports during the same period.

Nevertheless, there are solutions to these problems. Sufficient airspace capacity actually exists to accommodate likely growth to the year 2010 if properly organised. This requires however a commitment to the timely implementation of development plans and procedural changes. Primary among these is the proper integration of the European ATC network to reduce the number of handover points, improve communication and realign networks to respond to the actual requirements of traffic flow rather than national boundaries. The solution proposed is that ECAC, Eurocontrol and ICAO co-operatively undertake the required restructuring. Needless to say a great deal of political will is required to implement such a fundamental change. The combination of such political will and the capabilities provided in an ECAC/Eurocontrol/ICAO joint effort would permit the required system redesign effort to begin with a minimal delay. If voluntary co-operation cannot be achieved the only recourse is to use the legislative authority of the EC to mandate the recommended re-routing/resectorisation process.

For IATA's part, a fundamental prerequisite is a commitment from its members to the increased funding required to support additional efforts which include technical research, continued consensus building among affected parties, public relations programmes and an airport-focused support programme.

In an effort to bring together all the interested parties, IATA is proposing that a European Air Traffic Assembly (EATA) be convened. The major participants are seen to be ECAC, ICAO, EC and Eurocontrol. It would also include IATA, Association of European Airlines (AEA) and Airport representatives. EATA's mission would be to offer a forum where the major stakeholders with an interest in a safe and expanding European air transport system could meet to exchange facts and opinions, develop strategies to remedy deficiencies and adopt the means to implement these strategies.

The remedy for the airport constraints is in some respects even more difficult given the frequent presence of severe geographical and/or environmental constraints. This brings us back to the earlier comment on the difficulty in putting across arguments for the benefit of a disparate group of air travellers in the face of a cohesive local lobbying group. For example, despite the massive improvements made in the field of jet noise, very few airports have responded by reducing the night curfews which were introduced when the first noisy jets started operating. These airport problems, unlike the ATC, can usually only be solved on an individual and local basis, but a general need exists to balance the often negative image of airports that lobby groups have sought to foster. Of particular importance is the demonstration of airports vital contribution to local and national economies. An important section of the SRI report mentioned above sets out an analysis of the economic value of airports to the surrounding communities' economy and also quantifies the economic cost of delays, present and projected: the Western European economic activity attributable to the provision or use of commercial aviation approaches $75 billion annually, while providing 2.5 million jobs – a level of activity equivalent to the economies of Greece and Ireland combined. To maintain and expand this activity, European airlines are acquiring $5 billion of aircraft annually. To provide supporting infrastructure, governments are annually spending $1.5 billion in capital resources. The cost of these delays at the present levels to airlines and the travelling public has been estimated by other researchers at $1.5 billion annually. Currently, the total loss due to delays, inefficient routings arising from poor route structure and military airspace restrictions, non-optimal flight profiles, low ATC system productivity, and other inefficiencies has been estimated at $5 billion. By the year 2000, annual losses to national economies are calculated to be almost $10 billion. The message is that the level of government investment is inadequate to support the present system or to permit significant growth.

So what is likely to happen if moves are not made to resolve this and other related problems?

First, the consumer is not going to benefit to the same extent and maybe not at all from liberalization moves. Some observers believe it is already too late. New routing opportunities may emerge but the price liberalization which had already begun in the tariff co-ordination process as early as 1985 may soon see a slowing down in the introduction of innovative pricing initiatives. It has been argued that the era of cheap air fares is over. The shortage of airport infrastructure and an integrated air traffic control system means there is insufficient scope for the sort of economies of scale that could engender such scope for low fares. When a resource becomes scarce, it is not going to become cheaper and essential business travel will be prepared to price out tourism to get to its destination.

Second, the distribution of air tourism traffic may change considerably. It has been seen in the past how swiftly transatlantic travel to and from Europe has responded to changes in the currency exchange values. The tourist aided by entrepreneurial tour developers can just as rapidly respond to other negative values affecting his holiday. The perceived wisdom is for example that the high mortgage rates in Great Britain are largely to blame for the massive drop in package tours being sold this year but certainly the memory of a day or more spent trapped in a crowded air terminal must be just as big a disincentive as any financial pressures. Long distance tourism is actually on the increase. Given the right kind of marketing, the Eastern European countries which have comparatively free airspace could also start to benefit from Europe's crowded skies and wrest the laurels for tourism growth from the OECD camp.

In conclusion, it is fair to say that there are some potentially severe growth constraints facing the air transport industry. Their solution will require innovation, co-operation, financial investment and political will. These environmental and infrastructural problems are now receiving widening recognition both in industry and government and it is a well-known axiom that recognition of a problem is a starting part for solving it. We can therefore look forward optimistically to continued growth in air transport and the international tourism which it supports.

# THE CHANNEL TUNNEL

## Contribution of the United Kingdom

Provision of an adequate transport network to service traffic using the Channel Tunnel is especially important. For, although the proportion of tourists travelling by rail has diminished the following factors suggest that it will enjoy a surge in popularity:

- Increasing congestion on Europe's roads;
- Increasing congestion of airspace, runways and airports;
- Expansion of an efficient high-speed rail network in Europe;
- Opening of the Channel Tunnel in 1993.

The French experience already indicates that the delays and congestion facing many air/road travellers are encouraging a transfer to high-speed trains, which are efficient and comfortable. It is currently estimated that one-third of TGV passengers have been attracted from the airlines. Furthermore, due to public desire for travel, one-quarter of people are travelling simply because the opportunity exists.

The success of high speed rail travel means that 14 European national railways are planning extensive networks. Thus, rail travelling times between major cities, such as Rome, Lisbon, Madrid, Paris, Milan, Brussels, Munich, Barcelona and London, will be greatly reduced. For example, the journey between Paris and London should take only about three hours when the Tunnel opens. However, the potential tourism benefits are not being fully realised due to lack of investment in a supporting transport infrastructure.

In October 1988 15.4 million through rail passengers were expected to travel via the Channel Tunnel during its first year of operation. By October 1989 this forecast had been reduced to 13.6 million – a loss of 1.8 million potential passengers. This revision was largely caused by the belief that the high-speed rail links between Brussels-Lille and Ashford-London will not be operational until 1995 and 1998 respectively.

**Channel Tunnel passenger forecasts**

|  | 1993 million[1] | 2003 million | 2013 million |
|---|---|---|---|
| Shuttle Trains (Calais-Ashford) | 15.8 | 22.9 | 29.0 |
| Through Trains | 13.6 | 21.0 | 25.0 |
| TOTAL | 29.4 | 43.9 | 54.0 |

1. 1993 figures are for the first full year of operation.
*Source:* Eurotunnel

This example suggests that, to reap the maximum social and economic benefits of transport developments, the viability of new services should not be simply assessed according to existing levels of demands as new opportunities and ease of travel generate additional travellers. However, a general policy of supplying transport links to stimulate business and more traffic would not be wise. This applies especially to the tourist industry which is often reliant on an aesthetically pleasing environment.

# II

# INTERNATIONAL TOURIST FLOWS IN MEMBER COUNTRIES

This Chapter brings together, in the form of summary tables, the most recent data available on international tourist flows to OECD Member countries and Yugoslavia. The tables give regional totals for each of the three geographical areas of the OECD – Europe, North America and Australasia-Japan – plus the OECD total.

Annual data by country of origin of foreign tourists or visitors, for 1988 and 1989, are set out in the Statistical Annex. The statistics given in the 1989 OECD publication *National and International Tourism Statistics, 1974-1985*, together with the more recent annual reports, provide the reader with a series of historical data on international tourism in the OECD area since 1974.

Section A outlines the general trends noted in 1989 over the whole OECD area.

Section B records changes in international tourist flows in each Member country and Yugoslavia in 1989. The data cover:

a) Arrivals at frontiers either of tourists (persons spending more than one night in the country being visited) or, where such figures are not available, all visitors (tourists plus excursionists). For further details of how travellers are classified, please refer to Chart A in the Statistical Annex.

b) The number of nights spent by foreign tourists in hotels and similar establishments (generally speaking, hotels, motels, inns and boarding houses).

c) The number of nights spent in all forms of accommodation without distinction.

For further details on the types of accommodation covered by the data for each receiving country, please refer to Table C in the Statistical Annex.

Lastly, Section C describes international flows from the OECD's main generating countries: Canada, France, Germany, Italy, Japan, the Netherlands, the United Kingdom and the United States. To reflect the importance of the new generating countries that have emerged in recent years, two new tables have been introduced – Tables 5 and 7.

## A.  INTERNATIONAL TOURISM IN THE OECD AREA

In 1989 international tourism in the OECD area continued to expand. Growth rates remained strong in most Member countries and Yugoslavia, resulting in a satisfactory situation in all regions:

– Arrivals at frontiers in Europe; + 5% (as against + 5% the previous year);
– Nights spent in hotels in Europe: + 3% (as against + 1%);
– Nights spent in all forms of accommodation in Europe: + 5% (as against + 1%);

– Arrivals at frontiers in North America: + 7% (as against + 8%);
– Arrivals at frontiers in Australasia-Japan: + 6% (as against + 14%).

### Arrivals at frontiers (Table 1)

Of the 19 European Member countries, only 12 collect data or provide estimates on tourist or foreign

Table 1. **Annual growth rates of number of arrivals of foreign tourists at frontiers[1]**

| | T/V | %<br>87/86 | %<br>88/87 | %<br>89/88 | 1989<br>Millions<br>of<br>arrivals |
|---|---|---|---|---|---|
| Austria | | | | | |
| Belgium | | | | | |
| Denmark | | | | | |
| Finland | | | | | |
| France | T | 2.5 | 3.6 | 12.3 | 43.0 |
| Germany | | | | | |
| Greece[4] | T | 6.9 | 2.7 | 3.9 | 8.1 |
| Iceland[4] | T | 13.9 | −0.4 | 1.3 | 0.1 |
| Ireland | V | 12.5 | 15.0 | 16.5 | 2.7 |
| Italy | T | 4.4 | 1.6 | −0.8 | 25.9 |
| Luxembourg | | | | | |
| Netherlands | | | | | |
| Norway | | | | | |
| Portugal | T | 12.8 | 8.6 | 7.4 | 7.1 |
| Spain | V | 6.7 | 7.2 | −0.2 | 54.1 |
| Sweden | | | | | |
| Switzerland[2] | T | 1.7 | 0.0 | 7.7 | 12.6 |
| Turkey[3] | V | 19.4 | 46.1 | 6.9 | 4.5 |
| United Kingdom | V | 12.0 | 1.5 | 8.9 | 17.2 |
| **EUROPE[1]** | | 5.9 | 5.0 | 4.9 | |
| Canada | T | −4.1 | 3.4 | −2.3 | 15.1 |
| United States | T | 17.0 | 9.7 | 11.7 | 35.2 |
| **NORTH AMERICA[1]** | | 8.8 | 7.5 | 7.1 | |
| Australia | V | 24.9 | 26.0 | −7.5 | 2.1 |
| New Zealand | T | 15.1 | 2.4 | 4.2 | 0.9 |
| Japan | V | 4.5 | 9.3 | 20.4 | 2.8 |
| **AUSTRALASIA-<br>JAPAN[1]** | | 13.3 | 14.3 | 6.3 | |
| **OECD[1]** | | 6.7 | 5.7 | 5.4 | |
| Yugoslavia | V | 5.7 | 13.3 | 15.1 | 34.1 |

V Visitors.
T Tourists.
Note: Canada, Italy and Portugal dispose of both series (V and T); see annex.
1. Overall trend for all countries with data available from 1986 to 1989.
2. Estimates.
3. Travellers.
4. Preliminary data for 1989.

visitor movements at frontiers. Two of these 12 countries, Austria and Germany, record all traveller arrivals at frontiers, a much broader yardstick than is used for analysing tourist flows, since it includes travellers in transit. These figures have not therefore been included in Table 1, but are shown for information in Table 6 of the Statistical Annex.

Sixteen countries, including 11 European countries, have data concerning arrivals at frontiers. Although the regional trends in 1989 were satisfactory (in the vicinity of + 6%), the increases varied widely from one destination to another.

In *Europe*, only Italy and Spain recorded a downturn in tourism (- 0.8 and - 0.2% respectively). There was a steep fall in the number of Germans going to

Italy and, to a lesser extent, Spain, which also lost a number of its British and French tourists.

France, with 43 million tourists in 1989, recorded the largest increase in gross terms (+ 5 million arrivals); this was largely ascribable to the French Revolution Bicentenary celebrations, but excellent weather and a major promotion campaign also played their part. The promotional campaign that Ireland has been conducting for several years also seems to have borne fruit (+ 17%). Ireland benefits as well from the growing demand for "green" holiday destinations; in particular, there was an increase in the number of German tourists in 1989 (+ 15%).

*Australasia-Japan* recorded an increase of 6%. Japan, which in 1989 had 20% more visitors than the previous year, accounted for a large share of the growth of tourism in the region. Most of the growth was attributable to increased demand from non-OECD Member countries (60% of total arrivals in Japan), but visitors from Europe also increased.

Table 2. **Annual growth rates of nights spent by foreign tourists in hotels and similar establishments[1]**

| | %<br>87/86 | %<br>88/87 | %<br>89/88 | 1989<br>Millions<br>of<br>beds-<br>nights |
|---|---|---|---|---|
| Austria | 1.6 | 1.7 | 9.0 | 61.4 |
| Belgium[2] | −0.1 | 2.0 | 10.0 | 6.0 |
| Denmark | 3.3 | −2.3 | 17.2 | 5.1 |
| Finland | 9.2 | 4.1 | 9.5 | 2.5 |
| France | 0.0 | 10.9 | 26.2 | 51.0 |
| Germany | 3.9 | 3.4 | 12.5 | 28.4 |
| Greece[2] | 0.1 | −1.2 | −1.2 | 32.9 |
| Iceland | | | | |
| Ireland | 4.8 | 11.9 | 20.2 | 7.4 |
| Italy | 7.7 | 0.3 | −4.0 | 67.6 |
| Luxembourg | 3.8 | 2.9 | 5.0 | 1.0 |
| Netherlands | −0.9 | −4.0 | 6.2 | 7.2 |
| Norway | 17.2 | −13.2 | 2.2 | 3.4 |
| Portugal | 1.7 | 3.3 | 3.1 | 15.5 |
| Spain | 5.4 | −4.4 | −11.4 | 78.3 |
| Sweden | −2.0 | −1.6 | 5.5 | 3.4 |
| Switzerland | −0.1 | −2.2 | 7.3 | 20.5 |
| Turkey | 29.4 | 44.6 | 3.3 | 9.7 |
| United Kingdom | | | | |
| **EUROPE[1]** | 3.9 | 1.1 | 2.9 | |
| Canada | | | | |
| United States | | | | |
| **NORTH AMERICA** | | | | |
| Australia | 24.6 | 28.1 | | |
| New Zealand | | | | |
| Japan | | | | |
| **AUSTRALASIA-JAPAN[1]** | | | | |
| **OECD[1]** | 3.9 | 1.1 | 2.9 | |
| Yugoslavia | 3.0 | −0.4 | −1.1 | 27.9 |

1. Overall trend for all countries with data available from 1986 to 1989.
2. Preliminary data for 1989.

**North America** also recorded an increase of 7% in arrivals, despite a 2% fall in Canada, ascribable to the strength of the Canadian dollar in 1989 (making Canadian tourism less competitive), and to fewer visitors from the United States. Arrivals in the United States increased by nearly 4 million (+ 12% over the previous year).

### Nights spent in hotels and similar establishments (Table 2)

Eighteen countries, all of them European, have data on nights spent in hotels and similar establishments; generally speaking, these data concern nights recorded in hotels, motels, boarding houses and inns (see Table C in the Statistical Annex).

After a 1% rise in 1988, hotel occupancy in Europe increased by 3% in 1989. However, although this seems a fairly satisfactory result, in fact 1989 was quite an uneven year.

Hotel occupancy in three of the main receiving countries in the Mediterranean area fell steeply: Spain (- 11%, i.e. - 10 million nights spent); Italy (- 4%, i.e. - 3 million nights); Greece (- 1%, i.e. - 400 000 nights). By contrast, France had an exceptionally good year (+ 26%, i.e. + 10 million nights) and good results were recorded in Ireland and Denmark.

### Nights spent in all forms of accommodation (Table 3)

This category includes hotel and non-hotel accommodation (see Table C in the Statistical Annex).

In 1989 most countries registered an increase in the number of nights spent (4% overall), particularly the Scandinavian countries, which after a fairly lacklustre year in 1988 recorded a marked increase in the number of nights spent; the Dutch and German markets were the most buoyant.

Demand in the Mediterranean area, which had been expanding for several years, marked time in 1989, and even fell in Italy (- 6%), Yugoslavia (- 6%) and Greece (- 2%). Turkey recorded a slower rate of increase (+ 2%) after several years of very rapid growth (annual rates of over 35% from the early 1980s).

The moderate growth in OECD Europe as a whole can be explained by a swing of the pendulum in tourism markets. On the one hand, there was a fall in the number of nights spent in Italy, Greece and Yugoslavia, due in large part to the sluggishness of the traditional markets. On the other hand, the number of nights spent in the Scandinavian countries and the United Kingdom and Ireland picked up quite markedly, tending to suggest that Northern Europe is coming back into fashion as a holiday destination. The emergence of new generating countries such as Italy and Japan, and to a lesser extent Spain, was confirmed in 1989 for most destinations.

Table 3. **Annual growth rates of nights spent by foreign tourists in all means of accommodation[1]**

| | %<br>87/86 | %<br>88/87 | %<br>89/88 | 1989<br>Millions<br>of<br>beds-<br>nights |
|---|---|---|---|---|
| Austria | 0.3 | 2.2 | 8.4 | 95.0 |
| Belgium[3] | 2.1 | 5.1 | 1.9 | 10.8 |
| Denmark | -3.7 | -2.3 | 13.4 | 9.1 |
| Finland | | | | |
| France | 2.3 | 2.1 | | |
| Germany | 4.6 | 3.5 | 11.5 | 33.6 |
| Greece[3] | 0.9 | -2.7 | -2.0 | 34.1 |
| Iceland | | | | |
| Ireland | 19.2 | 15.8 | 19.9 | 31.4 |
| Italy[2] | | 0.3 | -6.3 | 86.5 |
| Luxembourg | -7.9 | -1.4 | | |
| Netherlands | | | 12.1 | 14.2 |
| Norway | 8.3 | -1.3 | 2.8 | 5.5 |
| Portugal | 2.6 | 4.0 | 2.5 | 18.2 |
| Spain | | | | |
| Sweden | -1.2 | 0.3 | 6.6 | 7.6 |
| Switzerland | -1.0 | -0.4 | 4.4 | 35.9 |
| Turkey | 40.3 | 40.0 | 1.8 | 11.9 |
| United Kingdom | 12.7 | -3.0 | 7.0 | 185.0 |
| **EUROPE**[1] | 4.1 | 0.9 | 4.8 | |
| Canada | -7.2 | 8.3 | -2.0 | 90.0 |
| United States | | | | |
| **NORTH AMERICA** | | | | |
| Australia | 24.9 | 26.0 | | |
| New Zealand | 12.5 | 2.0 | 1.8 | 18.9 |
| Japan | | | | |
| **AUSTRALASIA-JAPAN** | | | | |
| **OECD**[1] | 2.6 | 1.9 | 3.7 | |
| Yugoslavia | 1.8 | 0.1 | -6.1 | 49.2 |

1. Overall trend for all countries with data available from 1986 to 1989.
2. New series from 1987.
3. Preliminary data for 1989.

## B. INTERNATIONAL TOURISM IN EACH COUNTRY IN 1989

*Australia.* Following 1988, which was an exceptional year (+ 26%) because of the Bicentennial celebrations, 1989 marked a return to normal rates. Combined with the effects of the pilots' strike, the overall result was that visitor arrivals went down by 8 % and totalled 2.1 million, a figure still 17% higher than in 1987.

Only the United Kingdom, out of Australia's four main markets, showed an increase in the number of visitors (+ 5%, as against + 31% in 1989. But New Zealand and the United States, together accounting for 34% of the market, were down by 16 and 19% respectively in 1989.

At the time of going to press, the 1989 figures for nights spent in hotels and similar establishments and for all forms of accommodation broken down by country of origin were not available.

*Austria*. Nights spent in all forms of accommodation (95 million in 1989) were 8% up on 1988; the number of nights spent in hotels increased in similar proportions (+ 9%). This was partly explainable by the sharp increase in demand from non-Member countries (+ 16%) and particularly from East European countries (+ 26%) and OECD countries in the Australasia-Japan area (+ 20%).

The number of nights spent by Italian tourists increased by one-third, making Italy Austria's sixth largest market; demand from Ireland and Turkey increased markedly for the second year running, + 75% and 66% respectively.

On the other hand, the Norwegian, Portuguese and Canadian markets declined for the second year running.

*Belgium*. (At the time of going to press, provisional data only was available on Belgium.) In 1989, nights spent in all forms of accommodation increased by 2% to nearly 11 million, of which 6 million in hotels and similar establishments (10% up on 1988). Trends in the four main markets varied: Netherlands (+ 3%); Germany (- 3%); the United Kingdom (+ 10%); France (- 7%).

The overall trend of Belgium as a destination in 1989 was uncertain, with marked increases in some markets (the Soviet Union, Japan, Sweden and Ireland) and a few substantial decreases for the second year running in others (Luxembourg, the United States and Austria).

*Canada*. In 1989 all indicators showed a fall in tourism: arrivals of foreign tourists at frontiers were down 2%, arrivals of foreign visitors at frontiers down 3% and nights spent in all forms of accommodation down 2%.

In all forms of accommodation, the most significant development was the decline in Canada's main market, the United States (- 5%, for a market representing 60% of total demand), together with an appreciable fall in demand from Europe and particularly Iceland, Austria, Spain and Norway.

In contrast, demand from Australasia and Japan taken together remained very strong, up for the second year running (+ 11% in 1989).

*Denmark*. In 1989 there was a reversal of trend after several consecutive years of decline: nights spent in all forms of accommodation increased by 13% on 1988 to 9 million; nights spent in hotels increased by an even larger percentage, + 17% on 1988. All markets picked up, particularly Denmark's three main markets, Germany (+ 14%), Sweden (+ 17%) and Norway (+ 6%).

*Finland*. Nights spent in hotels were up by 10% in 1989 following an increase of 4% the previous year. The reasons for this were the 46% increase in the Soviet market, Finland's third largest market, which had fallen by 18% in 1988, and the positive trend of its other main markets (Sweden, Germany and the United Kingdom).

However, the number of nights spent by tourists from the United States (who account for 8% of total demand) fell slightly (- 0.4%). The number of nights spent by tourists from Norway was also down (- 5%), for the second year running.

*France*. 1989 was an exceptional year for France on account of the French Revolution Bicentenary celebrations; other factors – excellent weather and a major promotional campaign – were also important.

In 1989 France carried out a survey at its frontiers; while the final figures are not yet available, the number of tourist arrivals for 1989 is estimated at 43 million. International demand measured by the number of nights spent in hotels and similar establishments increased by 26%. Since 1985 a new statistical series that shows nights spent by international tourists in licensed hotels over practically the whole of France (with the exception of three regions: Champagne-Ardennes, Corsica and the Loire) has been compiled.

Japanese demand in particular increased markedly (+ 69%), while demand from the United Kingdom, Spain, the United States and Italy increased by over 30%.

At the time of going to press, 1989 figures broken down by country of origin for arrivals of tourists at frontiers and nights spent in all forms of accommodation were not available.

*Germany*. In terms of nights spent in all forms of accommodation, international tourism demand increased quite substantially (1989/88 + 12%, as against 1988/87 + 4%), to 34 million nights, of which 28 million in hotels and similar establishments.

This good performance was largely ascribable to the buoyancy of Germany's main markets (United Kingdom + 16%, Italy + 18% and France + 13%); the upward trend of nights spent by Americans (+ 9%) should be noted, after a fall of 9% in 1988. There was also a large increase in demand from the Australasia-Japan area (+ 20%) and from Eastern Europe (+ 26%).

*Greece*. Greece had 8 million tourists in 1989, an overall increase of 4% on 1988.

Although Germany, the main market, grew by 20%, the Netherlands by 10% and Italy by 5%, the other main markets were stagnant or down (United Kingdom - 8%, Yugoslavia - 5%). The biggest falls were in demand from Norway (- 36%), Switzerland (- 21%) and North America (- 11%).

At the time of going to press, the 1989 figures for nights spent in hotels and all forms of accommodation, broken down by country of origin, were not available.

*Iceland*. At the time of going to press, the 1989 figures, broken down by country of origin, for tourist arrivals at frontiers were unavailable.

*Ireland*. Tourism continued to expand; in 1989, Ireland had a total of 3 million foreign visitors (+ 17% on 1988), while the number of nights spent in hotels increased by 20% to more than 7 million.

The increase in demand as expressed in terms of nights spent was ascribable mainly to the fact that there were more visitors from the United Kingdom (+ 38%), Ireland's main market, and to a considerable expansion in two other major markets, Canada (+ 121%) and the Netherlands (+ 60%). In contrast, there was a sharp fall in visitors from the United States (- 9%), Ireland's second market.

*Italy*. 1989 was a poor year for tourism in Italy; this was reflected in the 1% decline in arrivals of visitors at frontiers (which totalled 55 million in 1989) and the 6% fall-off in the number of nights spent in all forms of accommodation.

In the case of visitors at frontiers, three of Italy's five main markets declined: Switzerland (- 13%), Germany (- 3%) and Austria (- 2%). As throughout the Mediterranean area, market trends varied quite a lot. Demand from the Australasia-Japan area grew by 19%, that from France by 5% and that from Yugoslavia by 8%; these variations explain why the average overall trend of tourism was more or less unchanged on 1988.

It should be noted that, since 1987, arrivals/nights spent in all forms of accommodation no longer include private homes, which had accounted for about 15% of the total.

At the time of going to press, the 1989 data for nights spent, broken down by country of origin, were unavailable.

*Japan*. International tourism demand continued to grow and in fact accelerated in 1989, with visitors up by 20% (nearly 3 million frontier arrivals). With 60% of total demand and growth of 30%, the Asia-Oceania region accounted for most of this expansion. The increase in demand was particularly marked from the dynamic Asian economies: the number of tourists from South Korea and Taiwan, which together account for about 40% of the market, increased by 78% and 28% respectively.

*Netherlands*. After a poor year in 1988, the number of nights spent in all forms of accommodation in 1989 increased by 12%, to 14 million, and nights spent in hotels were up by 6%.

This was due mainly to the buoyancy of the Netherland's main markets, particularly the German market, which accounts for 45% of demand (up by 13% or 740 000 nights). Tourism from non-Member countries, however, declined by 6%.

*New Zealand*. In 1989 there were 900 000 tourist arrivals at frontiers, more than 4% up on the previous year. This was partly ascribable to the 14% increase in the number of tourists from the Australasia-Japan region, which accounts for nearly half of demand; Australia, the leading main market picked up considerably (+ 17%, after falling by 10% in 1988). The number of tourists from New Zealand's two main European markets, the United Kingdom and Germany, also increased (+ 2% and + 18% respectively).

The overall increase, however, was fairly modest because many other significant markets declined. There were falls in demand from North America (- 18%), Latin America (- 16%), Norway (- 14%) and Italy (- 7%).

*Norway*. After falling by 13% in 1988, demand in terms of nights spent in hotels picked up slightly (+ 2%). The reason for this was that the moderate increase in its two main markets (Denmark and Germany: + 4%) was offset by a marked fall in its third and fourth markets (Sweden and the United States: - 7%).

*Portugal*. Every indicator on international tourist demand was again up in 1989, although not as sharply as in 1988: nights spent in all forms of accommodation (+ 3%, against + 4% in 1988); nights spent in hotels and similar establishments (+ 3%, as in 1988); tourist arrivals at frontiers (+ 7%, against + 9% in 1988).

Regarding nights spent in all forms of accommodation, Portugal's two main markets shrank for the second year running; in 1989, nights spent by German and United Kingdom nationals (44% of the market) were down by 1 and 3% respectively, or by 204 000 nights.

The country's other major markets, Spain, the Netherlands and France increased their presence appreciably (up from + 6 to + 9%). Tourism from Ireland (- 4%), Africa (- 3%) and Norway (- 28%) was in decline, however.

*Spain*. In 1989, arrivals of visitors at frontiers levelled off (- 0.2%) and nights spent in hotels were once again down (- 11% in 1989 and - 4% in 1988). Data on nights spent in camping sites and vacation appartments indicate a global decrease of 5% from 1988 to 1989.

In the case of arrivals at frontiers, there were fewer crossings by French (- 1%), British (- 4%) and German (- 2%) visitors, which make up 22, 14 and 13% of demand respectively. Arrivals of Portuguese visitors, however, remained steady, accounting for 19% of the total.

According to the information drawn from the number of nights recorded as spent in "gold star" and "silver star" hotels, there was a decline for the second year running. This was due mainly to a drop of 19% in British and 12% in German clients, these two markets making up the bulk (60%) of the total. On the other hand, the only marked increase was that of the Japanese market recording + 34% over 1988.

*Sweden*. Following a lacklustre year in 1988, in 1989 the number of nights spent in all forms of accommodation increased by 7% to nearly 8 million, of which 3.4 million in hotels and similar establishments (+ 6%). Taking all types of accommodation into account, demand from all OECD countries expanded; however, a fall in the Norwegian clientele of hotels may be noted (down by 6%).

In terms of nights spent in all forms of accommodation, a pick-up in the North American clientele (+ 3%), after a fall in 1988, may be noted in particular; as for Europe, the Italian market surged by 23%, the German market, Sweden's second largest, grew by 10%, and so did the UK market. Demand from Japan expanded still further (+ 10%, after a 19% increase in 1988).

*Switzerland*. After a slowdown for two years running (- 1% and - 0.4%), demand in terms of nights spent in all forms of accommodation increased by 4% on 1988 to 36 million; the number of nights spent in hotels and similar establishments increased slightly more (+ 7%) than that for all forms of accommodation.

Some markets that had increased the previous year expanded again (Japan + 19%, Italy + 15%); others showed a reversal of trend (in particular, North America, + 8% as against - 12% the previous year).

Demand from two Scandinavian countries fell (Denmark down by 11% and Sweden down by 7%).

*Turkey*. Overall statistics on arrivals and nights spent show that international demand fell off somewhat in 1989. The number of nights spent in all forms of accommodation increased by only 2% (against + 40% in 1988), nights spent in hotels or similar establishments increased by 3% (against + 45%) and visitor arrivals at frontiers were up by 7 per cent (against + 46%).

Regarding nights spent in all forms of accommodation, the most notable fall-off was that of the European market which accounted for 85% of demand (+ 3%, against + 44% the previous year). Some outright decreases were noted, from Greece (- 47%), the United Kingdom (- 14%), France (- 3%) and Italy (0.4%), these four countries accounting for about 25% of the market. On the other hand, there were substantial increases in tourism from Denmark (+ 68%), Turkey's fourth-largest European market, and Spain (+ 26%).

*United Kingdom*. International demand expressed in terms of nights spent in all forms of accommodation was up by 7% (as against - 6% in 1988), and by 9% in terms of arrivals at frontiers. Demand from all the OECD regions picked up, particularly North America (+ 5% as against - 8% in 1988) and Europe (+ 6% as against - 1%); these two regions accounted for 67% of total demand. The largest increases were from Finland (+ 80%) and Austria (+ 69%).

There was a fall-off in demand from New Zealand (- 21%), Switzerland (- 17%) and Canada (- 4%).

*United States*. International tourism as measured by frontier arrivals remained buoyant in the United States, with a marked increase for the second year running (+ 12% in 1989 and + 10% in 1988).

The expansion was largely due to strong demand from the Asia-Oceania area (+ 21%) and Canada (+ 11%), which together made up 54% of demand. Demand from the East European countries also increased markedly (+ 40% in 1989). The growth of demand from the OECD Europe Member countries slowed (+ 8% in 1989, as against + 23% in 1988).

*Yugoslavia*. After a flat year in 1988, the number of nights spent in all forms of accommodation fell by 6% in 1989, although the number of nights in hotels and similar establishments fell by only 1%. This was primarily ascribable to the fall-off in demand from European countries (- 6%), which account for 86% of total demand. Demand from Germany, Yugoslavia's largest market (36% of total demand), declined (- 11%), as did that from most European countries and North America (- 13%).

In contrast, the Italian market expanded (by 15% to 13% of total demand), further confirming Italy's rise as a generating country. Demand from the Australasia-Japan region also continued to grow (+ 8%).

# C. MAIN GENERATING COUNTRIES

To give a clearer picture of the recent trends in tourism from the international tourism generating countries to the OECD area, new tables have been added to the 1990 Report. Tables 4 and 6 relate to "traditional" generating countries: France, Germany, the United Kingdom and the United States. Tables 5 and 7 relate to four "new" major generating countries: Canada, Italy, Japan and the Netherlands. In the Annex, summary tables covering the period 1978-1989 give an historical overview of the trends in the main generating countries.

These countries, eight in all, were selected not at random but on the basis of the contribution that they have made to the development of international tourism as expressed in terms of dollar expenditures, the standard unit of account for the "Travel" item in the balance of payments. They accounted for about 79% of the total expenditure by the 24 OECD Member countries in 1988; Japan has made considerable headway in the recent period (moving up from seventh place in 1975 to third place in 1988), while France now ranks fifth among the generating countries (third in 1975) (see Table 2 in Chapter III).

These few figures give an idea of recent trends and show that countries like Japan can no longer be omitted from an analysis of the generating countries. The data in the summary tables were compiled by adding up the totals for arrivals in the individual countries.

### Table 4. Annual growth rates of number of arrivals at frontiers from main generating countries

| | T/V | Total Variation % 89/88 | From France | | From Germany | | From United Kingdom | | From United States | |
|---|---|---|---|---|---|---|---|---|---|---|
| | | | Relative share % 88 | Variation % 89/88 | Relative share % 88 | Variation % 89/88 | Relative share % 88 | Variation % 89/88 | Relative share % 88 | Variation % 89/88 |
| Austria | | | | | | | | | | |
| Belgium | | | | | | | | | | |
| Denmark | | | | | | | | | | |
| Finland | | | | | | | | | | |
| France (R) | T | 12.3 | | | 23.8 | | 17.4 | | 5.1 | |
| Germany | | | | | | | | | | |
| Greece (N) | T | 3.9 | 6.0 | 1.9 | 17.8 | 19.8 | 23.0 | −8.8 | 3.8 | −5.4 |
| Iceland (N) | T | 1.3 | 4.8 | 33.3 | 12.3 | 15.2 | 8.2 | 13.9 | 22.3 | −20.1 |
| Ireland (R) | V | 16.5 | 4.6 | 27.1 | 4.8 | 34.8 | 62.4 | 13.9 | 15.9 | 1.9 |
| Italy (N) | V | −1.0 | 16.1 | 4.6 | 18.8 | −3.3 | 3.3 | 4.8 | 2.4 | 0.4 |
| Luxembourg | | | | | | | | | | |
| Netherlands | | | | | | | | | | |
| Norway | | | | | | | | | | |
| Portugal (N) | T | 7.4 | 8.5 | 8.0 | 8.0 | 6.6 | 16.1 | −3.5 | 2.9 | −3.8 |
| Spain (N) | V | −0.2 | 22.3 | −0.8 | 12.7 | −1.7 | 14.1 | −3.9 | 1.6 | 11.0 |
| Sweden | | | | | | | | | | |
| Switzerland | | | | | | | | | | |
| Turkey (N) | V | 6.9 | 5.9 | 14.9 | 18.4 | 16.8 | 11.1 | −12.7 | 4.0 | 23.6 |
| United Kingdom (R) | V | 8.9 | 12.5 | 14.5 | 11.6 | 9.9 | | | 16.6 | 7.4 |
| **EUROPE** | | 1.5 | 16.6 | 3.0 | 15.0 | 0.9 | 9.7 | −1.8 | 4.0 | 5.3 |
| Canada (R) | T | −2.3 | 1.5 | 5.7 | 1.7 | −0.1 | 3.4 | 6.4 | 82.4 | −4.4 |
| United States (R) | T | 11.7 | 2.0 | 5.7 | 3.7 | −6.7 | 5.8 | 22.2 | | |
| **NORTH AMERICA** | | 7.1 | 1.8 | 5.7 | 3.0 | −5.5 | 5.0 | 18.7 | 27.1 | −4.4 |
| Australia (R) | V | −7.5 | 0.9 | −4.3 | 2.9 | 3.3 | 11.6 | 4.8 | 14.3 | −19.1 |
| New Zealand (R) | T | 4.2 | 0.4 | 18.5 | 2.3 | 18.2 | 8.4 | 2.2 | 19.4 | −17.9 |
| Japan (N) | V | 20.4 | 1.7 | 16.8 | 2.4 | 8.1 | 6.6 | 14.7 | 21.9 | 3.0 |
| **AUSTRALASIA-JAPAN** | | 6.3 | 1.2 | 10.1 | 2.6 | 7.3 | 8.9 | 7.6 | 18.4 | −7.6 |
| **OECD** | | 2.9 | 12.7 | 3.1 | 11.8 | 0.5 | 8.6 | 1.2 | 9.9 | −1.7 |
| Yugoslavia (N) | | | | | | | | | | |

V  Visitors.
T  Tourists.
(R) Tourist count by country of residence.
(N) Tourist count by country of nationality.

| | T/V | Total Variation % 89/88 | From Japan | | From Netherlands | | From Canada | | From Italy | |
|---|---|---|---|---|---|---|---|---|---|---|
| | | | Relative share % 88 | Variation % 89/88 | Relative share % 88 | Variation % 89/88 | Relative share % 88 | Variation % 89/88 | Relative share % 88 | Variation % 89/88 |
| Austria | | | | | | | | | | |
| Belgium | | | | | | | | | | |
| Denmark | | | | | | | | | | |
| Finland | | | | | | | | | | |
| France (R) | T | 12.3 | 1.7 | | 10.6 | | 0.9 | | 9.0 | |
| Germany | | | | | | | | | | |
| Greece (N) | T | 3.9 | 1.3 | −1.0 | 5.0 | 10.0 | 1.4 | −26.2 | 7.0 | 4.6 |
| Iceland (N) | T | 1.3 | 0.8 | | 2.2 | | 1.0 | | 2.2 | |
| Ireland (R) | V | 16.5 | | | | | 1.2 | 32.1 | | |
| Italy (N) | V | −1.0 | 0.7 | 18.7 | 3.2 | 2.1 | 0.6 | 19.4 | | |
| Luxembourg | | | | | | | | | | |
| Netherlands | | | | | | | | | | |
| Norway | | | | | | | | | | |
| Portugal (N) | T | 7.4 | 0.4 | 6.8 | 4.2 | 15.0 | 1.1 | 9.3 | 2.1 | 20.4 |
| Spain (N) | V | −0.2 | 0.3 | 27.2 | 3.7 | 1.5 | 0.3 | 2.6 | 2.5 | 13.4 |
| Sweden | | | | | | | | | | |
| Switzerland | | | | | | | | | | |
| Turkey (N) | V | 6.9 | 0.7 | 15.3 | 1.9 | 31.7 | 0.7 | 8.1 | 3.5 | 6.8 |
| United Kingdom (R) | V | 8.9 | 2.5 | 28.7 | 5.6 | 7.3 | 4.1 | −2.8 | 4.2 | 5.9 |
| **EUROPE** | | 1.3 | 0.8 | 21.2 | 3.8 | 4.4 | 1.0 | 2.6 | 2.0 | 10.0 |
| Canada (R) | T | −2.3 | 2.1 | 19.4 | 0.6 | −0.7 | | | 0.6 | 4.9 |
| United States (R) | T | 11.7 | 8.0 | 21.6 | 0.8 | 5.2 | 43.9 | 11.0 | 1.1 | −0.5 |
| **NORTH AMERICA** | | 7.1 | 6.1 | 21.3 | 0.7 | 3.7 | 29.4 | 11.0 | 0.9 | 0.6 |
| Australia (R) | V | −7.5 | 15.7 | −0.8 | 1.0 | −10.3 | 3.0 | −18.7 | 1.1 | −18.7 |
| New Zealand (R) | T | 4.2 | 10.8 | 3.8 | 0.8 | 0.9 | 4.3 | −16.7 | 0.3 | −6.6 |
| Japan (N) | V | 20.4 | | | 0.7 | 3.7 | 2.5 | 2.7 | 1.0 | 17.9 |
| **AUSTRALASIA-JAPAN** | | 6.3 | 8.2 | 0.2 | 0.8 | −3.7 | 3.0 | −10.6 | 0.9 | −1.3 |
| **OECD** | | 2.8 | 2.2 | 19.2 | 3.0 | 4.3 | 7.8 | 10.0 | 1.7 | 8.5 |
| Yugoslavia (N) | | | | | | | | | | |

V    Visitors.
T    Tourists.
(R) Tourist count by country of residence.
(N) Tourist count by country of nationality.

Although gross national statistics are not always comparable with one another, they do give an order of magnitude and an idea of recent trends.

In *Europe*, the German market predominates with 25% of all nights in accommodation. In 1989, the growth of the German market (up by 3% on 1988) was less than that of overall total nights in accommodation (+ 6%); the United Kingdom, which accounts for 13% of nights in Europe, went down by 1%. The virtual stagnation in both markets was ascribable to the steep fall in nights spent in Spain.

The other major markets in Europe are the United States (8% of nights), France (6%), the Netherlands (7%) and Italy (5%). In 1989, the US market increased in all European countries (+ 10% on average), the only exceptions being Belgium, Finland,

Norway and Portugal. The Japanese and the Italians spent more nights in almost all countries (respectively + 27% and + 10%). The Dutch and the Canadian markets are flat, primarily on account of a drop in the numbers going to Spain and the United Kingdom.

The pattern in *North America* was more or less the same as in Europe, 56% of the tourism being generated by countries within the area.

Overall, the number of arrivals at frontiers in the area increased by 7%, with 12% more tourist arrivals in the United States and 2% less in Canada. In particular, there was a fall-off in the German market in North America (- 6%) and in the American market in Canada (- 4%). In contrast, the Japanese and British markets expanded strongly (+ 21% and + 19% respectively).

Table 6.  **Annual growth rates of nights spent in the various means of accommodation from main generating countries**

| | H/A | Total Variation % 89/88 | From France | | From Germany | | From the United Kingdom | | From the United-States | |
|---|---|---|---|---|---|---|---|---|---|---|
| | | | Relative share % 88 | Variation % 89/88 | Relative share % 88 | Variation % 89/88 | Relative share % 88 | Variation % 89/88 | Relative share % 88 | Variation % 89/88 |
| Austria (R) | A | 8.4 | 3.0 | 9.3 | 64.0 | 6.9 | 4.8 | 12.0 | 1.8 | 6.7 |
| Belgium (R) | A | 1.9 | 9.6 | −7.1 | 16.0 | −3.2 | 9.2 | 9.5 | 5.4 | −4.7 |
| Denmark (N) | A | 13.4 | 1.7 | 11.0 | 35.2 | 13.9 | 4.3 | 8.2 | 5.0 | 12.2 |
| Finland (R) | H | 9.5 | 2.9 | 7.3 | 14.0 | 9.9 | 5.7 | 7.3 | 8.8 | −0.4 |
| France (R) | H | 26.2 | | | 16.0 | 15.0 | 16.2 | 35.3 | 9.7 | 33.0 |
| Germany (R) | A | 11.5 | 4.9 | 13.0 | | | 8.5 | 15.8 | 12.9 | 9.2 |
| Greece (N) | A | −2.0 | 7.5 | | 23.9 | | 20.9 | | 2.4 | |
| Iceland | | | | | | | | | | |
| Ireland (R) | A | 19.9 | 6.0 | 37.8 | 6.7 | 26.3 | 52.7 | 16.9 | 15.7 | 10.5 |
| Italy (N) | A | −6.3 | 7.4 | | 42.8 | | 6.6 | | 5.3 | |
| Luxembourg (R) | H | 5.0 | 8.8 | | 12.8 | | 5.7 | | 6.5 | |
| Netherlands (R) | A | 12.1 | 4.9 | 8.7 | 44.6 | 13.1 | 11.9 | 11.9 | 6.6 | 9.5 |
| Norway (N) | H | 2.2 | 3.6 | 16.7 | 16.1 | 7.7 | 9.9 | 1.3 | 10.4 | −0.2 |
| Portugal (N) | A | 2.5 | 7.1 | 6.0 | 15.6 | −1.0 | 30.4 | −3.2 | 3.8 | −5.2 |
| Spain (N) | H | −11.4 | 8.1 | −0.9 | 27.9 | −11.5 | 35.4 | −19.3 | 2.0 | 4.5 |
| Sweden (N) | A | 6.6 | 2.1 | 10.1 | 19.4 | 9.9 | 4.4 | 9.5 | 4.8 | 2.3 |
| Switzerland (R) | A | 4.4 | 7.2 | 0.1 | 43.0 | 2.0 | 7.5 | 1.4 | 6.6 | 8.7 |
| Turkey (N) | A | 1.8 | 13.1 | −3.4 | 39.4 | 2.5 | 8.4 | −14.2 | 2.8 | 20.8 |
| United Kingdom (R) | A | 7.0 | 8.1 | 15.8 | 10.0 | 2.3 | | | 14.8 | 7.5 |
| **EUROPE** | | 6.2 | 6.2 | 9.5 | 25.4 | 3.2 | 12.8 | −0.6 | 8.4 | 9.7 |
| Canada (R) | A | −2.0 | 3.1 | 2.8 | 3.9 | −9.3 | 7.4 | 0.3 | 61.1 | −4.6 |
| United States | | | | | | | | | | |
| **NORTH AMERICA** | | | | | | | | | | |
| Australia | H | | 0.9 | | 3.7 | | 11.7 | | 20.0 | |
| New Zealand | A | 1.8 | | | 3.4 | 18.3 | 15.7 | −1.7 | 12.2 | −5.3 |
| Japan | | | | | | | | | | |
| **AUSTRALASIA-JAPAN** | | | | | | | | | | |
| **OECD** | | 5.0 | 5.7 | 9.0 | 22.4 | 2.9 | 12.1 | −0.5 | 16.0 | 1.9 |
| Yugoslavia (N) | A | −6.1 | 2.3 | −8.1 | 37.8 | −11.4 | 11.2 | 0.3 | 1.4 | −12.1 |

H   Hotels and similar establishments.
A   All means of accommodation.
(R) Tourist count by country of residence.
(N) Tourist count by country of nationality.

Most visitors to *Australasia-Japan* (from the OECD countries) came from the United States (18% of the total) and Japan (8%).

In 1989 the region had 6% more visitors than in 1988, with the largest increases from France (+ 10%), the United Kingdom (+ 8%) and Germany (+ 7%). In contrast, there was a drop in the Canadian market (- 11%), the US market (- 8%), the Dutch market (- 4%) and the Italian market (- 1%).

A quick look at the main regional and intra-regional tourist flows shows once again, that despite some factors that have made travel easier (liberalization, lower transport costs, etc.), most tourists still prefer by far to go on holiday within their own geographical area.

The trend of demand from each generating country of the OECD area from 1984 to 1989 (or 1988 when more recent data are not available) is described below.

*France* (population, 56 million) is a country with a long tradition of tourism. It is, of course, a major receiving country on account of its cultural and geographical diversity, but it is also a major generating market. It has a high net departure rate (58%) but only 15% of holidays are taken abroad; this is partly due to the fact that the country itself offers a very wide range of tourism products.

Spain is still the favourite holiday destination of the French, who travel mainly to the Mediterranean countries. They travel much less to other countries; only two out of ten French tourists went to the United Kingdom[1].

Table 7. **Annual growth rates of nights spent in the various means of accommodation from main generating countries**

| | H/A | Total Variation % 89/88 | From Japan | | From Netherlands | | From Canada | | From Italy | |
|---|---|---|---|---|---|---|---|---|---|---|
| | | | Relative share % 88 | Variation % 89/88 | Relative share % 88 | Variation % 89/88 | Relative share % 88 | Variation % 89/88 | Relative share % 88 | Variation % 89/88 |
| Austria (R) | A | 8.4 | 0.4 | 15.6 | 10.6 | 4.2 | 0.3 | −1.3 | 2.4 | 33.3 |
| Belgium (R) | A | 1.9 | 1.2 | 26.5 | 38.5 | 3.3 | 0.9 | 7.6 | 2.9 | 7.2 |
| Denmark (N) | A | 13.4 | | | 6.4 | 18.3 | | | 1.9 | 14.0 |
| Finland (R) | H | 9.5 | 2.4 | 9.1 | 2.0 | 12.8 | 1.3 | 9.2 | 3.6 | 6.2 |
| France (R) | H | 26.2 | 4.2 | 68.7 | 5.4 | 9.8 | 1.8 | 27.7 | 12.2 | 30.8 |
| Germany (R) | A | 11.5 | 3.5 | 19.9 | 18.9 | 4.8 | 1.2 | 15.5 | 4.7 | 17.8 |
| Greece (N) | A | −2.0 | 0.8 | | 5.0 | | 0.7 | | 5.2 | |
| Iceland | | | | | | | | | | |
| Ireland (R) | | | | | | | | | | |
| Italy (N) | A | −6.3 | 1.3 | | 3.9 | | 0.7 | | | |
| Luxembourg (R) | | | | | | | | | | |
| Netherlands (R) | A | 12.1 | 1.3 | 1.6 | | | 1.6 | 3.2 | 3.7 | 15.5 |
| Norway (N) | H | 2.2 | 2.0 | 20.1 | 3.2 | 9.7 | | | | |
| Portugal (N) | A | 2.5 | 0.4 | 1.3 | 9.3 | 5.7 | 1.8 | 8.7 | 2.4 | 8.7 |
| Spain (N) | H | −11.4 | 0.7 | 34.1 | 3.8 | −15.5 | 0.2 | −2.8 | 5.3 | −1.4 |
| Sweden (N) | A | 6.6 | 1.1 | 9.5 | 4.8 | 16.1 | 0.4 | 8.9 | 1.6 | 23.2 |
| Switzerland (R) | A | 4.4 | 2.0 | 19.8 | 8.6 | 4.7 | 0.7 | 5.2 | 4.4 | 14.9 |
| Turkey (N) | A | 1.8 | 1.0 | 15.1 | | | 0.3 | 1.8 | 4.2 | −0.4 |
| United Kingdom (R) | A | 7.0 | 1.7 | 10.8 | 3.2 | −6.5 | 5.1 | −3.6 | 4.9 | −3.6 |
| **EUROPE** | | 5.5 | 1.6 | 27.4 | 7.0 | 1.2 | 2.2 | 0.0 | 4.9 | 10.1 |
| Canada (R) | A | −2.0 | 2.4 | 13.9 | 1.3 | −4.8 | | | 1.2 | −6.0 |
| United States | | | | | | | | | | |
| **NORTH AMERICA** | | | | | | | | | | |
| Australia | H | | 12.4 | | 0.6 | | 4.2 | | 1.3 | |
| New Zealand | | | | | | | | | | |
| Japan | | | | | | | | | | |
| **AUSTRALASIA-JAPAN** | | | | | | | | | | |
| **OECD** | | 4.4 | 1.7 | 24.4 | 6.1 | 1.0 | 1.9 | 0.0 | 4.3 | 9.5 |
| Yugoslavia (N) | A | −6.1 | 0.1 | 7.1 | 6.9 | −3.5 | 0.2 | −19.4 | 10.2 | 14.5 |

H Hotels and similar establishments.
A All means of accommodation.
(R) Tourist count by country of residence.
(N) Tourist count by country of nationality.

Since 1984, the most popular holiday destinations with the French have been Turkey (nights spent up by 257%, 1988/84), Canada (arrivals up by 113%, 1989/84), the United States, Australia and Ireland (up by about 80%). On the other hand, the French made fewer visits to Yugoslavia (nights spent down by 25%, 1989/84).

With a net departure rate of 60%, and 66% abroad, *Germany* (population, 61 million) was one of the three main generating countries.

Austria, Italy and Spain accounted for more than half (53%) of foreign holidays taken by Germans. It can be seen that although Austria was slightly less popular in 1985 than in 1978, by and large German tourists still tend take their holidays in the same places. All the same, in the past six years the number of German tourists has increased substantially in Turkey (nights spent up by 524%, 1988/84), Portugal (nights spent up by 79%, 1989/84) and Ireland (nights spent up by 44%, 1988/84).

The *United Kingdom* (population, 57 million) is still one of the main generating countries. By tradition, culture and the specific geographical features of their country, the British like to travel. The United Kingdom has a net departure rate of 61%, with 28% of holidays being taken abroad. In 1989, foreign holidays taken by residents totalled about 275 million nights[2].

The British are particularly keen on holidays in the sun, the two most popular destinations being Spain, which accounts for one-third of all foreign holidays (between 1984 and 1989 the number of British arrivals in Spain increased by 20%) and France (number of nights spent between 1984 and 1988 up by 25%). At the same time, nights spent in Turkey increased by 477% (1988/1984), arrivals in the United States by 96% (1988/1984), in New Zealand by 85% (1989/1984), and nights spent in Yugoslavia by 64% (1989/1984). In contrast, there was a fall in the number of British tourists in Japan, Austria, Belgium, Denmark, Switzerland and Sweden (ranging from - 3% for Austria to - 22% for Belgium between 1984 and 1988).

In terms of expenditure, in 1988, the *United States* (population, 247 million) was the largest generating country. The US market has grown fairly briskly (+ 7% a year in real terms from 1975 to 1988 compared with the OECD average of + 5%). This was largely ascribable to the strength of the dollar at the beginning of the 1980s, when Americans travelled more abroad. Since 1985 the choice of destinations has changed radically.

In 1986 the number of American tourists in Europe fell sharply (down by 20% on 1985) on account of international events (the wave of terrorism in Europe, Chernobyl) and the fall in the dollar; many went to the Asian countries instead. Since 1987 the trend has been reversed, with the number of American tourists on the increase again. The main beneficiaries have been Ireland (+ 23% in terms of nights spent, 1988/84), Turkey (+ 25% in terms of nights spent, 1988/84) and Yugoslavia (+ 20% in terms of nights spent, 1988/84). Over the same period, arrivals in Australia increased by 100% and those in New Zealand by 66%.

Other new markets have emerged alongside the traditional generating markets; historically these have played a smaller role in international tourism but as their economies have expanded they have gradually caught up with the main generating countries. Whereas in 1975 the ratio of expenditure by the first-placed generating country to that of the ninth-placed was 8 to 1, in 1988 it was only 5 to 1; clearly, the group of main generating countries is now larger than it used to be, and in the space of 15 years has changed considerably. Some of the "new" main countries generating international tourism towards the OECD area are described below.

*Canada* (population, 26 million) is a major market. With one of the highest standards of living in the world but with a harsh climate, particularly in winter, the Canadians have been keen travellers abroad (34% of departures) for many years.

In 1985, Canadians made more than 7 million non-business person/trips (number of trips multiplied by the number of people from the same household on the trip), representing about 106 million nights[3].

While most Canadians (71%) still tend to take their holidays in the United States, more of them are travelling to Europe. They tend to prefer holidays in the sun (40%), the most popular destinations being Florida, Hawaii, California, Mexico, the Bermudas and the Caribbean.

The most popular European destinations are the United Kingdom, France, Germany, Italy and Switzerland. The main reasons for travelling to Europe are business, family and cultural ties (particularly in the case of the United Kingdom and France). The biggest increases have been to Turkey (nights spent up by 120%, 1988/84), Australia (arrivals up by 57%, 1989/84), New Zealand (arrivals up by 34%, 1989/84) and the United States (arrivals up by 40%, 1989/84).

With a net departure rate of 57%, of which 10% abroad, *Italy* (population, 57 million) is a rapidly expanding market; this is ascribable to increased purchasing power and the easing of exchange controls. Italy is probably one of the largest growth markets in Europe. It was estimated that in 1985 the Italians made 3 million trips abroad, representing 47.2 million days. The average length of stay was thus 16 days[4].

The small proportion of foreign journeys can be explained, as in the case of France, by the wide range and diversity of holidays to be had in Italy itself.

It is estimated that only 46% of Italians have been to countries outside the European Economic Community. France, and Mediterranean countries in general, are the most popular destinations.

Since 1984 the trend of international tourism has been positive in all OECD Member countries, particularly Australia (nights spent up by 230%, 1988/84), New Zealand (arrivals up by 175%, 1989/84), Turkey (nights spent up by 138%, 1988/84) and Portugal (nights spent up by 110%, 1988/84).

In the past 15 years, *Japan* (population, 123 million) has experienced unprecedented economic growth; as a result, the purchasing power of the Japanese has increased, together with their desire for leisure. In recent years the government has launched a major programme, known as the "ten million Programme" to encourage the Japanese to take holidays abroad; this has probably helped to increase spending by the Japanese abroad considerably (up by 75% in 1988 on 1987 in dollar terms). Japan is the OECD country with the largest average annual real increase (+ 11% from 1975 to 1988, compared with the OECD average of + 5%).

A recent study shows that the number of Japanese travelling abroad increased by over 50% from 1986 to 1988. It also indicates that 62% of these were men; however, in the space of 10 years the number of women travelling abroad increased 2.8 times, compared with only 1.8 times for men[5]. Moreover, the number of overseas journeys (for all reasons) by the Japanese increased 13-fold in 15 years; in 1985 they made 4 million overseas journeys[6].

The Japanese travel mostly to Asian countries and the United States. The biggest increases (1988/1987) have been in journeys to Australia (+ 63%), the Philippines (+ 43%), Spain (+ 30%) and Canada (+ 30%). This may be ascribed partly to the fact that these countries, with the exception of Spain, are not far from Japan; as for Spain, a number of Japanese firms appear to have invested in holiday/retirement villages there, leading to an increase in the number of Japanese tourists.

Despite the fact that it has a relatively small population (15 million), the *Netherlands* has become one of the main generating countries. One of the reasons is that the Dutch have always been keen travellers. The net departure rate is accordingly very high (72% in 1989); and 71% of the Dutch who travel do so abroad, the second-highest figure in Europe, exceeded only by Luxembourg. In 1989, the Dutch made 11 million non-business journeys abroad, totalling 132 million days.

Unlike other Europeans, quite often the Dutch (35% of them) take their holidays in Northern countries. Four destinations alone account for 62% of Dutch tourism abroad. Between 1984 and 1989 the number of Dutch tourists increased particularly in Turkey (arrivals up by 294%), Greece, Portugal and the United States (+ 100%).

## NOTES

1. "The Europeans and their holidays", European Economic Community, 1986.
2. "The International Passenger Survey", Department of Employment, United Kingdom.
3. "Questionnaire for residents returning from a foreign journey of at least 24 hours", Canada Statistics, 1985.
4. "Survey on the holidays, the travel and the sports of Italians", Central Statistical Institute, Rome, 1985.
5. "Annual Tourism Report", Prime Minister's Office, Japan, 1985.
6. "Annual Report of Statistics on Legal Migrants", Japanese Ministry of Justice, 1985.

### Trends of international tourism in Europe, from:

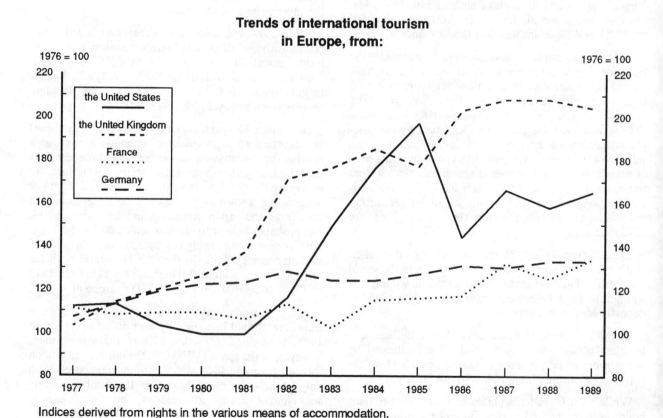

Indices derived from nights in the various means of accommodation.

Source: OECD.

# Trends of international tourism
# in Europe, from:

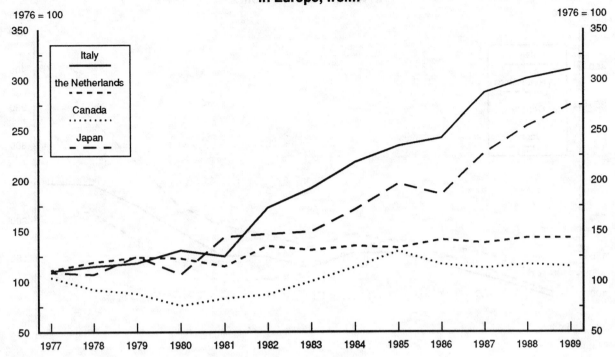

Indices derived from nights in the various means of accommodation.
Source: OECD.

# Trends of international tourism
# in North America, from:

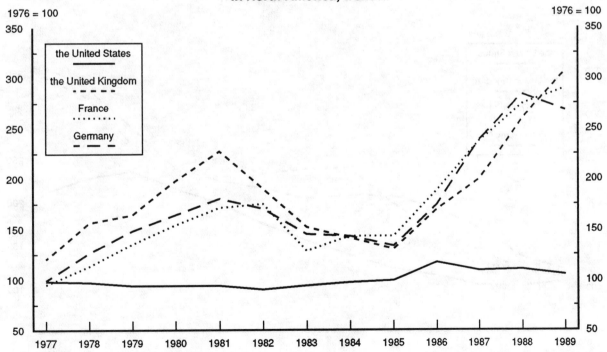

Indices derived from arrivals at frontiers.
Source: OECD.

## Trends of international tourism
## in North America, from:

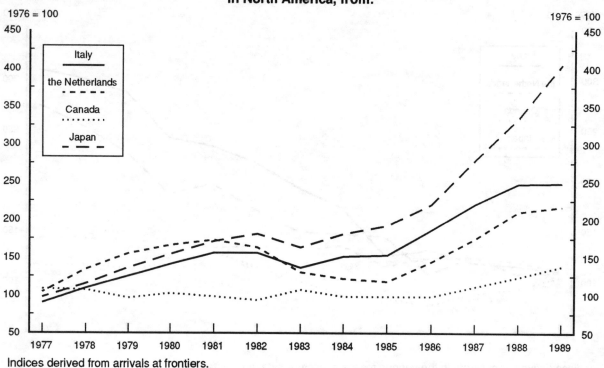

1976 = 100

1976 = 100

Indices derived from arrivals at frontiers.
Source: OECD.

## Trends of international tourism
## in Australasia-Japan, from:

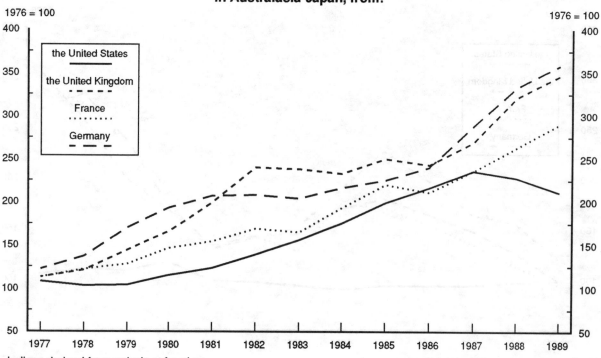

1976 = 100

1976 = 100

Indices derived from arrivals at frontiers.
Source: OECD.

# Trends of international tourism
## in Australasia-Japan

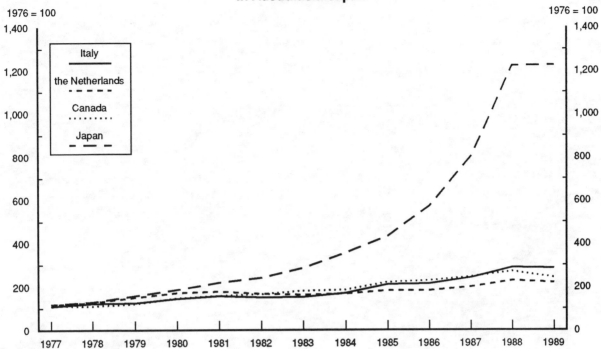

Indices derived from arrivals at frontiers.

Source: OECD.

# III

# THE ECONOMIC IMPORTANCE
# OF INTERNATIONAL TOURISM
# IN MEMBER COUNTRIES

This chapter provides the most recent information on international tourism receipts and expenditure in 1989 for the 24 OECD Member countries and Yugoslavia. The figures do not include international fare payments, except where explicitly stated (see Table 18 of the Statistical Annex).

The first part of the Chapter (Section A) considers:

a) Receipts in both national currencies and in US dollars (in current terms) and then in real terms, i.e. adjusted for the effects of inflation and for changes in parities between the dollar and national currencies;

b) Expenditure, again in both national currencies and US dollars, in current terms;

c) The tourism balance sheet for the OECD area and its three constituent regions.

The United States dollar is used as the common unit of account in order to evaluate trends for a range of countries. However, when considering the tables which give figures in "current dollars", the reader must take into account the marked fluctuations in recent years in most OECD currencies against the dollar. In 1989, the positive changes were less than 10% for most countries (17 out of 24), reflecting the appreciation of the dollar against these currencies. Only the Canadian and Australian currencies rose against the US dollar. In this context, some cases of very marked depreciation are to be noted: Yugoslavia (1 039%), Turkey (49%), Iceland (33%), Greece (14%) and Switzerland (12%) (see Table 17 in the Annex). The limits to the use of these figures are thus obvious and great care must be taken in drawing any conclusions based on data expressed in dollars.

Section B compares the information on receipts and expenditure with a number of major macroeconomic indicators, i.e. gross domestic product, private final consumption and the export and import of goods and services. They cover the period 1986-1988, as comprehensive 1989 data for these indicators are not yet available.

The comparability of the figures provided by Member countries on receipts and expenditure for international tourism is still insufficient and its improvement is a continuing priority for the Statistical Working Party of the OECD Tourism Committee.

The main source of divergence lies in the different survey methods used. Most countries use the "bank reporting method", which is based on the sales and purchases of foreign currency before or after travel abroad. The main drawback of this method is that it gives data on the currency concerned but not on the country visited. The "estimation method" is based on sample surveys carried out among residents at entry or departure points. Such surveys can provide extensive information but because of their cost are conducted by only a few countries. Last, some countries use a "mixed method" involving limited surveys to give adjustment factors to apply to bank-derived data. Progress towards greater comparability is being made, however. For further information, the notes in the Statistical Annex should be consulted.

## A. INTERNATIONAL TOURIST RECEIPTS AND EXPENDITURE[1]

Dollar receipts and expenditure for the OECD area as a whole were up respectively by 5% and 4% (as against 15% and 19% respectively in 1988); the increase was limited since the US dollar rose against all OECD currencies (except the Canadian and Australian dollars).

51

The increased percentage in receipts in North America was nearly twice that of expenditure, while in Australasia-Japan the rise in expenditure was three times that of receipts. In real terms, receipts in the OECD area were up 5%, or much less than in 1988 (up 9%).

## International tourist receipts

The growth in international tourist flows (see Chapter II) was confirmed by the increase in receipts expressed in national currency (see Table 1) in 18 of the 24 OECD countries. The six countries which recorded declines in their national currency receipts included two Mediterranean countries, Spain (down 1%) and Greece (4%).

Receipts expressed in current dollars (see Table 2) rose again in 1989 but more slowly than in 1988, mainly because the dollar was firmer against almost all the other currencies. France (up 20%), the United States (19%), Canada, Japan and Turkey (all 9%) recorded the highest growth, while Italy, Greece and Spain taken together show a decrease of some $1.25 billion.

For the OECD area as a whole receipts in current dollars amounted to $148.2 billion. Provisional estimates published by the World Tourism Organisation gave a total figure for world international tourism receipts in 1989 of $209 billion, or 8% more than the

$194 billion of 1988. On this basis the OECD share amounted to 71% of the 1989 total.

The countries earning most from international tourism – in dollar terms – were the United States, which accounted for 23% of the OECD total, and France and Spain (11% each).

In real terms (see Table 3), i.e. once the effects of inflation and exchange fluctuations against the dollar are removed, North America (up 12%) recorded higher growth than the OECD area as a whole (5%), and Australasia-Japan saw a modest rise of 1% in 1989 following very good progress (21%) in 1988.

## International tourist expenditure

Expenditure in terms of national currency (see Table 1) was up in nearly all the OECD countries, the exceptions being Austria (down 15%) and Norway (down 12%). The highest increases were recorded by Turkey (up 136%), Australia (30%), Greece and Spain (both 27%) and Japan (22%).

In terms of dollar expenditure (see Table 2), some generating countries confirmed their economic impact on international tourism, with Japan, the United States, Canada, Italy and Spain in decreasing order of volume growth. Turkey's expenditure rose by 58%. Expenditure by the OECD countries as a whole rose by 4% to $164.7 billion in 1989.

Table 1. **International tourist receipts and expenditure in national currencies**

In millions

| | | Receipts | | | Expenditure | | |
|---|---|---|---|---|---|---|---|
| | Currency | 1988 | 1989 | %89/88 | 1988 | 1989 | %89/88 |
| Austria | Schilling | 124 617 | 123 257 | −1.1 | 77 891 | 66 508 | −14.6 |
| Belgium-Luxembourg | Franc[1] | 126 300 | 120 700 | −4.4 | 169 900 | 168 300 | −0.9 |
| Denmark | Krone | 16 307 | 16 894 | 3.6 | 20 732 | 21 407 | 3.3 |
| Finland | Markka | 4 120 | 4 344 | 5.4 | 7 717 | 8 782 | 13.8 |
| France | Franc | 82 097 | 105 272 | 28.2 | 57 852 | 65 663 | 13.5 |
| Germany | Deutsche Mark | 14 889 | 16 276 | 9.3 | 43 806 | 45 362 | 3.6 |
| Greece | Drachma | 338 878 | 323 800 | −4.4 | 104 580 | 132 650 | 26.8 |
| Iceland | Krona | 4 628 | 6 143 | 32.7 | 8 594 | 10 406 | 21.1 |
| Ireland | Pound | 655 | 755 | 15.3 | 631 | 698 | 10.6 |
| Italy | Lira | 16 138 883 | 16 443 000 | 1.9 | 7 878 750 | 9 291 000 | 17.9 |
| Netherlands | Guilder | 5 679 | 6 405 | 12.8 | 13 316 | 13 680 | 2.7 |
| Norway | Krone | 9 563 | 9 167 | −4.1 | 22 442 | 19 653 | −12.4 |
| Portugal | Escudo | 349 093 | 406 437 | 16.4 | 76 883 | 87 546 | 13.9 |
| Spain | Peseta | 1 944 400 | 1 924 200 | −1.0 | 286 200 | 364 700 | 27.4 |
| Sweden | Krona | 14 382 | 16 394 | 14.0 | 27 947 | 32 026 | 14.6 |
| Switzerland | Franc | 8 395 | 9 190 | 9.5 | 7 365 | 8 100 | 10.0 |
| Turkey | Lira | 3 343 183 | 5 419 754 | 62.1 | 508 156 | 1 197 794 | 135.7 |
| United Kingdom | Pound | 6 184 | 6 877 | 11.2 | 8 216 | 9 290 | 13.1 |
| Canada | Dollar | 5 665 | 5 936 | 4.8 | 7 781 | 8 734 | 12.2 |
| United States | Dollar[2] | 28 935 | 34 432 | 19.0 | 33 098 | 34 977 | 5.7 |
| Australia | Dollar | 4 222 | 4 262 | 0.9 | 3 668 | 4 760 | 29.8 |
| New Zealand | Dollar | 1 544 | 1 676 | 8.5 | 2 060 | 2 258 | 9.6 |
| Japan | Yen | 370 931 | 435 388 | 17.4 | 2 396 985 | 2 915 378 | 21.6 |
| Yugoslavia | Dinar | 5 754 695 | 72 203 909 | 1154.7 | | | |

Notice: for statistical coverage, see notes in table 18 in annex.
1. Preliminary data for 1989.
2. New series from 1984 affecting regional as well as overall OECD volumes and trends.

## Table 2. International tourist receipts and expenditure in current dollars
In millions

| | Receipts | | | Expenditure | | |
|---|---|---|---|---|---|---|
| | 1988 | 1989 | %89/88 | 1988 | 1989 | %89/88 |
| Austria | 10 094.7 | 9 316.1 | −7.7 | 6 309.6 | 5 026.9 | −20.3 |
| Belgium-Luxembourg | 3 434.7 | 3 063.5 | −10.8 | 4 620.4 | 4 271.6 | −7.5 |
| Denmark | 2 423.0 | 2 311.1 | −4.6 | 3 080.5 | 2 928.4 | −4.9 |
| Finland | 984.1 | 1 013.0 | 2.9 | 1 843.3 | 2 048.0 | 11.1 |
| France | 13 784.1 | 16 500.0 | 19.7 | 9 713.4 | 10 291.8 | 6.0 |
| Germany | 8 478.4 | 8 657.6 | 2.1 | 24 944.8 | 24 129.3 | −3.3 |
| Greece | 2 392.6 | 1 997.7 | −16.5 | 738.4 | 818.4 | 10.8 |
| Iceland | 107.5 | 107.6 | 0.0 | 199.7 | 182.2 | −8.8 |
| Ireland | 997.1 | 1 070.0 | 7.3 | 960.5 | 989.2 | 3.0 |
| Italy | 12 398.5 | 11 987.4 | −3.3 | 6 052.7 | 6 773.4 | 11.9 |
| Netherlands | 2 872.9 | 3 019.9 | 5.1 | 6 736.3 | 6 450.0 | −4.2 |
| Norway | 1 467.3 | 1 327.9 | −9.5 | 3 443.5 | 2 846.9 | −17.3 |
| Portugal | 2 425.2 | 2 587.1 | 6.7 | 534.1 | 557.3 | 4.3 |
| Spain | 16 691.4 | 16 252.0 | −2.6 | 2 456.8 | 3 080.3 | 25.4 |
| Sweden | 2 346.5 | 2 543.2 | 8.4 | 4 559.7 | 4 968.2 | 9.0 |
| Switzerland | 5 738.1 | 5 619.2 | −2.1 | 5 034.1 | 4 952.7 | −1.6 |
| Turkey | 2 355.4 | 2 556.5 | 8.5 | 358.0 | 565.0 | 57.8 |
| United Kingdom | 10 999.8 | 11 248.4 | 2.3 | 14 614.2 | 15 195.3 | 4.0 |
| **EUROPE** | 99 991.3 | 101 178.5 | 1.2 | 96 200.2 | 96 075.0 | −0.1 |
| Canada | 4 600.1 | 5 013.3 | 9.0 | 6 318.4 | 7 376.4 | 16.7 |
| United States | 28 935.0 | 34 432.0 | 19.0 | 33 098.0 | 34 977.0 | 5.7 |
| **NORTH AMERICA** | 33 535.1 | 39 445.3 | 17.6 | 39 416.4 | 42 353.4 | 7.5 |
| Australia | 3 295.1 | 3 369.7 | 2.3 | 2 862.8 | 3 763.5 | 31.5 |
| New Zealand | 1 009.9 | 1 001.0 | −0.9 | 1 347.4 | 1 349.0 | 0.1 |
| Japan | 2 894.2 | 3 155.6 | 9.0 | 18 702.8 | 21 129.9 | 13.0 |
| **AUSTRALASIA-JAPAN** | 7 199.3 | 7 526.3 | 4.5 | 22 912.9 | 26 242.4 | 14.5 |
| **OECD** | 140 725.7 | 148 150.1 | 5.3 | 158 529.5 | 164 670.7 | 3.9 |
| Yugoslavia | 2 024.2 | 2 230.4 | 10.2 | | | |

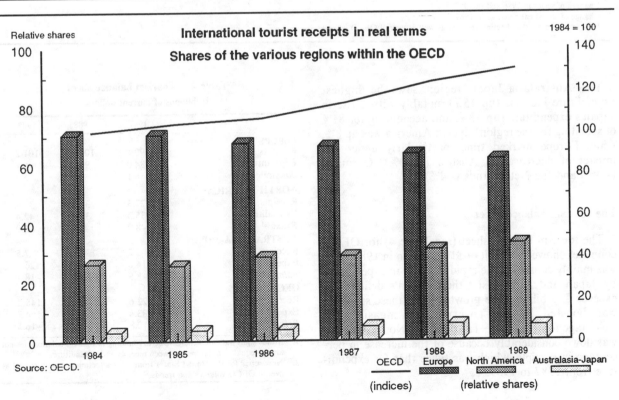

Relative shares     **International tourist receipts in real terms**     1984 = 100

**Shares of the various regions within the OECD**

Source: OECD.

OECD — (indices)    Europe    North America    Australasia-Japan    (relative shares)

Table 3. **Trends in international tourist receipts in real prices**[1]

| | 1984 = 100 | | | | | Relative share in percentage of total | |
|---|---|---|---|---|---|---|---|
| | 1985 | 1986 | 1987 | 1988 | 1989 | 1988 | 1989 |
| Austria | 100.6 | 99.6 | 104.2 | 113.6 | 109.5 | 6.1 | 5.6 |
| Belgium-Luxembourg | 97.1 | 96.2 | 107.7 | 119.8 | 111.0 | 2.1 | 1.9 |
| Denmark | 100.3 | 98.3 | 100.8 | 103.3 | 102.2 | 1.4 | 1.3 |
| Finland | 101.1 | 95.9 | 108.9 | 117.1 | 115.8 | 0.6 | 0.6 |
| France | 101.6 | 93.4 | 95.9 | 107.6 | 133.3 | 8.8 | 10.3 |
| Germany | 111.9 | 109.9 | 110.6 | 117.6 | 125.0 | 5.4 | 5.5 |
| Greece | 112.7 | 120.3 | 125.5 | 121.2 | 101.8 | 1.7 | 1.4 |
| Iceland | 121.6 | 138.8 | 158.3 | 180.2 | 198.0 | 0.1 | 0.1 |
| Ireland | 112.3 | 107.1 | 114.0 | 129.5 | 143.5 | 0.7 | 0.7 |
| Italy | 96.7 | 84.1 | 86.2 | 84.0 | 80.3 | 7.7 | 7.0 |
| Netherlands | 99.2 | 97.9 | 98.6 | 101.6 | 113.3 | 1.8 | 2.0 |
| Norway | 102.7 | 110.0 | 103.5 | 110.0 | 100.8 | 0.8 | 0.7 |
| Portugal | 114.7 | 120.3 | 144.6 | 153.1 | 158.3 | 1.6 | 1.5 |
| Spain | 101.8 | 113.8 | 118.0 | 119.9 | 111.1 | 10.0 | 8.8 |
| Sweden | 102.1 | 106.0 | 117.1 | 123.2 | 132.0 | 1.5 | 1.5 |
| Switzerland | 100.7 | 98.4 | 101.9 | 104.6 | 111.0 | 3.6 | 3.6 |
| Turkey | 167.9 | 147.2 | 197.6 | 256.6 | 245.2 | 2.4 | 2.2 |
| United Kingdom | 112.0 | 109.5 | 118.9 | 112.3 | 115.8 | 7.4 | 7.3 |
| **EUROPE** | 104.2 | 102.0 | 107.2 | 111.7 | 114.2 | 63.7 | 61.9 |
| Canada | 110.9 | 134.4 | 127.0 | 132.7 | 132.4 | 4.1 | 3.9 |
| United States[4] | 100.3 | 112.4 | 123.9 | 147.3 | 167.3 | 26.9 | 29.1 |
| **NORTH AMERICA** | 101.8 | 115.5 | 124.4 | 145.2 | 162.3 | 31.0 | 33.0 |
| Australia[3] | 117.6 | 135.0 | 198.0 | 255.3 | 239.5 | 3.0 | 2.6 |
| New Zealand[2] | 143.2 | 191.6 | 236.1 | 217.5 | 223.0 | 0.7 | 0.7 |
| Japan | 114.3 | 102.4 | 127.0 | 156.4 | 179.5 | 1.6 | 1.8 |
| **AUSTRALASIA-JAPAN** | 119.6 | 129.0 | 173.7 | 209.6 | 212.6 | 5.3 | 5.1 |
| **OECD** | 104.0 | 106.4 | 113.8 | 123.6 | 129.9 | 100.0 | 100.0 |
| Yugoslavia | 129.4 | 123.5 | 140.7 | 205.7 | 190.9 | | |

1. After correcting for the effects of inflation in each country. For the regional and OECD totals, the receipts of the individual countries are weighted in proportion to their share in the total expressed in dollars.
2. Changes of series in 1986 and in 1987.
3. Change of statistical coverage in 1987.
4. New series from 1984 affecting regional as well as overall OECD volumes and trends.

The Australasia-Japan region saw the highest expenditure increase (up 15%), notably with a rise in Japan's expenditure (up 13%, and accounting for 81% of spending for the region); North America was up 8%, while Europe marked time, particularly under the impact of decreases in Austria (- 20%), Germany (- 3%) and the Netherlands (- 4%).

### The tourism balance sheet

The tourism balance sheet (see Table 4) for OECD countries showed a deficit of $16.5 billion in 1989. This was mainly caused by the rapid increase in expenditure by Japan and Australasia; their region's deficit now exceeds $18 billion. The growth in Japanese spending was boosted by the government's measures to encourage foreign travel. The deficit in North America was down considerably because of the increase in percentage in receipts, which was twice that for expenditure from 1987 to 1989.

Table 4. **Tourism balance sheet**
In billions of current dollars

| | 1987 | 1988 | 1989 |
|---|---|---|---|
| **EUROPE** | | | |
| Receipts | 90.1 | 100.0 | 101.2 |
| Expenditure | 84.0 | 96.2 | 96.1 |
| *Balance*[1] | 6.1 | 3.8 | 5.1 |
| **NORTH AMERICA**[2] | | | |
| Receipts | 27.3 | 33.5 | 39.4 |
| Expenditure | 35.3 | 39.4 | 42.4 |
| *Balance*[1] | −8.0 | −5.9 | −2.9 |
| **AUSTRALASIA-JAPAN** | | | |
| Receipts | 5.2 | 7.2 | 7.5 |
| Expenditure | 14.0 | 22.9 | 26.2 |
| *Balance*[1] | −8.9 | −15.7 | −18.7 |
| **OECD**[2] | | | |
| Receipts | 122.6 | 140.7 | 148.2 |
| Expenditure | 133.4 | 158.5 | 164.7 |
| *Balance*[1] | −10.8 | −17.8 | −16.5 |

1. Minus signs indicate deficits. Due to rounding of figures, balances are not always equal to difference between receipts and expenditure.
2. New series for the United States from 1984 affecting regional as well as overall OECD volumes and trends.

54

# B.  THE ECONOMIC IMPORTANCE OF THE "TRAVEL" ACCOUNT IN THE BALANCE OF PAYMENTS

For some years, the Tourism Committee's Statistical Working Party has been working to apply the tried and tested approach of the System of National Accounts (SNA) to pinpoint the economic importance of tourism. The SNA is the only available framework for coherent analysis of the economic contribution of tourism because it brings together commodities, supply and use, and sets them against activities and final users. It also allows links with other parts of the system, such as income and outlay.

The preliminary version of a user's manual should be ready by the end of 1990, so that it can subsequently serve as an OECD contribution to the Internation Conference on Statistics to be held by the World Tourism Organisation (WTO) in Ottawa, Canada, in June 1991. A system of this kind could then be gradually introduced, with a test period to develop a pilot project for use of the manual. There is no doubt that the use of such a system will be a very useful contribution to assessing the part which tourism plays in countries' economies since it will take both national and international tourism into account.

As data on this basis are not yet available, other indicators are still being used that are admittedly less satisfactory but are the only ones that give an idea of tourism's importance at macroeconomic level.

A recent study for the purposes of the current Uruguay Round in GATT discusses the importance of services in the world economy and provides some interesting information concerning the place of the "travel account" and passenger transport expenditure (part of the "transport account") within the balance of payments.

**World exports of private services, by category**

| Category of services | Share in exports of private services (%) | | | Average annual percentage change | |
|---|---|---|---|---|---|
| | 1970 | 1980 | 1987 | 1970-79 | 1980-87 |
| Passenger transport | 5 | 5 | 6 | 19 | 7.5 |
| Travel | 29 | 27 | 29 | 18 | 6.5 |
| Private services[1] | 100 | 100 | 100 | 19 | 5.0 |

1.  Other services include freight transport, insurance, communications, professional services, etc.
*Source*:  World Bank and UN Centre on Transnational Corporations.

This table shows the importance of tourism activities (passenger transport, travel) in total exports of services; tourism accounted for over a third of the total in 1987. The increase for these two items has also been considerably higher than for services as a whole over the past twenty years.

The final section of this paper considers the importance of tourism in individual Member countries with the use of four indicators. The tables cover the period 1986 to 1988; the data for 1989 are not yet available. It would admittedly have been instructive to include international passenger transport payments, but only a few Member countries break down their "transport" account in this way (see Table 16 of the Statistical Annex) so the data would not be comparable.

### Share of "travel account" receipts in gross domestic product

"Travel account" receipts (see Table 5) amounted to 1% of GDP for the entire OECD area. The increase from 1986 to 1988 was particularly marked in Turkey (from 1.6 to 3.3%), Portugal (from 5.3 to 5.8%) and Ireland (from 2.6 to 3.1%), three countries where tourism is particularly important and has developed considerably in recent years.

### Share of "travel account" expenditure in private final consumption

From 1986 to 1988 "travel account" expenditure as a proportion of private final consumption in Member countries as a whole rose from 1.6 to 1.9% (see Table 6). During this same period the highest increases were in Austria (from 7.6 to 8.9%) and New Zealand (from 3.8 to 5.2%), with no country recording a decline.

### Share of "travel account" receipts in the export of goods and services

The share of international tourism receipts in the export of goods and services for the OECD area has

| Table 5. Ratio of the "Travel" account receipts to the gross domestic product (%) | | | |
|---|---|---|---|
| | 1986 | 1987 | 1988 |
| Austria | 7.5 | 7.6 | 7.9 |
| Belgium-Luxembourg | 2.0 | 2.2 | 2.3 |
| Denmark | 2.1 | 2.2 | 2.3 |
| Finland | 0.9 | 0.9 | 0.9 |
| France | 1.3 | 1.3 | 1.5 |
| Germany | 0.7 | 0.7 | 0.7 |
| Greece | 4.7 | 4.9 | 4.6 |
| Iceland | 1.5 | 1.6 | 1.8 |
| Ireland | 2.6 | 2.8 | 3.1 |
| Italy | 1.6 | 1.6 | 1.5 |
| Netherlands | 1.3 | 1.3 | 1.3 |
| Norway | 1.5 | 1.5 | 1.7 |
| Portugal | 5.3 | 5.8 | 5.8 |
| Spain | 5.2 | 5.1 | 4.9 |
| Sweden | 1.2 | 1.3 | 1.3 |
| Switzerland | 4.0 | 3.9 | 3.9 |
| Turkey | 1.6 | 2.2 | 3.3 |
| United Kingdom | 1.5 | 1.5 | 1.3 |
| **EUROPE** | 1.8 | 1.8 | 1.8 |
| Canada | 1.3 | 1.2 | 1.2 |
| United States | 0.5 | 0.5 | 0.6 |
| **NORTH AMERICA** | 0.5 | 0.6 | 0.7 |
| Australia | 0.9 | 1.1 | 1.3 |
| New Zealand | 2.2 | 2.7 | 2.4 |
| Japan | 0.1 | 0.1 | 0.1 |
| **AUSTRALASIA-JAPAN** | 0.2 | 0.2 | 0.2 |
| **OECD** | 0.9 | 1.0 | 1.0 |

*Source:* OECD, Balance of Payments Division and *National Accounts of OECD Member Countries.*

| Table 6. Ratio of the "Travel" account expenditure to the private final consumption (%) | | | |
|---|---|---|---|
| | 1986 | 1987 | 1988 |
| Austria | 7.6 | 8.5 | 8.9 |
| Belgium-Luxembourg | 4.1 | 4.4 | 4.9 |
| Denmark | 4.7 | 5.2 | 5.4 |
| Finland | 2.8 | 3.1 | 3.3 |
| France | 1.5 | 1.6 | 1.7 |
| Germany | 3.7 | 3.7 | 3.8 |
| Greece | 1.9 | 1.6 | 2.0 |
| Iceland | 5.5 | 6.2 | 6.3 |
| Ireland | 4.6 | 4.8 | 5.1 |
| Italy | 0.8 | 1.0 | 1.2 |
| Netherlands | 4.7 | 4.9 | 5.0 |
| Norway | 7.0 | 7.1 | 7.5 |
| Portugal | 1.8 | 1.7 | 2.0 |
| Spain | 1.0 | 1.1 | 1.1 |
| Sweden | 4.1 | 4.4 | 4.7 |
| Switzerland | 5.0 | 5.2 | 5.6 |
| Turkey | 0.8 | 1.0 | 0.8 |
| United Kingdom | 2.6 | 2.8 | 2.8 |
| **EUROPE** | 2.7 | 2.9 | 3.0 |
| Canada | 2.6 | 2.8 | 2.8 |
| United States | 1.0 | 1.0 | 1.0 |
| **NORTH AMERICA** | 1.1 | 1.1 | 1.2 |
| Australia | 2.0 | 2.1 | 2.0 |
| New Zealand | 3.8 | 4.3 | 5.2 |
| Japan | 0.6 | 0.8 | 1.1 |
| **AUSTRALASIA-JAPAN** | 0.8 | 0.9 | 1.3 |
| **OECD** | 1.6 | 1.8 | 1.9 |

*Source:* OECD, Balance of Payments Division and *National Accounts of OECD Member Countries.*

increased steadily since the mid 1980s to reach 4.9% in 1988 (see Table 7). The main increases were in Turkey (from 8.7 to 13.1%) and in Australia (from 5.1 to 7.5%); the most important declines were recorded in Greece (from 23.2 to 21.1%), Spain (from 25.8 to 25.1%) and Italy (from 7.7 to 7.3%).

### Share of "travel account" expenditure in the import of goods and services

From 1986 to 1988 the share of "travel account" expenditure in the import of goods and services rose slightly more than the share of receipts in exports (from 5 to 5.5%) (see Table 8); the Australasia-Japan region, up from 4.5 to 6.4%, was mainly responsible for this increase. Japan's share rose from 4.2 to 6.5% and New Zealand's from 6.5 to 10.4%. In Europe, the percentages decreased in only three countries, Spain (from 3.5 to 3.3%), Portugal (from 2.9 to 2.7%) and Turkey (from 2.2 to 1.9%).

## NOTES

1. A revision of US data from 1984 has had a considerable impact on regional as well as overall OECD volumes and trends (for details, see table 18 in Annex).

| Table 7. Share of "Travel" account receipts in exports of goods and services | | | | Table 8. Share of "Travel" account expenditure in imports of goods and services | | | |
|---|---|---|---|---|---|---|---|
| | 1986 | 1987 | 1988 | | 1986 | 1987 | 1988 |
| Austria | 18.1 | 19.0 | 18.9 | Austria | 10.5 | 12.0 | 11.7 |
| Belgium-Luxembourg | 2.1 | 2.4 | 2.4 | Belgium-Luxembourg | 2.9 | 3.2 | 3.3 |
| Denmark | 5.9 | 6.1 | 6.0 | Denmark | 6.3 | 7.4 | 7.4 |
| Finland | 3.1 | 3.5 | 3.6 | Finland | 5.3 | 6.0 | 6.1 |
| France | 5.2 | 5.4 | 5.6 | France | 3.6 | 3.9 | 4.0 |
| Germany | 2.1 | 2.1 | 2.1 | Germany | 7.3 | 7.8 | 7.6 |
| Greece | 23.2 | 22.2 | 21.1 | Greece | 4.1 | 3.5 | 4.6 |
| Iceland | 3.8 | 4.5 | 5.5 | Iceland | 8.4 | 10.1 | 10.4 |
| Ireland | 4.5 | 4.5 | 4.5 | Ireland | 4.1 | 4.2 | 4.2 |
| Italy | 7.7 | 7.8 | 7.3 | Italy | 2.3 | 2.9 | 3.4 |
| Netherlands | 2.2 | 2.2 | 2.1 | Netherlands | 5.1 | 5.5 | 5.2 |
| Norway | 3.7 | 3.9 | 4.1 | Norway | 8.0 | 8.7 | 9.1 |
| Portugal | 15.6 | 16.6 | 16.4 | Portugal | 2.9 | 2.5 | 2.7 |
| Spain | 25.8 | 26.1 | 25.1 | Spain | 3.5 | 3.3 | 3.3 |
| Sweden | 3.3 | 3.6 | 3.7 | Sweden | 6.2 | 6.7 | 7.1 |
| Switzerland | 8.4 | 8.5 | 8.1 | Switzerland | 7.1 | 7.4 | 7.7 |
| Turkey | 8.7 | 10.2 | 13.1 | Turkey | 2.2 | 2.5 | 1.9 |
| United Kingdom | 3.8 | 4.0 | 3.7 | United Kingdom | 4.2 | 4.7 | 4.7 |
| **EUROPE** | 5.4 | 5.6 | 5.5 | **EUROPE** | 5.0 | 5.4 | 5.4 |
| Canada | 4.3 | 4.1 | 4.1 | Canada | 4.8 | 5.4 | 5.2 |
| United States | 5.4 | 5.4 | 5.4 | United States | 5.2 | 5.2 | 5.1 |
| **NORTH AMERICA** | 5.2 | 5.1 | 5.1 | **NORTH AMERICA** | 5.1 | 5.2 | 5.1 |
| Australia | 5.1 | 6.0 | 7.5 | Australia | 5.1 | 5.5 | 5.2 |
| New Zealand | 7.8 | 9.1 | 8.3 | New Zealand | 6.4 | 7.6 | 10.4 |
| Japan | 0.6 | 0.7 | 0.8 | Japan | 4.2 | 5.0 | 6.5 |
| **AUSTRALASIA-JAPAN** | 1.2 | 1.5 | 1.7 | **AUSTRALASIA-JAPAN** | 4.5 | 5.2 | 6.4 |
| **OECD** | 4.8 | 4.9 | 4.9 | **OECD** | 5.0 | 5.3 | 5.5 |

*Source:* OECD, Balance of Payments Division.        *Source:* OECD, Balance of Payments Division.

# IV

# TRANSPORT

During 1989, economic conditions remained favourable for passenger transport, although economic growth appears to be moderate and some concerns emerged about a possible pick-up in inflation. In this economic environment, international passenger transport maintained its positive trend.

Airport and airspace congestion continued in 1989. According to the Association of European Airlines (AEA), 24 per cent of all European flights were delayed by more than 15 minutes, almost 5 points worse than in 1988 and more than 10 points over 1986. In order to combat air traffic congestion, various attempts in the field of air traffic control have been made, in particular on the European continent.

As the importance of the computer reservation systems (CRS) was widely recognised, global co-operation in this field between airlines developed promptly and proposals for the set up of codes of conduct for CRSs have been made.

Liberalization of European air transport is in progress. In December 1989, European Community Transport Ministers adopted the principles of a second package of European air liberalization measures following the first series of measures taken in December 1987. In response to the liberalization move, an increasing number of airlines are taking steps to form alliances with other carriers, including a tripartite shareholding agreement among British Airways, KLM and Sabena and the acquisition of UTA by Air France.

For rail transport, high-speed rail projects are in progress as a way to recover competitiveness. In January 1989, the Community of European Railways published "Proposals for a European High-Speed Network" and projects such as TGV-Nord and the Alpine crossings are under way. Outside Europe, developments were made in Australia, Japan, Canada and the United States.

As far as road transport is concerned, one of the main issues was the balance between transport activities and environmental protection.

On the other hand, the cruise market continued to grow, at a double-digit rate.

At the beginning of this new decade, more comprehensive transportation policies aiming at the 21st century have been considered in a number of Member countries. These will inevitably affect tourism in the future.

The text of this Chapter presents the situation on the basis of the information available as of 1st May 1990.

## A. AIR TRANSPORT

### World air traffic

#### Scheduled services

World scheduled airline traffic growth was sustained in 1988, with more than 1 billion passengers carried for the second year in a row. Passenger-kilometers increased by 7 per cent over 1987, compared with an average annual growth rate of about 5 per cent during the past decade. The passenger load factor increased from 67 in 1987 to 68 per cent in 1988. For international services, the number of passengers was 243 million, a 10 per cent increase over 1987, and the figure for passenger-kilometers increased by 11 per cent over 1987 (see Table 1).

Between 1987 and 1988, the growth of international traffic varied considerably among regions. Expressed in terms of passenger-kilometers, North American airlines recorded a growth rate of 16 per cent as a group, followed by those of Asia and the Pacific (14 per cent),

Table 1. **Trend in world scheduled passenger traffic**

| | Passengers | | | | Passenger-kilometers | | | | Passenger load factor | | | |
|---|---|---|---|---|---|---|---|---|---|---|---|---|
| | Total | | International | | Total | | International | | Total | | International | |
| | Volume in millions | Annual change (%) | Volume in millions | Annual change (%) | Volume in billions | Annual change (%) | Volume in billions | Annual change (%) | Load factor (%) | Annual change (point) | Load factor (%) | Annual change (point) |
| 1980 | 748 | -0.8 | 163 | 3.1 | 1 089 | 2.7 | 466 | 6.0 | 63 | -3.0 | 61 | 2.0 |
| 1981 | 752 | 0.5 | 173 | 6.0 | 1 119 | 2.7 | 495 | 6.0 | 64 | 1.0 | 63 | 2.0 |
| 1982 | 766 | 1.8 | 170 | -1.8 | 1 142 | 2.1 | 497 | 0.4 | 64 | 0.0 | 62 | -1.0 |
| 1983 | 798 | 4.2 | 172 | 1.7 | 1 190 | 4.2 | 511 | 2.9 | 64 | 0.0 | 63 | 1.0 |
| 1984 | 848 | 6.3 | 185 | 6.9 | 1 278 | 7.4 | 556 | 8.9 | 65 | 1.0 | 65 | 2.0 |
| 1985 | 899 | 6.0 | 194 | 5.1 | 1 367 | 7.0 | 591 | 6.2 | 66 | 1.0 | 65 | 0.0 |
| 1986 | 960 | 6.8 | 199 | 2.2 | 1 452 | 6.2 | 603 | 2.2 | 65 | -1.0 | 63 | -2.0 |
| 1987 | 1 027 | 7.0 | 222 | 11.9 | 1 589 | 9.4 | 688 | 14.0 | 67 | 2.0 | 67 | 4.0 |
| 1988 | 1 081 | 5.2 | 243 | 9.6 | 1 705 | 7.3 | 760 | 10.8 | 68 | 1.0 | 68 | 1.0 |
| 1989[1] | 1 099 | 1.7 | 259 | 6.7 | 1 778 | 4.3 | 821 | 8.0 | 68 | 0.0 | 68 | 0.0 |

1. Provisional data.
*Source:* International Civil Aviation Organisation (ICAO).

Latin America and the Caribbean (7 per cent), while those of both Africa and Europe recorded identical growth rates of 6 per cent, and those of the Middle East remained at the same level.

According to preliminary estimates for 1989 by the International Civil Aviation Organisation (ICAO), the scheduled airlines carried close to 1.1 billion passengers, an increase of 2 per cent over 1988. Passenger-kilometers increased 4 per cent over 1988 and the passenger load factor stood at 68 per cent.

### Non-scheduled services

Total non-scheduled passenger-kilometers performed throughout the world rose by 6 per cent in 1988 and non-scheduled passenger traffic accounted for 19 per cent of total traffic. Provisional data available concerning the following year suggest that the same trends prevailed in 1989 (see Table 2).

Travel between states within the 22 countries of the European Civil Aviation Conference (ECAC) constitutes the world's largest international charter market,

with the volume of non-scheduled traffic being comparable to that of scheduled traffic. For the year 1988, several new charter carriers were either formed or began operations in Europe, e.g. Spanair in Spain, Air Columbus in Portugal, Unifly in Italy, Nesu Air in Turkey, Air Liberté in France, Norway Airlines in Norway, Air City in Switzerland, Swan Airlines in the United Kingdom.

In Europe and over the North Atlantic route, non-scheduled passenger traffic increased by 6 per cent and 12 per cent respectively in 1988; however, a fall was recorded on routes to and from South America (down by 13 per cent), to and from the Caribbean and Central America (down by 6 per cent) and to and from Asia and the Pacific (down by 1 per cent).

### International traffic forecasts

Based on forecasts made in 1989, it was expected that continuing economic growth in the major traffic generating markets, lower oil price and improvements in aircraft technology and airline service standards

Table 2. **International non-scheduled passenger traffic**

| Category of traffic | Billions of passenger-kilometers | | | | | Annual change (%) | | | |
|---|---|---|---|---|---|---|---|---|---|
| | 1985 | 1986 | 1987 | 1988 | 1989[1] | 1986/85 | 1987/86 | 1988/87 | 1989/88[1] |
| Non-scheduled traffic | 122.6 | 134.3 | 163.2 | 172.5 | 183.0 | 9.5 | 21.5 | 5.7 | 6.1 |
| Total traffic | 712.8 | 737.4 | 850.7 | 934.2 | 1007.8 | 3.5 | 15.4 | 9.8 | 7.9 |
| Non-scheduled traffic, as percentage of total | 17.2 | 18.2 | 19.2 | 18.5 | 18.2 | | | | |

1. Provisional data.
Source: International Civil Aviation Organisation (ICAO).

would enable international air traffic to sustain its growth. According to the International Air Transport Association (IATA), worldwide international scheduled passenger traffic growth should attain 8.0 per cent or more in 1989-1990, settling down to 6.5-7.0 per cent in 1991-93. Asia and Pacific will remain the fastest growing region during the period, with an 11 per cent average annual increase in passenger traffic expected in the North Pacific area and 9 per cent in Southeast Asia and Southwest Pacific. Europe and North America are forecast to show consistent growth of 6 per cent on average during 1989-93.

**Air congestion**

For the year 1989, airport and airspace congestion continued. According to the AEA, 23.8 per cent of all European flights were delayed on departure by more than 15 minutes, almost 5 points worse than in 1988 and more than 10 points than in 1986 (see Diagram 1). There is also severe congestion in North America and the Asia/Pacific region. IATA estimates that passenger traffic on international services will show an average annual growth of about 7 per cent during the period 1989-1993 and there is a fear that air transport services could not be provided to keep pace with the growth of the number of travellers.

It is often pointed out that the existing European air traffic control systems aggravate European air congestion. In Europe there are 22 different national air traffic control systems which operate with different levels of performance and technology, without commonly agreed standards and compatibility between the different systems. A number of initiatives were taken to remedy this situation:

- Since early summer of 1989, the five major air traffic flow management units (London, Paris, Frankfurt, Rome and Madrid) have been working effectively as a single executive;
- In July 1989, Transport Ministers from eleven European countries agreed to set up an Ecu 60 million ($64.2 million) centralised information system for air traffic controllers. The new system will pull together information from 22 ECAC Member States. The information will facilitate route planning across Europe and find alternatives quickly for airlines in saturated airspace. The system will not remove national responsibility for air traffic control at the first stage; however, by 1993, it will replace the existing ten national or regional flow management systems;
- In October 1989, ECAC established a Task Force on the integration of European air traffic control systems; and finally,
- In April 1990, the Transport Ministers of ECAC countries adopted a new Strategy and Action Programme to harmonize and integrate the operations of their air traffic control systems in the 1990s. It states that harmonization will achieve comparable levels of operational system performance by closer compatibility between standards, specifications and procedures and will lead on to integration of systems in such a way that their operation in a given area will be such that, from the user's perspective, they will function as a single unit. This initiative will prepare the way for the introduction of a new generation of air navigation technology on the eve of the 21st century.

At the international level, ICAO adopted in September 1989 a resolution on airport and aerospace congestion which:

- Urges States to take measures that have positive effects on airport and airspace capacity;
- Invites States to recognise that airports and airspace constitute an integrated system and developments in both areas should be harmonized;
- Urges States to take into account the effects on other States of their airport and airspace congestion problems and the implication of actions taken to deal with those problems;
- Invites States to consider the possible relaxation of operating restrictions for aircraft.

**Computer Reservation Systems**

Computer Reservation Systems (CRSs) are recognised as a powerful marketing tool for the sale of

Diagram 1. **International short/medium haul departure delays over 15 minutes**

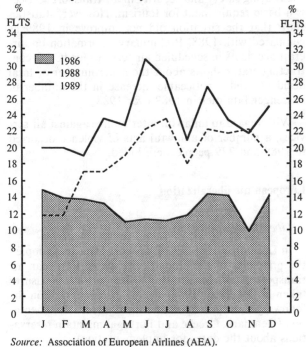

*Source:* Association of European Airlines (AEA).

61

airline tickets. In the United States, the proportion of airline tickets sold through agents rose from 50 per cent in 1976 to 70 per cent in 1989, with over 95 per cent of tickets sold by agents being handled through CRSs.

### International CRS arrangements

In order to strengthen the marketing power of their CRSs, airlines are developing new "co-operative" CRSs or seeking tie-ups with other CRSs. At present, international arrangements are in progress as a way to link advanced US airlines' CRSs – in particular the Sabre system (owned by American Airlines) and the Apollo system (owned by United) – with other airlines' CRSs. The present situation is shown in Diagram 2.

### Code of conduct for CRSs

CRSs could have negative impact on fair airline competition by giving unfavourable treatment to non-vendor airlines in participating in a CRS or when displaying their flights and fares. Travel agencies could be bound to a CRS by long-term or high-termination penalty clauses in the contract. Consumers could be affected by information manipulation. Therefore, it has been felt necessary to devise rules of conduct for CRSs. At present, the following instruments have been developed:

- The International Civil Aviation Organisation published "Guidance material on the regulation of computer reservation systems", in November 1988;
- The European Civil Aviation Conference elaborated the "ECAC code of conduct for computer reservation systems", effective August 1989: this code was adopted by way of resolution and ECAC has the intention to transform it into a more binding instrument in due course.
- The European Community has developed a "Regulation on a code of conduct for computerised reservation systems" (No. 2299/89), which came into effect in August 1989.

In the latter case, and since the Regulation covers only scheduled services, the Commission is studying the opportunity to introduce a similar code of conduct for non-scheduled services.

The United States and Canada also have legislation to regulate CRSs. On the one hand, the current US CRS Rules were adopted in 1984 and, unless extended will expire at the end of 1990. On the other hand, the Government of Canada is developing regulations for all CRS systems operating in Canada, which are intended to enhance competition and ensure fair treatment for consumers of air services. An extensive public consultation process with 200 airlines, travel organisations and other governments was conducted by the government in the spring of 1990. The government Working Group will be making policy recommendations to the Minister of Transport in the fall of 1990. The regulations are expected to be put in place by the spring of 1991 and will be enforced by the National Transportation Agency.

### Facilitation

For the promotion of international tourism, the effort to facilitate controls and procedures to process air passengers appears to be important. Specific provisions of the ICAO constituent Convention (The Chicago Convention, 1944) provide a mandate in this field and detailed provisions are set forth in the Convention's Annex 9 on "Facilitation" (8th edition).

On the basis of the recommendations of the 10th Session of the ICAO Facilitation Division in September 1988, a 9th edition of Annex 9 was adopted in December 1989. This comprehensive revision was undertaken for the first time since it was drafted in 1946. Amendments to the 8th edition cover in particular the following subjects:

- Harmonization of facilitation and security requirements;
- Improvement of access to air transport for elderly and disabled persons;
- Issuance and use of machine-readable passports and visas;
- Consolidation of public health, immigration, agriculture and customs controls.

### Safety and security

Ensuring safety and security in air transport services is a basic requirement for tourism. However, statistics show that the situation did not improve in 1989 as compared with 1988. Preliminary information on aircraft accidents in scheduled air services for ICAO contracting states shows about the same number of fatal accidents and a noticeable increase in the number of passenger fatalities in 1989 over 1988.

With regard to unlawful interference against air services, a number of unlawful acts of violence occurred in 1989 and 279 people were killed.

### European air liberalization

### Liberalization measures

In December 1989, EC Transport Ministers adopted the principles of the second package of European air transport measures following a first series of measures taken in December 1987. The Ministers agreed on the following three principles and the date for implementation (Denmark, Greece and Portugal maintain reservations about the dates for implementation):

# Diagram 2. **International CRS arrangements**

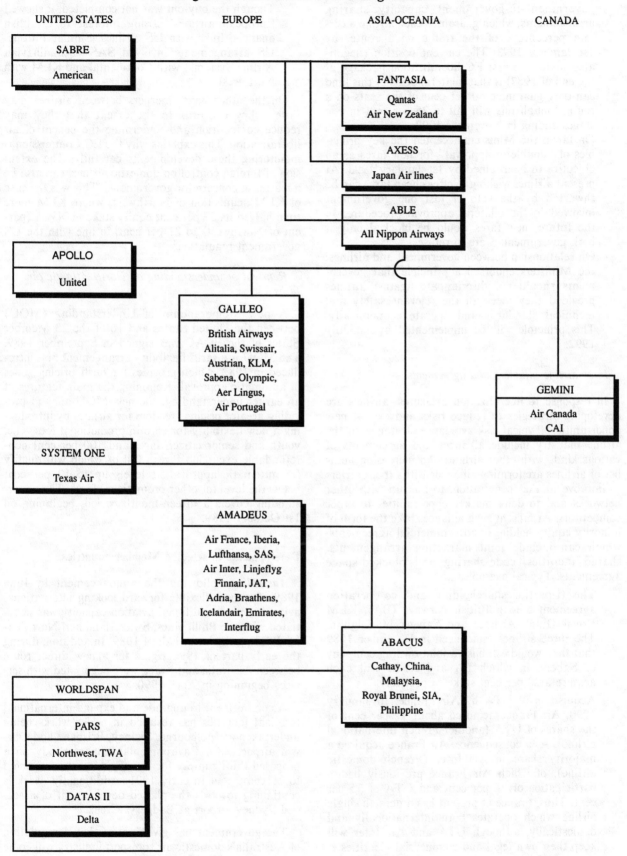

| UNITED STATES | EUROPE | ASIA-OCEANIA | CANADA |
|---|---|---|---|

**SABRE**
American

**FANTASIA**
Qantas
Air New Zealand

**AXESS**
Japan Air lines

**ABLE**
All Nippon Airways

**APOLLO**
United

**GALILEO**
British Airways
Alitalia, Swissair,
Austrian, KLM,
Sabena, Olympic,
Aer Lingus,
Air Portugal

**GEMINI**
Air Canada
CAI

**SYSTEM ONE**
Texas Air

**AMADEUS**
Air France, Iberia,
Lufthansa, SAS,
Air Inter, Linjeflyg
Finnair, JAT,
Adria, Braathens,
Icelandair, Emirates,
Interflug

**ABACUS**
Cathay, China,
Malaysia,
Royal Brunei, SIA,
Philippine

**WORLDSPAN**

**PARS**
Northwest, TWA

**DATAS II**
Delta

– On capacity: the Ministers agreed to eliminate the government-to-government capacity sharing arrangements, which guarantee each airline a certain percentage of the traffic on a route, by 1st January 1993. The current position (negotiated under the first EC liberalization package at the end of 1987) is that bilateral deals of this kind can only guarantee 40 per cent of the seats on a route, though this will fall to 25 per cent in two stages ending in November 1992.

– On fares: the Ministers accepted the key principles of "double disapproval" for new fares as an objective to be attained by 1st January 1993. At present airlines wishing to offer cheap fares can be thwarted by the veto of just one government involved in the bilateral approval procedure. In the future, new fares would be blocked only if both governments were to refuse.

– On relationship between government and airlines: the Ministers endorsed a principle that governments should not discriminate against airlines provided they meet all the relevant safety and technical standards and operate economically. This principle will be implemented by 1st July 1992.

### Inter-airline alliances and agreements

In response to liberalization measures, airlines are developing strategies to reduce risks and exploit new opportunities. Typical risk avoidance strategies in the airline industry include alliances and agreements of various kinds with other airlines. An increasing number of airlines are forming alliances with other carriers to improve market penetration, to link up with other networks and to deny market opportunities to other competitors. At present such alliances take the form of minority equity holdings and commercial agreements, which can include joint marketing arrangements, shared facilities, code-sharing and blocked-space agreements. Typical examples are:

– The tripartite shareholding and co-operation agreement among British Airways (BA), KLM Royal Dutch Airlines and Sabena of Belgium. The three airlines announced in December 1989 that they would establish a joint owning company of Sabena in which BA and KLM will each acquire a 20 per cent stake respectively.

– Acquisition of UTA by Air France: In January 1990, Air France acquired about 72 per cent of the shares of UTA (another French international airline). As a consequence, Air France acquired a majority share in Air Inter (French domestic airline), of which Air France previously had a participation of 36 per cent and UTA of 35 per cent. Thus, France at present has a defacto single airline which operates both internationally and domestically, although UTA and Air Inter will keep their own legal and commercial identities.

– United Airlines buy-out by British Airways: Though the buy-out was not completed, it showed European airlines' strong interest to establish financial links with US airlines. Similar Europe-US arrangements involved SAS (Scandinavian Airline Systems) with Continental and KLM with Northwest.

On the other hand, mergers between airlines may raise policy concerns to the extent that they may reduce competition and undermine the benefit of air liberalization. This explains why the EC Commission is monitoring these developments carefully. The extension of foreign control on domestic airlines can also be a matter of concern for governments. This was the case of KLM acquisition of Northwest, where KLM more than halved its 57 per cent equity stake in NWA (parent of Northwest) to 21 per cent, in line with the US government regulations.

### Renewal of understanding on North Atlantic air fares

A new Memorandum of Understanding (MOU) between the United States and 16 of the 23 Member States of the ECAC was signed in September 1989. The MOU is a tariff flexibility arrangement first introduced in 1982, which provides for tariff pricing zones of automatic approval. Retaining the main features of an earlier understanding, the new MOU aims at providing greater pricing freedom for airlines by introducing a new flexibility for certain promotional fees – i.e. youth and senior citizen fares and 100 per cent non-refundable excursion fares – all of which will qualify for automatic approval at levels up to 12 per cent below the level for other promotional fares. The understanding covers a fifteen-month period, beginning on 1st October 1989.

### Developments in selected Member countries

*Australia*. Following the announcement in June 1989 of a more flexible forward looking international aviation policy, additional aviation capacity was negotiated with the Philippines, Switzerland and New Zealand during the latter half of 1989. In addition, during the early part of 1990 rights for a new direct route between Australia and Korea were negotiated with services beginning in April 1990.

A commitment to upgrade and expand international terminal facilities has resulted in major works being undertaken at Melbourne, Sydney, Brisbane and Darwin airports. An Environmental Impact Study on a proposed third runway for Sydney Airport is expected to be completed in early 1991. Additionally, work is continuing towards the phased development of a second Sydney airport at Badgerys Creek.

The government has given notice that deregulation of Australia's domestic air transport industry will come into effect from 1st November 1990. The objective of the government's decision to deregulate domestic aviation is to foster increased responsiveness by airlines to consumer needs and to open up the industry to increased competition.

*Canada*. Air transportation agreements for improvements in services were initialled in 1989 with the following countries: Norway, Sweden, Denmark, Luxembourg, Venezuela, United Kingdom, Argentina and France.

Revised agreements were signed with the Netherlands, Czechoslovakia, Japan and the Soviet Union. New agreements were signed with Korea and Thailand.

Non-smoking regulations were introduced which will ban all smoking on flights to and from Canada effective July 1990. Non-smoking regulations are already in effect for all domestic flights and for international flights of less than six hours. The regulations are designed to protect the health of passengers and crews.

*Greece*. Greece has realised the need for adjusting to the situation that is expected to prevail in air transport in 1992 and thus understands that substantial measures are necessary in order to be able to survive within the competitive spirit which will prevail. Moreover, as far as charter flights are concerned, Greece in line with the rest of the European countries of the Mediterranean (especially Portugal and Spain), agrees that a specific policy in charter flights must be formulated which will create conditions of healthy competition among the regular and charter air companies.

*Ireland*. During 1989 and 1990 negotiations with the US authorities resulted in agreement on revised bilateral air services arrangements which, inter alia, provide traffic rights for Irish airlines at Los Angeles. Formal conclusion of the revised arrangements is expected by mid-1990. Passenger services on the route will commence in 1991. Air services to Los Angeles will represent an important expansion in the Ireland-US route network, covering a major market segment which has not hitherto enjoyed direct services.

In April 1990, the Irish Government announced a change in policy on transatlantic charter services, in order to allow such services to operate directly to and from Cork and Connaught Regional Airports. Hitherto, a stop at Shannon Airport in either the inbound or outbound direction had been mandatory for such services. This decision, which relates solely to charter services, should enable the airports concerned to generate new business in the transatlantic charter market.

*Norway*. With regard to international flights, by investing in hotel accommodation worldwide, SAS is now aiming at being able to offer combined transport plus overnighting facilities. Due to the availability on domestic flights, airlines are now offering seats at reduced prices to members of the Travel Trade, particularly on the routes between Northern and Southern Norway.

*Turkey*. Tourism has developed considerably in Turkey in recent years.

Since most tourists visiting the country travel by air, the Turkish authorities are doing everything in their power to facilitate inbound and outbound traffic at the international airports, and construction work on a turn-key project for an eighth international airport at Milas-Mugla and on the extension of Istanbul's Atatürk Airport is currently in progress.

In addition to its international airports, the country has twelve airports run by the National Airports Authority and 32 STOLports run by the Turkish Air Transport Association.

Airline activity has also been stimulated in line with the increase in tourism. Thus, airlines using wide-body aircraft for charter services have been set up, air taxi operations have attracted more passengers and helicopters are now widely used.

Various steps have been taken to increase the quality and safety of services and to improve passenger movements within airports.

*United Kingdom*. The government is committed to the creation of a liberal market in aviation and has therefore been in the lead in pressing for a Single Market in air transport with the European Community, with free, fair and open competition, subject only to effective safeguards to protect the consumer and airlines against unfair practices.

With regard to charter services, the government believes that the charter market operates effectively as it is in what is already a very liberal market. The EC is already committed to liberalizing air transport, and it is felt that the correct approach would be to further reduce regulations on scheduled services so that scheduled and charter business be considered on a more equal basis.

# B. RAIL TRANSPORT

## High-speed rail network

Rail transport exhibits a steady decline in relative importance in tourism reflecting the strong growth of air and road transport. In order to recover competitiveness, a reduction of journey time is essential for rail transport. This is one of the chief reasons why high-speed rail network projects are under consideration in several OECD Member countries.

In January 1989, the Community of European Railways (national railways of the EC Member countries, Austria and Switzerland) published its "Proposals for a European High-Speed Network". The final network is made up of about 30 000 km of lines, 19 000 km of which are new or upgraded lines. Travel times on the most technologically advanced lines will generally be halved. The network will be completed in 25 to 30 years. In 1989 and 1990, there were some developments in Europe along the lines of this proposal:

- TGV-Nord: In November 1989, transport Ministers from Belgium, France, Germany and the Netherlands agreed on a timetable for completion of TGV-Nord and its associated links. The French section (Paris to the Channel Tunnel via Lille) is already going ahead and due to open in 1993, with the Lille-Brussels section following in 1995. Completion of upgrading and sections of new line east of Brussels to provide high-speed routes to Rotterdam (via Antwerp) and Cologne (via Aachen) is scheduled for 1998, together with the Cologne-Frankfurt line – and the link from the British Channel Tunnel portal to London.
  Of the FF 90 billion total cost of infrastructure work, FF 16 billion will be spent in France, FF 24 billion in Germany, and FF 12.5 billion in Belgium. More than one-third of the total is set aside for the 109 km line in Britain.
- Transrapid magnetic rail system: In December 1989, the German Government decided to give its support to the first commercial stretch of the transrapid magnetic rail system between Cologne/Bonn airport and Essen, which is capable of speeds approaching 500 km per hour. The first part of the Cologne-Essen track, i.e. between the airports in Cologne and Düsseldorf, would be completed by 1996.
- The Alpine crossings: For the completion of the European high-speed network, it is essential to combine the Italian lines with those of Germany, France and the Benelux countries. At present, however, the only connections between the two parts are over difficult mountains which require trains to run at low speeds. Therefore, studies for improved Alpine crossings have been undertaken. In May 1989, the Swiss Government decided to

build two new Alpine railway tunnels, i.e. a new 49 km-tunnel alongside the existing Saint-Gothard tunnel and a complementary 28.4 km-tunnel at Lotschborg. The Gothard tunnel will shorten the journey time between Basel (Switzerland) and Milan (Italy) from 5 hours to nearly 3 hours. The Austrian Government also has a project to construct a new Brenner crossing between Innsbruck (Austria) and Bolzano (Italy).

High-speed train projects are also under construction or consideration outside Europe:

- In Australia: In 1989, the Cabinet decided to commission a Senate inquiry on a "Very Fast Train" project, a plan to build a 350 km/hour railway between Melbourne and Sydney. A feasibility study is under way.
- In Canada: The feasibility of a high-speed rail service linking Quebec City/Montreal/Ottawa/Toronto is being closely examined.
- Japan: In 1989, construction of Hokuriku (Takasaki-Komatsu) Shinkansen lines (Japanese high-speed rail) was started.
- United States: Florida State has a high-speed rail plan to link Miami, Orlando and Tampa with 500 km steel rail and 30 km magnetic levitation route between Disney World and Orlando Airport. Other States such as Texas and California also have plans for high-speed rail.

## Developments in Europe

### Traffic trends

Rail passenger transport was up by 4.1 per cent in 1988, which was the highest annual increase ever recorded in the 1970-1988 period and enabled the European Conference of Ministers of Transport (ECMT) countries as a whole to set an all-time record with 278 billion passenger-kilometers. Notwithstanding this highly favourable overall trend, the situation differed considerably from country to country: while there were increases of at least 5 per cent in France, Germany, Turkey and the United Kingdom, traffic declined by more than 1 per cent in Ireland, Norway, Sweden and Yugoslavia.

### The Channel Tunnel

Construction of the Channel Tunnel linking the United Kingdom and the rest of Europe [between Folkestone (United Kingdom) and Calais (France)] is under way. When it opens in 1993, the tunnel company Eurotunnel will operate shuttle trains conveying cars,

66

coaches and lorries. The national railway companies British Rail (United Kingdom) and SNCF (France) will provide direct rail-link services both for passengers and freight. The direct rail-link service will significantly reduce journey times, e.g. between Paris and London from 7 hours to 2.5 hours – city centre to city centre – journey time will thus be shorter than by air.

In 1989, difficulties arose among Eurotunnel, Transmanche Link (TML; a consortium of five British and five French construction companies) and 200 international banks. The dispute started in October when Eurotunnel and TML announced different revised tunnel completing costs [from original cost of £4.87 billion (i.e. $7.8 billion) to £7 billion (by Eurotunnel) and £7.5 billion (by TML)]. There was also a dispute over who should bear the increased cost. In April 1990, Eurotunnel announced a plan to raise as much as £2.5 billion (i.e. $3.26 billion) to cover the increased cost of building the Channel Tunnel. The money would be in addition to the £6 billion already raised by Eurotunnel from international banks and shareholders. So this finance should then give Eurotunnel £8.5 billion, allowing it a £1 billion cushion over the latest cost estimate of £7.5 billion by Eurotunnel. Although bankers were worried by the escalating costs, Eurotunnel expected them to react positively to this new proposal, as the new management of Eurotunnel had settled down and tunnelling was progressing quickly.

### Developments in selected Member countries

*Canada*. In October 1989, the Canadian Government announced that Via Rail would be reducing passenger train services by approximately half in 1990. Transcontinental rail service is now available tri-weekly. Service was reduced between many urban areas and some regional routes were abandoned. Other modes of transportation, particularly buses have moved quickly to provide new replacement services.

A weekly daylight rail service through the Rocky Mountains was sold to private interests and additional frequencies will be offered in 1991. Other companies have announced plans to introduce scenic rail trips for tourists in 1991.

*Denmark*. The Danish Railways (DSB) have brought a new train into service, the "IC3". This train uses high performance technology among the best available and provides a faster and pleasanter rail service.

Tourists on cycling trips may now put their bicycles on most trains travelling within the Danish borders.

DSB have also introduced a product for tourists combining a rail fare with an entrance ticket to an event or for visiting a monument.

DSB have been holding talks with foreign airlines on the sale of a combined air and rail ticket in Denmark.

In view of the possibilities opened by tourist destinations in Eastern and Central Europe, a rail ticket valid for multiple trips in several countries has been introduced. Many other countries are also looking into this idea.

*Greece*. A firm Greek policy until now has been the development and upgrading of the role of its railroads (at the national as well as the international level) provided that this development does not result in artificial limitations/restrictions on road transport.

Greece is particularly interested in participating in the TGV system of railroads (high-speed trains) being developed in the context of the European Community.

*Ireland.* In response to the government's development plans for tourism the national public transport authority – Coras Iompair Eireann (CIE) – introduced a wide range of service improvements directed towards the tourist market. These include special concessionary fares, travel and accommodation package deals and foreign language brochures.

As part of its tourism drive, Irish Rail, a CIE subsidiary company, identified the home packaged holiday market as one of considerable growth potential. Since the establishment of this company in 1987 it has become the single biggest provider in this market segment generating approximately 75 000 bednights annually.

*Norway*. The Norwegian State Railways have increased their marketing for holiday and leisure traffic and offered rebates and other ways of cheap travel. In view of the Olympic Games in 1994, plans are under way for the improvement of both road and rail routes between Oslo and Lillehammer.

## C. ROAD TRANSPORT

### Environment

Environmental protection was one of the main international concerns for the year 1989. The basic issue is how to balance the need for economic and social activities with that for protection of the environment. These considerations apply to transport as well. While transport makes an important contribution to economic and social activities, undesirable effects such as air and noise pollution are also caused by transport. These issues have been discussed extensively in recent years, notably at the special ECMT (European Conference of Ministers of Transport) Ministerial Session "Transport and Environment" held in November 1989.

During the session, road transport was a subject of concern. Statistics show that emissions from the road transport sector represent a high share of overall man-made air pollutant emissions. The prime offending source of noise in terms of the number of people disturbed is road transport. The ECMT adopted a resolution which recommends to:

- Fostering technical progress to reduce noise and air pollution emissions;
- Harmonizing and strengthening rules concerning emissions on the lines of those adopted by the most advanced countries;
- Influencing traffic demand in such a way as to provide less environmentally harmful modes of transport.

### Developments in Europe

#### Traffic trends

Public and private road passenger traffic in 1988 topped the 1987 peak by 4 per cent. This growth was mainly attributable to an increase of almost 5 per cent in private car traffic, while transport by buses and coaches was maintained at the 1987 level (see Diagram 3). Private car traffic now accounts for almost

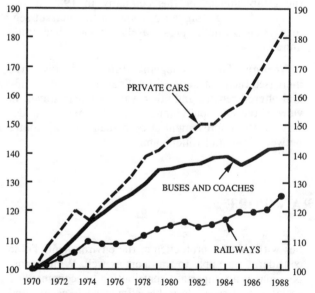

Diagram 3. **Passenger traffic trends**
1970 = 100
passenger-kilometres

*Source:* European Conference of Ministers of Transport (ECMT).

83 per cent of the total passenger kilometers in ECMT Member countries. Among the countries providing data on this subject, there was not one in which private car traffic did not increase in 1988, the highest growth being in Italy (9 per cent), Spain (8 per cent) and Finland (6 per cent). The situation of public passenger transport varied across countries in 1988: bus and coach traffic increased sharply in Spain (7 per cent) and Portugal (6 per cent) but diminished appreciably in Yugoslavia (-16 per cent) and, to a lesser extent, in Denmark, Germany and Norway. Comparison over the longer term shows that the period 1970 to 1979 was marked by substantially similar growth in private and public road transport; since 1980, they have developed at a different pace, with the gap between them widening, especially over the past four years, to the advantage of private transport. From 1980 to 1988, private car traffic expanded by 25 per cent, while coach and bus traffic increased by only 5 per cent.

#### Road accidents

The road safety situation deteriorated considerably in Europe in 1988. The number of road accidents was up 3 per cent, the number of casualties up 4 per cent and the number of fatalities rose by 2 per cent from 1987. These poor results for road safety could be explained to some extent by the sharp increase in traffic.

### Developments in selected Member countries

*Australia.* In February 1990, the Federal Government announced a new A$300 million Provincial Cities and Rural Highways Programme which, inter alia, is designed to provide funds for the upgrading of roads of tourism significance. This programme is in addition to the government's major road funding programme, the Australian Centennial Roads Development Programme which commenced on 1st January 1989.

*Greece.* As a consequence of the complete liberalization in the transportation sector which is anticipated for 1992, Greece is particularly interested in the solution of the transit problem through Austria and Yugoslavia, which are not members of the EEC, without which distortion of competition will subsist at the expense of Greek interests.

*Ireland.* An Operational Programme for road development is currently being negotiated by the Irish authorities with the EC Commission to cover the period up to 1993.

The fundamental aim of road development policy is to assist economic and social development by ensuring the efficient and safe movement of persons and goods by road, having regard to overall transportation requirements and to the preservation of the environment.

One of the main objectives of the Programme will be to ensure upgrading and development of roads/railways linking major tourist access points, e.g. ports/airports, to tourist centres. Other objectives include, inter alia:

- The reduction of urban congestion by providing new river crossings, ring roads and relief roads;
- The improvement of non-national roads which contribute to economic and regional development;
- The improvement of road surfaces and the strengthening of bridges to cater for increased EC vehicle weight limits;
- The maximisation of road usage through effective traffic management and enforcement;
- The improvement of road safety.

On domestic bus transport, the main development is the proposed legislation to liberalize access by private bus operators to the market. The fundamental objective of the new law will be to maximise the talents of both the public and private transport systems to provide the best quality, efficient and cost-effective bus transport for the general public. It is hoped that the

new proposals will be before the Irish Parliament later in 1990.

On the other hand, and as mentioned previously (see under B. Rail transport) the national public transport authority – CIE – has introduced a wide range of service improvements directed to tourists.

*Norway.* In an effort to promote tourism, the Directorate of Public Roads has also to take into account the needs of local residents. New guidelines for improving signposts are now being drawn up and efforts are being made to ensure that ferry capacity in the high season meets the needs of tourism.

*United Kingdom.* The White Paper "Roads for Prosperity", published in May 1989, and the report "Trunk Roads, England - into the 1990s", published in February 1990, announced a major increase in the government's programme for building trunk roads in England, which will add over 2 700 miles of new or widened roads to the trunk road network. Although the encouragement of tourism is not as such an objective of the road programme, many of these better roads will improve access to important tourist areas.

# D.   CRUISES AND FERRIES

## Cruises

### Traffic trends

The cruise market is continuing to exhibit double-digit growth. In 1988, there were 3.7 million cruise passengers, a 16 per cent increase over 1987 (see Table 3). On the supply side, the world cruise fleet is comprised of about 250 ships with 150 000 berths. Their average size has increased steadily and the newest ships carry more than 1 500 passengers with extensive amenities of all kinds.

Table 3.   **World cruise population**

In thousands

| Cruise Areas | 1984 | 1985 | 1986 | 1987 | 1988 |
|---|---|---|---|---|---|
| North America | 1 630 | 1 950 | 2 340 | 2 730 | 3 200 |
| Europe | 220 | 250 | 200 | 300 | 330 |
| Other | 150 | 160 | 160 | 170 | 190 |
| Total | 2 000 | 2 360 | 2 700 | 3 200 | 3 720 |
| Growth Rate (%) | – | 18.0 | 14.4 | 18.5 | 16.3 |

*Source:* World cruise market 1987/88, published by MRC/Hawkedon, London, United Kingdom.

The major cruise areas are the Caribbean, Mediterranean and the United States Pacific Coast. The leading segment of the world cruise market is the Caribbean with 3.5 million cruise passengers in 1989, which represents a share of more than 80 per cent of the world market. The second largest is the Mediterranean with a share of about 15 per cent of the world market followed by the United States Pacific Coast. Other areas, including those closer to Japan, are expected to grow in importance.

Cruising is changing character from a holiday choice of older tourists with high incomes to a mass market product. The advent of air/sea packages which provides cheap airline seats for cruisers and short-duration cruises has contributed to this shift in the market. Cruise operators divide cruisers into targetable segments such as budget cruisers and rich cruisers or younger cruisers and older cruisers and offer different types of services.

## Ferries

### Traffic trends

Short-sea and cross-channel ferry services mainly in the North Sea, the Baltic and Japan have increased greatly during the last few decades, and some ferries are being used for short mini-cruises. More than 2 000 ships are registered as passenger, passenger-vehicle or rail ferries. Their average size has steadily increased, and the largest can carry more than 2 000 passengers, 500 cars and 80 heavy freight vehicles.

### Developments in selected Member countries

*Canada.* The Pacific Coast continues to be the most popular cruise destination. In 1989, 333 000 cruise passengers visited the Port of Vancouver. This represented approximatively 198 sailings and 17 vessels. In 1990, Vancouver will see 19 cruise ships utilising its port facilities.

Cruises on the Atlantic Coast, are gaining in popularity and represent approximately 20 per cent of cruise activity in Canada. Cruises are often popular for whale watching, seeing the autumn colours and experiencing the culture and heritage of the region.

*Ireland.* There has been a consistent increase in international demand for water-based activities over the last decade, and Ireland, in this regard, has particular appeal for the Continental market.

In response to the growing market demand, funding for cruising developments will be made available from the EC Structural Funds under the Operational Programme for Tourism 1989-1993 for improvement of navigation and shore facilities. This money will be used by the public and private sector to extend and improve cruising waters and develop shore infrastructure, and to extend the cruiser fleet.

Expenditure will cover major navigational improvements on the main waterways, i.e. the Shannon, Grand Canal and Barrow systems. It is hoped, thereby, to effect by 1992 a 100 per cent increase in the numbers of overseas visitors engaging in cruising activities, thus bringing the total figure to 32 000.

*United Kingdom.* The United Kingdom is continuing to both promote a free and fair market in shipping, aimed at increasing competition and consumer choice, and to improve maritime and river-boat safety. To these ends the Government has been arguing strenuously within the EC and other international groupings for the levelling down of subsidies and tax breaks that distort competition and is promoting passenger safety both through the IMO and own flag requirements. The United Kingdom continues to exceed the internationally agreed standard of inspection of 25 per cent of visiting foreign ships and enforces additional safety requirements in domestic legislation for visiting passenger ships. High standards are also applied to boats operating on inland waterways.

# E.   COMPREHENSIVE TRANSPORT POLICY DEVELOPMENTS

Entering a new decade, some Member countries have made or have been considering overall transportation policies in order to prepare for the future. Because of the close relation between tourism and transport, these developments will inevitably affect tourism.

### Developments in selected Member countries

*New Zealand.* Since 1983, New Zealand's transport system has undergone the most extensive structural reform in the country's history. This reform, which aims at maximising economic efficiency, has centred on seeking to remove restrictions on the introduction of improved transport services and reduce transport costs through the restructuring of the public and private transport sectors.

To do so, particular attention has been paid to the separation of regulatory functions from the delivery of commercial services in governmental structures, the removal of quantitive controls on access to the transport industry in favour of unrestricted entry subject to quality controls and safety audit systems, and the government's withdrawal of direct public involvement in operational ownership.

The net effect should be increased competition and downward pressure on the transport sector prices.

Below are examples of domestic applications of this new policy, which could have an impact on tourism:

- Operator licences for all sectors of the land transport industry are now issued on the "fit and proper person" principle and are unrestricted as to number;
- Quantitative licensing of air transport services and price control ceased in December 1983 allowing operators to vary routes, fares and fleets in response to market demand. In 1986, restrictions on overseas investment in domestic air services were revoked.
- The state owned airlines, Air New Zealand, was sold to foreign and local institutional and private shareholders. The overseas ownership amounts to 35 per cent.
- Air Traffic Control Services were separated from the Ministry ofTransport in April 1987 and are

now provided by the Airways Corporation of New Zealand Ltd on a fully commercial basis.

- Joint venture airport partnerships between Cenral and Local Government have progressively been restructured since April 1988 as public companies. Airport companies have complete commercial freedom although there is a legislative requirement for consultation with airlines before setting charges.
- At the remaining joint venture airports, a new cost-related charging methodology has been implemented to avoid the necessity for government subsidy.
- The Ministry of Transport is no longer totally reliant on taxpayer funding. In the 1990/91 fiscal year, the Air Transport Division will expend some $29 million on policy advice and safety regulation services. The government will "purchase" policy advice, search and rescue co-ordination and standards development at a cost of $3.2 million. The balance of $25.8 million muyst be recovered from the aviation industry through specific charges for operator and aircraft certification, personnel examinations, testing and licensing and operator safety audit inspections.

The Ministry of Transport was also reorganised in 1988 and its role is now clearly focused on the development of transport safety and efficiency.

As for the outcome, it is safe to say that the fundamental aim of achieving reductions in transport costs has been achieved. Examples of the savings include the following:

- Through the most dramatic restructuring process, New Zealand Railways' staff was reduced from 23 000 in 1982 to under 10 000 in 1989, with almost unaltered networks.
- Airways charges to airlines on a typical sector have fallen by 70 per cent since 1986, through efficiency gains and expansion of the airways client base to include private, corporate and flight training operators.
- Domestic air fares have fallen by 18.5 per cent in real terms over the period June 1987 – June 1990. The increase in the Consumer Price Index for all goods over the same period was 19.5 per cent.

Other experience arising from these policies includes:

- Government expenditure to maintain a civil aviation regulatory body and an airport and airways system is no longer required.
- Substantive competition with Air New Zealand on main trunk routes occurred from 1987 as a result of the change in overseas investment policy. Ansett New Zealand was established that year with 50 per cent Australian ownership and the government allowed 100 per cent Australian ownership in 1988.

- Uneconomic air services are being rationalised through changes in aircraft type or divestment to other operators.

On the other hand, the government's revised External Aviation Policy was released in December 1986. The objective of the policy is to maximise economic benefits to New Zealand, including trade and tourism, by fostering the liberalization of air services to and from New Zealand consistent with foreign policy and strategic considerations. The government seeks to attain a less regulated environment in order to promote competition and achieve a mix of prices and services which can provide a better deal for New Zealand consumers and businesses.

In implementing this policy, the government responds favourably to approaches from foreign governments or ailines to discuss proposals for new or additionl air services to or from New Zealand. While taking a flexible and pragmatic approach at bilateral discussions, New Zealand expects increased access by foreign carriers to the New Zealand market to be balanced by fair and equal opportunity for New Zealand airlines to compete.

Since the policy was released, New Zealand has successfully entered into or expanded air services agreements with a number of countries. Whereas in 1985, New Zealand has twelve agreements, by mid 1990 there were twenty. Over the same five-year period, the number of foreign airlines licensed to serve New Zealand increased from eleven to twenty four. As a result, air services to New Zealand have increased substantially in terms of capacity, frequency, and points of origin around the world.

*United States*. In February 1990, the US Government released its statement of national transportation policy to prepare for the challenges and opportunities in the 21st century. In this report, the United States presents an ambitious agenda to fulfil both short and long-term needs and which evolves around six key themes:

- Maintain and expand the Nation's transportation system, by the reduction of congestion in the aviation and highway systems through improved management and use of key transportation facilities, new technology, and enhanced capacity;
- Foster a sound financial base for transportation, through greater reliance to user charges and the infusions of private capital;
- Keep the transportation industry strong and competitive, with the elimination of economic regulations of transportation industries where they are unnecessary and outmoded;
- Ensure that the transportation system supports public safety and national security, by keeping safety as the top priority of the Department of Transportation;

- Protect the environment and the quality of life, through support given to national efforts for environmental protection;
- Advance US technology and expertise for the 21st century; by the renewal of focus on technology and innovation, the fostering of research, the evaluation and demonstration of promising new technologies.

The fifth theme mentioned above also includes policies to improve the quality of travel; with the following action-orientated objectives, i.e.:

- To review Federal programmes and standards affecting transportation service to leisure travellers, to ensure that the Federal Government is not an obstacle to attractive, high-quality service;
- To promote standardised signs and increased information for travellers, particularly at airports and passenger terminals and along scenic highways and other passenger routes; and
- To incorporate in Federal-aid programmes transportation provisions for adequate service facilities for travellers.

# NOTE

Thanks are expressed to the following organisations which have provided a certain amount of information and statistical data which has helped in the drafting of this chapter:

International Civil Aviation Organisation (ICAO)
European Conference of Ministers of Transport (ECMT)
European Civil Aviation Conference (ECAC)
International Air Transport Association (IATA)
Association of European Airlines (AEA).

# STATISTICAL ANNEX

# INTERNATIONAL TOURIST FLOWS FROM MAIN GENERATING COUNTRIES

# INTERNATIONAL TOURIST FLOWS BY RECEIVING COUNTRY

# NOTES

This Annex reproduces the main tourism statistical series available in Member countries. For 1989, data are in certain cases provisional. It illustrates recent tourism developments in the OECD (over a two or three-year period).

Some of the data contained in the text itself may not always correspond exactly to that included in the Annex: the discrepancies can be explained by a different statistical coverage (e.g. the use of GNP instead of GDP) or by the use of material of a more analytical nature (data derived from gross figures).

Finally, certain tables are prepared from data available for other OECD work (e.g. Balance of Payments and National Accounts), in some cases, these statistics, which have been standardised to follow existing international guidelines, may differ from the ones supplied by countries in response to the annual questionnaire of the Tourism Committee.

Three tables of general interest for the use of the statistical series are presented at the beginning of the Annex:

A. Classification of travellers;
B. Series available by country;
C. Types of establishments covered by the statistics.

## Main elements of the terminology used

This section indicates the main methods used for collecting statistics and deals with international tourism.

Table A gives an overview of the international classification of travellers.

International inbound tourism (i.e. tourism performed in a given country by non-residents) is usually measured by the receiving country as monthly, quarterly or annual number of arrivals and/or nights spent, using one of three methods:

- *Border controls*: these can provide only a limited amount of information about volumes, means of transport, etc. (as used in Japan, New Zealand and Spain);
- *Sample surveys*: these provide a large amount of quantitative and qualitative information (as used in Canada, Portugal and the United Kingdom);
- *Registration in means of accommodation*: this method, which is used in Finland, Italy and Switzerland among others, provides more accurate information, but with a more limited scope. However, by definition, it excludes excursionists and certain types of accommodation that are not registered for tax or other reasons, such as that provided by relatives or friends.

In estimating tourism supply, it is necessary to take account of all the goods and services required by tourism i.e. the resources, infrastructure and industries producing such goods and services, whether in the tourism field itself or indirectly related to the tourist industries.

The various means of accommodation are an essential part of this supply. They can be divided into two broad categories: hotels and similar establishments, and supplementary means of accommodation.

The first category (hotels and similar establishments) normally covers four types of establishment: hotels, motels, boarding houses and inns. However, in order to reflect the actual situation in a country more accurately, similar establishments are also often included (in which case the statistical coverage is indicated in Table C or in the methodological notes for each country).

The second category (supplementary means of accommodation) can include seven types of establishment: youth hostels, camping sites, holiday villages, mountain huts and shelters, rented rooms, houses and flats, sanatoria and health establishments and children's holiday camps. The list can also be extended in some cases.

The data on international tourism receipts and expenditure are those found under the "travel" heading in the Balance of Payments. They are available in varying degrees of disaggregation by country/region of origin or country/region of destination.

Data concerning international tourism payments follow, in practice, the recommendations of the World Tourism Organisation.

International tourism receipts: They are defined as the receipts of a country resulting from consumption expenditures, i.e., payments for goods and services, made by visitors out of foreign currency. They should, however, exclude all forms of remuneration resulting from employment, as well as international fare receipts.

International tourism expenditure: They are defined as consumption expenditures, i.e., payments for goods and services, made by residents of a country visiting abroad. They should, however, exclude all forms of remuneration resulting from employment, as well as international fare payments.

Three different methods are currently used by the Member countries.

In most countries, data are collected by the central bank using a method called the *bank reporting method*. When a traveller purchases or sells currency before or after a trip abroad, the bank or authorised agency records the transaction. Under this method, data are broken down according to the currency used and not according to the traveller's country of origin or destination.

The *estimation method* is based on sample surveys that are usually carried out at the points of entry or departure for non-residents, or at the re-entry points for returning residents. Data are broken down according to tourists' country of origin or destination. These surveys provide the most reliable and most detailed statistics.

The *mixed method*, which is used by only a few countries, was developed to remedy the shortcomings of the bank reporting method. It uses parallel sources (surveys of visitors, comparison with data provided by receiving countries, etc.), allowing the statistics obtained by the bank reporting method to be adjusted.

However, these data have their limitations. First, the volumes obtained by the bank reporting method in most countries are not an accurate measure of international tourist trade, since they represent net balances and not gross volumes; tourist transactions therefore tend to be understated. Second, it was noted that items unrelated to international tourism were included under the "travel" heading. Third, large discrepancies are found when any attempt is made to compile bilateral balances by comparing a given country's receipts, broken down by country of origin, with the expenditure reported by generating countries, broken down by country of destination.

### Geographic coverage

Belgium-Luxembourg: Balance of payments statistics refer to the Belgo-Luxembourg Economic Union.

Other OECD-Europe: include OECD European countries for which no breakdown is available.

Other European countries: include non-OECD European countries for which no breakdown is available.

Origin country unspecified: includes non-OECD countries which cannot be broken down into any specific large geographic region (Other European countries, Latin America, Asia-Oceania, Africa).

### Conventional signs:

/ *Break of series.*

# SOURCES

The principal national bodies for each OECD Member country dealing with tourism statistics are as follows:

Australia

  Bureau of Tourism Research
  Australian Bureau of Statistics
  Australian Tourist Commission

Austria

  Osterreichisches Statistisches Zentralamt
  Osterreichische Nationalbank

Belgium

  Institut National de Statistiques
  Banque nationale de Belgique
  Institut Belgo-Luxembourgeois du Change

Canada

  Statistics Canada, International Travel Section
  Industry, Science and Technology Canada, Tourism

Denmark

  Danmarks Stastistik
  Danmarks National Bank

Finland

  Central Statistical Office
  Bank of Finland

France

  Ministère du Tourisme, Direction des Industries touristiques
  Banque de France

Germany

  Statistisches Bundesamt
  Deutsche Bundesbank

Greece

  National Statistical Service of the National Tourist Organisation of Greece
  Bank of Greece

Iceland

  Icelandic Immigration Authorities
  Iceland Tourist Board
  Central Bank of Iceland

Ireland

  Central Statistics Office
  Irish Tourist Board (Board Failte)

Italy

  Istituto Centrale di Statistica
  Banca d'Italia

Japan

  Ministry of Transport, Department of Tourism
  Japan National Tourist Organisation
  Bank of Japan

Luxembourg

  Service Central de la Statistique et des Études Économiques (STATEC)
  Institut Belgo-Luxembourgeois du Change

Netherlands

  Ministry of the Economy
  Central Bureau of Statistics
  Dutch Central Bank

New Zealand

  New Zealand Tourism Department

Norway

  Central Bureau of Statistics
  Bank of Norway

Portugal

  Direcçao-Geral de turisme
  Instituto Nacional de Estatistica
  Banco de Portugal

Spain

  Instituto Nacional de Estadisticas
  Banco de Espana

Sweden

  Central Bureau of Statistics
  Swedish Tourist Board
  Central Bank of Sweden

Switzerland

  Office Fédéral de la Statistique, Section du Tourisme

Turkey

  Ministry of Tourism
  Central Bank

United Kingdom

  Department of Employment, Office of Population Censuses and Surveys
  British Tourist Authority

United States

  Department of Commerce, United States Travel and Tourism Administration (USTTA)
  Department of Commerce, Bureau of Economic Analysis

Yugoslavia

  Federal Bureau of Statistics
  National Bank of Yugoslavia

77

## A. Classification of travellers

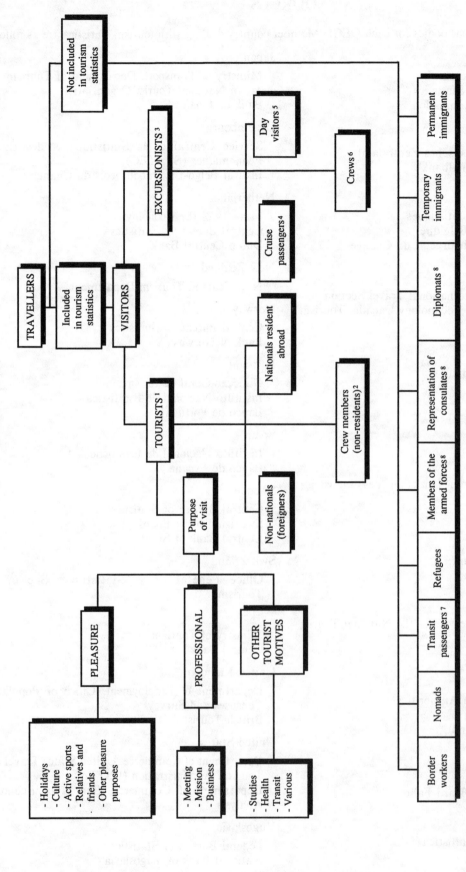

1. Visitors who spend at least one night in the country visited.
2. Foreign air or ship crews docked or in lay over and who use the accommodation establishments of the country visited.
3. Visitors who do not spend the night in the country visited although they may visit the country during one day or more and return to their ship or train to sleep.
4. Normally included in excursionists. Separate classification of these visitors is nevertheless recommended.
5. Visitors who come and leave the same day.
6. Crews who are not residents of the country visited and who stay in the country for the day.
7. Who do not leave the transit area of the airport or the port. In certain countries, transit may involve a stay of one day or more. In this case, they should be included in the visitors statistics.
8. When they travel from their country of origin to the duty station and vice versa (including household servants and dependants accompanying or joining them).

*Source*: World Tourism Organisation.

78

# B. Series available by country

### ARRIVALS OF TOURISTS AT FRONTIERS

| | | |
|---|---|---|
| Canada | Iceland* | Portugal |
| France* | New Zealand | United States |
| Greece | | |

### ARRIVALS OF VISITORS AT FRONTIERS

| | | |
|---|---|---|
| Australia | Italy | Spain |
| Canada | Japan | Turkey (Travellers) |
| Ireland | Portugal | United Kingdom |

### ARRIVALS OF FOREIGN TOURISTS AT HOTELS AND SIMILAR ESTABLISHMENTS

| | | |
|---|---|---|
| Austria | Ireland | Spain |
| France | Italy* | Switzerland |
| Germany | Netherlands | Turkey |
| Greece* | Portugal | Yugoslavia |

### ARRIVALS OF FOREIGN TOURISTS AT ALL MEANS OF ACCOMMODATION

| | | |
|---|---|---|
| Austria | Italy* | Switzerland |
| Germany | Netherlands | Turkey |
| Greece* | Portugal | Yugoslavia |

### NIGHTS SPENT BY FOREIGN TOURISTS IN HOTELS AND SIMILAR ESTABLISHMENTS

| | | |
|---|---|---|
| Australia* | Germany | Portugal |
| Austria | Greece* | Spain |
| Belgium | Ireland | Sweden |
| Denmark | Italy* | Switzerland |
| Finland | Netherlands | Turkey |
| France | Norway | Yugoslavia |

### NIGHTS SPENT BY FOREIGN TOURISTS IN ALL MEANS OF ACCOMMODATION

| | | |
|---|---|---|
| Australia* | Germany | Sweden |
| Austria | Greece* | Switzerland |
| Belgium | Italy* | Turkey |
| Canada | Netherlands | United Kingdom |
| Denmark | Portugal | Yugoslavia |
| France* | | |

\* As 1989 statistical series are not available for these tables, they show 1987 and 1988 data.

## C. Types of accommodation covered by the statistics

| Countries | Hotels and similar establishments | | | | | Supplementary means of accommodation | | | | | | | |
|---|---|---|---|---|---|---|---|---|---|---|---|---|---|
| | Hotels[1] | Motels[2] | Boarding houses[3] | Inns[4] | Others[5] | Youth hostels[6] | Camping and caravan sites[7] | Holiday villages[3] | Mountain huts and shelters | Rented rooms, houses and flats | Sanatoria, health establishments | Recreation homes for children[8] | Others[9] |
| Australia | x | x | x | | x | x | x | | | x | | | x |
| Austria[10] | x | | | | | x | x | x | x | x | x | x | x |
| Belgium | x | | | | x | | x | | | x | x | x | x |
| Canada | x | x | | | | | x | | | | | | x |
| Denmark[10] | x | | x | | | x | x | | | | | | x |
| Finland | x | | x | | x | | | | | | | | |
| France | x | | x | | | | x | | | | | | |
| Germany | x | x | x | | | x | x | x | | x | x | | x |
| Greece | x | | x | x | x | | x | | | | | | |
| Ireland | x | | x | x | | | | | | x | | | |
| Italy | x | | | | x | x | x | | | | | | x |
| Netherlands | x | | x | | x | x | x | | | | | | |
| Norway[10] | x | | | | | x | x | | | | | x | |
| Portugal | x | x | x | x | x | | x | | | | | | |
| Spain | x | x | | | | | x | | | | | | |
| Sweden | x | x | x | | | x | x | x | | | | | |
| Switzerland | x | x | x | x | | x | x | | | x | x | | x |
| Turkey | x | x | x | x | x | | x | x | | x | | | |
| Yugoslavia | x | x | x | x | x | x | x | x | | x | x | | x |

Countries not listed in this table do not dispose of data by type of accommodation.

1. "Hotels" includes:
Germany: hotels serving breakfast only; Belgium: motels, boarding houses and inns; Finland: motels; France: motels; Ireland: motels; Portugal: studio-hotels; Spain: "Paradores" and boarding houses ("Fondas" and "Casas de Huespedes"); Sweden: motels (since 1986); Switzerland: boarding houses; Turkey: thermal hotels.

2. "Motels" includes:
Greece: bungalows.

3. "Boarding houses" includes:
Finland: inns; Ireland: inns; Sweden: resort hotels.

4. "Inns" includes:
Portugal: private and state-owned inns.

5. "Other" hotels and similar establishments include:
Australia: hotels and motels without facilities in most rooms and not necessarily providing meals and alcoholic drinks; Belgium: non-licensed establishments; Finland: lodging houses and part of youth hostels; Greece: bungalow-hotels, studio-hotels and recreation homes for children; Netherlands: youth hostels in Amsterdam; Portugal: holiday flats and villages; Sweden: boarding houses, inns, and resort hotels; Turkey: special licensed hotels and studio-hotels.

6. "Youth hostels" includes:
Germany: mountain huts and shelters.

7. "Camping and caravan sites" includes:
Australia: cabins and flats; Finland: holiday village cottages (since 1986).

8. "Recreation homes for children" includes:
Portugal: youth hostels.

9. "Other" supplementary means of accommodation includes:
Australia: rented farms, house-boats, rented camper-vans, boats, cabin cruisers, camping outside commercial grounds; Belgium: youth hostels, holiday villages and social tourism establishments; Canada: homes of friends or relatives, private cottages, commercial cottages and others (universities, hostels); Germany: recreation and holiday homes, institutions providing educational services; Greece: holiday centres; Italy: recreation homes for children, mountain huts and shelters, holiday homes and religious establishments; Spain: secondary residences and private apartments; Switzerland: dormitories in recreation homes for children, tourist camps, mountain huts and shelters, holiday villages; Yugoslavia: children and student homes, sleeping cars, cabins on ships.

10. Total available without breakdown for "hotels and similar establishments".

## 1. Tourism from European Member countries[1]

| | Arrivals at frontiers[2] | | | Arrivals at all means of accommodation[3] | | | Nights spent in all means of accommodation[4] | | |
|---|---|---|---|---|---|---|---|---|---|
| | Volume 1989 (thousands) | % 89/88 | % 88/87 | Volume 1989 (thousands) | % 89/88 | % 88/87 | Volume 1989 (thousands) | % 89/88 | % 88/87 |
| Austria | | | | 16 028.5 | 9.7 | 5.3 | 89 271.2 | 8.2 | 2.2 |
| Belgium | | | | | | | 9 205.4 | 1.8 | 7.5 |
| Denmark | | | | | | | 7 709.6 | 13.1 | - 0.7 |
| Finland | | | | | | | 1 641.0 | 6.1 | 7.9 |
| France | | | 3.3 | | | 3.3 | | | 2.4 |
| Germany | 6 478.0 | 4.2 | 2.4 | 9 526.2 | 10.1 | 4.6 | 21 546.1 | 10.1 | 4.3 |
| Greece | | | | | | 0.5 | | | - 1.6 |
| Iceland | | | 7.0 | | | | | | |
| Ireland | 2 206.0 | 18.4 | 17.1 | 892.0 | 27.2 | 19.4 | 4 221.0 | 29.5 | 19.9 |
| Italy | 44 404.0 | - 2.6 | 6.8 | | | 1.8 | | | 0.1 |
| Luxembourg | | | | | | | | | |
| Netherlands | | | | 4 125.3 | 7.7 | | 12 107.1 | 13.7 | |
| Norway | | | | | | | 2 707.1 | 2.0 | 1.6 |
| Portugal | 6 499.2 | 7.3 | 7.8 | 3 538.7 | 4.5 | 4.3 | 16 436.8 | 2.4 | 3.9 |
| Spain | 48 598.9 | - 0.4 | 7.4 | 10 513.2 | - 6.3 | - 3.0 | 70 834.9 | - 12.8 | - 4.4 |
| Sweden | | | | | | | 6 232.1 | 5.8 | 0.1 |
| Switzerland | | | | 7 325.9 | 6.5 | 2.5 | 29 527.2 | 3.3 | 1.2 |
| Turkey | 2 689.8 | 4.6 | 65.0 | 2 954.6 | 9.5 | 29.6 | 10 069.9 | 2.9 | 44.4 |
| United Kingdom | 10 485.7 | 10.0 | 4.0 | | | | 88 229.0 | 5.7 | - 0.5 |
| Canada | 1 528.8 | 3.3 | 17.1 | | | | 18 718.1 | - 2.4 | 18.1 |
| United States | 6 082.0 | 7.9 | 23.4 | | | | | | |
| Australia | 510.9 | - 0.1 | 28.6 | | | | | | 28.2 |
| New Zealand | 142.2 | 5.0 | 16.2 | | | | | | |
| Japan | 428.3 | 12.2 | 5.3 | | | | | | |
| Yugoslavia | | | | 6 987.0 | - 4.7 | 0.7 | 42 477.9 | - 6.1 | 1.2 |

1. Derived from tables by receiving country (see corresponding notes).
2. *Tourist* or *visitor arrivals.* When both available : *tourist arrivals.*
3. Arrivals *in all means of accommodation* or *in hotels and similar establishments.* When both available: arrivals *in all means of accommodation.*
4. Nights spent *in all means of accommodation* or *in hotels and similar establishments.* When both available: nights spent *in all means of accommodation.*

## 2. Tourism from Canada and the United States[1]

| | Arrivals at frontiers[2] | | | Arrivals at all means of accommodation[3] | | | Nights spent in all means of accommodation[4] | | |
|---|---|---|---|---|---|---|---|---|---|
| | Volume 1989 (thousands) | % 89/88 | % 88/87 | Volume 1989 (thousands) | % 89/88 | % 88/87 | Volume 1989 (thousands) | % 89/88 | % 88/87 |
| Austria | | | | 766.0 | 8.7 | - 6.8 | 1 918.6 | 5.7 | - 6.8 |
| Belgium | | | | | | | 643.8 | - 3.0 | - 18.9 |
| Denmark | | | | | | | 447.2 | 12.2 | - 14.7 |
| Finland | | | | | | | 235.7 | 0.9 | 2.2 |
| France | | | 6.6 | | | 6.6 | | | 2.7 |
| Germany | 358.0 | - 10.9 | 14.5 | 2 262.6 | 10.5 | - 8.5 | 4 635.4 | 9.7 | - 8.1 |
| Greece | | | | | | 8.3 | | | 4.1 |
| Iceland | | | - 18.8 | | | | | | |
| Ireland | 417.0 | 4.0 | 4.7 | 415.0 | 2.7 | 0.0 | 2 202.0 | - 2.0 | 6.1 |
| Italy | 1 779.6 | 4.3 | - 8.7 | | | - 1.0 | | | - 4.6 |
| Luxembourg | | | | | | | | | |
| Netherlands | | | | 563.3 | 1.3 | | 1 120.3 | 8.2 | |
| Norway | | | | | | | 347.3 | - 0.2 | - 23.9 |
| Portugal | 269.8 | - 0.2 | 20.5 | 364.3 | 6.6 | - 0.3 | 1 044.2 | 5.4 | - 1.9 |
| Spain | 1 126.1 | 9.7 | - 1.7 | 902.1 | 5.7 | - 4.5 | 2 013.7 | 3.8 | - 9.1 |
| Sweden | | | | | | | 375.7 | 2.7 | - 7.4 |
| Switzerland | | | | 1 235.2 | 10.5 | - 10.0 | 2 734.6 | 8.3 | - 11.9 |
| Turkey | 236.1 | 21.3 | 28.6 | 186.1 | 40.9 | 28.1 | 420.6 | 19.1 | 20.2 |
| United Kingdom | 3 447.5 | 5.4 | - 3.6 | | | | 35 969.0 | 4.6 | - 7.5 |
| Canada | 12 195.4 | - 4.4 | 0.3 | | | | 53 598.0 | - 4.6 | 1.5 |
| United States | 15 365.9 | 11.0 | 11.5 | | | | | | |
| Australia | 314.9 | - 19.0 | 7.5 | | | | | | 8.5 |
| New Zealand | 168.4 | - 17.7 | - 5.2 | | | | | | |
| Japan | 591.4 | 3.0 | - 5.6 | | | | | | |
| Yugoslavia | | | | 299.3 | - 12.7 | 24.6 | 735.1 | - 13.2 | 20.0 |

1. Derived from tables by receiving country (see corresponding notes).
2. *Tourist* or *visitor arrivals.* When both available : *tourist arrivals.*
3. Arrivals *in all means of accommodation* or *in hotels and similar establishments.* When both available: arrivals *in all means of accommodation.*
4. Nights spent *in all means of accommodation* or *in hotels and similar establishments.* When both available: nights spent *in all means of accommodation.*

# 3. Tourism from Australia, New Zealand and Japan [1]

| | Arrivals at frontiers [2] | | | Arrivals at all means of accommodation [3] | | | Nights spent in all means of accommodation [4] | | |
|---|---|---|---|---|---|---|---|---|---|
| | Volume 1989 (thousands) | % 89/88 | % 88/87 | Volume 1989 (thousands) | % 89/88 | % 88/87 | Volume 1989 (thousands) | % 89/88 | % 88/87 |
| Austria | | | | 294.0 | 19.7 | 2.5 | 608.1 | 19.5 | 3.1 |
| Belgium | | | | | | | 158.6 | 26.5 | 13.8 |
| Denmark | | | | | | | 118.7 | 10.2 | 29.9 |
| Finland | | | | | | | 60.9 | 9.1 | 8.7 |
| France | | | 11.4 | | | 11.4 | | | 4.3 |
| Germany | | | | 916.7 | 22.6 | 4.6 | 1 555.5 | 20.3 | 6.8 |
| Greece | 232.0 | 4.5 | 2.8 | | | 1.6 | | | − 4.4 |
| Iceland | | | 4.7 | | | | | | |
| Ireland | 59.0 | 40.5 | 27.3 | 198.0 | 52.3 | 1.6 | 1 011.0 | 49.3 | − 1.9 |
| Italy | 731.0 | 19.4 | − 0.6 | | | 12.8 | | | 12.0 |
| Luxembourg | | | | | | | | | |
| Netherlands | | | | 164.0 | 0.4 | | 328.6 | 7.6 | |
| Norway | | | | | | | 80.1 | 20.1 | − 11.2 |
| Portugal | 50.1 | 8.4 | 1.6 | 57.1 | 3.7 | 0.9 | 130.6 | 1.3 | 1.9 |
| Spain | 287.4 | 21.2 | 20.0 | 471.8 | 32.3 | 8.8 | 857.1 | 34.1 | 8.3 |
| Sweden | | | | | | | 83.8 | 9.5 | 19.1 |
| Switzerland | | | | 637.4 | 18.2 | 4.8 | 1 123.7 | 18.9 | |
| Turkey | 75.5 | 13.3 | 34.5 | 89.8 | 20.7 | 21.2 | 166.1 | 10.6 | 27.0 |
| United Kingdom | 1 151.1 | 15.3 | 7.7 | | | | 18 051.0 | 1.5 | − 1.4 |
| Canada | 536.0 | 18.9 | 24.7 | | | | 4 228.0 | 11.0 | 23.4 |
| United States | 3 653.6 | 20.9 | 19.0 | | | | | | |
| Australia | 798.8 | − 9.9 | 37.9 | | | | | | 34.0 |
| New Zealand | 429.1 | 13.9 | − 0.1 | | | | | | |
| Japan | 71.2 | 17.8 | − 0.3 | | | | | | |
| Yugoslavia | | | | 56.6 | 5.5 | 13.1 | 113.2 | 7.8 | 4.8 |

1. Derived from tables by receiving country (see corresponding notes).
2. *Tourist* or *visitor arrivals*. When both available : *tourist arrivals*.
3. Arrivals *in all means of accommodation* or *in hotels and similar establishments*. When both available: arrivals *in all means of accommodation*.
4. Nights spent *in all means of accommodation* or *in hotels and similar establishments*. When both available: nights spent *in all means of accommodation*.

# 4. Tourism from all OECD countries [1]

| | Arrivals at frontiers [2] | | | Arrivals at all means of accommodation [3] | | | Nights spent in all means of accommodation [4] | | |
|---|---|---|---|---|---|---|---|---|---|
| | Volume 1989 (thousands) | % 89/88 | % 88/87 | Volume 1989 (thousands) | % 89/88 | % 88/87 | Volume 1989 (thousands) | % 89/88 | % 88/87 |
| Austria | | | | 17 088.5 | 9.8 | 4.6 | 91 797.9 | 8.2 | 2.0 |
| Belgium | | | | | | | 10 007.7 | 1.7 | 5.3 |
| Denmark | | | | | | | 8 156.8 | 13.1 | − 1.6 |
| Finland | | | | | | | 1 937.6 | 5.5 | 7.2 |
| France | | | 3.7 | | | 3.7 | | | 2.4 |
| Germany | | | | 12 705.6 | 11.0 | 2.0 | 27 737.0 | 10.6 | 2.1 |
| Greece | 7 068.0 | 3.3 | 3.1 | | | 1.1 | | | − 1.5 |
| Iceland | | | − 0.6 | | | | | | |
| Ireland | 2 682.0 | 16.3 | 14.9 | 1 505.0 | 21.9 | 10.4 | 7 434.0 | 20.2 | 11.9 |
| Italy | 46 914.6 | − 2.0 | 6.1 | | | 1.9 | | | 0.0 |
| Luxembourg | | | | | | | | | |
| Netherlands | | | | 4 852.6 | 6.7 | | 13 556.0 | 13.1 | |
| Norway | | | | | | | 3 134.4 | 2.1 | − 2.4 |
| Portugal | 6 819.2 | 7.0 | 8.2 | 3 960.1 | 4.7 | 3.8 | 17 611.7 | 2.5 | 3.5 |
| Spain | 50 012.4 | − 0.1 | 7.3 | 11 887.1 | − 4.3 | − 2.8 | 73 705.6 | − 12.1 | − 4.4 |
| Sweden | | | | | | | 6 691.6 | 5.7 | − 0.1 |
| Switzerland | | | | 9 198.5 | 7.8 | 0.8 | 33 385.5 | 4.1 | 0.0 |
| Turkey | 3 001.4 | 5.9 | 61.0 | 3 230.5 | 11.3 | 29.3 | 10 656.6 | 3.6 | 43.1 |
| United Kingdom | 15 084.3 | 9.3 | 2.3 | | | | 142 249.0 | 4.9 | − 2.5 |
| Canada | 14 260.2 | − 2.9 | 2.4 | | | | 76 544.1 | − 3.3 | 6.0 |
| United States | 25 101.5 | 11.6 | 15.3 | | | | | | |
| Australia | 1 624.6 | − 9.1 | 27.4 | | | | | | 24.5 |
| New Zealand | 739.8 | 3.2 | 1.0 | | | | | | |
| Japan | 1 090.8 | 7.3 | − 1.5 | | | | | | |
| Yugoslavia | | | | 7 343.0 | − 5.0 | 1.6 | 43 326.1 | − 6.2 | 1.5 |

1. Derived from tables by receiving country (see corresponding notes).
2. *Tourist* or *visitor arrivals*. When both available : *tourist arrivals*.
3. Arrivals *in all means of accommodation* or *in hotels and similar establishments*. When both available: arrivals *in all means of accommodation*.
4. Nights spent *in all means of accommodation* or *in hotels and similar establishments*. When both available: nights spent *in all means of accommodation*.

## 5. Tourism from non-Member countries[1]

| | Arrivals at frontiers[2] | | | Arrivals at all means of accommodation[3] | | | Nights spent in all means of accommodation[4] | | |
|---|---|---|---|---|---|---|---|---|---|
| | Volume 1989 (thousands) | % 89/88 | % 88/87 | Volume 1989 (thousands) | % 89/88 | % 88/87 | Volume 1989 (thousands) | % 89/88 | % 88/87 |
| Austria | | | | 1 113.3 | 9.8 | 14.2 | 3 170.6 | 16.4 | 10.0 |
| Belgium | | | | | | | 767.1 | 3.5 | 2.5 |
| Denmark | | | | | | | 931.0 | 16.8 | − 8.0 |
| Finland | | | | | | | 579.7 | 25.5 | − 6.5 |
| France | | | 1.6 | | | 1.6 | | | − 0.5 |
| Germany | | | | 1 947.6 | 17.2 | 7.4 | 5 840.6 | 16.0 | 11.0 |
| Greece | 1 013.9 | 8.3 | − 0.1 | | | − 27.0 | 34 157.7 | 1393.5 | − 17.5 |
| Iceland | | | 0.7 | | | | | | |
| Ireland | 50.0 | 25.0 | 21.2 | | | | | | |
| Italy | 8 216.5 | 5.4 | 3.0 | | | 4.3 | | | 3.1 |
| Luxembourg | | | | | | | | | |
| Netherlands | | | | 297.5 | − 9.4 | | 615.7 | − 6.1 | |
| Norway | | | | | | | 296.9 | 3.7 | − 60.3 |
| Portugal | 296.7 | 17.5 | 18.1 | 202.7 | − 1.2 | 11.7 | 618.1 | 1.4 | 17.2 |
| Spain | 4 045.1 | − 1.4 | 6.1 | 1 297.4 | 7.2 | − 9.3 | 4 595.8 | 1.5 | − 5.3 |
| Sweden | | | | | | | 892.4 | 14.5 | 4.4 |
| Switzerland | | | | 904.9 | 10.8 | − 4.3 | 2 561.2 | 7.4 | − 5.3 |
| Turkey | 1 457.7 | 8.8 | 22.2 | 553.5 | 8.8 | 21.9 | 1 208.1 | − 11.8 | 20.4 |
| United Kingdom | 2 119.6 | 6.5 | − 4.1 | | | | 42 795.0 | 14.7 | − 4.9 |
| Canada | 862.1 | 8.9 | 25.6 | | | | 13 487.5 | 6.1 | 25.2 |
| United States | 10 147.5 | 12.1 | − 2.0 | | | | | | |
| Australia | 455.7 | − 1.4 | 20.8 | | | | | | 32.0 |
| New Zealand | 161.3 | 8.9 | 10.0 | | | | | | |
| Japan | 1 744.2 | 30.3 | 19.2 | | | | | | |
| Yugoslavia | | | | 1 301.1 | 1.1 | − 0.9 | 5 849.8 | − 5.0 | − 9.1 |

1. Derived from tables by receiving country (see corresponding notes).
2. *Tourist* or *visitor arrivals.* When both available : *tourist arrivals.*
3. Arrivals *in all means of accommodation* or *in hotels and similar establishments.* When both available: arrivals *in all means of accommodation.*
4. Nights spent *in all means of accommodation* or *in hotels and similar establishments.* When both available: nights spent *in all means of accommodation.*

## 6. Tourism from all countries[1]

| | Arrivals at frontiers[2] | | | Arrivals at all means of accommodation[3] | | | Nights spent in all means of accommodation[4] | | |
|---|---|---|---|---|---|---|---|---|---|
| | Volume 1989 (thousands) | % 89/88 | % 88/87 | Volume 1989 (thousands) | % 89/88 | % 88/87 | Volume 1989 (thousands) | % 89/88 | % 88/87 |
| Austria[5] | 170 950.0 | 9.1 | 5.4 | 18 201.8 | 9.8 | 5.1 | 94 968.5 | 8.4 | 2.2 |
| Belgium | | | | | | | 10 774.8 | 1.9 | 5.1 |
| Denmark | | | | | | | 9 087.8 | 13.4 | − 2.3 |
| Finland | | | | | | | 2 517.3 | 9.5 | 4.1 |
| France | 43 000.0 | 12.3 | 3.6 | | | 3.6 | 350 000.0 | 0.8 | 2.1 |
| Germany[5] | | | | 14 653.2 | 11.7 | 2.6 | 33 577.6 | 11.5 | 3.5 |
| Greece | 8 081.9 | 3.9 | 2.7 | | | − 2.8 | 34 158.0 | − 1.8 | − 2.7 |
| Iceland | | | − 0.6 | | | | | | |
| Ireland | 2 732.0 | 16.5 | 15.0 | 1 505.0 | 21.9 | 10.4 | 7 434.0 | 20.2 | 11.9 |
| Italy | 55 131.1 | − 1.0 | 5.6 | | | 2.1 | 91 000.0 | − 1.6 | 0.3 |
| Luxembourg | | | | | | | 2 100.0 | | |
| Netherlands | | | | 5 150.1 | 5.6 | | 14 171.7 | 12.1 | |
| Norway | | | | | | | 3 431.4 | 2.2 | −13.2 |
| Portugal | 7 115.9 | 7.4 | 8.6 | 4 162.8 | 4.4 | 4.2 | 18 229.8 | 2.5 | 4.0 |
| Spain | 54 057.6 | − 0.2 | 7.2 | 13 184.4 | − 3.3 | − 3.4 | 78 301.4 | −11.4 | − 4.4 |
| Sweden | | | | | | | 7 584.0 | 6.6 | 0.3 |
| Switzerland[6] | 12 600.0 | 7.7 | 0.0 | 10 103.4 | 8.0 | 0.3 | 35 946.7 | 4.4 | − 0.4 |
| Turkey[5] | 4 459.2 | 6.9 | 46.1 | 3 783.9 | 10.9 | 28.2 | 11 864.7 | 1.8 | 40.0 |
| United Kingdom | 17 203.9 | 8.9 | 1.5 | | | | 185 044.0 | 7.0 | − 3.0 |
| Canada | 15 122.3 | − 2.3 | 3.4 | | | | 90 031.6 | − 2.0 | 8.3 |
| United States | 35 249.0 | 11.7 | 9.7 | | | | | | |
| Australia | 2 080.3 | − 7.5 | 26.0 | | | | | | 26.0 |
| New Zealand | 901.1 | 4.2 | 2.4 | | | | | | |
| Japan | 2 835.1 | 20.4 | 9.3 | | | | | | |
| Yugoslavia | 34 118.1 | 15.1 | 13.3 | 8 644.1 | − 4.1 | 1.2 | 49 175.9 | − 6.1 | 0.1 |

1. Derived from tables by receiving country. See corresponding notes, except for the countries mentioned in notes 5 and 6 below.
2. *Tourist* or *visitor arrivals.* When both available : *tourist arrivals.*
3. Arrivals *in all means of accommodation* or *in hotels and similar establishments.* When both available: arrivals *in all means of accommodation.*
4. Nights spent *in all means of accommodation* or *in hotels and similar establishments.* When both available: nights spent *in all means of accommodation.*
5. *Traveller* arrivals at frontiers.
6. *Tourist* arrivals at frontiers : estimates.

## 7. Tourism from the United States
## Expenditure of US residents travelling abroad

In millions of dollars

|  | 1985 | 1986 | 1987 | 1988 | 1989[p] |
|---|---|---|---|---|---|
| Expenditure abroad[1] | 24 517 | 26 000 | 29 215 | 32 112 | 34 229 |
| Canada[2] | 2 503 | 3 030 | 2 949 | 3 241 | 3 302 |
| Mexico | 3 280 | 3 579 | 3 928 | 4 720 | 5 684 |
|   *Of which:*   Persons visiting Mexican border only | 2 048 | 2 215 | 2 254 | 2 740 | .. |
| Overseas areas | 18 734 | 19 391 | 22 338 | 24 151 | 25 153 |
|   *Of which:*   Europe and Mediterranean area | 9 317 | 9 149 | 10 042 | 11 248 | 11 560 |
|     Caribbean and Central America | 2 787 | 2 768 | 3 252 | 3 170 | 4 950 |
|     South America | 626 | 861 | 914 | 1 316 | |
|     Other overseas countries | 6 004 | 6 613 | 8 130 | 8 417 | 8 643 |
|     *Of which:*   Japan | 1 009 | 1 321 | 1 522 | 1 793 | 1 884 |
|       Australia – New Zealand[3] | 450 | 615 | 821 | 1 007 | 1 120 |
| Fare payments | | | | | |
|   Foreign-flag carriers | 6 671 | 6 774 | 7 423 | 7 872 | 8 349 |

*p.* Preliminary data.
1. Excludes travel by military personnel and other Government employees stationed abroad, their dependents and United States citizens residing abroad; includes shore expenditure of United States cruise travellers.
2. Excluding fare payments and crew spending.
3. Australia-New-Zealand include South Africa.
*Source: US Department of Commerce, Bureau of Economic Analysis.*

## 8. Tourism from the United States
## Number and expenditure of US residents travelling overseas

| Countries visited | Number of travellers In thousands[1] | | | Total expenditure Millions of dollars[2] | | | Average expenditure per traveller | | |
|---|---|---|---|---|---|---|---|---|---|
| | 1987 | 1988 | 1989 | 1987 | 1988 | 1989[p] | 1987 | 1988 | 1989 |
| Europe and Mediterranean area[3] | 6 062 | 6 415 | 6 909 | 10 042 | 11 248 | 11 560 | 1 657 | 1 753 | 1 673 |
| Carribean and Central America | 4 078 | 4 301 | 4 301 | 3 252 | 3 170 | 4 950 | 797 | 737 | 959 |
| South America | 762 | 887 | 863 | 914 | 1 376 | | 1 119 | 1 551 | |
| Other overseas countries | 2 809 | 2 643 | 2 827 | 8 130 | 8 417 | 8 643 | 2 894 | 3 185 | 3 057 |
| Total | 13 711 | 14 247 | 14 900 | 22 338 | 24 211 | 25 153 | 1 629 | 1 699 | 1 688 |

*p.* Preliminary data.
1. Excludes travel by military personnel and other Government employees stationed abroad, their dependents and United States citizens residing abroad and cruise travellers.
2. Includes shore expenditure of cruise travellers; excludes fares.
3. Includes all European countries Algeria, Cyprus, Egypt, Israel, Lebanon, Lybia, Malta, Morocco, Syria, Tunisia and Turkey.
*Source: US Department of Commerce, Bureau of Economic Analysis, based on data of the US Department of Justice, Immigration and Naturalization Service.*

# 9. Average length of stay of foreign tourists

| | Tourists from all foreign countries | | | Tourists from Europe (OECD) | | | Tourists from North America (OECD) | | | Tourists from Pacific (OECD) | | |
|---|---|---|---|---|---|---|---|---|---|---|---|---|
| | 1987 | 1988 | 1989 | 1987 | 1988 | 1989 | 1987 | 1988 | 1989 | 1987 | 1988 | 1989 |
| | **Average length of stay in tourist accommodation[1]** | | | | | | | | | | | |
| Austria | 5.4 | 5.3 | 5.2 | 5.8 | 5.6 | 5.6 | 2.6 | 2.6 | 2.5 | 2.1 | 2.1 | 2.1 |
| Germany | 2.3 | 2.3 | 2.3 | 2.3 | 2.3 | 2.3 | 2.1 | 2.1 | 2.0 | 1.7 | 1.7 | 1.7 |
| Italy | 4.6 | 4.5 | | 5.1 | 5.0 | | 2.6 | 2.6 | | 2.1 | 2.1 | |
| Netherlands | 2.1 | 2.6 | 2.8 | 2.1 | 2.8 | 2.9 | 1.9 | 1.9 | 2.0 | 2.0 | 1.9 | 2.0 |
| Portugal | 4.5 | 4.5 | 4.4 | 4.8 | 4.7 | 4.6 | 2.9 | 2.9 | 2.9 | 2.3 | 2.3 | 2.3 |
| Spain[2] | 6.5 | 6.5 | 5.9 | 7.3 | 7.2 | 6.7 | 2.4 | 2.3 | 2.2 | 1.8 | 1.8 | 1.8 |
| Switzerland | 3.7 | 3.7 | 3.6 | 4.2 | 4.2 | 4.0 | 2.3 | 2.3 | 2.2 | 1.8 | 1.8 | 1.8 |
| Turkey | 3.1 | 3.4 | 3.1 | 3.3 | 3.6 | 3.4 | 2.8 | 2.7 | 2.3 | 1.9 | 2.0 | 1.9 |
| Yugoslavia | 5.9 | 5.8 | 5.7 | 6.1 | 6.2 | 6.1 | 2.6 | 2.5 | 2.5 | 2.1 | 2.0 | 2.0 |

1. Unless otherwise stated below, the average length of stay in all means of accommodation is obtained by dividing the number of nights recorded in particular means of accommodation by the number of arrivals of tourists at the same means of accommodation (see country tables).
2. Hôtellerie.

| | Tourists from all foreign countries | | | Tourists from Europe (OECD) | | | Tourists from North America (OECD) | | | Tourists from Pacific (OECD) | | |
|---|---|---|---|---|---|---|---|---|---|---|---|---|
| | 1987 | 1988 | 1989 | 1987 | 1988 | 1989 | 1987 | 1988 | 1989 | 1987 | 1988 | 1989 |
| | **Average length of stay in the country visited[1]** | | | | | | | | | | | |
| France | 9.2 | 9.1 | 9.1 | 8.4 | 8.4 | 8.4 | 14.5 | 13.9 | 13.9 | 7.3 | 6.8 | 6.8 |
| Greece[2] | 14.0 | 13.0 | | | | | | | | | | |
| Ireland[3] | 9.2 | 8.8 | 9.2 | 9.1 | 8.7 | 9.1 | 11.0 | 10.5 | 11.1 | 14.8 | 14.4 | 15.2 |
| Portugal[2] | 7.8 | 7.6 | 7.7 | 7.8 | 7.6 | 7.7 | 11.1 | 9.5 | 10.3 | 5.4 | 7.7 | 7.5 |
| Turkey | 3.1 | 3.4 | 3.2 | 3.3 | 3.6 | 3.4 | 2.8 | 2.7 | 2.3 | 1.9 | 2.0 | 1.9 |
| United Kingdom | 11.0 | 11.0 | 11.0 | 9.0 | 9.0 | 8.0 | 11.0 | 11.0 | 10.0 | 19.0 | 18.0 | 16.0 |
| Canada | 5.7 | 5.9 | 6.0 | 12.9 | 13.0 | 12.2 | 4.4 | 4.4 | 4.4 | 8.5 | 8.5 | 7.9 |
| Australia | | 28.0 | | | 46.0 | | | 25.0 | | | 21.0 | |
| Japan | 13.0 | 15.6 | 13.8 | | | | | | | | | |
| New Zealand[2] | 25.0 | 21.0 | 21.0 | | | | 21.0 | 15.0 | 16.0 | 16.0 | 16.0 | 15.0 |

1. Unless otherwise stated below, the average length of stay in the country visited is expressed in number of nights spent.
2. Greece, New Zealand and Portugal: number of days.
3. Ireland : excluding visitors from Northern Ireland.

## 10. Nights spent by foreign and domestic tourists in all means of accommodation[1]

In thousands

| | Nights spent by foreign tourists | | | Nights spent by domestic tourists | | | Total nights | | | Proportion spent by foreign tourists (%) | |
|---|---|---|---|---|---|---|---|---|---|---|---|
| | 1988 | 1989 | % 89/88 | 1988 | 1989 | % 89/88 | 1988 | 1989 | % 89/88 | 1988 | 1989 |
| Austria | 87 575.1 | 94 968.5 | 8.4 | 28 137.1 | 28 815.6 | 2.4 | 115 712.2 | 123 784.2 | 7.0 | 75.7 | 76.7 |
| Belgium | 10 577.0 | 10 798.7 | 2.1 | 21 897.6 | 19 320.4 | −11.8 | 32 474.6 | 30 119.0 | −7.3 | 32.6 | 35.9 |
| Denmark | 8 010.9 | 9 087.8 | 13.4 | 12 322.1 | 13 160.3 | 6.8 | 20 333.0 | 22 248.0 | 9.4 | 39.4 | 40.8 |
| Finland | 2 611.2 | 2 846.0 | 9.0 | 9 505.5 | 10 130.3 | 6.6 | 12 116.8 | 12 976.4 | 7.1 | 21.6 | 21.9 |
| Germany | 34 474.5 | 38 028.2 | 10.3 | 216 165.6 | 222 833.6 | 3.1 | 250 640.1 | 260 861.8 | 4.1 | 13.8 | 14.6 |
| Greece | 34 779.1 | 34 157.7 | −1.8 | 11 255.0 | 11 985.8 | 6.5 | 46 034.0 | 46 143.5 | 0.2 | 75.6 | 74.0 |
| Italy | 107 030.1 | | | 250 835.8 | | | 357 865.9 | | | 29.9 | |
| Netherlands | 12 645.9 | 14 171.9 | 12.1 | 34 274.9 | 36 787.1 | 7.3 | 46 920.8 | 50 959.0 | 8.6 | 27.0 | 27.8 |
| Norway | 5 388.0 | 5 538.6 | 2.8 | 11 397.8 | 11 122.7 | −2.4 | 16 785.7 | 16 661.3 | −0.7 | 32.1 | 33.2 |
| Portugal | 17 786.6 | 18 229.8 | 2.5 | 11 995.6 | 12 588.6 | 4.9 | 29 782.1 | 30 818.3 | 3.5 | 59.7 | 59.2 |
| Sweden | 7 112.4 | 7 584.0 | 6.6 | 27 521.5 | 28 634.9 | 4.0 | 34 633.9 | 36 218.9 | 4.6 | 20.5 | 20.9 |
| Switzerland | 34 495.6 | 35 946.7 | 4.2 | 38 960.2 | 39 804.6 | 2.2 | 73 455.8 | 75 751.3 | 3.1 | 47.0 | 47.5 |
| Turkey[2] | 11 655.2 | 11 864.7 | 1.8 | 5 577.7 | 5 565.6 | −0.2 | 17 232.8 | 17 430.3 | 1.1 | 67.6 | 68.1 |
| Canada | | | | 257 444.0 | | | | | | | |
| Australia | 31 490.2 | | | 122 070.0 | | | 153 560.2 | | | 20.5 | |
| Yugoslavia | 52 351.0 | 49 175.9 | −6.1 | 55 147.9 | 51 112.9 | −7.3 | 107 498.9 | 100 288.8 | −6.7 | 48.7 | 49.0 |

1. For the "Types of accommodation covered by the statistics" see Table C.
2. Turkey: figures based on a monthly sample survey carried out amoung establishments licenced by the Ministry of Tourism.

## 11. Nights spent by foreign and domestic tourists in hotels and similar establishments[1]

In thousands

| | Nights spent by foreign tourists | | | Nights spent by domestic tourists | | | Total nights | | | Proportion spent by foreign tourists (%) | |
|---|---|---|---|---|---|---|---|---|---|---|---|
| | 1988 | 1989 | % 89/88 | 1988 | 1989 | % 89/88 | 1988 | 1989 | % 89/88 | 1988 | 1989 |
| Austria | 56 339.8 | 61 428.4 | 9.0 | 14 415.2 | 14 875.6 | 3.2 | 70 755.0 | 76 304.0 | 7.8 | 79.6 | 80.5 |
| Belgium | 5 424.2 | 5 989.9 | 10.4 | 2 422.7 | 2 431.0 | 0.3 | 7 846.9 | 8 420.9 | 7.3 | 69.1 | 71.1 |
| Denmark | 4 377.7 | 5 131.9 | 17.2 | 4 655.6 | 4 843.5 | 4.0 | 9 033.3 | 9 975.4 | 10.4 | 48.5 | 51.4 |
| Finland | 2 298.3 | 2 517.3 | 9.5 | 7 609.9 | 8 054.1 | 5.8 | 9 908.2 | 10 571.4 | 6.7 | 23.2 | 23.8 |
| France[2] | 40 377.9 | 50 953.3 | 26.2 | 82 370.7 | 86 750.1 | 5.3 | 122 748.6 | 137 703.4 | 12.2 | 32.9 | 37.0 |
| Germany | 25 226.1 | 28 388.7 | 12.5 | 115 033.6 | 118 591.1 | 3.1 | 140 259.8 | 146 979.9 | 4.8 | 18.0 | 19.3 |
| Greece | 33 341.1 | 32 938.5 | −1.2 | 10 733.4 | 11 396.2 | 6.2 | 44 074.5 | 44 334.7 | 0.6 | 75.6 | 74.3 |
| Italy | 70 406.4 | | | 117 965.0 | | | 188 371.4 | | | 37.4 | |
| Netherlands | 6 761.5 | 7 178.5 | 6.2 | 5 471.3 | 5 941.1 | 8.6 | 12 232.8 | 13 119.6 | 7.2 | 55.3 | 54.7 |
| Norway | 3 356.3 | 3 431.4 | 2.2 | 8 496.9 | 8 192.9 | −3.6 | 11 853.2 | 11 624.3 | −1.9 | 28.3 | 29.5 |
| Portugal | 15 005.3 | 15 467.5 | 3.1 | 6 264.0 | 6 585.5 | 5.1 | 21 269.3 | 22 053.0 | 3.7 | 70.5 | 70.1 |
| Spain | 88 351.0 | 78 301.4 | −11.4 | 48 987.3 | 53 123.1 | 8.4 | 137 338.3 | 131 424.5 | −4.3 | 64.3 | 59.6 |
| Sweden | 3 192.0 | 3 366.9 | 5.5 | 12 987.5 | 13 607.9 | 4.8 | 16 179.5 | 16 974.8 | 4.9 | 19.7 | 19.8 |
| Switzerland | 19 101.3 | 20 489.4 | 7.3 | 13 239.4 | 13 659.9 | 3.2 | 32 340.7 | 34 149.3 | 5.6 | 59.1 | 60.0 |
| Turkey[4] | 9 365.6 | 9 673.3 | 3.3 | 5 054.1 | 4 975.2 | −1.6 | 14 419.7 | 14 648.5 | 1.6 | 65.0 | 66.0 |
| Canada[3] | | | | 51 538.0 | | | | | | | |
| Australia | 15 115.3 | | | 40 173.0 | | | 55 288.3 | | | 27.3 | |
| Yugoslavia | 28 246.7 | 27 931.0 | −1.1 | 21 505.5 | 20 705.5 | −3.7 | 49 752.2 | 48 636.5 | −2.2 | 56.8 | 57.4 |

1. For the "Types of accommodation covered by the statistics" see Table C.
2. France: data covering all France except 3 regions (Pays de la Loire, Champagne-Ardennes and Corse).
3. Canada: includes nights spent by canadians in the United States with final destination in Canada.
4. Turkey: does not include thermal hotels.

## 12. Nights spent by foreign and domestic tourists in supplementary means of accommodation[1]

In thousands

| | Nights spent by foreign tourists | | | Nights spent by domestic tourists | | | Total nights | | | Proportion spent by foreign tourists (%) | |
|---|---|---|---|---|---|---|---|---|---|---|---|
| | 1988 | 1989 | % 89/88 | 1988 | 1989 | % 89/88 | 1988 | 1989 | % 89/88 | 1988 | 1989 |
| Austria | 31 235.3 | 33 540.1 | 7.4 | 13 721.9 | 13 940.0 | 1.6 | 44 957.2 | 47 480.1 | 5.6 | 69.5 | 70.6 |
| Belgium | 5 152.9 | 4 808.8 | −6.7 | 19 475.0 | 16 889.4 | −13.3 | 24 627.9 | 21 698.2 | −11.9 | 20.9 | 22.2 |
| Denmark | 3 633.2 | 3 955.9 | 8.9 | 7 666.5 | 8 316.8 | 8.5 | 11 299.7 | 12 272.6 | 8.6 | 32.2 | 32.2 |
| Finland | 312.9 | 328.7 | 5.0 | 1 895.6 | 2 076.2 | 9.5 | 2 208.5 | 2 404.9 | 8.9 | 14.2 | 13.7 |
| Germany | 9 248.4 | 9 639.5 | 4.2 | 101 132.0 | 104 242.4 | 3.1 | 110 380.4 | 113 881.9 | 3.2 | 8.4 | 8.5 |
| Greece | 1 438.0 | 1 219.2 | −15.2 | 521.5 | 589.6 | 13.0 | 1 959.5 | 1 808.8 | −7.7 | 73.4 | 67.4 |
| Italy | 36 623.7 | | | 132 870.8 | | | 169 494.5 | | | 21.6 | |
| Netherlands | 5 884.4 | 6 993.4 | 18.8 | 28 803.6 | 30 846.0 | 7.1 | 34 688.0 | 37 839.4 | 9.1 | 17.0 | 18.5 |
| Norway | 2 031.7 | 2 107.3 | 3.7 | 2 900.9 | 2 929.8 | 1.0 | 4 932.6 | 5 037.1 | 2.1 | 41.2 | 41.8 |
| Portugal | 2 781.2 | 2 762.3 | −0.7 | 5 731.6 | 6 003.0 | 4.7 | 8 512.9 | 8 765.3 | 3.0 | 32.7 | 31.5 |
| Sweden | 3 920.4 | 4 217.1 | 7.6 | 14 534.0 | 15 027.0 | 3.4 | 18 454.4 | 19 244.1 | 4.3 | 21.2 | 21.9 |
| Switzerland | 15 345.6 | 15 457.3 | 0.7 | 25 720.8 | 26 144.7 | 1.6 | 41 066.4 | 41 602.0 | 1.3 | 37.4 | 37.2 |
| Turkey | 2 289.6 | 2 191.4 | −4.3 | 523.6 | 590.3 | 12.7 | 2 813.2 | 2 781.8 | −1.1 | 81.4 | 78.8 |
| Canada[2] | | | | 205 906.0 | | | | | | | |
| Australia | 16 374.9 | | | 81 897.0 | | | 98 271.9 | | | 16.7 | |
| Yugoslavia | 24 104.3 | 21 245.0 | −11.9 | 33 642.4 | 30 407.4 | −9.6 | 57 746.7 | 51 652.4 | −10.6 | 41.7 | 41.1 |
| *Of which:* **on camping sites** | | | | | | | | | | | |
| Austria | 5 422.9 | 5 472.9 | 0.9 | 1 194.0 | 1 208.4 | 1.2 | 6 616.9 | 6 681.3 | 1.0 | 82.0 | 81.9 |
| Belgium | 2 041.7 | 2 280.9 | 11.7 | 8 341.2 | 8 843.6 | 6.0 | 10 382.9 | 11 124.5 | 7.1 | 19.7 | 20.5 |
| Denmark | 3 213.8 | 3 506.2 | 9.1 | 7 203.2 | 7 806.9 | 8.4 | 10 417.0 | 11 313.1 | 8.6 | 30.9 | 31.0 |
| Finland | 312.9 | 328.7 | 5.0 | 1 895.6 | 2 076.2 | 9.5 | 2 208.5 | 2 404.9 | 8.9 | 14.2 | 13.7 |
| Germany | 4 357.8 | 4 450.6 | 2.1 | 11 951.4 | 13 017.0 | 8.9 | 16 309.2 | 17 467.7 | 7.1 | 26.7 | 25.5 |
| Greece | 1 438.0 | 1 219.2 | −15.2 | 521.5 | 589.6 | 13.0 | 1 959.5 | 1 808.8 | −7.7 | 73.4 | 67.4 |
| Italy | 16 447.1 | | | 26 747.8 | | | 43 194.9 | | | 38.1 | |
| Netherlands | 2 612.4 | 3 191.8 | 22.2 | 12 223.3 | 13 376.3 | 9.4 | 14 835.7 | 16 568.1 | 11.7 | 17.6 | 19.3 |
| Norway | 1 828.2 | 1 908.7 | 4.4 | 2 767.2 | 2 798.0 | 1.1 | 4 595.4 | 4 706.7 | 2.4 | 39.8 | 40.6 |
| Portugal | 2 679.8 | 2 666.3 | −0.5 | 4 884.9 | 5 127.3 | 5.0 | 7 564.6 | 7 793.6 | 3.0 | 35.4 | 34.2 |
| Sweden | 2 999.8 | 3 256.0 | 8.5 | 10 653.1 | 11 147.6 | 4.6 | 13 652.9 | 14 403.6 | 5.5 | 22.0 | 22.6 |
| Switzerland | 2 158.8 | 2 373.1 | 9.9 | 5 116.3 | 5 451.6 | 6.6 | 7 275.1 | 7 824.7 | 7.6 | 29.7 | 30.3 |
| Turkey | 331.9 | 280.3 | −15.5 | 37.8 | 56.0 | 48.1 | 369.7 | 336.3 | −9.0 | 89.8 | 83.4 |
| Canada[2] | | | | 26 702.0 | | | | | | | |
| Australia | 3 419.0 | | | 25 466.0 | | | 28 885.0 | | | 11.8 | |
| Yugoslavia | 12 135.7 | 10 607.8 | −12.6 | 6 987.7 | 6 343.2 | −9.2 | 19 123.4 | 16 951.0 | −11.4 | 63.5 | 62.6 |
| *Of which:* **in youth hostels** | | | | | | | | | | | |
| Austria | 607.4 | 742.8 | 22.3 | 648.5 | 543.8 | −16.1 | 1 255.9 | 1 286.6 | 2.4 | 48.4 | 57.7 |
| Denmark | 419.4 | 449.7 | 7.2 | 463.3 | 509.9 | 10.1 | 882.7 | 959.5 | 8.7 | 47.5 | 46.9 |
| Germany | 1 036.6 | 1 166.0 | 12.5 | 9 119.5 | 9 313.1 | 2.1 | 10 156.1 | 10 479.1 | 3.2 | 10.2 | 11.1 |
| Italy | 595.3 | | | 167.0 | | | 762.3 | | | 78.1 | |
| Netherlands | 605.7 | 630.0 | 4.0 | 317.5 | 317.2 | −0.1 | 923.2 | 947.2 | 2.6 | 65.6 | 66.5 |
| Norway | 203.5 | 198.6 | −2.4 | 133.7 | 131.8 | −1.4 | 337.2 | 330.4 | −2.0 | 60.3 | 60.1 |
| Sweden | 231.8 | 262.2 | 13.1 | 796.0 | 858.7 | 7.9 | 1 027.8 | 1 120.9 | 9.1 | 22.6 | 23.4 |
| Switzerland | 491.0 | 532.2 | 8.4 | 360.5 | 371.6 | 3.1 | 851.5 | 903.8 | 6.1 | 57.7 | 58.9 |
| Australia | 4 408.6 | | | 2 244.0 | | | 6 652.6 | | | 66.3 | |
| Yugoslavia | 457.6 | 450.3 | −1.6 | 4 242.4 | 3 983.8 | −6.1 | 4 700.1 | 4 434.1 | −5.7 | 9.7 | 10.2 |
| *Of which:* **in private rooms, rented apartments and houses** | | | | | | | | | | | |
| Austria | 15 380.5 | 16 088.8 | 4.6 | 4 251.2 | 4 357.7 | 2.5 | 19 631.7 | 20 446.5 | 4.2 | 78.3 | 78.7 |
| Belgium | 677.6 | 139.9 | −79.3 | 6 071.9 | 2 849.7 | −53.1 | 6 749.5 | 2 989.6 | −55.7 | 10.0 | 4.7 |
| Germany | 1 734.6 | 1 770.7 | 2.1 | 18 286.7 | 19 699.8 | 7.7 | 20 021.3 | 21 470.5 | 7.2 | 8.7 | 8.2 |
| Italy | 18 494.1 | | | 96 943.8 | | | 115 437.9 | | | 16.0 | |
| Switzerland | 10 350.0 | 10 250.0 | −1.0 | 13 850.0 | 13 810.0 | −0.3 | 24 200.0 | 24 060.0 | −0.6 | 42.8 | 42.6 |
| Australia | 5 668.2 | | | 15 777.0 | | | 21 445.2 | | | 26.4 | |
| Yugoslavia | 10 192.2 | 9 007.7 | −11.6 | 8 996.0 | 7 543.9 | −16.1 | 19 188.2 | 16 551.6 | −13.7 | 53.1 | 54.4 |

1. For the "Types of accommodatiom covered by the statistics" see Table C.
2. Canada: person-nights: includes nights spent by Canadians in the United States with final destination in Canada.

# 13. Capacity in hotels and similar establishments[1]

In thousands

| | Hotels | | | Motels | | | Boarding houses | | | Inns | | | Others | | | Total | | |
|---|---|---|---|---|---|---|---|---|---|---|---|---|---|---|---|---|---|---|
| | 1988 | 1989 | % 89/88 | 1988 | 1989 | % 89/88 | 1988 | 1989 | % 89/88 | 1988 | 1989 | % 89/88 | 1988 | 1989 | % 89/88 | 1988 | 1989 | % 89/88 |
| Austria[2] | 653.9 | 656.9 | 0.5 | | | | | | | | | | | | | 653.9 | 656.9 | 0.5 |
| Belgium | 87.2 | 84.6 | -3.0 | | | | | | | | | | | | | 87.2 | 84.6 | -3.0 |
| Denmark[3] | 68.5 | 77.3 | 12.8 | | | | 9.2 | 14.8 | 61.9 | 6.3 | | | | | | 84.0 | 89.1 | 6.1 |
| Finland[4] | | | | | | | | | | | | | | | | 84.0 | 92.1 | 9.7 |
| France[5] | 549.8 | 564.8 | 2.7 | | | | 138.3 | 137.0 | -0.9 | 243.5 | 243.0 | -0.2 | 245.4 | 246.2 | 0.3 | 1 177.0 | 1 191.0 | 1.2 |
| Germany[6] | 341.6 | 356.6 | 4.4 | 3.3 | 3.3 | 0.0 | 16.7 | 18.5 | 10.7 | 5.1 | 5.1 | 0.0 | 29.1 | 35.0 | 20.2 | 395.8 | 418.5 | 5.7 |
| Greece | | | | | | | | | | | | | | | | 105.0 | 108.2 | 3.1 |
| Netherlands | | | | | | | | | | | | | 105.9 | 105.3 | -0.6 | 105.9 | 105.3 | -0.6 |
| Norway[7] | 77.5 | 81.2 | 4.8 | 1.0 | 1.2 | 15.8 | 43.2 | 44.8 | 3.6 | 3.9 | 4.0 | 2.4 | 33.3 | 37.3 | 12.0 | 158.9 | 168.4 | 6.0 |
| Portugal[8] | | | | | | | | | | | | | | | | | | |
| Spain[9] | 683.2 | 708.0 | 3.6 | 224.8 | 210.7 | -6.3 | | | | | | | 173.3 | 94.8 | -45.3 | 1 081.1 | 1 093.6 | 1.2 |
| Sweden[14] | 106.4 | 110.0 | 3.3 | | | | 46.9 | 46.3 | -1.4 | | | | | | | 153.4 | 156.2 | 1.9 |
| Switzerland[10] | 235.9 | 235.7 | -0.1 | 6.3 | 6.1 | -3.2 | | | | 30.0 | 29.5 | -1.8 | | | | 272.2 | 271.2 | -0.4 |
| Turkey[11] | 84.9 | 105.8 | 24.7 | 3.7 | 3.2 | -15.4 | 3.7 | 4.4 | 16.7 | 2.4 | 2.4 | 0.0 | 1.7 | 2.5 | 44.3 | 96.4 | 118.2 | 22.6 |
| Australia[12] | 125.3 | 125.7 | 0.3 | 278.0 | 286.0 | 2.9 | | | | | | | | | | 403.3 | 421.7 | 4.6 |
| Japan | 108.7 | 112.5 | 3.5 | | | | 94.1 | 94.3 | 0.2 | 94.1 | | | | | | | | |
| New Zealand | | | | | | | | | | | | | | | | | | |
| Yugoslavia[13] | 333.1 | 336.7 | 1.1 | 11.3 | 11.4 | 1.5 | 5.7 | 5.9 | 3.6 | 2.3 | 2.1 | -9.1 | 5.7 | 6.1 | 6.6 | 358.1 | 362.3 | 1.2 |

Notice : this table contains data on available bed capacity unless otherwise stated in the following notes by country.
1. For the "Types of accommodation covered by the statistics" see Table C.
2. Austria : position at 31st August.
3. Denmark : position at 31st July.
4. Finland : position at 31st December.
5. France : position at 31st December.
6. Germany : position at April.
7. Norway : position at 31st December.
8. Portugal : position at 31st July.
9. Spain : position at 31st December.
10. Switzerland : position at 31st December.
11. Turkey : position at 31st December of accommodation establishments approved by Ministry of Culture and Tourism.
12. Australia : position at December.
13. Yugoslavia : position at 31st August.
14. Sweden : position at December.

# 14. Capacity in supplementary means of accommodation[1]

## In thousands

| | Youth hostels | | | Camping sites Places | | | Holiday villages | | | Rented rooms, houses and flats | | | Sanatoria and health establishments | | | Recreational camps | | | Others | | | Total | | |
|---|---|---|---|---|---|---|---|---|---|---|---|---|---|---|---|---|---|---|---|---|---|---|---|---|
| | 1988 | 1989 | %89/88 | 1988 | 1989 | %89/88 | 1988 | 1989 | %89/88 | 1988 | 1989 | %89/88 | 1988 | 1989 | %89/88 | 1988 | 1989 | %89/88 | 1988 | 1989 | %89/88 | 1988 | 1989 | %89/88 |
| Austria[2] | 10.2 | 11.5 | 12.7 | | | | 104.9 | 110.7 | 5.6 | 323.4 | 313.6 | -3.0 | 16.6 | 17.8 | 7.3 | 28.4 | 28.5 | 0.3 | 31.4 | 32.3 | 3.0 | 514.9 | 514.6 | -0.1 |
| Belgium | | | | 354.1 | 356.8 | 0.8 | | | | | | | 3.5 | 3.5 | 0.2 | 24.8 | 23.5 | -5.3 | 62.3 | 66.8 | 7.3 | 444.6 | 450.6 | 1.3 |
| Denmark | 10.4 | 10.4 | 0.2 | | | | | | | | | | | | | | | | | | | 10.4 | | |
| Germany | 94.1 | 93.5 | -0.6 | | | | 24.6 | 23.9 | -3.2 | 196.9 | 204.5 | 3.8 | 126.7 | 126.7 | 0.0 | | | | 159.9 | 161.5 | 1.0 | 602.3 | 610.0 | 1.3 |
| Greece | | | | 75.4 | 79.6 | 5.5 | | | | 219.1 | 219.6 | 0.2 | | | | | | | 7.4 | 7.4 | 0.0 | 301.9 | 306.6 | 1.6 |
| Italy | 6.2 | | | 1 172.8 | | | | | | 156.1 | | | | | | | | | 184.7 | | | 1 519.7 | | |
| Norway | 5.6 | 5.8 | 3.9 | | | | | | | | | | | | | | | | | | | 5.6 | 5.8 | 3.9 |
| Portugal | | | | 247.8 | 257.0 | 3.7 | | | | | | | | | | 11.2 | 12.0 | 6.5 | | | | 259.0 | 268.9 | 3.8 |
| Spain | | | | 457.4 | 470.4 | 2.8 | | | | 328.4 | 335.8 | 2.3 | | | | | | | 10 393.0 | 10 808.7 | 4.0 | 11 378.7 | 11 614.9 | 2.1 |
| Sweden | 15.4 | 15.3 | -0.3 | 364.0 | 395.0 | 8.5 | 47.0 | 45.9 | -2.4 | | | | | | | | | | | | | 426.4 | 456.2 | 7.0 |
| Switzerland | 8.2 | 8.1 | -1.0 | 272.0 | 269.5 | -0.9 | | | | 360.0 | 360.0 | 0.0 | 7.0 | 6.9 | -1.4 | | | | 235.0 | 228.1 | -2.9 | 882.1 | 872.6 | -1.1 |
| Turkey[3] | | | | 9.8 | 8.7 | -11.1 | 16.0 | 19.1 | 19.2 | | | | | | | | | | | | | 25.9 | 27.9 | 7.9 |
| Australia[4] | | | | 592.8 | 564.1 | -4.8 | | | | 133.8 | 135.6 | 1.3 | | | | | | | | | | 726.6 | 702.7 | -3.3 |
| Japan | 30.3 | 29.3 | -3.2 | | | | | | | | | | | | | | | | | | | | | |
| Yugoslavia[5] | 59.9 | 58.9 | -1.8 | 372.0 | 372.2 | 0.1 | 118.0 | 111.5 | -5.4 | 474.8 | 455.0 | -4.2 | 18.4 | 17.2 | -6.8 | | | | 24.2 | 24.1 | -0.2 | 1 067.2 | 1 038.8 | -2.7 |

Notice: this table contains data on available bed capacity, unless otherwise stated in the following notes by country.

1. For the "Types of accommodation covered by the statistics" see Table C.
2. Austria: others includes mountain huts and shelters.
3. Turkey: the total doesn't include licenced yacht bed capacity (9 358) and beds registered by local municipalities in social tourism establishments (223 576).
4. Australia: assuming 3 beds per place.
5. Yugoslavia: others includes mountain huts and shelters.

## 15. Monthly hotel occupancy rates

| Year | Month | Belgium (B) | Finland[1] (R) | Germany[10] (B) | Italy (B) | Netherlands[11] (R) | Norway[2] (B) | Portugal[8] (B) | Spain (B) | Sweden[3] (B) | Switzerland[9] (B) | Turkey[4] (B) | United Kingdom[5] (B) | Australia[6] (B) | Japan[7] (R) | Yugoslavia (B) |
|---|---|---|---|---|---|---|---|---|---|---|---|---|---|---|---|---|
| 1987 | January | 17.9 | 42.0 | 25.1 | 23.3 | | 34.6 | 34.8 | 42.3 | 22.2 | 28.9 | 27.8 | 26.0 | | 56.0 | 26.7 |
| | February | 20.9 | 52.0 | 30.8 | 26.4 | | 45.6 | 40.4 | 48.0 | 32.6 | 38.4 | 31.3 | 34.0 | 36.2 | 67.8 | 27.8 |
| | March | 24.4 | 56.2 | 30.4 | 30.3 | | 47.7 | 48.3 | 48.8 | 34.1 | 40.2 | 30.9 | 36.0 | | 71.2 | 27.3 |
| | April | 19.3 | 51.5 | 34.4 | 35.5 | | 40.1 | 58.6 | 53.6 | 31.3 | 31.2 | 46.8 | 42.0 | | 65.4 | 39.7 |
| | May | 26.3 | 53.8 | 41.4 | 31.8 | | 34.1 | 60.9 | 58.0 | 31.7 | 26.4 | 49.3 | 45.0 | 32.2 | 71.9 | 58.3 |
| | June | 19.3 | 55.9 | 46.8 | 44.1 | | 45.9 | 60.2 | 61.9 | 37.6 | 35.9 | 58.0 | 51.0 | | 65.5 | 72.6 |
| | July | 47.8 | 57.1 | 52.2 | 58.8 | | 55.8 | 63.8 | 68.0 | 52.5 | 45.7 | 63.1 | 57.0 | | 66.7 | 75.9 |
| | August | 42.6 | 56.7 | 52.8 | 68.7 | | 47.9 | 76.3 | 78.0 | 38.1 | 48.5 | 69.0 | 58.0 | 35.6 | 75.4 | 84.8 |
| | September | 16.3 | 58.7 | 49.8 | 46.0 | | 39.6 | 70.5 | 68.0 | 31.2 | 42.6 | 63.1 | 56.0 | | 67.5 | 76.2 |
| | October | 12.9 | 52.1 | 42.4 | 33.8 | | 37.3 | 60.0 | 59.3 | 29.0 | 30.7 | 52.7 | 51.0 | | 78.5 | 48.9 |
| | November | 10.6 | 53.1 | 28.1 | 20.9 | | 36.2 | 39.6 | 47.1 | 27.0 | 16.0 | 35.7 | 39.0 | 34.3 | 75.9 | 23.1 |
| | December | 29.7 | 39.9 | 25.1 | 21.8 | | 29.7 | 30.5 | 40.8 | 22.5 | 20.4 | 31.5 | 32.0 | | 57.0 | 20.0 |
| 1988 | January | 18.1 | 43.8 | 25.8 | 24.2 | 20.0 | 32.5 | 34.3 | 44.6 | 22.2 | 27.3 | 32.1 | | 35.2 | | 25.4 |
| | February | 21.8 | 53.2 | 31.9 | 31.3 | 24.2 | 43.0 | 41.3 | 50.0 | 32.1 | 39.7 | 33.7 | | | | 26.6 |
| | March | 7.6 | 56.0 | 32.4 | 32.1 | 26.7 | 42.5 | 49.7 | 52.4 | 34.5 | 39.3 | 37.2 | | | | 29.2 |
| | April | 14.4 | 54.1 | 34.1 | 35.9 | 37.7 | 37.6 | 54.0 | 51.8 | 34.1 | 30.0 | 43.0 | | | | 36.9 |
| | May | 16.4 | 54.6 | 41.1 | 32.7 | 41.9 | 29.4 | 57.5 | 54.9 | 28.7 | 25.6 | 55.2 | | 33.5 | | 56.6 |
| | June | 14.6 | 57.7 | 47.5 | 42.8 | 39.8 | 44.0 | 56.8 | 59.2 | 34.8 | 34.5 | 60.1 | | | | 67.7 |
| | July | 36.3 | 60.0 | 53.1 | 60.5 | 41.4 | 53.5 | 64.3 | 66.9 | 49.7 | 45.8 | 63.4 | | | | 75.3 |
| | August | 33.1 | 58.8 | 52.9 | 71.0 | 41.4 | 45.3 | 76.9 | 76.5 | 37.7 | 49.1 | 67.2 | | 38.5 | | 81.1 |
| | September | 13.1 | 59.1 | 50.8 | 47.2 | 39.2 | 35.3 | 65.1 | 65.2 | 30.2 | 43.9 | 65.6 | | | | 71.7 |
| | October | 12.3 | 53.3 | 43.6 | 35.6 | 34.6 | 31.0 | 56.2 | 55.7 | 28.2 | 30.3 | 52.4 | | | | 43.1 |
| | November | 15.6 | 54.3 | 28.8 | 22.8 | 28.5 | 30.4 | 40.5 | 46.9 | 28.0 | 16.7 | 33.3 | | 34.4 | | 22.2 |
| | December | 20.2 | 38.7 | 25.3 | 26.2 | 22.9 | 24.8 | 34.0 | 40.2 | 22.0 | 20.4 | 29.9 | | | | 19.3 |
| 1989 | January | | 43.2 | 27.0 | | 21.1 | | | 43.0 | 23.0 | | 23.7 | 26.0 | 35.2 | | 25.0 |
| | February | | 52.8 | 33.0 | | 25.2 | | | 48.5 | 32.0 | | 27.9 | 33.0 | | | 25.0 |
| | March | | 52.4 | 34.9 | | 30.4 | | | 53.5 | 33.0 | | 34.0 | 40.0 | | | 30.1 |
| | April | | 54.1 | 34.5 | | 36.9 | | | 48.2 | 33.0 | | 39.2 | 40.0 | | | 35.6 |
| | May | | 52.6 | 43.4 | | 43.6 | | | 52.7 | 29.0 | | 56.0 | 45.0 | 32.8 | | 55.5 |
| | June | | 54.8 | 46.0 | | 40.7 | | | 53.6 | 35.0 | | 54.0 | 53.0 | | | 64.6 |
| | July | | 58.5 | 53.5 | | 44.7 | | | 62.8 | 49.0 | | 58.7 | 56.0 | | | 73.2 |
| | August | | 56.5 | 54.0 | | 49.4 | | | 74.8 | 39.0 | | 66.4 | 60.0 | 35.3 | | 80.4 |
| | September | | 56.9 | 51.8 | | 42.8 | | | 60.7 | 32.0 | | 61.7 | 59.0 | | | 68.7 |
| | October | | 52.9 | 44.2 | | 35.8 | | | 51.8 | 28.0 | | 51.3 | 51.0 | | | 42.1 |
| | November | | 52.5 | 30.3 | | 30.1 | | | 44.1 | 29.0 | | 32.5 | 40.0 | 32.0 | | 20.3 |
| | December | | 37.4 | 27.2 | | 27.6 | | | 38.4 | 22.0 | | 28.5 | 36.0 | | | 18.6 |

B = Beds.
R = Rooms.
Occupancy rates registered in hotels only, unless otherwise stated.
1. Finland: room occupancy rates in hotels and similar establishments.
2. Norway: Bed occupancy rates covers registered accommodation with 20 beds or more.
3. Sweden: occupancy rates in hotels, motels, resort hotels, holiday villages and youth hostels.
4. Turkey: bed occupancy rates in hotels, motels, boarding houses, inns, holiday villages and thermal resorts. Since 1987 campings are included.
5. United Kingdom: figures apply to England only.
6. Australia: quarterly figures in bed-places in hotels and motels with facilities in most rooms.
7. Japan: rates concerning hotels which are members of the "Japan Hotel Association".
8. Portugal: bed occupancy rates in hotels, studio-hotels, motels and state-owned inns.
9. Switzerland: bed occupancy rates in hotels, motels and inns.
10. Germany: bed occupancy rates cover registered accommodation with 9 beds or more.
11. Netherlands: room occupancy rates in hotels and similar establishments with 20 beds or more.

## 16. International fare payments
### Rail, air, sea and road transport
#### In million dollars

| | Receipts | | | Expenditure | | |
|---|---|---|---|---|---|---|
| | 1987 | 1988 | 1989 | 1987 | 1988 | 1989 |
| Austria[1] | 451.7 | | | 140.2 | | |
| Germany[2] | 2 933.8 | 3 535.6 | 3 918.7 | 3 471.3 | 4 117.0 | 4 004.9 |
| Greece | 27.6 | 28.8 | 15.8 | 126.2 | 113.5 | 113.9 |
| Ireland | 248.3 | 283.1 | 333.1 | 196.3 | 236.0 | |
| Italy[3] | 1 302.3 | 1 344.4 | 1 421.6 | 798.8 | 1 051.7 | 1 189.8 |
| Spain | 834.7 | 906.5 | 792.2 | 173.3 | 211.2 | 287.2 |
| Sweden[4] | 683.7 | 732.9 | 731.0 | 570.3 | 717.1 | 737.3 |
| Switzwerland | 1 351.7 | 1 438.8 | 1 440.0 | 865.4 | 956.9 | 877.4 |
| Turkey[5] | 263.7 | 286.4 | | 2.1 | 1.6 | 1.4 |
| Canada | 764.6 | 968.8 | 1 047.3 | 1 320.3 | 1 469.0 | 1 635.1 |
| Australia | 919.0 | 1 269.8 | 1 117.2 | 991.8 | 1 304.9 | 1 701.5 |

1. Austria: rail, air, inland waterways and road transport.
2. Germany: air, sea and rail transport.
3. Italy: air and sea transport.
4. Sweden: sea and rail transport.
5. Turkey: air, sea and rail transport for receipts; rail transport only for expenditure.

## 17. Nominal exchange rates of national currencies against the dollar

| | Exchange rates (units per dollar) | | | Per cent changes[1] | |
|---|---|---|---|---|---|
| | 1987 | 1988 | 1989 | 88/87 | 89/88 |
| Austria | 12.64 | 12.34 | 13.23 | −2.4 | 7.2 |
| Belgium-Luxembourg | 37.34 | 36.77 | 39.40 | −1.5 | 7.1 |
| Denmark | 6.84 | 6.73 | 7.31 | −1.6 | 8.6 |
| Finland | 4.40 | 4.19 | 4.29 | −4.8 | 2.4 |
| France | 6.01 | 5.96 | 6.38 | −0.9 | 7.1 |
| Germany | 1.80 | 1.76 | 1.88 | −2.3 | 7.1 |
| Greece | 135.18 | 141.64 | 162.08 | 4.8 | 14.4 |
| Iceland | 38.68 | 43.03 | 57.11 | 11.3 | 32.7 |
| Ireland | 0.67 | 0.66 | 0.71 | −2.3 | 7.4 |
| Italy | 1 296.97 | 1 301.68 | 1 371.69 | 0.4 | 5.4 |
| Netherlands | 2.03 | 1.98 | 2.12 | −2.4 | 7.3 |
| Norway | 6.74 | 6.52 | 6.90 | −3.3 | 5.9 |
| Portugal | 140.79 | 143.94 | 157.10 | 2.2 | 9.1 |
| Spain | 123.52 | 116.49 | 118.40 | −5.7 | 1.6 |
| Sweden | 6.34 | 6.13 | 6.45 | −3.3 | 5.2 |
| Switzwerland | 1.49 | 1.46 | 1.64 | −1.9 | 11.8 |
| Turkey | 854.61 | 1 419.40 | 2 119.96 | 66.1 | 49.4 |
| United Kingdom | 0.61 | 0.56 | 0.61 | −8.1 | 8.7 |
| Canada | 1.33 | 1.23 | 1.18 | −7.1 | −3.9 |
| United States | 1.00 | 1.00 | 1.00 | 0.0 | 0.0 |
| Australia | 1.43 | 1.28 | 1.26 | −10.3 | −1.3 |
| New Zealand | 1.70 | 1.53 | 1.67 | −9.8 | 9.5 |
| Japan | 144.62 | 128.16 | 137.97 | −11.4 | 7.7 |
| Yugoslavia | 801.00 | 2 842.95 | 32 372.60 | 254.9 | 1038.7 |

*Source:* OECD Balance of Payments Division, except for Yugoslavia.
1. Minus signs indicate an appreciation of national currencies against the dollar.

## 18. International tourist receipts (R) and expenditure (E) in dollars

Regional breakdown

In million

| | R/E | Europe | | | North America | | | Australasia-Japan | | |
|---|---|---|---|---|---|---|---|---|---|---|
| | | 1988 | 1989 | % 89/88 | 1988 | 1989 | % 89/88 | 1988 | 1989 | % 89/88 |
| Austria[1] | R | 8 705.8 | | | 608.5 | | | 54.0 | | |
| | E | 4 053.4 | | | 608.9 | | | 31.5 | | |
| Belgium-Luxembourg | R | | | | | | | | | |
| | E | | | | | | | | | |
| Denmark | R | 1 962.7 | 1 815.5 | −7.5 | 287.7 | 337.8 | 17.4 | 25.1 | 24.2 | −3.6 |
| | E | 2 495.0 | 2 313.5 | −7.3 | 373.6 | 419.8 | 12.4 | 8.0 | 5.9 | −26.7 |
| Finland | R | 717.1 | 695.7 | −3.0 | 144.8 | 137.8 | −4.8 | 6.7 | 6.8 | 1.1 |
| | E | 1 316.1 | 1 420.9 | 8.0 | 280.0 | 274.0 | −2.1 | 9.1 | 9.6 | 5.3 |
| France | R | 8 953.3 | | | 2 663.6 | | | 495.1 | | |
| | E | 5 475.6 | | | 2 074.9 | | | 153.1 | | |
| Germany | R | 6 426.1 | 6 392.2 | −0.5 | 869.0 | 941.0 | 8.3 | 421.4 | 480.9 | 14.1 |
| | E | 19 601.2 | 19 115.8 | −2.5 | 1 345.6 | 1 366.0 | 1.5 | 263.1 | 272.9 | 3.7 |
| Greece | R | 1 655.5 | 1 274.0 | −23.0 | | 634.3 | | 6.6 | 35.4 | 434.7 |
| | E | | 516.7 | | | 278.3 | | | 8.0 | |
| Iceland | R | 60.0 | | | 45.2 | | | 2.4 | | |
| | E | 108.7 | | | 90.9 | | | 0.1 | | |
| Ireland[2] | R | 701.8 | 759.6 | 8.2 | 242.0 | 248.0 | 2.5 | | | |
| | E | 855.5 | 877.3 | 2.5 | 92.9 | 99.2 | 6.8 | | | |
| Italy | R | 10 953.3 | | | 2 183.4 | | | 232.3 | | |
| | E | 4 401.5 | | | 1 612.6 | | | 34.3 | | |
| Netherlands | R | 2 259.3 | 2 401.3 | 6.3 | 535.2 | 555.4 | 3.8 | 32.4 | 27.3 | −15.5 |
| | E | 5 612.2 | 5 255.3 | −6.4 | 779.6 | 816.6 | 4.8 | 33.4 | 30.6 | −8.2 |
| Norway | R | 1 226.1 | 1 129.5 | −7.9 | 233.7 | 182.1 | −22.1 | 3.7 | 7.0 | 88.8 |
| | E | 2 982.6 | 2 480.1 | −16.8 | 377.9 | 313.9 | −16.9 | 10.1 | 7.5 | −25.6 |
| Portugal | R | 1 786.5 | | | 604.4 | | | 9.6 | | |
| | E | 387.9 | | | 134.9 | | | 2.8 | | |
| Spain | R | | | | | | | | | |
| | E | | | | | | | | | |
| Sweden | R | 1 791.8 | 1 890.3 | 5.5 | 249.5 | 278.9 | 11.8 | 14.5 | 16.6 | 14.3 |
| | E | 3 485.7 | 3 681.6 | 5.6 | 738.6 | 872.3 | 18.1 | 38.3 | 39.4 | 2.8 |
| Switzerland | R | | | | | | | | | |
| | E | | | | | | | | | |
| Turkey | R | | | | | | | | | |
| | E | | | | | | | | | |
| United Kingdom[3] | R | 4 541.2 | 4 714.0 | 3.8 | 2 808.7 | 2 757.7 | −1.8 | 919.6 | 1 082.8 | 17.7 |
| | E | 9 921.9 | 9 800.9 | −1.2 | 1 741.4 | 2 147.6 | 23.3 | 467.8 | 502.1 | 7.3 |
| Canada[4] | R | 704.8 | 553.2 | −21.5 | 3 187.2 | 3 309.0 | 3.8 | 270.4 | 332.8 | 23.1 |
| | E | 1 227.0 | 1 330.2 | 8.4 | 3 961.1 | 3 139.2 | −20.7 | 186.0 | 161.3 | −13.3 |
| United States[6] | R | | | | | | | | | |
| | E | | | | | | | | | |
| Australia | R | 521.4 | | | 497.2 | | | 855.4 | | |
| | E | 832.0 | | | 484.7 | | | 338.7 | | |
| New Zealand[5] | R | | | | | | | | | |
| | E | | | | | | | | | |
| Japan | R | | | | | | | | | |
| | E | | | | | | | | | |
| Yugoslavia | R | | | | | | | | | |
| | E | | | | | | | | | |

*Important notice:* the amounts, excluding those concerning Canada, United States, Ireland, Italy, United Kingdom and Switzerland, refer to receipts and expenditure registered in foreign currency grouped regionally according to the denomination of the currency.
1. Austria: including international fare payments.

In million

| Total OECD countries | | | Non-Member countries | | | All countries | | | |
|---|---|---|---|---|---|---|---|---|---|
| 1988 | 1989 | % 89/88 | 1988 | 1989 | % 89/88 | 1988 | 1989 | % 89/88 | |
| 9 368.4 | | | 726.3 | 9 316.1 | 1182.7 | 10 094.7 | 9 316.1 | -7.7 | Austria[1] |
| 4 693.9 | | | 1 615.7 | 5 026.9 | 211.1 | 6 309.6 | 5 026.9 | -20.3 | |
| | | | | | | 3 434.7 | 3 063.5 | -10.8 | Belgium-Luxembourg |
| | | | | | | 4 620.4 | 4 271.6 | -7.5 | |
| 2 275.5 | 2 177.4 | -4.3 | 147.5 | 133.7 | -9.4 | 2 423.0 | 2 311.1 | -4.6 | Denmark |
| 2 876.5 | 2 739.3 | -4.8 | 204.0 | 189.2 | -7.3 | 3 080.5 | 2 928.4 | -4.9 | |
| 868.8 | 840.2 | -3.3 | 115.4 | 172.8 | 49.8 | 984.1 | 1 013.0 | 2.9 | Finland |
| 1 608.0 | 1 709.6 | 6.3 | 235.3 | 338.4 | 43.8 | 1 843.3 | 2 048.0 | 11.1 | |
| 12 112.0 | | | 1 672.1 | | | 13 784.1 | 16 500.0 | 19.7 | France |
| 7 703.6 | | | 2 009.8 | | | 9 713.4 | 10 291.8 | 6.0 | |
| 7 716.5 | 7 814.0 | 1.3 | 761.9 | 843.6 | 10.7 | 8 478.4 | 8 657.6 | 2.1 | Germany |
| 21 209.9 | 20 754.7 | -2.1 | 3 734.9 | 3 374.5 | -9.6 | 24 944.8 | 24 129.3 | -3.3 | |
| 1 662.2 | 1 943.7 | 16.9 | | 32.2 | | 2 392.6 | 1 975.9 | -17.4 | Greece |
| | 803.0 | | | 13.3 | | 734.3 | 816.3 | 11.2 | |
| 107.5 | | | | | | 107.5 | 107.6 | 0.0 | Iceland |
| 199.7 | | | | | | 199.7 | 182.2 | -8.8 | |
| 943.8 | 1 007.7 | 6.8 | 53.3 | 62.4 | 17.0 | 997.1 | 1 070.0 | 7.3 | Ireland[2] |
| 948.4 | 976.5 | 3.0 | 12.2 | 12.8 | 4.7 | 960.5 | 989.2 | 3.0 | |
| 13 369.1 | | | 1.2 | | | 12 398.5 | 11 987.4 | -3.3 | Italy |
| 6 048.4 | | | 4.4 | | | 6 052.7 | 6 773.4 | 11.9 | |
| 2 832.9 | 2 989.7 | 5.5 | 40.0 | 30.2 | -24.5 | 2 872.9 | 3 019.9 | 5.1 | Netherlands |
| 6 483.8 | 6 179.4 | -4.7 | 252.4 | 270.6 | 7.2 | 6 736.3 | 6 450.0 | -4.2 | |
| 1 463.5 | 1 318.5 | -9.9 | 3.8 | 9.4 | 145.5 | 1 467.3 | 1 327.9 | -9.5 | Norway |
| 3 370.6 | 2 801.6 | -16.9 | 72.9 | 45.3 | -37.8 | 3 443.5 | 2 846.9 | -17.3 | |
| 2 401.8 | | | 23.4 | | | 2 425.2 | 2 587.1 | 6.7 | Portugal |
| 525.8 | | | 8.3 | | | 534.1 | 557.3 | 4.3 | |
| | | | | | | 16 691.4 | 16 252.0 | -2.6 | Spain |
| | | | | | | 2 456.8 | 3 080.3 | 25.4 | |
| 2 056.3 | 2 185.9 | 6.3 | 290.3 | 357.3 | 23.1 | 2 346.5 | 2 543.2 | 8.4 | Sweden |
| 4 269.5 | 4 607.1 | 7.9 | 290.3 | 361.1 | 24.4 | 4 559.7 | 4 968.2 | 9.0 | |
| | | | | | | 5 738.1 | 5 619.2 | -2.1 | Switzerland |
| | | | | | | 5 034.1 | 4 952.7 | -1.6 | |
| | | | | | | 2 355.4 | 2 556.5 | 8.5 | Turkey |
| | | | | | | 358.0 | 565.0 | 57.8 | |
| 8 283.7 | 8 564.3 | 3.4 | 2 716.2 | 2 684.1 | -1.2 | 10 999.8 | 11 248.4 | 2.3 | United Kingdom[3] |
| 12 136.4 | 12 468.6 | 2.7 | 2 477.8 | 2 726.6 | 10.0 | 14 614.2 | 15 195.3 | 4.0 | |
| 4 162.5 | 4 194.9 | 0.8 | 437.7 | 818.4 | 87.0 | 4 600.1 | 5 013.3 | 9.0 | Canada[4] |
| 5 374.0 | 4 630.7 | -13.8 | 944.4 | 2 745.7 | 190.7 | 6 318.4 | 7 376.4 | 16.7 | |
| | | | | | | 28 935.0 | 34 432.0 | 19.0 | United States[6] |
| | | | | | | 33 098.0 | 34 977.0 | 5.7 | |
| 1 873.9 | | | 355.1 | | | 3 295.1 | 3 369.7 | 2.3 | Australia |
| 1 655.4 | | | 310.6 | | | 2 862.8 | 3 763.5 | 31.5 | |
| | | | | | | 1 009.9 | 1 001.0 | -0.9 | New Zealand[5] |
| | | | | | | 1 347.4 | 1 349.0 | 0.1 | |
| | | | | | | 2 894.2 | 3 155.6 | 9.0 | Japan |
| | | | | | | 18 702.8 | 21 129.9 | 13.0 | |
| | | | | | | 2 024.2 | 2 230.4 | 10.2 | Yugoslavia |

2. Ireland: receipts from and expenditure to Northern Ireland are included. The expenditure include passenger fares paid by Irish residents to foreign transportation companies because the relevant data are not compiled separately.
3. United Kingdom: including estimates for the Channel Islands receipts and expenditure, and cruise expenditure.
4. Canada: excluding crew spending.
5. New Zealand: includes international airfares payments.
6. United States: all data revised from 1984 to include the results of the new travel survey administered by the US Travel and Tourism Administration; this also takes into account students' expenditure not previously included. In millions of dollars, from 1984 to 1987 : receipts (17 050, 17 663, 20 273, 23 366) and expenditure (23 305, 25 155, 26 746, 30 022).

## 19.  Foreign tourism by purpose of visit

| | 1988 | | | | | | 1989 | | | | | |
|---|---|---|---|---|---|---|---|---|---|---|---|---|
| | Business journeys (%)[1] | Private journeys (%) | | | | Total volume in thousands | Business journeys (%)[1] | Private journeys (%) | | | | Total volume in thousands |
| | | Holidays | VFR[2] | Others | Total | | | Holidays | VFR[2] | Others | Total | |
| Greece[3] | 9.0 | 83.0 | 4.0 | 4.0 | 91.0 | 7 778.0 | 9.3 | 82.6 | 4.1 | 4.0 | 90.7 | 7 935.0 |
| Ireland[4] | 18.7 | 34.5 | 39.2 | 7.6 | 81.3 | 2 345.0 | 17.2 | 38.8 | 37.3 | 6.6 | 82.8 | 2.7 |
| Portugal[5] | 2.4 | 92.3 | 0.7 | 4.6 | 97.6 | 6 623.9 | 2.4 | 92.2 | 0.8 | 4.6 | 97.6 | 7 115.9 |
| Spain[6] | 7.0 | 84.0 | 3.0 | 6.0 | 93.0 | 35 600.0 | 7.0 | 84.0 | 3.0 | 6.0 | 93.0 | 35 350.0 |
| Turkey[12] | 6.3 | 83.7 | 2.5 | 7.5 | 93.7 | 4 126.8 | 8.4 | 79.9 | 2.4 | 9.4 | 91.6 | 4 361.2 |
| United Kingdom[7] | | 56.5 | 27.0 | 16.6 | 100.0 | 11 781.0 | | 56.1 | 27.0 | 16.9 | 100.0 | 12 952.0 |
| Canada[8] | 16.3 | 57.0 | 23.3 | 3.4 | 83.7 | 15 485.0 | 17.7 | 54.2 | 24.1 | 3.9 | 82.3 | 15 111.2 |
| Australia[9] | 12.9 | 55.0 | 19.9 | 12.1 | 87.1 | 2 249.2 | 12.3 | 53.2 | 22.1 | 12.4 | 87.7 | 2 080.3 |
| New zealand[10] | 11.5 | 51.0 | 23.9 | 13.6 | 88.5 | 865.6 | 11.7 | 49.9 | 24.4 | 14.0 | 88.3 | 901.1 |
| Japan[11] | 29.7 | 47.4 | | 22.9 | 70.3 | 2 355.4 | 29.2 | 52.9 | | 18.0 | 70.8 | 2 835.1 |
| Yugoslavia[13] | | | | | | | | 83.7 | | 16.3 | 100.0 | 8.4 |

1. Includes : business, congresses, seminars, on missions, etc.
2. VFR : visits to friends and relatives.
3. Greece : number of tourists. "Others" includes journeys combining visiting relatives and holiday or business and holiday.
4. Ireland : number of journeys. Excluding visitors from Northern Ireland.
5. Portugal : number of tourists. "Others" includes visits for cultural purposes and journeys for educational reasons.
6. Spain : number of tourists. "Others" includes journeys for educational reasons.
7. United Kingdom : number of visits. "Others" includes visits for religion, sports, health and visits of more than one purpose where none predominates.
8. Canada : number of tourists.
9. Australia : short-term visitors (less than one year). "Others" includes journeys for educational reasons.
10. New Zealand : number of tourists. "Others" includes journeys for educational reasons.
11. Japan : number of visitors. "Others" includes journeys for educational reasons.
12. Turkey : "Others" includes journeys combining shopping and transit.
13. Yugoslavia : number of tourists. "Others" includes visits to friends and relatives, tours(cruises) and visits for sports, health and religion purposes. Estimate on the basis of sample survey of foreign tourists in accommodation establishments.

## 20.  Foreign tourism by mode of transport

| | 1988 | | | | | 1989 | | | | |
|---|---|---|---|---|---|---|---|---|---|---|
| | Breakdown of arrivals (%) | | | | Total volume in thousands | Breakdown of arrivals (%) | | | | Total volume in thousands |
| | Air | Sea | Rail | Road | | Air | Sea | Rail | Road | |
| Belgium[1] | | | | | 3 221.6 | | | | | |
| Iceland | 96.0 | 4.0 | | | 128.8 | | | | | |
| Ireland[2] | 55.4 | 36.4 | 4.0 | 4.2 | 2 556.0 | 57.6 | 35.0 | 3.3 | 4.1 | 2 950.0 |
| Italy[2] | 9.1 | 2.2 | 8.1 | 80.5 | 55 690.4 | 11.2 | 2.4 | 8.7 | 77.7 | 55 131.1 |
| Portugal[2] | 15.3 | 1.2 | 0.9 | 82.5 | 16 076.7 | 16.2 | 1.5 | 0.9 | 81.4 | 16 475.8 |
| Spain[3] | 31.6 | 3.1 | 4.7 | 60.5 | 54 206.1 | 31.3 | 3.3 | 4.9 | 60.5 | 54 256.4 |
| Turkey[4] | 50.6 | 17.0 | 1.6 | 30.8 | 4 172.7 | 52.6 | 16.7 | 1.7 | 29.0 | 4 459.2 |
| United Kingdom[2] | 69.4 | 30.6 | | | 15 798.0 | 67.8 | 32.2 | | | 17 292.0 |
| Canada[5] | 27.8 | 1.6 | 0.4 | 70.2 | 15 485.0 | 29.2 | 2.1 | 0.4 | 68.2 | 15 111.2 |
| Australia[6] | 99.6 | 0.4 | | | 2 249.3 | 99.5 | 0.5 | | | 2 080.2 |
| New Zealand[5] | 98.9 | 1.1 | | | 864.9 | 98.9 | 1.1 | | | 901.1 |
| Japan[7] | 97.3 | 2.7 | | | 2 414.4 | 96.7 | 3.3 | | | 2 985.8 |
| Yugoslavia[2] | 5.3 | 2.2 | 4.2 | 88.3 | 29 635.0 | 4.3 | 2.1 | 4.9 | 88.7 | 34 118.1 |

1. Belgium: air and sea include both arrivals and departures of foreign and domestic visitors. Rail refers to international traffic only.
2. Ireland, Italy, Portugal, United Kingdom and Yugoslavia : visitor arrivals.
3. Spain: visitor arrivals, including Spaniards living abroad.
4. Turkey: traveller arrivals.
5. Canada and New Zealand: tourist arrivals.
6. Australia: arrivals of short-term visitors (less than one year).
7. Japan: visitor arrivals, including those of returning residents and excluding crew members.

# 21.  Staff employed in tourism

| | | 1987 | | | 1988 | | | 1989 | | |
|---|---|---|---|---|---|---|---|---|---|---|
| | | Total | Men % | Women % | Total | Men % | Women % | Total | Men % | Women % |
| Austria [1] | HR | 116 695 | 37.4 | 62.6 | 119 587 | 37.6 | 62.4 | 123 047 | 38.0 | 62.0 |
| Belgium | H | 17 682 | | | | | | | | |
| | R | 87 023 | | | | | | | | |
| | HR | 119 131 | | | | | | | | |
| | V | 3 646 | | | | | | | | |
| | A | 8 721 | | | | | | | | |
| | O | 2 059 | | | | | | | | |
| Finland [2] | HR | 64 000 | 20.3 | 78.1 | 66 000 | 19.7 | 80.3 | 73 000 | 20.5 | 78.1 |
| Germany | HR | 671 000 | 41.1 | 59.0 | 683 000 | 42.2 | 57.7 | | | |
| Netherlands [3] | H | 21 800 | 53.2 | 46.8 | 23 200 | 53.9 | 46.1 | | | |
| | R | 42 100 | 57.5 | 42.5 | 51 200 | 53.7 | 46.3 | | | |
| | HR | 109 800 | 52.1 | 47.9 | 126 000 | 57.5 | 42.5 | | | |
| | V | 6 700 | 38.8 | 61.2 | 7 200 | 41.7 | 58.3 | | | |
| | O | 39 200 | 48.0 | 77.6 | 44 400 | 66.2 | 33.6 | | | |
| Norway [4] | HR | 55 000 | | | 56 000 | | | 58 000 | | |
| Sweden | HR | 87 000 | 35.6 | 64.4 | 88 500 | 37.3 | 62.7 | 94 500 | 37.6 | 62.4 |
| Turkey [5] | HR | 110 336 | | | 128 796 | | | 134 034 | | |
| | V | 1 889 | | | 2 408 | | | 9 910 | 63.6 | 36.4 |
| | A | 9 600 | 65.2 | 34.8 | 9 594 | 65.0 | 34.7 | 1 635 | 66.2 | 33.8 |
| | O | 1 262 | | | 1 456 | | | 1 868 | | |
| United Kingdom [6] | H | 265 400 | 38.4 | 61.6 | 275 200 | 40.2 | 59.8 | 283 900 | 40.8 | 59.2 |
| | R | 240 400 | 37.5 | 62.3 | 258 600 | 42.3 | 57.7 | 272 400 | 43.2 | 56.8 |
| | O | 775 100 | 39.8 | 60.2 | 788 800 | 41.6 | 58.4 | 815 200 | 43.4 | 56.6 |
| Canada | H | 150 000 | 40.0 | 60.7 | 152 000 | 40.8 | 59.2 | 168 000 | 39.3 | 60.1 |
| | R | 506 000 | 43.1 | 56.9 | 521 000 | 43.2 | 56.8 | 573 000 | 43.1 | 56.9 |
| | HR | 656 000 | 33.2 | 57.8 | 673 000 | 42.6 | 57.4 | 768 000 | 41.7 | 58.2 |
| | V | 20 000 | 25.0 | 75.0 | 25 000 | 28.0 | 72.0 | 27 000 | 25.9 | 74.1 |
| Australia [7] | H | 90 200 | 57.0 | 43.0 | 94 000 | 39.4 | 60.6 | | | |
| | HR | 90 200 | 57.0 | 43.0 | 94 000 | 39.4 | 60.6 | | | |
| | O | 420 000 | 64.3 | 35.7 | 336 000 | 70.8 | 29.2 | | | |
| Yugoslavia | H | 121 670 | | | 124 083 | | | 123 717 | | |
| | R | 171 596 | | | 171 120 | | | 167 309 | | |
| | V | 12 260 | | | 12 773 | | | 12 280 | | |

H: staff employed in hotels.
R: staff employed in restaurants.
HR: staff employed in hotels and restaurants.
V: staff employed in travel agencies.
A: staff employed in national tourism administrations.
O: staff employed in other sectors of tourist industry.

1. Austria: weighted average of peak season (August) and low season (November).
2. Finland: weighted average of peak season (July) and low season (January).
3. Netherlands: data registered at September. Includes staff employed less than 15 hours a week. O = holiday centers, youth hostels, camping sites, cafés, librairies, museums and cultural sites.
4. Norway: average of 1st and 4th quarters.
5. Turkey: data registered at 31 December of each year, except for O registered at 31 March and V registered at 31 October. V = minimum number of persons which travel agencies (central and local offices) have to employ. A includes regional tourism administrations and staff working at the Ministry of Tourism. O = tourist guides whose licences have been renewed.
6. United Kingdom: data registered at September. O = "pubs", bars, night clubs, clubs, librairies, museums, art galleries, sports and other recreational services.
7. Australia: data registered at December of each year.

## 22. Trends in tourism prices

| | | %84/83 | %85/84 | %86/85 | %87/86 | %88/87 | %89/88 |
|---|---|---|---|---|---|---|---|
| Austria | H | 3.7 | 4.5 | 3.9 | 3.0 | 3.8 | 2.2 |
| | R | 6.1 | 3.3 | 4.3 | 4.0 | 2.8 | 2.2 |
| | T | 5.1 | 3.5 | 1.9 | 0.9 | 2.1 | 2.8 |
| | C | 5.7 | 3.2 | 1.7 | 1.4 | 1.9 | 2.6 |
| Belgium [1] | H | | | 6.0 | 9.3 | 6.3 | |
| | R | | | 6.0 | 3.7 | 2.5 | |
| | T | | | 6.1 | 4.0 | 2.7 | |
| | C | 6.3 | 4.9 | 1.3 | 1.6 | 1.2 | 3.1 |
| Finland [2] | H | 7.0 | 11.0 | 7.0 | 5.0 | 6.0 | 6.0 |
| | R | 7.0 | 7.0 | 5.0 | 7.0 | 7.0 | 8.0 |
| | T | 7.0 | 4.0 | | | | |
| | C | 7.1 | 5.9 | 2.9 | 4.1 | 5.1 | 6.6 |
| France | H | 6.5 | 7.1 | 5.4 | 9.2 | 7.8 | 6.3 |
| | R | 6.8 | 6.1 | 5.1 | 7.1 | 5.4 | 5.0 |
| | T | | | | | | 2.5 |
| | C | 7.7 | 5.8 | 2.5 | 3.3 | 2.7 | 3.5 |
| Germany | H | 2.7 | 2.7 | 3.2 | 3.4 | 4.3 | 4.4 |
| | R | 2.5 | 1.5 | 1.8 | 1.7 | 1.5 | 1.9 |
| | T | 2.9 | 4.9 | 4.4 | 1.3 | 1.0 | 1.8 |
| | C | 2.4 | 2.2 | -0.1 | 0.2 | 1.3 | 2.8 |
| Greece | H | 12.0 | 21.0 | 18.0 | 40.0 | 10.0 | |
| | R | | | | | | |
| | T | | | | | | |
| | C | 18.4 | 19.3 | 23.0 | 16.4 | 13.5 | 13.7 |
| Italy [3] | H | 15.8 | 9.8 | 8.8 | 9.0 | 7.3 | |
| | R | 11.5 | 11.2 | 9.7 | 5.8 | 7.2 | |
| | T | 12.4 | 11.2 | 9.6 | 6.4 | 7.1 | |
| | C | 10.6 | 8.6 | 6.2 | 4.6 | 5.0 | 6.6 |
| Netherlands [4] | H | 1.0 | 3.0 | 1.0 | 2.0 | 2.0 | 2.0 |
| | R | 4.0 | 2.0 | 2.0 | 2.0 | 1.0 | 2.0 |
| | T | | | | | | |
| | C | 3.3 | 2.3 | 0.1 | -0.7 | 0.7 | 1.1 |
| Norway [5] | H | 9.4 | 9.1 | 10.8 | 12.0 | 11.5 | 9.0 |
| | R | 5.1 | 4.9 | 8.2 | 8.6 | 5.7 | 3.9 |
| | T | | | | | | |
| | C | 6.3 | 5.7 | 7.2 | 8.7 | 6.7 | 4.6 |
| Portugal [6] | H | 25.0 | 28.0 | 30.0 | 23.0 | 12.0 | 14.0 |
| | R | 13.0 | 24.0 | 13.0 | 14.0 | 17.0 | 17.0 |
| | T | | | | | | |
| | C | 28.8 | 19.6 | 11.8 | 9.4 | 9.7 | 12.6 |
| Spain [7] | H | 17.2 | 16.5 | 11.6 | 13.1 | 10.9 | 10.6 |
| | R | 13.5 | 10.7 | 10.2 | 5.1 | 8.7 | 10.9 |
| | T | 12.3 | 9.7 | 9.6 | 4.8 | 6.9 | 8.6 |
| | C | 11.3 | 8.8 | 8.8 | 5.2 | 4.8 | 6.8 |
| Sweden [8] | H | 12.4 | 11.6 | 11.0 | -1.4 | 5.8 | 6.0 |
| | R | 11.8 | 10.3 | 10.4 | 6.6 | 9.5 | 9.3 |
| | T | | | | | | |
| | C | 8.0 | 7.4 | 4.2 | 4.2 | 5.8 | 6.4 |
| Switzerland [9] | H | 6.2 | 6.3 | 6.3 | 5.6 | 5.5 | 6.6 |
| | R | 2.8 | 5.0 | 3.4 | 2.2 | 3.0 | 4.3 |
| | T | | | | | | |
| | C | 2.9 | 3.4 | 0.8 | 1.4 | 1.9 | 3.2 |
| Turkey [10] | H | 50.0 | 50.0 | | | | |
| | R | 55.0 | 45.0 | 50.0 | | | |
| | T | | | | | | |
| | C | 48.4 | 45.0 | 34.6 | 38.9 | 75.4 | 69.6 |
| United Kingdom [11] | H | 14.1 | 9.1 | 12.5 | 9.9 | 10.9 | 8.7 |
| | R | 6.5 | 5.4 | 7.0 | 7.0 | 6.8 | 6.7 |
| | T | 6.7 | 7.4 | 7.0 | 6.3 | 8.1 | 7.5 |
| | C | 5.0 | 6.1 | 3.4 | 4.1 | 4.9 | 7.8 |
| Canada [12] | H | 4.2 | 5.7 | 13.5 | 3.0 | 7.2 | 5.3 |
| | R | 4.1 | 4.2 | 4.7 | 4.0 | 4.6 | 5.3 |
| | T | 5.1 | 4.9 | 5.6 | 4.2 | 1.4 | 5.7 |
| | C | 4.3 | 4.0 | 4.2 | 4.4 | 4.0 | 5.0 |
| Australia [13] | H | 8.4 | -1.9 | 27.2 | 16.2 | 16.6 | |
| | R | 0.1 | 9.4 | 8.7 | 6.7 | 7.3 | |
| | T | 3.5 | 13.2 | 6.3 | 6.6 | 13.5 | |
| | C | 4.1 | 6.7 | 8.9 | 8.6 | 7.2 | 7.6 |
| Yugoslavia [14] | H | 36.0 | 92.0 | 132.0 | 155.0 | 196.0 | 1664.0 |
| | R | 45.0 | 83.0 | 114.0 | 120.0 | 186.0 | 1300.0 |
| | T | | | | | | |
| | C | 53.8 | 73.8 | 88.3 | 120.7 | 194.6 | 1252.0 |

# NOTES TO TABLE 22

H: average increase in hotel prices.
R: average increase in restaurant prices.
T: average increase in travel prices.
C: average increase in consumer prices (CPI). Source: OECD Balance of Payments Division.
 1. Belgium : H = hotels and campings, R = cafés, restaurants and bars, T = hotels, campings, cafés, restaurants, bars and package tours.
 2. Finland: H = hotels, R = food and alcoholic beverages, T = transports and communications.
 3. Italy: T = hotels, restaurants and public establishments (bars, night club, sea-side resorts....).
 4. Netherlands: H = price of a night spent in an hotel, R = price of a certain number of typical expenses made in bars and restaurants (cup of coffee, fruit drinks, beer, jenever, croquette, fried potatoes, several hot meals, ham roll, ice cream).
 5. Norway: H = approved hotels and boarding houses, R = restaurants and cafés.
 6. Portugal: H = hotels of from 1 to 5 stars, R concerns Lisbon only.
 7. Spain: H takes into account the types of accommodation presented in the official guide, R = hotels, restaurants, cafeteria and bars.
 8. Sweden: position at December of each year H = hotel room, R = meals not taken at home (lunch, dinner, coffee with bread, hot sausage with bread).
 9. Switzerland: H = hotels and similar establishments. R is estimated.
10. Turkey: H = hotels, motels, inns, boarding houses, holiday villages, health resorts. R = 1st and 2nd class restaurants. In 1984 H and R = freely determined prices approved by the Ministry of Culture and Tourism. C concerns the city of Ankara only.
11. United Kingdom: H = all holiday accommodation. R = meals and snacks including take-away. T = accommodation, meals, food, alcohol, tobacco, durable household goods, clothes, footwear, motoring and cycling fares, entertainment and other services.
12. Canada: H = hotels and motels. R = food purchases for restaurants, T is calculated from domestic tourist spending patterns only.
13. Australia: position every fourth quarter of each year. H = change in the price of a room in hotels, motels, and similar establishments. R = change in the price of meals taken outside home and take-away food (one component of the CPI). C = weighted average of eight State capital cities. T = air, bus and rail fares, hotel, motel and caravan park charges, package tours.
14. Yugoslavia: H = all categories of hotel.

# INTERNATIONAL TOURIST FLOWS FROM MAIN GENERATING COUNTRIES

Tables 23 to 49 gather data available for the period 1978 to 1989 concerning physical flows to OECD Member countries and Yugoslavia.

These tables contain data on arrivals at frontiers and arrivals and nights spent at/in accommodation:

- from all the foreign countries;
- from the eight main generators of tourism to the OECD area (Canada, France, Germany, Italy, Japan, the Netherlands, the United Kingdom and the United States).

Data used in the synthesis tables are derived from data broken down by country of origin; when these data are not available, the tables are derived from monthly or quarterly statistics.

## Methodological notes

These notes present on a country-by-country basis, and where appropriate, the main methodological and statistical changes affecting the series available between 1978 and 1989. For more detailed information, refer to the book "National and International Tourism Statistics 1974-1985", published in 1989.

*Canada.* Arrivals of foreign visitors at frontiers: change of series in 1980.

*Finland.* Arrivals of foreign visitors at frontiers: series discontinued from 1979.

*France.* Arrivals and nights spent at/in hotels and similar establishments: change of series in 1986.

*Germany.* Arrivals and nights spent at/in hotels and similar establishments and in all means of accommodation: changes of series in 1981 and in 1984.

*Ireland.* Arrivals and nights spent at/in hotels and similar establishments: series available from 1985.

*Japan.* Arrivals and nights spent at/in hotels and similar establishments: series discontinued from 1986.

*Netherlands.* Arrivals and nights spent at/in hotels and similar establishments: change of series in 1986. Arrivals and nights spent at/in all means of commodations: new series from 1988.

*Norway.* Arrivals of foreign visitors at frontiers: series discontinued from 1984.

*Portugal.* Arrivals and nights spent at/in hotels and similar establishments and in all means of accommodation: change of series in 1979.

*Sweden.* Nights spent in all means of accommodation: change of series in 1985.

*Switzerland.* Arrivals of foreign tourists/visitors at frontiers: annual estimates.

*Turkey.* Arrivals and nights spent at/in all means of accommodation: change of series in 1980.

*United States.* Arrivals of foreign tourists at frontiers: estimates in 1979 and in 1980. Change of series in 1984.

## Conventional signs

/ Break of series

## Table/Tableau 23

### ARRIVALS OF FOREIGN TOURISTS/VISITORS AT FRONTIERS
### ARRIVÉES DE TOURISTES/VISITEURS ÉTRANGERS AUX FRONTIÈRES

1984=100

| Country | T/V | Volume 1978 | 1979 | 1980 | 1981 | 1982 | 1983 | Volume 1984 | 1985 | 1986 | 1987 | 1988 | 1989 | Volume 1989 | T/V |
|---|---|---|---|---|---|---|---|---|---|---|---|---|---|---|---|
| Finland (R) | V | 297 037 | 81.3 | 85.1 | 86.1 | 94.6 | 96.2 | 35 379 000 | 103.9 | 102.0 | 104.5 | 108.2 | 121.5 | 43 000 000 | V |
| France (R) | T | 26 846 000 | 94.7 | 86.8 | 92.2 | 91.1 | 86.5 | 5 523 212 | 119.0 | 128.4 | 137.2 | 140.8 | 146.3 | 8 081 851 | T |
| Greece (N) | T | 4 532 411 | 96.2 | 87.5 | 92.5 | 90.7 | 87.2 | 6 027 266 | 116.8 | 121.8 | 132.8 | 136.6 | 141.7 | 8 540 962 | T |
| Iceland (N) | T | 75 700 | 90.1 | 77.3 | 84.3 | 85.1 | 90.9 | 85 330 | 114.2 | 133.0 | 151.5 | 151.0 | 152.9 | 130 503 | T |
| Ireland (R) | V | 1 673 000 | 92.4 | 89.6 | 89.1 | 93.8 | 94.7 | 1 873 000 | 102.0 | 96.8 | 108.9 | 125.3 | 145.9 | 2 732 000 | V |
| Italy (N) | T | 42 648 600 | 99.2 | 97.2 | 88.6 | 98.3 | 94.8 | 49 150 736 | 109.1 | 108.5 | 107.3 | 113.3 | 112.2 | 55 131 098 | T |
| Norway (N) | V | 3 389 252 | 54.8 | 65.8 | 73.4 | 76.8 | 90.2 | 4 118 626 | 121.1 | 131.3 | 148.1 | 160.8 | 172.8 | 7 115 900 | V |
| Portugal (N) | T | 1 680 600 | 53.9 | 71.1 | 74.2 | 74.4 | 90.5 | 9 811 012 | 119.2 | 133.1 | 164.8 | 163.9 | 167.9 | 16 475 799 | T |
| Spain (N) | V | 39 833 085 | 91.1 | 89.1 | 94.0 | 98.4 | 96.7 | 42 688 538 | 100.7 | 111.0 | 118.4 | 126.9 | 126.6 | 54 057 562 | V |
| Switzerland (R)[1] | T | 82 900 000 | 77.2 | 89.9 | 94.9 | 97.0 | 97.0 | 102 900 000 | 99.0 | 108.8 | 118.5 | 110.9 | 119.9 | 122 900 000 | T |
| Turkey (N) | V | 1 644 177 | 72.0 | 60.8 | 66.4 | 65.7 | 76.8 | 2 117 094 | 123.5 | 112.9 | 134.9 | 197.1 | 210.6 | 4 459 151 | V |
| United Kingdom (R) | V | 12 646 000 | 91.5 | 91.0 | 83.9 | 85.3 | 91.4 | 13 644 300 | 105.9 | 101.9 | 114.1 | 115.8 | 126.1 | 17 203 900 | V |
| Canada (R) | T | 12 688 900 | 97.0 | 98.5 | 98.7 | 93.9 | 96.3 | 12 975 000 | 101.5 | 120.4 | 115.4 | 119.3 | 116.5 | 15 122 300 | T |
| United States (R) | T | 19 842 142 | 95.2 | 116.6 | 120.3 | 98.7 | 98.3 | 26 913 000 | 103.0 | 116.0 | 113.6 | 112.6 | 131.0 | 35 249 046 | T |
| Australia (R) | V | 630 700 | 78.0 | 88.9 | 92.1 | 93.9 | 92.8 | 1 017 000 | 112.4 | 140.6 | 175.5 | 221.2 | 204.5 | 2 080 000 | V |
| Japan (N) | V | 1 038 875 | 52.7 | 62.4 | 75.0 | 85.0 | 93.3 | 2 110 346 | 110.3 | 97.7 | 102.1 | 111.6 | 134.3 | 2 835 064 | V |
| New Zealand (R) | T | 406 976 | 76.2 | 82.0 | 84.2 | 84.9 | 89.6 | 567 595 | 118.0 | 129.2 | 148.8 | 152.4 | 158.8 | 901 078 | T |
| Yugoslavia (N) | V | 29 229 089 | 112.7 | 103.5 | 104.0 | 90.8 | 95.0 | 19 716 574 | 118.5 | 125.5 | 132.6 | 150.3 | 173.0 | 34 118 072 | V |

V   Visitors (travellers in Austria, Germany and Turkey) — Visiteurs (voyageurs en Allemagne, en Autriche et en Turquie)
T   Tourists — Touristes
(R)   Tourist count by country of residence — Recensement des touristes par pays de résidence
(N)   Tourist count by country of nationality — Recensement des touristes par pays de nationalité
1.   Estimates — Estimations

## Table/Tableau 24

## ARRIVALS AND NIGHTS OF FOREIGN TOURISTS AT/IN HOTELS
## ARRIVÉES ET NUITÉES DE TOURISTES ÉTRANGERS DANS L'HÔTELLERIE

1984=100

| Country | AH/NH | Volume 1978 | 1979 | 1980 | 1981 | 1982 | 1983 | Volume 1984 | 1985 | 1986 | 1987 | 1988 | 1989 | Volume 1989 | AH/NH | Pays |
|---|---|---|---|---|---|---|---|---|---|---|---|---|---|---|---|---|
| Austria (R) | NH | 49 560 762 | 93.8 | 100.1 | 102.4 | 100.8 | 99.0 | 55 523 913 | 98.3 | 98.2 | 99.8 | 101.5 | 110.6 | 61 428 409 | NH | Autriche (R) |
| | AH | 8 491 958 | 82.2 | 89.1 | 90.8 | 91.8 | 94.2 | 10 867 149 | 100.7 | 99.1 | 104.7 | 109.7 | 120.7 | 13 120 640 | AH | |
| Belgium (R) | NH | 4 179 029 | 81.2 | 83.3 | 83.1 | 90.0 | 93.8 | 5 256 533 | 105.3 | 101.2 | 101.1 | 103.2 | 113.5 | 5 968 327 | NH | Belgique (R) |
| Denmark (N) | NH | 4 276 500 | 92.4 | 94.4 | 97.2 | 96.5 | 97.7 | 4 608 300 | 99.6 | 94.1 | 97.2 | 95.0 | 111.4 | 5 132 000 | NH | Danemark (N) |
| Finland (R) | NH | 1 586 059 | 81.6 | 87.3 | 97.2 | 95.8 | 97.5 | 2 112 508 | 99.3 | 95.7 | 104.5 | 108.8 | 119.2 | 2 517 300 | NH | Finlande (R) |
| France (R) | NH | 15 296 448 | 89.6 | 92.9 | 92.5 | 89.1 | 92.8 | 17 942 391 | 101.2 | 203.0 | 202.9 | 225.0 | 284.0 | 50 953 307 | NH | France (R) |
| | AH | 5 733 379 | 90.7 | 89.6 | 93.2 | 93.3 | 93.8 | 6 523 598 | 106.2 | 261.7 | 263.2 | 290.4 | 368.6 | 24 046 230 | AH | |
| Germany (R) | NH | 16 247 946 | 77.0 | 85.4 | 87.4 | 85.1 | 86.1 | 22 240 675 | 106.5 | 105.5 | 106.3 | 108.8 | 127.6 | 28 388 733 | NH | Allemagne (R) |
| | AH | 8 011 007 | 74.6 | 82.2 | 83.0 | 83.1 | 85.8 | 11 084 288 | 106.1 | 101.9 | 106.3 | 114.9 | 121.5 | 13 466 784 | AH | |
| Greece (N) | NH | 30 221 402 | 94.1 | 95.2 | 93.5 | 91.2 | 87.0 | 29 006 165 | 117.4 | 116.2 | 116.4 | 108.8 | 113.6 | 32 938 451 | NH | Grèce (N) |
| | AH | 4 790 531 | 87.5 | 84.8 | 87.8 | 86.5 | 82.2 | 6 096 237 | 107.4 | 96.6 | 101.2 | 98.5 | | | AH | |
| Ireland (R) | NH | | | | | | | | | | | | | 7 434 000 | NH | Irlande (R) |
| | AH | | | | | | | | | | | | | 1 505 000 | AH | |
| Italy (N) | NH | 56 534 808 | 105.1 | 104.9 | 93.5 | 102.4 | 100.5 | 63 072 518 | 101.4 | 103.3 | 111.3 | 111.6 | 107.2 | 67 588 960 | NH | Italie (N) |
| | AH | 12 445 889 | 90.8 | 92.3 | 84.0 | 93.8 | 94.7 | 15 792 735 | 101.9 | 96.0 | 107.8 | 110.4 | 111.7 | 17 639 191 | AH | |
| Luxembourg (R) | NH | | | | 105.1 | 109.6 | 102.9 | 885 565 | 105.3 | 102.4 | 106.3 | 109.4 | 114.8 | 1 017 004 | NH | Luxembourg (R) |
| Netherlands (R) | NH | 5 708 994 | 91.8 | 92.8 | 93.3 | 96.1 | 91.9 | 6 538 712 | 103.2 | 108.7 | 107.7 | 103.4 | 109.8 | 7 178 400 | NH | Pays-Bas (R) |
| | AH | 2 663 126 | 85.4 | 85.7 | 87.4 | 92.1 | 90.0 | 3 218 231 | 103.4 | 104.3 | 104.2 | 103.2 | 108.4 | 3 487 000 | AH | |
| Norway (N) | NH | 2 348 356 | 68.3 | 70.2 | 71.9 | 66.2 | 67.6 | 3 459 837 | 107.3 | 95.3 | 111.7 | 97.0 | 99.2 | 3 431 354 | NH | Norvège (N) |
| | AH | 1 233 415 | 71.8 | 71.8 | 73.4 | 69.5 | 72.9 | 1 744 542 | 110.8 | 93.9 | 102.1 | 97.7 | 107.0 | 1 867 386 | AH | |
| Portugal (N) | NH | 6 796 528 | 81.3 | 86.9 | 84.9 | 86.7 | 89.7 | 11 025 239 | 117.3 | 129.6 | 131.7 | 136.1 | 140.3 | 15 467 488 | NH | Portugal (N) |
| | AH | 1 437 016 | 74.7 | 80.3 | 77.8 | 79.6 | 87.1 | 2 377 953 | 114.9 | 119.2 | 129.1 | 134.3 | 141.1 | 3 354 601 | AH | |
| Spain (N) | NH | 79 384 133 | 79.1 | 65.9 | 79.5 | 86.1 | 89.5 | 89 064 060 | 88.6 | 98.5 | 103.8 | 99.2 | 87.9 | 78 301 406 | NH | Espagne (N) |
| | AH | 12 177 296 | 79.7 | 70.9 | 81.4 | 86.0 | 88.6 | 13 010 544 | 95.6 | 104.4 | 108.5 | 104.8 | 101.3 | 13 184 412 | AH | |
| Sweden (N) | NH | 2 746 736 | 85.8 | 81.2 | 83.5 | 83.8 | 92.3 | 3 275 838 | 108.3 | 101.0 | 99.0 | 97.4 | 102.8 | 3 366 899 | NH | Suède (N) |
| Switzerland (R) | NH | 18 495 947 | 83.9 | 99.0 | 105.0 | 99.0 | 98.4 | 20 178 342 | 100.7 | 96.9 | 96.8 | 94.7 | 101.5 | 20 489 411 | NH | Suisse (R) |
| | AH | 6 032 908 | 79.6 | 91.5 | 95.2 | 93.5 | 94.6 | 7 281 388 | 100.7 | 94.5 | 97.0 | 96.3 | 105.4 | 7 673 125 | AH | |
| Turkey (N) | NH | 1 428 461 | 38.5 | 28.4 | 43.0 | 51.6 | 74.9 | 3 480 864 | 127.7 | 144.7 | 187.3 | 270.8 | 279.9 | 9 742 312 | NH | Turquie (N) |
| | AH | 575 137 | 40.0 | 29.4 | 46.2 | 55.2 | 79.6 | 1 336 800 | 125.6 | 143.2 | 179.6 | 231.9 | 259.4 | 3 467 825 | AH | |
| Australia (R) | NH | | 88.5 | | 101.9 | | 96.2 | 6 150 700 | 115.0 | 144.2 | 179.6 | 230.1 | | | NH | Australie (R) |
| Japan (N) | NH | 3 627 062 | 57.6 | 65.3 | 75.8 | 84.5 | 45.2 | 6 419 886 | 126.1 | | | | | | NH | Japon (N) |
| | AH | 1 529 622 | 56.2 | 62.1 | 72.4 | 85.2 | 44.2 | 3 046 124 | 117.5 | | | | | | AH | |
| Yugoslavia (N) | NH | 20 849 596 | 82.6 | 85.9 | 91.3 | 85.8 | 85.4 | 23 891 230 | 114.6 | 115.2 | 118.7 | 118.2 | 116.9 | 27 930 967 | NH | Yougoslavie (N) |
| | AH | 4 155 607 | 85.3 | 87.3 | 88.3 | 82.5 | 82.9 | 4 583 126 | 111.4 | 110.3 | 116.9 | 119.1 | 119.8 | 5 492 678 | AH | |

AH  Arrivals at hotels and similar establishments  
NH  Nights in hotels and similar establishments  
(R) Tourist count by country of residence  
(N) Tourist count by country of nationality  

AH  Arrivées dans les hôtels et les établissements assimilés  
NH  Nuitées dans les hôtels et établissements assimilés  
(R) Recensement des touristes par pays de résidence  
(N) Recensement des touristes par pays de nationalité

# Table/Tableau 25

## ARRIVALS AND NIGHTS OF FOREIGN TOURISTS AT/IN ALL MEANS OF ACCOMMODATION
## ARRIVÉES ET NUITÉES DE TOURISTES ÉTRANGERS DANS L'ENSEMBLE DES MOYENS D'HÉBERGEMENT

*1984=100*

| Country | AAA/NAA | Volume 1978 | 1979 | 1980 | 1981 | 1982 | 1983 | Volume 1984 | 1985 | 1986 | 1987 | 1988 | 1989 | Volume 1989 | AEH/NEH | |
|---|---|---|---|---|---|---|---|---|---|---|---|---|---|---|---|---|
| Austria (R) | NAA | 81 301 494 | 97.8 | 104.0 | 106.7 | 103.7 | 100.8 | 86 713 254 | 98.1 | 98.5 | 98.8 | 101.0 | 109.5 | 94 968 501 | NEH | Autriche (R) |
| Belgium (R) | AAA | 12 254 255 | 85.2 | 91.9 | 94.2 | 94.3 | 95.8 | 15 110 233 | 100.9 | 99.9 | 104.3 | 109.7 | 120.5 | 18 201 763 | AEH | Belgique (R) |
| Denmark (N) | NAA | 7 029 043 | 73.1 | 76.8 | 77.1 | 91.6 | 95.7 | 9 339 016 | 105.5 | 105.5 | 107.8 | 113.3 | 115.4 | 10 774 778 | NEH | Danemark (N) |
| Denmark (N) | AAA | 8 409 674 | 91.1 | 90.3 | 97.9 | 101.2 | 104.6 | 9 112 271 | 98.5 | 93.4 | 90.0 | 87.9 | 99.7 | 9 087 783 | AEH | |
| France (R) | NAA | 244 830 000 | 78.9 | 85.1 | 86.1 | 94.6 | 96.2 | 319 990 000 | 103.0 | 102.0 | 104.5 | 108.2 | | | NEH | France (R) |
| France (R) | AAA | 27 056 000 | 81.3 | 86.9 | 81.6 | 79.4 | 82.5 | 35 379 000 | 107.4 | 106.3 | 111.3 | 115.2 | | | AEH | |
| Germany (R) | NAA | 19 813 640 | 79.6 | 81.3 | 82.3 | 79.8 | 82.5 | 26 151 605 | 107.4 | 106.3 | 111.3 | 115.2 | 128.4 | 33 577 555 | NEH | Allemagne (R) |
| Germany (R) | AAA | 8 663 048 | 74.9 | 81.6 | 79.1 | 79.2 | 82.3 | 11 941 945 | 106.2 | 102.3 | 107.0 | 109.8 | 122.7 | 14 653 201 | AEH | |
| Greece (N) | NAA | 24 355 903 | 86.9 | 94.4 | 92.3 | 90.2 | 82.4 | 33 194 062 | 107.6 | 106.8 | 107.7 | 94.8 | 102.7 | 34 100 000 | NEH | Grèce (N) |
| Greece (N) | AAA | 5 772 844 | 93.6 | 92.0 | 89.5 | 88.5 | 83.4 | 6 863 951 | 102.8 | 93.5 | 97.5 | 94.7 | | | AEH | |
| Ireland (R) | NAA | 21 388 600 | 107.1 | 107.7 | 89.9 | 89.5 | 97.2 | 19 254 600 | 97.8 | 98.5 | 117.5 | 136.0 | 163.1 | 31 409 000 | NEH | Irlande (R) |
| Ireland (R) | AAA | 1 753 100 | 97.6 | 94.2 | 91.4 | 93.5 | 93.3 | 1 838 000 | 105.8 | 102.2 | 114.0 | 131.9 | 153.1 | 2 814 000 | AEH | |
| Italy (N) | NAA | 87 552 283 | 107.2 | 108.6 | 97.1 | 105.9 | 102.2 | 95 144 339 | 101.5 | 104.4 | 96.7 | 97.0 | 90.9 | 86 488 233 | NEH | Italie (N) |
| Italy (N) | AAA | 15 321 451 | 91.8 | 94.0 | 86.0 | 95.7 | 95.9 | 19 279 279 | 102.6 | 99.0 | 104.7 | 106.9 | 106.7 | 20 563 342 | AEH | |
| Luxembourg (R) | NAA | 2 410 271 | 101.9 | | 86.0 | 83.0 | 84.1 | 2 450 852 | 89.5 | 96.1 | 88.6 | 87.3 | | | NEH | Luxembourg (R) |
| Luxembourg (R) | AAA | 739 939 | 108.2 | 81.5 | 84.7 | 83.0 | 85.2 | 687 641 | 100.1 | 103.4 | 103.4 | 106.0 | | | AEH | |
| Netherlands (R) | NAA | 9 861 216 | 80.9 | 84.5 | 84.7 | 91.8 | 88.9 | 13 905 150 | 100.1 | 100.3 | | 90.9 | 101.9 | 14 171 700 | NEH | Pays-Bas (R) |
| Netherlands (R) | AAA | 3 824 352 | 83.2 | 84.8 | 87.4 | 91.9 | 90.4 | 4 932 948 | 101.2 | 97.9 | | 98.8 | 104.4 | 5 150 100 | AEH | |
| Norway (N) | NAA | 5 503 000 | 104.7 | 90.1 | 85.3 | 69.7 | 95.3 | 5 155 611 | 117.1 | 130.8 | 134.2 | 139.5 | 143.0 | 18 229 785 | NEH | Norvège (N) |
| Portugal (N) | AAA | 7 768 323 | 81.2 | 83.3 | 92.4 | 93.0 | 93.6 | 12 752 498 | 115.3 | 123.8 | 133.5 | 139.0 | 145.1 | 4 162 847 | AEH | Portugal (N) |
| Spain (N) | NAA | 1 735 164 | 74.8 | 61.4 | 81.8 | 83.5 | 89.1 | 2 868 600 | 82.1 | | 107.4 | 103.8 | | | NEH | Espagne (N) |
| Spain (N) | AAA | 83 351 618 | 73.6 | 71.5 | 73.5 | 79.4 | 83.3 | 99 288 005 | 95.8 | | 96.4 | 96.7 | | | AEH | |
| Sweden (N) | NAA | 15 144 039 | 102.2 | 76.7 | 81.7 | 86.3 | 90.6 | 13 140 814 | 101.8 | 99.9 | 98.9 | 98.5 | 103.1 | 7 584 021 | NEH | Suède (N) |
| Switzerland (R) | NAA | 5 082 985 | 79.7 | 103.1 | 82.3 | 83.6 | 98.8 | 7 354 369 | 100.5 | 96.6 | 98.3 | 98.6 | 102.8 | 35 946 700 | AEH | Suisse (R) |
| Switzerland (R) | AAA | 32 459 600 | 86.0 | 93.6 | 112.1 | 105.1 | 102.9 | 34 958 000 | 131.0 | 159.3 | 223.6 | 313.0 | 106.6 | 10 103 400 | NEH | Turquie (N) |
| Turkey (N) | NAA | 7 855 200 | 80.2 | 29.9 | 99.0 | 96.9 | 97.0 | 9 481 600 | 126.8 | 147.0 | 194.7 | 249.5 | 318.6 | 11 864 746 | AEH | Royaume-Uni (R) |
| Turkey (N) | AAA | 1 840 486 | 43.8 | 30.2 | 42.4 | 50.7 | 76.2 | 3 723 635 | 108.1 | 102.4 | 115.4 | 111.9 | 276.7 | 3 783 941 | NEH | |
| United Kingdom (R) | NAA | 670 100 | 43.7 | 88.1 | 45.9 | 54.8 | 80.0 | 1 367 351 | | | | | 119.8 | 185 044 000 | | Canada (R) |
| Canada (R) | NAA | 149 148 000 | 100.0 | 88.1 | 87.7 | 88.2 | 93.8 | 154 496 000 | | 119.0 | 110.4 | 119.5 | 117.1 | 90 031 600 | NEH | |
| Canada (R) | AAA | 70 429 200 | 98.6 | 96.9 | 99.8 | 94.3 | 91.4 | 76 889 800 | 100.3 | 120.4 | 115.4 | 119.3 | 116.5 | 15 111 100 | AEH | Australie (R) |
| | AAA | 12 688 900 | 97.0 | 98.5 | 98.7 | 93.9 | 96.3 | 12 975 000 | 101.5 | | | | | | | Nouvelle-Zélande (R) |
| Australia (R) | NAA | | 77.7 | 87.5 | 84.4 | 84.2 | 93.2 | 15 135 200 | 96.2 | 119.4 | 149.1 | 187.9 | | | NEH | Yougoslavie (N) |
| New Zealand (R) | NAA | | | 88.7 | | 82.4 | | 12 620 000 | 116.7 | 127.9 | 143.9 | 146.7 | 149.4 | 18 858 320 | NEH | |
| Yugoslavia (N) | NAA | 34 866 053 | 79.2 | 87.5 | 93.9 | 84.2 | 83.6 | 42 269 847 | 120.2 | 121.6 | 123.7 | 123.8 | 116.3 | 49 175 927 | NEH | |
| Yugoslavia (N) | AAA | 6 384 868 | 82.6 | 88.7 | 91.6 | 82.4 | 82.3 | 7 223 804 | 116.8 | 117.2 | 123.3 | 124.8 | 119.7 | 8 644 080 | AEH | |

AAA Arrivals in all means of accommodation
NAA Nights in all means of accommodation
(R) Tourist count by country of residence
(N) Tourist count by country of nationality

AEH Arrivées dans l'ensemble des moyens d'hébergement
NEH Nuitées dans l'ensemble des moyens d'hébergement
(R) Recensement des touristes par pays de résidence
(N) Recensement des touristes par pays de nationalité

101

## Table/Tableau 26

## ARRIVALS OF FOREIGN TOURISTS/VISITORS AT FRONTIERS
## ARRIVÉES DE TOURISTES/VISITEURS ÉTRANGERS AUX FRONTIÈRES

**From Germany** / *En provenance de l'Allemagne*

1984=100

| Country | T/V | Volume 1978 | 1979 | 1980 | 1981 | 1982 | 1983 | Volume 1984 | 1985 | 1986 | 1987 | 1988 | 1989 | Volume 1989 |
|---|---|---|---|---|---|---|---|---|---|---|---|---|---|---|
| Finland (R) / Finlande (R) | V | 82 952 | 87.9 | 90.8 | 93.2 | 101.4 | 97.2 | | 105.2 | 101.5 | 107.5 | 109.9 | | |
| France (R) / France (R) | T | 6 685 000 | 64.3 | 80.2 | 72.4 | 70.1 | 84.3 | 8 290 000 | 121.5 | 132.5 | 139.5 | 160.0 | | |
| Greece (N) / Grèce (N) | T | 520 547 | 100.7 | 94.1 | 94.6 | 88.6 | 91.2 | 864 000 | 98.0 | 113.1 | 145.5 | 165.3 | 191.6 | 1 655 277 |
| Iceland (N) / Islande (N) | T | 11 841 | 99.8 | 120.3 | 91.8 | 89.8 | 102.2 | 9 615 | 105.5 | | 111.0 | 145.7 | 190.5 | 18 316 |
| Ireland (R) / Irlande (R) | V | 88 641 | | 97.4 | 86.4 | 96.0 | 95.9 | 91 000 | 108.4 | 106.6 | | 123.1 | 165.9 | 151 000 |
| Italy (N) / Italie (N) | V | 9 090 600 | | | | | | 10 812 412 | | 88.4 | 89.0 | 96.9 | 93.7 | 10 134 213 |
| Norway (N) / Norvège (N) | V | 193 400 | 77.5 | 87.4 | 90.9 | 82.5 | 105.9 | 294 636 | 125.3 | 129.8 | 163.7 | 179.7 | 191.7 | 564 726 |
| Portugal (N) / Portugal (N) | T | 259 331 | 83.3 | 87.2 | 89.1 | 84.2 | 103.3 | 344 020 | 120.1 | 125.1 | 152.9 | 165.3 | 177.7 | 611 275 |
| Spain (N) / Espagne (N) | V | 5 104 984 | 88.8 | 89.4 | 86.9 | 91.0 | 94.7 | 5 250 065 | 107.5 | 113.1 | 125.6 | 131.5 | 129.2 | 6 783 753 |
| Turkey (N) / Turquie (N) | V | 218 122 | 82.1 | 64.3 | 64.1 | 70.0 | 72.4 | 241 712 | 123.9 | 160.6 | 216.7 | 317.5 | 371.1 | 896 989 |
| United Kingdom (R) / Royaume-Uni (R) | V | 1 507 000 | 104.2 | 102.3 | 98.9 | 97.1 | 92.6 | 1 484 700 | 100.0 | 107.7 | 110.7 | 123.3 | 135.5 | 2 011 700 |
| Canada (R) / Canada (R) | T | 141 100 | 106.5 | 111.3 | 117.7 | 108.1 | 95.9 | 169 900 | 92.1 | 116.7 | 137.8 | 154.8 | 154.6 | 262 700 |
| United States (R) / États-Unis (R) | T | 185 800 | 117.4 | 118.6 | 120.4 | 109.7 | 95.5 | 200 200 | 90.9 | 117.8 | 149.2 | 160.7 | 154.1 | 308 500 |
| United States (R) / États-Unis (R) | V | 485 784 | 102.2 | 115.3 | 128.3 | 122.1 | 103.2 | 545 247 | 93.4 | 122.9 | 174.6 | 211.5 | 197.4 | 1 076 385 |
| Australia (R) / Australie (R) | V | 18 400 | 84.2 | 103.4 | 114.2 | 113.7 | 101.2 | 34 200 | 109.1 | 122.5 | 155.8 | 192.7 | 199.1 | 68 100 |
| Japan (N) / Japon (N) | V | 35 675 | 78.0 | 81.0 | 83.5 | 84.4 | 88.6 | 48 978 | 99.2 | 100.3 | 109.3 | 116.3 | 125.7 | 61 580 |
| New Zealand (R) / Nouvelle-Zélande (R) | T | 4 792 | 62.2 | 82.1 | 91.7 | 94.3 | 100.2 | 9 511 | 112.0 | 126.6 | 172.8 | 211.4 | 249.9 | 23 768 |

V    Visitors (travellers in Turkey)
T    Tourists
(R)  Tourist count by country of residence
(N)  Tourist count by country of nationality

V    Visiteurs (voyageurs en Turquie)
T    Touristes
(R)  Recensement des touristes par pays de résidence
(N)  Recensement des touristes par pays de nationalité

## Table/Tableau 27

## ARRIVALS AND NIGHTS OF FOREIGN TOURISTS AT/IN HOTELS
## ARRIVÉES ET NUITÉES DE TOURISTES ÉTRANGERS DANS L'HÔTELLERIE

*From Germany* — *En provenance de l'Allemagne*
1984=100

| Country | AH/NH | Volume 1978 | 1979 | 1980 | 1981 | 1982 | 1983 | Volume 1984 | 1985 | 1986 | 1987 | 1988 | 1989 | Volume 1989 |
|---|---|---|---|---|---|---|---|---|---|---|---|---|---|---|
| Austria (R) | NH | 34 615 078 | 106.8 | 112.5 | 112.7 | 107.4 | 104.2 | 33 903 402 | 96.8 | 97.9 | 97.1 | 98.6 | 105.1 | 35 648 584 |
|  | AH | 4 897 725 | 96.2 | 101.9 | 102.6 | 100.5 | 101.7 | 5 370 986 | 98.8 | 102.0 | 105.7 | 110.7 | 118.5 | 6 362 138 |
| Belgium (R) | NH | 674 956 | 90.1 | 89.9 | 87.2 | 94.8 | 96.8 | 745 012 | 100.3 | 102.2 | 104.6 | 107.6 | 116.3 | 866 682 |
| Denmark (N) | NH | 1 304 900 | 128.9 | 134.1 | 138.3 | 115.3 | 108.0 | 1 070 700 | 90.3 | 86.9 | 88.1 | 86.8 | 107.1 | 1 147 200 |
| Finland (R) | NH | 257 993 | 105.7 | 112.2 | 119.6 | 97.1 | 91.8 | 277 889 | 98.4 | 90.0 | 101.1 | 115.7 | 127.2 | 353 506 |
| France (R) | NH | 2 427 278 | 129.5 | 124.2 | 118.0 | 100.2 | 107.3 | 1 950 545 | 101.0 | 298.5 | 316.5 | 330.3 | 379.9 | 7 410 610 |
|  | AH | 939 468 | 127.9 | 118.5 | 116.2 | 103.3 | 109.9 | 739 960 | 107.7 | 386.4 | 411.7 | 439.6 | 506.1 | 3 745 116 |
| Greece (N) | NH | 3 643 159 | 91.1 | 102.5 | 97.4 | 88.4 | 83.7 | 5 468 051 | 125.9 | 130.4 | 131.7 | 143.9 |  |  |
|  | AH | 742 223 | 102.9 | 105.3 | 98.0 | 94.1 | 87.9 | 887 353 | 115.3 | 114.4 | 116.4 | 119.6 |  |  |
| Ireland (R) | NH |  |  |  |  |  |  |  |  |  |  |  |  | 564 000 |
|  | AH |  |  |  |  |  |  |  |  |  |  |  |  | 87 000 |
| Italy (N) | NH | 22 555 567 | 111.6 | 110.7 | 96.2 | 105.6 | 103.2 | 24 625 661 | 101.2 | 109.0 | 115.0 | 115.3 |  |  |
|  | AH | 3 208 379 | 96.7 | 98.3 | 87.0 | 95.2 | 99.2 | 4 065 296 | 102.4 | 110.6 | 121.3 | 124.1 |  |  |
| Luxembourg (R) | NH |  |  |  |  | 104.2 | 94.9 | 104 024 | 104.7 | 107.3 | 118.9 | 119.1 |  |  |
|  | AH |  |  |  |  |  | 95.7 | 58 218 | 106.4 | 108.7 | 116.4 | 121.6 |  |  |
| Netherlands (R) | NH | 1 491 903 | 106.0 | 104.9 | 101.6 | 99.2 | 97.8 | 1 416 485 | 97.2 | 115.0 | 111.1 | 104.1 | 107.5 | 1 523 100 |
|  | AH | 627 327 | 101.5 | 99.1 | 97.6 | 95.4 | 95.6 | 614 210 | 99.1 | 112.5 | 108.4 | 108.2 | 109.9 | 675 000 |
| Norway (N) | NH | 415 777 | 87.0 | 90.9 | 93.8 | 74.5 | 70.7 | 496 695 | 102.7 | 99.9 | 101.7 | 108.6 | 116.9 | 580 599 |
| Portugal (N) | NH | 1 225 712 | 129.6 | 125.8 | 105.6 | 94.4 | 92.4 | 1 237 364 | 137.4 | 152.8 | 165.8 | 166.2 | 168.3 | 2 081 997 |
|  | AH | 179 026 | 102.2 | 103.5 | 89.7 | 87.6 | 94.3 | 214 104 | 134.7 | 143.2 | 172.9 | 175.4 | 175.8 | 376 477 |
| Spain (N) | NH | 23 067 873 | 95.0 | 78.3 | 90.6 | 93.6 | 96.7 | 23 159 596 | 102.0 | 101.9 | 112.6 | 106.4 | 94.1 | 21 791 970 |
|  | AH | 2 341 790 | 90.0 | 78.7 | 87.5 | 91.1 | 96.5 | 2 423 051 | 103.2 | 107.3 | 117.0 | 111.1 | 102.4 | 2 482 027 |
| Sweden (N) | NH | 457 870 | 108.8 | 107.0 | 103.2 | 92.9 | 92.2 | 413 625 | 101.7 | 109.5 | 102.5 | 115.0 | 123.5 | 510 670 |
| Switzerland (R) | NH | 6 579 594 | 99.5 | 124.8 | 126.5 | 109.8 | 106.8 | 6 043 347 | 99.3 | 102.5 | 102.4 | 103.0 | 107.4 | 6 492 704 |
|  | AH | 1 821 302 | 95.7 | 112.8 | 113.8 | 105.0 | 104.4 | 1 859 932 | 98.6 | 103.2 | 105.9 | 108.4 | 114.5 | 2 130 168 |
| Turkey (N) | NH |  |  |  |  | 48.4 | 71.1 | 685 692 | 154.3 | 234.7 | 332.2 | 513.3 | 538.1 | 3 689 697 |
|  | AH |  |  |  |  | 50.6 | 78.7 | 242 624 | 145.9 | 214.2 | 292.1 | 369.7 | 391.6 | 950 001 |
| Australia (R) | NH |  | 86.3 |  | 129.3 |  | 108.5 | 240 200 | 126.0 | 139.1 | 176.9 | 218.7 |  |  |
| Japan (N) | NH | 160 935 | 75.9 | 76.2 | 84.9 | 77.9 | 35.8 | 220 399 | 104.1 |  |  |  |  |  |
|  | AH | 61 250 | 77.5 | 78.4 | 84.6 | 83.0 | 36.9 | 79 967 |  |  |  |  |  |  |
| Yugoslavia (N) | NH |  |  |  |  |  |  |  |  |  |  |  |  | 8 781 176 |
|  | AH |  |  |  |  |  |  |  |  |  |  |  |  | 1 309 745 |

AH  Arrivals at hotels and similar establishments
NH  Nights in hotels and similar establishments
(R)  Tourist count by country of residence
(N)  Tourist count by country of nationality

AH  Arrivées dans les hôtels et les établissements assimilés
NH  Nuitées dans les hôtels et établissements assimilés
(R)  Recensement des touristes par pays de résidence
(N)  Recensement des touristes par pays de nationalité

## Table/Tableau 28

## ARRIVALS AND NIGHTS OF FOREIGN TOURISTS AT/IN ALL MEANS OF ACCOMMODATION
## ARRIVÉES ET NUITÉES DE TOURISTES ÉTRANGERS DANS L'ENSEMBLE DES MOYENS D'HÉBERGEMENT

*From Germany* / *En provenance de l'Allemagne*
1984=100

| | AAA/NAA | Volume 1978 | 1979 | 1980 | 1981 | 1982 | 1983 | Volume 1984 | 1985 | 1986 | 1987 | 1988 | 1989 | Volume 1989 | AEH/NEH |
|---|---|---|---|---|---|---|---|---|---|---|---|---|---|---|---|
| Austria (R) | NAA | 60 436 183 | 108.6 | 114.2 | 114.9 | 109.3 | 105.3 | 57 406 928 | 96.6 | 97.6 | 95.7 | 97.7 | 104.4 | 59 921 841 | NEH |
| Belgium (R) | AAA | 7 673 058 | 96.9 | 102.9 | 104.3 | 102.0 | 102.4 | 8 274 471 | 98.4 | 101.4 | 103.8 | 108.7 | 116.8 | 9 666 493 | AEH |
| Denmark (N) | NAA | 1 230 619 | 79.7 | 84.3 | 82.8 | 94.2 | 94.3 | 1 406 525 | 107.9 | 107.5 | 111.0 | 120.2 | 116.3 | 1 636 191 | NEH |
| France (R) | NAA | 3 439 073 | 97.2 | 100.2 | 111.6 | 109.1 | 111.9 | 3 677 135 | 94.6 | 89.1 | 79.4 | 76.6 | 87.3 | 3 210 790 | NEH |
| | AAA | 55 500 000 | 79.9 | 81.6 | 83.8 | 101.7 | 98.3 | 73 804 000 | 103.5 | 103.5 | 106.8 | 108.7 | | | AEH |
| Greece (N) | NAA | 6 685 000 | 87.9 | 90.8 | 100.4 | 97.3 | 88.8 | 8 290 000 | 105.2 | 101.5 | 107.5 | 109.9 | | | NEH |
| | AAA | 4 187 638 | 90.4 | 103.0 | 98.2 | 89.8 | 84.5 | 6 232 307 | 118.0 | 121.8 | 123.8 | 133.4 | | | AEH |
| Ireland (R) | NAA | 903 945 | 104.8 | 108.6 | 100.4 | 97.0 | 109.1 | 1 071 952 | 108.5 | 108.7 | 111.3 | 112.8 | | | NEH |
| | AAA | 1 314 600 | 114.4 | 124.7 | 84.9 | 96.3 | 107.7 | 1 223 000 | 103.3 | 108.9 | 124.6 | 144.4 | 182.4 | 2 231 000 | AEH |
| Italy (N) | NAA | 93 900 | 114.7 | 101.1 | 101.1 | 96.6 | 103.4 | 89 000 | 110.0 | 112.4 | 114.2 | 130.6 | 172.9 | 153 900 | NEH |
| | AAA | 37 892 722 | 108.3 | 109.7 | 96.1 | 105.9 | 103.3 | 41 352 681 | 101.0 | 108.4 | 94.9 | 95.5 | | | AEH |
| Luxembourg (R) | NAA | 4 522 628 | 94.4 | 97.0 | 87.0 | 99.3 | 100.0 | 5 782 562 | 102.9 | 111.1 | 110.0 | 112.2 | | | NEH |
| | AAA | 155 966 | 98.9 | 109.4 | | 80.3 | 78.5 | 163 551 | 101.0 | 96.3 | 107.6 | 107.5 | | | AEH |
| Netherlands (R) | NAA | 84 390 | 109.4 | 75.3 | 81.1 | 91.5 | 90.7 | 78 735 | 102.7 | 102.0 | 108.4 | 112.7 | 94.9 | 6 379 400 | NEH |
| | AAA | 4 123 998 | 75.2 | 83.9 | 89.8 | 92.5 | 95.2 | 6 721 130 | 97.6 | 103.1 | | 83.9 | | | AEH |
| Portugal (N) | NAA | 1 213 067 | 81.8 | 125.2 | 119.4 | 107.1 | 99.9 | 1 624 190 | 99.1 | 103.9 | 167.5 | 94.2 | 101.6 | 1 650 400 | NEH |
| | AAA | 1 507 899 | 119.6 | 101.8 | 97.3 | 92.6 | 95.9 | 1 665 844 | 134.6 | 152.0 | 167.0 | 167.0 | 165.2 | 2 752 402 | AEH |
| Spain (N) | NAA | 256 724 | 94.1 | 79.1 | 90.7 | 94.2 | 100.0 | 331 763 | 129.4 | 145.7 | 171.2 | 172.8 | 169.4 | 561 958 | NEH |
| | AAA | 24 559 602 | 95.5 | 79.3 | 87.4 | 91.4 | 97.3 | 24 166 437 | 102.2 | 103.2 | | | | | AEH |
| Sweden (N) | NAA | 2 529 208 | 90.0 | 104.1 | 108.2 | 97.0 | 109.1 | 2 576 729 | 103.2 | 96.0 | 89.2 | 102.8 | 113.0 | 1 514 151 | NEH |
| Switzerland (R) | NAA | 1 059 396 | 112.3 | 113.6 | 121.7 | 111.0 | 109.2 | 1 339 508 | 99.8 | 102.5 | 100.2 | 102.8 | 104.8 | 15 095 500 | NEH |
| | AAA | 13 997 900 | 90.6 | 107.2 | 112.3 | 105.8 | 105.9 | 14 405 800 | 100.6 | 103.5 | 104.5 | 108.3 | 113.2 | 3 272 000 | AEH |
| Turkey (N) | NAA | 2 591 600 | 88.5 | 22.1 | 39.3 | 46.6 | 75.4 | 2 891 100 | 99.7 | 278.5 | 441.0 | 624.4 | | | NEH |
| | AAA | 367 741 | 40.7 | 22.9 | 40.4 | 50.0 | 79.7 | 735 605 | 160.6 | 225.7 | 335.6 | 414.7 | 640.2 | 4 709 013 | AEH |
| United Kingdom (R) | NAA | 124 042 | 40.2 | 112.4 | 106.8 | 108.5 | 98.3 | 248 137 | 147.7 | 114.6 | 109.4 | 120.4 | 436.0 | 1 081 801 | NEH |
| | AAA | 15 564 000 | 115.8 | 112.4 | | | | 14 304 000 | 102.0 | | | | 123.2 | 17 624 000 | AEH |
| Canada (R) | NAA | 1 976 100 | 109.8 | 106.7 | 115.3 | 111.8 | 96.4 | 2 523 200 | 89.6 | 108.1 | 120.4 | 141.9 | 128.7 | 3 247 300 | NEH |
| | AAA | 141 100 | 106.5 | 111.3 | 117.7 | 108.1 | 95.9 | 169 900 | 92.1 | 116.7 | 137.8 | 154.8 | 154.6 | 262 700 | AEH |
| Australia (R) | NAA | | 82.8 | | 136.5 | | 142.8 | 540 000 | 127.5 | 145.4 | 185.0 | 228.8 | | | NEH |
| New Zealand (R) | NAA | | | | | | | 290 000 | 110.3 | 141.6 | 198.3 | 215.7 | 255.3 | 740 392 | NEH |
| Yugoslavia (N) | NAA | 14 459 072 | 85.0 | 102.0 | 109.7 | 93.5 | 91.8 | 16 039 523 | 121.6 | 123.0 | 125.0 | 123.4 | 109.3 | 17 530 275 | NEH |
| | AAA | 2 009 489 | 86.3 | 99.2 | 103.8 | 89.3 | 90.0 | 2 145 435 | 121.6 | 123.0 | 129.8 | 128.1 | 114.8 | 2 462 455 | AEH |

AAA  Arrivals in all means of accommodation
NAA  Nights in all means of accommodation
(R)  Tourist count by country of residence
(N)  Tourist count by country of nationality

AEH  Arrivées dans l'ensemble des moyens d'hébergement
NEH  Nuitées dans l'ensemble des moyens d'hébergement
(R)  Recensement des touristes par pays de résidence
(N)  Recensement des touristes par pays de nationalité

## Table/Tableau 29

### ARRIVALS OF FOREIGN TOURISTS/VISITORS AT FRONTIERS
### ARRIVÉES DE TOURISTES/VISITEURS ÉTRANGERS AUX FRONTIÈRES

**From Canada** 1984=100 — **En provenance du Canada** 1984=100

| | T/V | Volume 1978 | 1979 | 1980 | 1981 | 1982 | 1983 | Volume 1984 | 1985 | 1986 | 1987 | 1988 | 1989 | Volume 1989 | T/V | |
|---|---|---|---|---|---|---|---|---|---|---|---|---|---|---|---|---|
| Finland (R) | V | 8 254 | 82.2 | 84.9 | 94.7 | 66.3 | 75.1 | 377 000 | 126.5 | 102.4 | 92.6 | 91.2 | | | V | Finlande (R) |
| France (R) | T | 368 000 | 101.7 | 88.1 | 79.9 | 78.9 | 88.2 | 82 226 | 124.7 | 90.7 | 110.7 | 130.1 | 96.1 | 79 000 | T | France (R) |
| Greece (N) | T | 75 326 | 104.2 | 80.5 | 89.0 | 100.2 | 103.7 | 1 001 | 128.5 | 119.4 | 128.5 | 127.6 | | | T | Grèce (N) |
| Iceland (N) | T | 1 056 | | | 121.7 | 77.3 | 100.0 | | 119.0 | 133.3 | 119.0 | 133.3 | | | T | Islande (N) |
| Ireland (R) | V | 396 800 | | | | | | 21 000 | | | | | 176.2 | 37 000 | V | Irlande (R) |
| Italy (N) | V | 9 124 | 117.8 | 104.8 | 91.9 | 91.7 | 98.6 | 336 205 | 103.7 | 100.5 | 114.4 | 105.4 | 125.8 | 422 939 | V | Italie (N) |
| Norway (N) | V | 31 700 | 75.1 | 72.2 | 79.3 | 72.5 | 79.2 | 52 331 | 131.7 | 137.9 | 138.8 | 145.2 | 158.7 | 83 070 | V | Norvège (N) |
| Portugal (N) | T | 36 867 | 72.5 | 71.8 | 77.6 | 74.8 | 83.4 | 56 116 | 125.2 | 131.6 | 138.2 | 140.9 | 162.4 | 91 126 | T | Portugal (N) |
| Spain (N) | V | 175 537 | 91.3 | 73.9 | 87.3 | 85.8 | 89.0 | 155 570 | 122.8 | 113.7 | 114.9 | 108.0 | 110.8 | 172 357 | V | Espagne (N) |
| Turkey (N) | V | 17 982 | 115.9 | 64.1 | 63.9 | 47.4 | 79.9 | 18 048 | 119.3 | 72.6 | 115.4 | 161.9 | 175.0 | 31 587 | V | Turquie (N) |
| United Kingdom (R) | V | 511 000 | 84.2 | 68.3 | 68.7 | 72.1 | 91.5 | 566 700 | 111.4 | 98.0 | 104.8 | 114.9 | 111.8 | 633 400 | V | Royaume-Uni (R) |
| United States (R) | T | 11 938 839 | 97.6 | 103.7 | 99.5 | 95.0 | 108.9 | 10 981 949 | 99.1 | 99.6 | 113.1 | 126.1 | 139.9 | 15 365 937 | T | États-Unis (R) |
| Australia (R) | V | 19 000 | 67.2 | 82.6 | 89.7 | 94.0 | 95.7 | 34 500 | 118.6 | 136.2 | 152.8 | 193.3 | 157.1 | 54 200 | V | Australie (R) |
| Japan (N) | V | 34 464 | 65.1 | 77.5 | 84.7 | 91.1 | 101.2 | 52 989 | 115.2 | 104.2 | 110.0 | 109.8 | 112.8 | 59 754 | V | Japon (N) |
| New Zealand (R) | T | 12 672 | 62.0 | 80.5 | 79.6 | 78.2 | 88.8 | 23 041 | 129.5 | 149.0 | 154.3 | 161.2 | 134.2 | 30 919 | T | Nouvelle-Zélande (R) |

V   Visitors (travellers in Turkey)
T   Tourists
(R)   Tourist count by country of residence
(N)   Tourist count by country of nationality

V   Visiteurs (voyageurs en Turquie)
T   Touristes
(R)   Recensement des touristes par pays de résidence
(N)   Recensement des touristes par pays de nationalité

## Table/Tableau 30

### ARRIVALS AND NIGHTS OF FOREIGN TOURISTS AT/IN HOTELS
### ARRIVÉES ET NUITÉES DE TOURISTES ÉTRANGERS DANS L'HÔTELLERIE

From Canada — En provenance du Canada
1984=100

| Country | AH/NH | Volume 1978 | 1979 | 1980 | 1981 | 1982 | 1983 | Volume 1984 | 1985 | 1986 | 1987 | 1988 | 1989 | Volume 1989 | AH/NH | En provenance du Canada |
|---|---|---|---|---|---|---|---|---|---|---|---|---|---|---|---|---|
| Austria (R) | NH | 123 820 | 64.4 | 61.9 | 71.9 | 78.2 | 82.7 | 163 894 | 122.1 | 100.8 | 110.9 | 102.7 | 106.0 | 173 757 | NH | Autriche (R) |
| | AH | 44 937 | 58.6 | 60.0 | 62.3 | 68.5 | 80.6 | 66 384 | 119.4 | 92.7 | 103.9 | 101.5 | 108.9 | 72 314 | AH | |
| Belgium (R) | NH | 56 843 | 60.8 | 68.3 | 64.3 | 66.0 | 76.0 | 74 849 | 123.9 | 97.1 | 101.7 | 106.0 | 115.1 | 86 146 | NH | Belgique (R) |
| | AH | 14 259 | 58.9 | 52.4 | 67.6 | 77.5 | 96.3 | 27 559 | 108.6 | 92.3 | 105.4 | 110.4 | 120.6 | 33 223 | AH | |
| Finland (R) | NH | | | | | | | / | | | | | | / | NH | Finlande (R) |
| | AH | | | | | | | / | | | | | | / | AH | |
| France (R) | NH | 364 101 | 56.9 | 58.3 | 64.7 | 71.0 | 85.3 | 465 016 | 120.7 | 173.1 | 160.3 | 160.4 | 204.9 | 952 905 | NH | France (R)· |
| | AH | 129 200 | 58.3 | 59.9 | 66.5 | 72.2 | 81.0 | 163 634 | 128.2 | 233.1 | 201.7 | 200.8 | 262.4 | 429 411 | AH | |
| Germany (R) | NH | 204 826 | 59.4 | 65.6 | 65.7 | 69.0 | 76.8 | 313 079 | 108.7 | 95.6 | 92.6 | 86.3 | 113.8 | 356 156 | NH | Allemagne (R) |
| | AH | 108 908 | 57.7 | 63.4 | 61.2 | 65.7 | 74.3 | 172 659 | 106.9 | 88.9 | 85.8 | 91.6 | 99.0 | 171 013 | AH | |
| Greece (N) | NH | 298 433 | 109.1 | 81.4 | 81.1 | 73.2 | 81.2 | 258 378 | 140.9 | 76.0 | 89.0 | 90.4 | | | NH | Grèce (N) |
| | AH | 106 497 | 101.0 | 79.3 | 73.4 | 69.6 | 76.5 | 101 024 | 136.4 | 74.9 | 87.8 | | | | AH | |
| Ireland (R) | NH | | | | | | | | | | | | | 254 000 | NH | Irlande (R) |
| | AH | | | | | | | | | | | | | 37 000 | AH | |
| Italy (N) | NH | 432 413 | 70.2 | 66.5 | 63.3 | 75.9 | 89.7 | 587 636 | 114.1 | 89.0 | 103.3 | 97.6 | | | NH | Italie (N) |
| | AH | 162 234 | 59.5 | 61.2 | 56.7 | 69.1 | 85.3 | 241 881 | 110.5 | 84.7 | 98.0 | 95.9 | | | AH | |
| Luxembourg (R) | NH | | | | | | | | | | | | | | NH | Luxembourg (R) |
| | AH | | | | | | | | | | | | | | AH | |
| Netherlands (R) | NH | 124 804 | 69.8 | 72.8 | 66.1 | 69.2 | 87.6 | 172 283 | 112.8 | 95.4 | 101.2 | 101.8 | 104.6 | 180 200 | NH | Pays-Bas (R) |
| | AH | 65 508 | 62.0 | 68.7 | 61.6 | 63.6 | 87.6 | 98 804 | 115.1 | 95.0 | 100.0 | 104.1 | 95.0 | 93 900 | AH | |
| Portugal (N) | NH | 126 831 | 66.4 | 72.1 | 77.9 | 67.2 | 83.2 | 258 803 | 150.0 | 140.5 | 134.0 | 120.5 | 131.6 | 340 529 | NH | Portugal (N) |
| | AH | 35 750 | 63.5 | 65.5 | 71.7 | 68.4 | 81.6 | 75 318 | 130.6 | 122.7 | 133.9 | 121.8 | 132.2 | 99 598 | AH | |
| Spain (N) | NH | | | 58.8 | 67.6 | 70.6 | 86.3 | 411 963 | 117.4 | 82.9 | 55.0 | 44.4 | 43.2 | 177 846 | NH | Espagne (N) |
| | AH | | | | | | | | | | | | | 75 274 | AH | |
| Sweden (N) | NH | 25 084 | 85.0 | 87.9 | 95.4 | 74.4 | 80.4 | 28 792 | 97.5 | 76.4 | 97.5 | 79.4 | 87.1 | 25 075 | NH | Suède (N) |
| | AH | | | | | | | | | | | | | | AH | |
| Switzerland (R) | NH | 194 040 | 58.9 | 65.0 | 70.3 | 75.2 | 88.1 | 263 150 | 120.8 | 99.4 | 91.2 | 79.6 | 82.8 | 217 828 | NH | Suisse (R) |
| | AH | 82 649 | 53.0 | 60.2 | 61.0 | 66.5 | 82.7 | 125 876 | 113.1 | 90.3 | 83.3 | 74.2 | 79.5 | 100 031 | AH | |
| Turkey (N) | NH | | | | | 70.2 | 76.3 | 13 768 | 101.5 | 119.1 | 138.0 | 215.0 | 223.7 | 30 801 | NH | Turquie (N) |
| | AH | | | | | 55.9 | 87.6 | 5 036 | 110.3 | 139.0 | 152.8 | 209.4 | 313.8 | 15 802 | AH | |
| Australia (R) | NH | | 81.5 | | 97.8 | | 143.6 | 263 000 | 135.2 | 159.5 | 178.8 | 226.3 | | | NH | Australie (R) |
| Japan (N) | NH | 77 268 | | | | | | | | | | | | | NH | Japon (N) |
| | AH | 33 345 | | | | | | | | | | | | | AH | |
| Yugoslavia (N) | NH | | | | | | | | | | | | | 74 387 | NH | Yougoslavie (N) |
| | AH | | | | | | | | | | | | | 35 123 | AH | |

AH  Arrivals at hotels and similar establishments  
NH  Nights in hotels and similar establishments  
(R)  Tourist count by country of residence  
(N)  Tourist count by country of nationality  

AH  Arrivées dans les hôtels et les établissements assimilés  
NH  Nuitées dans les hôtels et établissements assimilés  
(R)  Recensement des touristes par pays de résidence  
(N)  Recensement des touristes par pays de nationalité

Table/Tableau 31

## ARRIVALS AND NIGHTS OF FOREIGN TOURISTS AT/IN ALL MEANS OF ACCOMMODATION
## ARRIVÉES ET NUITÉES DE TOURISTES ÉTRANGERS DANS L'ENSEMBLE DES MOYENS D'HÉBERGEMENT

From Canada — *En provenance du Canada*  
1984=100

| Country | Pays | AAA/NAA | AEH/NEH | Volume 1978 | 1979 | 1980 | 1981 | 1982 | 1983 | Volume 1984 | 1985 | 1986 | 1987 | 1988 | 1989 | Volume 1989 |
|---|---|---|---|---|---|---|---|---|---|---|---|---|---|---|---|---|
| Austria (R) | Autriche (R) | NAA | NEH | 159 511 | 66.4 | 67.5 | 71.8 | 80.7 | 84.3 | 209 823 | 117.2 | 99.9 | 108.4 | 106.5 | 105.2 | 220 697 |
| Belgium (R) | Belgique (R) | AAA | AEH | 56 470 | 61.2 | 62.4 | 62.8 | 70.0 | 79.7 | 80 695 | 117.4 | 94.9 | 104.7 | 104.9 | 111.5 | 89 938 |
|  |  | NAA | NEH | 66 151 | 61.7 | 70.5 | 64.6 | 68.5 | 76.9 | 86 053 | 123.1 | 101.9 | 99.8 | 105.4 | 113.5 | 97 631 |
| France (R) | France (R) | NAA | NEH | 3 500 000 | 57.1 | 59.5 | 66.4 | 66.1 | 79.4 | 5 375 000 | 123.7 | 109.5 | 105.7 | 105.8 | 106.0 | 5 700 000 |
| Germany (R) | Allemagne (R) | AAA | AEH | 368 000 | 82.2 | 84.9 | 94.7 | 66.3 | 75.1 | 377 000 | 126.5 | 102.4 | 92.6 | 91.2 |  |  |
|  |  | NAA | NEH | 214 854 | 56.2 | 63.4 | 60.0 | 63.1 | 70.4 | 350 346 | 108.5 | 96.9 | 93.5 | 100.1 | 115.6 | 404 892 |
| Greece (N) | Grèce (N) | AAA | AEH | 111 198 | 52.6 | 59.8 | 55.0 | 59.0 | 66.8 | 193 400 | 106.0 | 90.9 | 86.8 | 87.9 | 101.0 | 195 312 |
|  |  | NAA | NEH | 327 980 | 77.4 | 62.0 | 59.5 | 54.0 | 58.9 | 385 360 | 96.7 | 52.5 | 61.0 | 62.5 | 62.3 | 240 000 |
| Italy (N) | Italie (N) | AAA | AEH | 118 218 | 101.2 | 81.2 | 72.6 | 70.2 | 76.1 | 111 321 | 126.5 | 70.1 | 81.8 | 83.7 |  |  |
|  |  | NAA | NEH | 598 434 | 81.8 | 78.3 | 73.6 | 84.1 | 91.9 | 733 694 | 110.3 | 89.7 | 96.0 | 92.0 | 92.7 | 680 000 |
| Luxembourg (R) | Luxembourg (R) | NAA | NEH | 187 184 | 62.4 | 64.2 | 59.2 | 70.6 | 85.9 | 267 154 | 109.3 | 86.5 | 97.8 | 97.0 |  |  |
| Netherlands (R) | Pays-Bas (R) | AAA | AEH | 166 334 | 78.3 | 81.1 | 70.7 | 73.4 | 88.2 | 201 730 | 110.4 | 89.5 | / | 101.3 | 104.5 | 210 900 |
|  |  | NAA | NEH | 86 810 | 69.1 | 74.0 | 66.2 | 67.9 | 88.0 | 116 707 | 112.3 | 88.9 | / | 105.2 | 93.1 | 108 700 |
| Portugal (N) | Portugal (N) | AAA | AEH | 134 735 | 68.1 | 74.8 | 79.0 | 68.1 | 83.6 | 271 252 | 147.9 | 137.9 | 132.0 | 119.3 | 129.6 | 351 615 |
|  |  | NAA | NEH | 38 623 | 66.2 | 68.9 | 73.0 | 69.3 | 82.2 | 79 289 | 129.6 | 121.2 | 132.5 | 121.0 | 131.4 | 104 219 |
| Sweden (N) | Suède (N) | NAA | NEH | 26 730 | 85.4 | 89.8 | 94.3 | 75.5 | 82.5 | 31 929 | 97.8 | 78.8 | 96.4 | 80.8 | 88.0 | 28 101 |
| Switzerland (R) | Suisse (R) | AAA | AEH | 246 400 | 62.2 | 67.1 | 72.6 | 77.6 | 88.7 | 315 500 | 119.2 | 99.7 | 92.4 | 81.1 | 85.3 | 269 200 |
|  |  | NAA | NEH | 108 600 | 58.4 | 64.1 | 65.0 | 70.1 | 84.6 | 149 100 | 113.6 | 92.0 | 84.2 | 76.5 | 82.2 | 122 500 |
| Turkey (N) | Turquie (N) | AAA | AEH | 8 865 | 59.5 | 38.8 | 40.5 | 69.0 | 75.8 | 14 060 | 101.8 | 119.5 | 142.0 | 221.0 | 225.0 | 31 631 |
|  |  | NAA | NEH | 4 223 | 70.4 | 40.6 | 49.5 | 55.6 | 87.5 | 5 088 | 111.9 | 139.2 | 157.6 | 219.4 | 317.1 | 16 132 |
| United Kingdom (R) | Royaume-Uni (R) | NAA | NEH | 8 181 000 | 96.4 | 69.6 | 78.1 | 84.4 | 95.6 | 8 434 000 | 108.1 | 101.5 | 97.6 | 105.0 | 101.2 | 8 537 000 |
| Australia (R) | Australie (R) | NAA | NEH |  | 58.0 |  | 86.5 |  | 166.6 | 795 800 | 97.0 | 108.4 | 121.5 | 153.8 |  |  |
| Yugoslavia (N) | Yougoslavie (N) | NAA | NEH | 94 383 | 74.4 | 57.2 | 61.8 | 60.2 | 67.0 | 105 778 | 106.1 | 92.1 | 118.6 | 119.4 | 96.3 | 101 857 |
|  |  | AAA | AEH | 33 300 | 84.3 | 67.5 | 66.8 | 63.2 | 71.4 | 33 375 | 118.4 | 103.2 | 129.8 | 141.9 | 123.9 | 41 364 |

AAA  Arrivals in all means of accommodation  
NAA  Nights in all means of accommodation  
(R)  Tourist count by country of residence  
(N)  Tourist count by country of nationality  

AEH  Arrivées dans l'ensemble des moyens d'hébergement  
NEH  Nuitées dans l'ensemble des moyens d'hébergement  
(R)  Recensement des touristes par pays de résidence  
(N)  Recensement des touristes par pays de nationalité

# Table/Tableau 32

# ARRIVALS OF FOREIGN TOURISTS/VISITORS AT FRONTIERS
# ARRIVÉES DE TOURISTES/VISITEURS ÉTRANGERS AUX FRONTIÈRES

*From the United States*  
1984=100

*En provenance des États-Unis*  
1984=100

| | T/V | Volume 1978 | 1979 | 1980 | 1981 | 1982 | 1983 | Volume 1984 | 1985 | 1986 | 1987 | 1988 | 1989 | Volume 1989 | T/V | |
|---|---|---|---|---|---|---|---|---|---|---|---|---|---|---|---|---|
| Finland (R) | V | 46 369 | 44.6 | 46.9 | 54.0 | 53.4 | 80.7 | 2 539 000 | 109.4 | 65.7 | 71.0 | 76.8 | | | V | Finlande (R) |
| France (R) | T | 1 220 000 | 126.7 | 60.8 | 67.6 | 70.1 | 85.7 | 474 845 | 98.2 | 43.1 | 54.8 | 62.1 | 58.8 | 279 000 | T | France (R) |
| Greece (N) | T | 513 181 | 82.5 | 55.9 | 65.6 | 76.3 | 91.3 | | | | | | | | T | Grèce (N) |
| Iceland (N) | T | 23 512 | | 79.6 | 80.2 | 99.7 | 88.4 | 27 293 | 115.9 | 119.8 | 130.7 | 105.2 | 84.1 | 22 952 | T | Islande (N) |
| Ireland (R) | V | 89 893 | | | | | | 303 000 | 124.8 | 98.3 | 118.2 | 123.1 | 125.4 | 380 000 | V | Irlande (R) |
| Italy (N) | V | 1 789 500 | 99.6 | 97.1 | 81.3 | 90.3 | 96.8 | 1 774 821 | 103.4 | 89.7 | 83.5 | 76.1 | 76.4 | 1 356 662 | V | Italie (N) |
| Norway (N) | V | 124 000 | 80.0 | 69.8 | 65.9 | 77.1 | 69.5 | 165 399 | 99.7 | 69.2 | 91.7 | 117.4 | 112.9 | 186 736 | V | Norvège (N) |
| Portugal (N) | T | 161 545 | 73.5 | 64.7 | 67.7 | 73.6 | 89.2 | 209 398 | 109.6 | 71.5 | 93.2 | 106.6 | 112.5 | 235 503 | T | Portugal (N) |
| Spain (N) | V | 948 977 | 95.1 | 87.3 | 82.5 | 81.0 | 86.7 | 935 886 | 106.6 | 82.3 | 92.5 | 91.8 | 101.9 | 953 782 | V | Espagne (N) |
| Turkey (N) | V | 158 689 | 75.4 | 55.6 | 48.6 | 49.1 | 88.5 | 213 345 | 92.0 | 37.3 | 61.2 | 77.5 | 95.9 | 204 502 | V | Turquie (N) |
| United Kingdom (R) | V | 1 964 000 | 62.2 | 61.3 | 62.1 | 62.5 | 83.8 | 2 763 800 | 114.6 | 82.8 | 101.3 | 94.8 | 101.8 | 2 814 100 | V | Royaume-Uni (R) |
| Canada (R) | T | 11 276 500 | 96.6 | 97.1 | 97.1 | 92.6 | 96.6 | 11 294 700 | 102.3 | 120.5 | 112.6 | 113.0 | 108.0 | 12 195 400 | T | Canada (R) |
| Canada (R) | V | 31 597 200 | 94.6 | 116.7 | 120.7 | 98.3 | 98.5 | 32 977 800 | 103.5 | 115.8 | 112.1 | 109.6 | 105.2 | 34 705 100 | V | |
| Australia (R) | V | 81 000 | 60.5 | 69.1 | 71.0 | 78.2 | 87.1 | 160 400 | 122.5 | 153.0 | 192.6 | 200.9 | 162.5 | 260 700 | V | Australie (R) |
| Japan (N) | V | 313 620 | 59.1 | 62.4 | 69.1 | 80.4 | 90.3 | 511 125 | 109.2 | 108.0 | 107.7 | 101.0 | 104.0 | 531 625 | V | Japon (N) |
| New Zealand (R) | T | 58 392 | 59.6 | 77.0 | 76.0 | 75.5 | 85.8 | 101 032 | 121.7 | 152.4 | 178.5 | 165.8 | 136.1 | 137 509 | T | Nouvelle-Zélande (R) |

V  Visitors (travellers in Turkey)     V  Visiteurs (voyageurs en Turquie)  
T  Tourists     T  Touristes  
(R)  Tourist count by country of residence     (R)  Recensement des touristes par pays de résidence  
(N)  Tourist count by country of nationality     (N)  Recensement des touristes par pays de nationalité

108

## Table/Tableau 33
## ARRIVALS AND NIGHTS OF FOREIGN TOURISTS AT/IN HOTELS
## ARRIVÉES ET NUITÉES DE TOURISTES ÉTRANGERS DANS L'HÔTELLERIE

From the United States — En provenance des États-Unis  
1984=100

| Country | AH/NH | Volume 1978 | 1979 | 1980 | 1981 | 1982 | 1983 | Volume 1984 | 1985 | 1986 | 1987 | 1988 | 1989 | Volume 1989 | AH/NH | |
|---|---|---|---|---|---|---|---|---|---|---|---|---|---|---|---|---|
| Austria (R) | NH | 1 118 313 | 46.6 | 58.6 | 50.7 | 64.0 | 78.3 | 2 024 920 | 107.8 | 61.9 | 76.6 | 70.5 | 75.6 | 1 531 322 | NH | Autriche (R) |
| Belgium (R) | AH | 447 949 | 41.9 | 58.4 | 45.7 | 56.3 | 73.0 | 877 010 | 105.5 | 52.2 | 69.9 | 64.2 | 70.0 | 613 624 | AH | Belgique (R) |
| Denmark (N) | NH | 466 840 | 71.5 | 67.5 | 67.5 | 79.0 | 84.5 | 688 637 | 112.1 | 87.2 | 78.3 | 67.4 | 74.3 | 511 738 | NH | Danemark (N) |
| Finland (R) | NH | 455 000 | 72.4 | 68.3 | 63.6 | 77.9 | 94.6 | 530 600 | 108.0 | 78.1 | 83.7 | 71.3 | 80.1 | 425 200 | NH | Finlande (R) |
| France (R) | NH | 121 876 | 60.8 | 53.9 | 62.1 | 72.9 | 95.3 | 157 477 | 117.3 | 101.3 | 126.8 | 129.0 | 128.6 | 202 452 | NH | France (R) |
| France (R) | AH | 2 214 720 | 50.4 | 54.7 | 59.1 | 61.2 | 76.2 | 3 399 706 | 113.3 | 96.1 | 105.7 | 115.7 | 153.9 | 5 231 991 | AH | |
| Germany (R) | NH | 810 696 | 51.2 | 52.4 | 56.3 | 63.1 | 74.1 | 1 283 749 | 110.9 | 109.9 | 119.1 | 135.9 | 179.8 | 2 308 421 | NH | Allemagne (R) |
| Germany (R) | AH | 2 318 598 | 48.6 | 60.3 | 54.4 | 62.4 | 77.2 | 4 475 322 | 108.3 | 80.1 | 90.2 | 81.7 | 89.0 | 3 982 998 | AH | |
| Greece (N) | NH | 1 230 393 | 46.4 | 60.2 | 52.3 | 60.1 | 75.6 | 2 401 332 | 105.7 | 73.7 | 82.3 | 74.3 | 81.8 | 1 963 587 | NH | Grèce (N) |
| Greece (N) | AH | 1 623 201 | 80.4 | 65.8 | 63.7 | 66.3 | 83.6 | 1 954 464 | 85.5 | 26.0 | 40.4 | 42.4 | | | AH | |
| Ireland (R) | NH | 636 515 | 74.6 | 60.5 | 59.1 | 61.6 | 79.7 | 822 076 | 87.7 | 22.6 | 39.4 | 43.5 | | 1 948 000 | NH | Irlande (R) |
| Italy (N) | NH | 4 151 622 | 63.5 | 59.3 | 55.9 | 67.7 | 84.9 | 6 153 639 | 106.9 | 55.1 | 77.4 | 74.6 | 74.6 | | NH | Italie (N) |
| Italy (N) | AH | 1 587 498 | 56.4 | 55.8 | 51.5 | 63.4 | 82.1 | 2 656 343 | 106.2 | 48.3 | 71.0 | 70.2 | 70.2 | | AH | |
| Luxembourg (R) | NH | | | | | 59.3 | 81.8 | 86 256 | 115.6 | 86.4 | 89.5 | 73.4 | 73.4 | 378 000 | NH | Luxembourg (R) |
| Luxembourg (R) | AH | | | | | 62.0 | 82.3 | 48 477 | 118.8 | 88.5 | 92.2 | 68.6 | 68.6 | | AH | |
| Netherlands (R) | NH | 721 809 | 63.7 | 61.1 | 62.3 | 76.5 | 81.7 | 1 071 205 | 100.3 | 77.8 | 78.1 | 70.6 | 76.5 | 819 400 | NH | Pays-Bas (R) |
| Netherlands (R) | AH | 347 296 | 55.2 | 56.4 | 55.1 | 71.3 | 79.1 | 574 570 | 114.6 | 73.2 | 74.3 | 66.3 | 71.8 | 412 400 | AH | |
| Norway (N) | NH | 397 598 | 61.9 | 58.7 | 59.8 | 66.8 | 79.9 | 561 033 | 111.1 | 69.8 | 81.5 | 62.0 | 61.9 | 347 258 | NH | Norvège (N) |
| Portugal (N) | NH | 573 680 | 84.2 | 64.5 | 64.8 | 65.6 | 84.4 | 710 227 | 108.2 | 63.8 | 88.3 | 91.5 | 95.4 | 677 442 | NH | Portugal (N) |
| Portugal (N) | AH | 196 137 | 72.9 | 59.3 | 62.2 | 62.9 | 84.2 | 269 672 | 102.8 | 60.1 | 85.9 | 88.9 | 94.2 | 254 047 | AH | |
| Spain (N) | NH | 3 020 890 | 84.9 | 55.6 | 63.9 | 66.8 | 84.2 | 2 468 894 | 107.0 | 61.2 | 77.2 | 71.2 | 74.4 | 1 835 837 | NH | Espagne (N) |
| Spain (N) | AH | 1 076 129 | 70.4 | 47.5 | 54.0 | 56.2 | 83.6 | 1 160 266 | | | 69.4 | 66.8 | 71.3 | 826 781 | AH | |
| Sweden (N) | NH | 288 711 | 69.7 | 60.0 | 65.7 | 70.8 | 95.1 | 415 649 | 78.4 | 78.4 | 83.9 | 78.3 | 79.7 | 331 449 | NH | Suède (N) |
| Switzerland (R) | NH | 1 925 592 | 46.9 | 56.4 | 57.5 | 67.6 | 77.9 | 3 062 643 | 106.5 | 67.9 | 76.2 | 66.6 | 72.6 | 2 224 447 | NH | Suisse (R) |
| Switzerland (R) | AH | 819 397 | 43.4 | 55.7 | 53.5 | 64.3 | 76.2 | 1 454 463 | 104.5 | 61.4 | 71.3 | 63.8 | 71.0 | 1 032 600 | AH | |
| Turkey (N) | NH | | | | | 58.7 | 75.2 | 254 462 | 105.3 | 86.0 | 105.2 | 123.7 | 149.6 | 380 779 | NH | Turquie (N) |
| Turkey (N) | AH | | | | | 63.1 | 90.3 | 79 184 | 111.6 | 96.2 | 117.2 | 149.1 | 211.6 | 167 555 | AH | |
| Australia (R) | NH | 1 194 292 | 76.2 | | 85.2 | | 114.8 | 1 082 400 | 153.4 | 199.3 | 251.0 | 261.8 | | | NH | Australie (R) |
| Japan (N) | NH | 513 536 | 54.9 | 58.7 | 69.3 | 77.9 | 44.4 | 1 901 289 | 124.5 | | | | | | NH | Japon (N) |
| Japan (N) | AH | | 57.1 | 58.8 | 68.9 | 78.6 | 42.2 | 839 803 | | | | | | | AH | |
| Yugoslavia (N) | NH | | | | | | | | | | | | | 463 586 | NH | Yougoslavie (N) |
| Yugoslavia (N) | AH | | | | | | | | | | | | | 221 624 | AH | |

AH  Arrivals at hotels and similar establishments  
NH  Nights in hotels and similar establishments  
(R)  Tourist count by country of residence  
(N)  Tourist count by country of nationality  

AH  Arrivées dans les hôtels et les établissements assimilés  
NH  Nuitées dans les hôtels et établissements assimilés  
(R)  Recensement des touristes par pays de résidence  
(N)  Recensement des touristes par pays de nationalité

# ARRIVALS AND NIGHTS OF FOREIGN TOURISTS AT/IN ALL MEANS OF ACCOMMODATION
# ARRIVÉES ET NUITÉES DE TOURISTES ÉTRANGERS DANS L'ENSEMBLE DES MOYENS D'HÉBERGEMENT

From the United States / En provenance des États-Unis
1984=100

| Country | AAA/NAA | Volume 1978 | 1979 | 1980 | 1981 | 1982 | 1983 | Volume 1984 | 1985 | 1986 | 1987 | 1988 | 1989 | Volume 1989 | AEH/NEH | Pays |
|---|---|---|---|---|---|---|---|---|---|---|---|---|---|---|---|---|
| Austria (R) | NAA | 1 272 219 | 49.5 | 60.5 | 53.1 | 65.3 | 79.0 | 2 203 027 | 107.9 | 63.9 | 78.1 | 72.2 | 77.1 | 1 697 928 | NEH | Autriche (R) |
| | AAA | 493 566 | 44.0 | 59.4 | 47.3 | 57.5 | 73.8 | 931 505 | 106.0 | 54.7 | 72.1 | 66.6 | 72.6 | 676 085 | AEH | |
| Belgium (R) | NAA | 493 645 | 69.7 | 65.8 | 66.2 | 76.4 | 81.7 | 740 758 | 120.5 | 108.1 | 98.9 | 77.3 | 73.7 | 546 129 | NEH | Belgique (R) |
| Denmark (N) | NAA | 482 230 | 73.5 | 70.6 | 65.6 | 79.5 | 94.8 | 553 435 | 107.7 | 78.9 | 84.4 | 72.1 | 80.8 | 447 229 | NEH | Danemark (N) |
| France (R) | NAA | 10 250 000 | 35.0 | 34.9 | 40.1 | 55.1 | 83.3 | 27 306 000 | 113.3 | 85.0 | 93.3 | 96.3 | | | NEH | France (R) |
| | AAA | 1 220 000 | 44.6 | 46.9 | 54.0 | 53.4 | 80.7 | 2 539 000 | 109.4 | 65.7 | 71.0 | 76.8 | | | AEH | |
| Germany (R) | NAA | 2 418 577 | 48.3 | 60.8 | 52.5 | 60.2 | 75.0 | 4 702 424 | 108.3 | 80.7 | 90.8 | 82.4 | 90.0 | 4 230 468 | NEH | Allemagne (R) |
| | AAA | 1 249 246 | 45.3 | 60.1 | 50.4 | 58.0 | 73.1 | 2 498 993 | 105.3 | 74.1 | 82.9 | 75.2 | 82.7 | 2 067 317 | AEH | |
| Greece (N) | NAA | 1 757 068 | 81.9 | 68.0 | 64.3 | 66.2 | 82.8 | 2 078 846 | 81.0 | 25.1 | 38.5 | 40.2 | | | NEH | Grèce (N) |
| | AAA | 667 183 | 74.5 | 61.0 | 59.1 | 61.5 | 79.1 | 860 249 | 84.4 | 22.1 | 38.1 | 41.9 | | | AEH | |
| Ireland (R) | NAA | 3 500 100 | 106.7 | 88.8 | 77.7 | 91.8 | 106.5 | 3 356 200 | 122.0 | 98.1 | 119.2 | 122.5 | 135.4 | 4 544 000 | NEH | Irlande (R) |
| | AAA | 280 000 | 83.4 | 73.6 | 78.3 | 91.2 | 89.9 | 318 000 | 123.3 | 107.9 | 115.4 | 120.8 | 121.1 | 385 100 | AEH | |
| Italy (N) | NAA | 4 883 305 | 66.8 | 63.8 | 60.4 | 71.4 | 87.1 | 6 927 447 | 106.1 | 58.2 | 73.7 | 71.1 | | | NEH | Italie (N) |
| | AAA | 1 672 828 | 57.6 | 57.0 | 52.7 | 57.0 | 82.6 | 2 737 513 | 106.2 | 49.5 | 71.5 | 72.8 | | | AEH | |
| Luxembourg (R) | NAA | 55 747 | 73.0 | | | | 77.5 | 92 888 | 114.2 | 86.7 | 91.4 | 75.5 | | | NEH | Luxembourg (R) |
| | AAA | 45 024 | 97.6 | | | | 76.3 | 53 215 | 117.1 | 88.8 | 94.0 | 72.2 | | | AEH | |
| Netherlands (R) | NAA | 841 039 | 68.1 | 64.7 | 65.2 | 78.8 | 82.8 | 1 159 136 | 100.6 | 73.1 | | 71.7 | 78.5 | 909 400 | NEH | Pays-Bas (R) |
| | AAA | 408 506 | 59.4 | 60.1 | 58.3 | 73.8 | 80.5 | 627 275 | 100.2 | 68.5 | | 69.0 | 72.5 | 454 600 | AEH | |
| Portugal (N) | NAA | 586 161 | 84.8 | 66.1 | 66.2 | 67.0 | 85.1 | 724 859 | 111.3 | 70.4 | 89.9 | 92.0 | 87.3 | 632 615 | NEH | Portugal (N) |
| | AAA | 201 210 | 74.0 | 61.0 | 63.2 | 63.7 | 84.6 | 274 319 | 108.5 | 64.7 | 86.8 | 89.7 | 94.8 | 260 107 | AEH | |
| Spain (N) | NAA | 3 077 226 | 73.5 | 56.7 | 65.0 | 67.7 | 84.7 | 2 904 532 | 104.8 | | | | | | NEH | Espagne (N) |
| | AAA | 1 086 681 | 70.7 | 56.2 | 63.8 | 66.3 | 83.7 | 1 166 826 | 106.9 | | | | | | AEH | |
| Sweden (N) | NAA | 295 228 | 70.2 | 60.7 | 66.1 | 71.1 | 94.5 | 431 874 | 115.7 | 78.9 | 84.4 | 78.7 | 80.5 | 347 643 | NEH | Suède (N) |
| Switzerland (R) | NAA | 2 153 800 | 50.5 | 57.9 | 59.6 | 69.6 | 78.8 | 3 319 900 | 107.0 | 70.1 | 77.5 | 68.3 | 74.3 | 2 465 400 | NEH | Suisse (R) |
| | AAA | 907 100 | 46.2 | 57.6 | 55.7 | 58.4 | 77.6 | 1 536 800 | 104.9 | 62.9 | 72.7 | 65.3 | 72.4 | 1 112 700 | AEH | |
| Turkey (N) | NAA | 132 319 | 42.4 | 25.3 | 40.1 | 62.8 | 74.8 | 258 359 | 104.9 | 86.3 | 106.0 | 124.6 | 150.5 | 388 945 | NEH | Turquie (N) |
| | AAA | 51 573 | 53.6 | 29.4 | 45.1 | | 89.6 | 80 371 | 111.4 | 95.9 | 118.3 | 150.4 | 211.4 | 169 919 | AEH | |
| United Kingdom (R) | NAA | 20 893 000 | 72.1 | 69.0 | 67.7 | 71.9 | 86.7 | 26 678 000 | 117.0 | 92.3 | 108.5 | 95.7 | 102.8 | 27 432 000 | NEH | Royaume-Uni (R) |
| Canada (R) | NAA | 51 571 000 | 99.1 | 95.1 | 97.2 | 89.3 | 91.2 | 52 999 400 | 101.6 | 119.5 | 104.5 | 106.0 | 101.1 | 53 598 000 | NEH | Canada (R) |
| | AAA | 11 276 500 | 96.6 | 97.1 | 97.1 | 92.6 | 96.6 | 11 294 700 | 102.3 | 120.5 | 112.6 | 113.0 | 107.9 | 12 184 200 | AEH | |
| Australia (R) | NAA | | | | | | | 2 122 200 | 138.7 | 157.8 | 198.6 | 207.2 | 137.1 | 2 138 831 | NEH | Australie (R) |
| New Zealand (R) | NAA | | 70.0 | | 79.9 | | 104.9 | 1 560 000 | 126.3 | 146.5 | 157.0 | 144.8 | | | NEH | Nouvelle-Zélande (R) |
| Yugoslavia (N) | NAA | 438 231 | 75.0 | 55.2 | 56.5 | 60.1 | 73.9 | 604 225 | 98.4 | 62.5 | 96.0 | 119.2 | 104.8 | 633 199 | NEH | Yougoslavie (N) |
| | AAA | 191 466 | 79.9 | 62.6 | 62.2 | 59.7 | 73.9 | 226 756 | 105.1 | 64.9 | 102.2 | 130.3 | 113.8 | 257 978 | AEH | |

AAA  Arrivals in all means of accommodation
NAA  Nights in all means of accommodation
(R)  Tourist count by country of residence
(N)  Tourist count by country of nationality

AEH  Arrivées dans l'ensemble des moyens d'hébergement
NEH  Nuitées dans l'ensemble des moyens d'hébergement
(R)  Recensement des touristes par pays de résidence
(N)  Recensement des touristes par pays de nationalité

Table/Tableau 35

# ARRIVALS OF FOREIGN TOURISTS/VISITORS AT FRONTIERS
# ARRIVÉES DE TOURISTES/VISITEURS ÉTRANGERS AUX FRONTIÈRES

From France  
1984=100

En provenance de la France  
1984=100

| | T/V | Volume 1978 | 1979 | 1980 | 1981 | 1982 | 1983 | Volume 1984 | 1985 | 1986 | 1987 | 1988 | 1989 | Volume 1989 | T/V | |
|---|---|---|---|---|---|---|---|---|---|---|---|---|---|---|---|---|
| Finland (R) | V | 13 036 | | | | | | 405 907 | 108.7 | 115.4 | 125.6 | 115.5 | 117.8 | 478 031 | V | Finlande (R) |
| Greece (N) | T | 347 627 | 78.7 | 73.9 | 73.0 | 82.6 | 73.8 | | 92.5 | 115.9 | 109.6 | 126.7 | | | T | Grèce (N) |
| Iceland (N) | T | 3 438 | 79.0 | 89.8 | 87.7 | 91.4 | 80.9 | 4 846 | 114.8 | 106.2 | 137.0 | 132.1 | 168.9 | 8 187 | T | Islande (N) |
| Ireland (R) | V | 36 495 | | | | | | 81 000 | | | | | 167.9 | 136 000 | V | Irlande (R) |
| Italy (N) | V | 6 121 400 | 81.9 | 87.5 | 106.7 | 115.8 | 93.3 | 8 462 438 | 102.9 | 101.3 | 106.9 | 106.1 | 111.0 | 9 390 152 | V | Italie (N) |
| Norway (N) | V | 162 600 | 53.8 | 71.4 | 88.2 | 89.3 | 100.9 | 312 783 | 102.4 | 108.9 | 132.3 | 180.8 | 195.3 | 610 896 | V | Norvège (N) |
| Portugal (N) | T | 179 562 | 56.1 | 72.7 | 73.2 | 88.3 | 100.4 | 326 646 | 106.3 | 107.2 | 133.1 | 181.7 | 198.0 | 646 847 | T | Portugal (N) |
| Spain (N) | V | 11 994 407 | 107.6 | 100.8 | 106.8 | 108.9 | 103.5 | 9 981 673 | 110.2 | 113.0 | 116.9 | 121.1 | 120.2 | 11 994 421 | V | Espagne (N) |
| Turkey (N) | V | 140 580 | 116.5 | 84.5 | 93.6 | 96.1 | 85.3 | 103 359 | 145.1 | 139.3 | 163.1 | 238.8 | 274.3 | 283 545 | V | Turquie (N) |
| United Kingdom (R) | V | 1 435 000 | 84.4 | 98.2 | 86.6 | 93.1 | 92.9 | 1 631 700 | 99.3 | 107.6 | 123.1 | 120.7 | 138.2 | 2 254 300 | V | Royaume-Uni (R) |
| Canada (R) | T | 90 100 | 95.5 | 102.9 | 107.2 | 106.6 | 81.9 | 110 800 | 96.8 | 126.6 | 169.3 | 207.3 | 219.2 | 242 900 | T | Canada (R) |
| Canada (R) | V | 108 600 | 105.5 | 110.4 | 112.5 | 108.7 | 82.0 | 121 900 | 96.1 | 127.9 | 172.9 | 205.4 | 215.4 | 262 600 | V | |
| United States (R) | T | 259 818 | 93.8 | 109.1 | 124.3 | 128.0 | 92.2 | 330 660 | 101.5 | 132.9 | 164.7 | 187.0 | 197.7 | 653 685 | T | États-Unis (R) |
| Australia (R) | V | 5 600 | 67.0 | 72.5 | 74.8 | 91.5 | 89.3 | 11 200 | 107.1 | 124.1 | 152.7 | 187.5 | 179.5 | 20 100 | V | Australie (R) |
| Japan (N) | V | 23 038 | 65.2 | 75.8 | 81.0 | 86.8 | 84.5 | 34 109 | 116.3 | 103.6 | 109.0 | 118.6 | 138.6 | 47 261 | V | Japon (N) |
| New Zealand (R) | T | 1 400 | 79.4 | 90.3 | 84.5 | 82.5 | 87.0 | 2 216 | 109.6 | 119.6 | 172.0 | 155.1 | 183.8 | 4 074 | T | Nouvelle-Zélande (R) |

V   Visitors (travellers in Turkey)  
T   Tourists  
(R)   Tourist count by country of residence  
(N)   Tourist count by country of nationality

V   Visiteurs (voyageurs en Turquie)  
T   Touristes  
(R)   Recensement des touristes par pays de résidence  
(N)   Recensement des touristes par pays de nationalité

111

# Table/Tableau 36
## ARRIVALS AND NIGHTS OF FOREIGN TOURISTS AT/IN HOTELS
## ARRIVÉES ET NUITÉES DE TOURISTES ÉTRANGERS DANS L'HÔTELLERIE

**From France / En provenance de la France**
**1984=100**

| Country / Pays | AH/NH | Volume 1978 | 1979 | 1980 | 1981 | 1982 | 1983 | Volume 1984 | 1985 | 1986 | 1987 | 1988 | 1989 | Volume 1989 |
|---|---|---|---|---|---|---|---|---|---|---|---|---|---|---|
| Austria (R) / Autriche (R) | NH | 883 830 | 55.7 | 64.8 | 78.3 | 88.0 | 77.5 | 1 791 041 | 106.7 | 118.5 | 116.5 | 115.8 | 126.7 | 2 269 067 |
| | AH | 291 769 | 63.8 | 73.5 | 86.6 | 91.2 | 78.8 | 498 797 | 105.4 | 115.2 | 111.2 | 112.3 | 124.3 | 620 227 |
| Belgium (R) / Belgique (R) | NH | 488 339 | 95.8 | 103.1 | 99.6 | 107.5 | 91.3 | 529 427 | 109.0 | 111.9 | 114.4 | 124.1 | 134.5 | 711 885 |
| | AH | 83 100 | 104.6 | 105.7 | 106.2 | 111.1 | 89.2 | 80 900 | 104.1 | 94.7 | 94.8 | 112.9 | 102.2 | 82 700 |
| Denmark (N) / Danemark (N) | NH | 37 670 | 74.1 | 79.6 | 79.7 | 86.3 | 79.0 | 58 842 | 98.3 | 92.4 | 105.2 | 112.9 | 121.1 | 71 269 |
| Finland (R) / Finlande (R) | NH | | | | | | | | | | | | | |
| Germany (R) / Allemagne (R) | NH | 995 793 | 102.3 | 105.1 | 109.0 | 101.8 | 88.5 | 1 051 455 | 106.0 | 110.6 | 112.9 | 116.2 | 132.5 | 1 393 211 |
| | AH | 543 918 | 101.2 | 105.1 | 107.5 | 101.9 | 88.8 | 564 031 | 105.4 | 108.7 | 110.4 | 113.4 | 128.7 | 725 665 |
| Greece (N) / Grèce (N) | NH | 1 893 645 | 86.9 | 83.5 | 80.9 | 87.6 | 73.3 | 2 319 078 | 113.7 | 104.1 | 110.0 | 105.4 | | |
| | AH | 648 140 | 87.9 | 84.4 | 82.3 | 89.9 | 73.0 | 759 292 | 106.0 | 100.5 | 102.5 | 95.1 | | |
| Ireland (R) / Irlande (R) | NH | | | | | | | | | | | | | 470 000 |
| | AH | | | | | | | | | | | | | 77 000 |
| Italy (N) / Italie (N) | NH | 4 443 599 | 108.1 | 109.8 | 102.2 | 116.5 | 94.4 | 5 054 166 | 104.1 | 110.6 | 113.6 | 109.4 | | |
| | AH | 1 349 488 | 103.5 | 106.3 | 95.8 | 110.2 | 90.1 | 1 626 147 | 101.6 | 106.6 | 110.9 | 110.4 | | |
| Luxembourg (R) | NH | | | | | 115.0 | 92.2 | 59 446 | 111.7 | 115.6 | 127.7 | 143.0 | | |
| | AH | | | | | 132.2 | 93.3 | 32 885 | 109.6 | 118.0 | 128.4 | 146.1 | | |
| Netherlands (R) / Pays-Bas (R) | NH | 361 413 | 99.8 | 110.1 | 106.3 | 112.1 | 87.2 | 395 460 | 101.7 | 112.7 | 116.3 | 112.5 | 122.5 | 464 700 |
| | AH | 208 385 | 96.6 | 101.3 | 98.6 | 107.3 | 85.7 | 232 826 | 100.4 | 110.0 | 113.3 | 110.7 | 111.3 | 259 100 |
| Norway (N) / Norvège (N) | NH | 83 119 | 75.2 | 80.7 | 85.8 | 89.5 | 72.0 | 102 290 | 99.6 | 107.3 | 116.8 | 117.2 | 136.8 | 139 979 |
| | AH | | | | | | | | | | | | | |
| Portugal (N) | NH | 426 179 | 90.0 | 79.9 | 82.3 | 88.4 | 79.1 | 652 463 | 107.3 | 114.8 | 104.0 | 113.5 | 122.5 | 799 573 |
| | AH | 148 424 | 75.6 | 78.0 | 78.9 | 97.6 | 79.5 | 212 536 | 103.1 | 117.9 | 119.3 | 131.8 | 139.8 | 297 166 |
| Spain (N) / Espagne (N) | NH | 8 448 655 | 97.1 | 86.8 | 95.7 | 100.6 | 94.6 | 6 363 778 | 103.7 | 97.5 | 107.0 | 111.8 | 110.8 | 7 049 426 |
| | AH | 2 025 681 | 100.9 | 90.7 | 100.3 | 101.2 | 100.8 | 1 377 518 | 94.1 | 113.1 | 121.6 | 125.5 | 126.7 | 1 745 352 |
| Sweden (N) / Suède (N) | NH | 84 071 | 113.9 | 106.2 | 101.6 | | 87.7 | 83 257 | 97.8 | 106.0 | 101.2 | 109.2 | 115.5 | 96 153 |
| Switzerland (R) / Suisse (R) | NH | 1 689 553 | 99.8 | 110.6 | 119.4 | 107.8 | 93.5 | 1 611 806 | 101.4 | 105.2 | 100.0 | 96.7 | 97.8 | 1 576 870 |
| | AH | 534 778 | 98.5 | 109.9 | 119.0 | 109.7 | 91.2 | 531 541 | 100.1 | 106.1 | 102.5 | 101.5 | 105.5 | 561 007 |
| Turkey (N) / Turquie (N) | NH | | | | | 72.4 | 86.6 | 351 276 | 154.6 | 179.5 | 241.3 | 319.1 | 322.8 | 1 133 899 |
| | AH | | | | | 67.6 | 84.7 | 192 266 | 154.8 | 179.8 | 236.6 | 282.1 | 341.1 | 655 816 |
| Australia (R) / Australie (R) | NH | | 75.4 | | 76.2 | 78.9 | | 90 500 | 92.4 | 93.9 | 115.5 | 141.9 | | |
| Japan (N) / Japon (N) | NH | 123 948 | 68.8 | 83.0 | 84.3 | 91.7 | 38.2 | 156 981 | 126.9 | | | | | |
| | AH | 46 032 | 74.8 | 84.6 | 85.0 | 91.2 | 37.0 | 58 521 | | | | | | |
| Yugoslavia (N) / Yougoslavie (N) | NH | | | | | | | | | | | | | 808 225 |
| | AH | | | | | | | | | | | | | 209 226 |

AH  Arrivals at hotels and similar establishments
NH  Nights in hotels and similar establishments
(R) Tourist count by country of residence
(N) Tourist count by country of nationality

AH  Arrivées dans les hôtels et les établissements assimilés
NH  Nuitées dans les hôtels et établissements assimilés
(R) Recensement des touristes par pays de résidence
(N) Recensement des touristes par pays de nationalité

Table/Tableau 37

# ARRIVALS AND NIGHTS OF FOREIGN TOURISTS AT/IN ALL MEANS OF ACCOMMODATION
# ARRIVÉES ET NUITÉES DE TOURISTES ÉTRANGERS DANS L'ENSEMBLE DES MOYENS D'HÉBERGEMENT

From France — 1984=100
En provenance de la France — 1984=100

| Country | AAA/NAA | Volume 1978 | 1979 | 1980 | 1981 | 1982 | 1983 | Volume 1984 | 1985 | 1986 | 1987 | 1988 | 1989 | Volume 1989 | AEH/NEH | |
|---|---|---|---|---|---|---|---|---|---|---|---|---|---|---|---|---|
| Austria (R) | NAA | 1 244 510 | 59.7 | 68.1 | 81.3 | 91.0 | 77.7 | 2 362 341 | 104.9 | 114.4 | 112.9 | 112.2 | 122.6 | 2 897 071 | NEH | Autriche (R) |
|  | AAA | 378 809 | 65.8 | 74.2 | 86.5 | 92.3 | 77.0 | 639 070 | 104.0 | 113.1 | 108.5 | 109.8 | 121.8 | 778 415 | AEH | |
| Belgium (R) | NAA | 814 054 | 72.1 | 91.4 | 92.4 | 105.1 | 93.6 | 956 212 | 98.8 | 101.7 | 101.7 | 105.7 | 98.2 | 939 061 | NEH | Belgique (R) |
| Denmark (N) | NAA | 154 025 | 98.7 | 96.0 | 98.7 | 103.2 | 76.2 | 149 341 | 96.3 | 88.1 | 91.8 | 92.9 | 103.1 | 154 036 | NEH | Danemark (N) |
| Germany (R) | NAA | 1 149 347 | 102.0 | 103.9 | 99.0 | 93.1 | 81.1 | 1 210 212 | 106.9 | 111.2 | 115.4 | 121.2 | 137.0 | 1 657 966 | NEH | Allemagne (R) |
|  | AAA | 570 849 | 96.7 | 99.5 | 99.7 | 94.5 | 82.3 | 617 894 | 105.5 | 108.9 | 111.3 | 115.6 | 130.8 | 808 102 | AEH | |
| Greece (N) | NAA | 2 374 136 | 89.2 | 86.3 | 84.7 | 91.3 | 76.1 | 2 778 399 | 100.7 | 92.9 | 98.3 | 93.4 |  |  | NEH | Grèce (N) |
|  | AAA | 779 104 | 90.3 | 86.8 | 83.8 | 91.9 | 75.0 | 886 962 | 98.8 | 94.8 | 96.0 | 89.3 |  |  | AEH | |
| Ireland (R) | NAA | 1 291 900 | 119.1 | 149.5 | 117.6 | 126.3 | 124.2 | 868 000 | 125.8 | 120.7 | 167.2 | 180.4 | 248.6 | 2 158 000 | NEH | Irlande (R) |
|  | AAA | 83 900 | 108.0 | 95.7 | 105.7 | 106.9 | 93.1 | 87 000 | 109.2 | 103.4 | 127.4 | 126.8 | 158.3 | 137 700 | AEH | |
| Italy (N) | NAA | 6 453 699 | 115.5 | 114.7 | 106.5 | 120.0 | 96.1 | 7 013 428 | 103.2 | 108.2 | 102.1 | 97.5 |  |  | NEH | Italie (N) |
|  | AAA | 1 606 455 | 104.3 | 106.6 | 96.4 | 110.6 | 90.4 | 1 945 977 | 101.9 | 105.9 | 108.1 | 107.2 |  |  | AEH | |
| Luxembourg (R) | NAA | 90 349 | 113.5 |  |  |  | 81.2 | 82 504 | 105.3 | 107.0 | 116.1 | 131.5 |  |  | NEH | Luxembourg (R) |
|  | AAA | 50 202 | 126.4 |  |  | 105.2 | 83.4 | 40 385 | 105.2 | 111.3 | 119.2 | 137.3 |  |  | AEH | |
| Netherlands (R) | NAA | 509 472 | 96.0 | 106.1 | 103.7 | 105.9 | 84.2 | 582 995 | 97.2 | 100.1 |  | 106.1 | 115.4 | 672 800 | NEH | Pays-Bas (R) |
|  | AAA | 285 798 | 94.0 | 102.0 | 99.7 | 105.2 | 84.5 | 326 724 | 97.7 | 101.5 |  | 111.3 | 107.0 | 349 500 | AEH | |
| Portugal (N) | NAA | 689 920 | 89.7 | 92.1 | 103.7 | 108.7 | 93.9 | 997 855 | 102.6 | 119.1 | 113.7 | 125.7 | 133.3 | 1 329 929 | NEH | Portugal (N) |
|  | AAA | 232 836 | 74.8 | 83.0 | 86.5 | 96.9 | 85.7 | 329 472 | 102.3 | 125.3 | 127.8 | 138.8 | 146.5 | 482 700 | AEH | |
| Spain (N) | NAA | 10 004 963 | 98.3 | 88.6 | 97.6 | 100.5 | 97.0 | 7 081 909 | 95.3 |  |  |  |  |  | NEH | Espagne (N) |
|  | AAA | 2 236 035 | 100.4 | 91.4 | 101.0 | 101.8 | 101.9 | 1 500 807 | 98.5 |  |  |  |  |  | AEH | |
| Sweden (N) | NAA | 147 644 | 102.4 | 94.2 | 95.5 | 96.4 | 78.8 | 150 698 | 94.7 | 104.1 | 97.4 | 100.4 | 110.6 | 166 622 | NEH | Suède (N) |
| Switzerland (R) | NAA | 2 628 100 | 95.8 | 111.2 | 121.7 | 116.2 | 97.7 | 2 496 400 | 100.4 | 106.7 | 104.4 | 99.9 | 100.1 | 2 498 000 | NEH | Suisse (R) |
|  | AAA | 675 900 | 93.8 | 106.8 | 117.0 | 110.9 | 91.7 | 700 200 | 99.6 | 106.7 | 103.6 | 102.8 | 106.2 | 743 300 | AEH | |
| Turkey (N) | NAA | 331 974 | 70.9 | 38.8 | 52.3 | 67.5 | 87.2 | 428 240 | 152.8 | 193.0 | 254.9 | 357.0 | 344.9 | 1 476 849 | NEH | Turquie (N) |
|  | AAA | 120 993 | 55.4 | 32.6 | 54.1 | 66.7 | 85.2 | 201 570 | 157.0 | 184.9 | 243.9 | 294.9 | 352.1 | 709 696 | AEH | |
| United Kingdom (R) | NAA | 11 000 000 | 93.3 | 91.8 | 80.0 | 85.6 | 86.5 | 13 043 000 | 98.1 | 93.6 | 128.1 | 107.7 | 124.7 | 16 259 000 | NEH | Royaume-Uni (R) |
| Canada (R) | NAA | 1 048 600 | 86.7 | 95.8 | 113.0 | 106.5 | 85.3 | 1 417 700 | 96.8 | 127.5 | 163.8 | 200.5 | 206.1 | 2 922 100 | NEH | Canada (R) |
|  | AAA | 90 100 | 95.5 | 102.9 | 107.2 | 106.6 | 81.9 | 110 800 | 96.8 | 126.6 | 169.3 | 207.3 | 219.2 | 242 900 | AEH | |
| Australia (R) | NAA |  | 58.3 |  | 73.8 |  | 65.7 | 225 400 | 77.8 | 85.5 | 105.1 | 129.1 |  |  | NEH | Australie (R) |
| Yugoslavia (N) | NAA | 1 432 410 | 86.6 | 79.9 | 89.8 | 89.8 | 69.8 | 1 499 969 | 102.9 | 96.0 | 90.9 | 81.5 | 74.8 | 1 122 647 | NEH | Yougoslavie (N) |
|  | AAA | 414 531 | 85.1 | 83.6 | 89.6 | 83.6 | 61.6 | 431 894 | 105.6 | 95.5 | 94.2 | 86.0 | 73.0 | 315 177 | AEH | |

AAA  Arrivals in all means of accommodation
NAA  Nights in all means of accommodation
(R)  Tourist count by country of residence
(N)  Tourist count by country of nationality

AEH  Arrivées dans l'ensemble des moyens d'hébergement
NEH  Nuitées dans l'ensemble des moyens d'hébergement
(R)  Recensement des touristes par pays de résidence
(N)  Recensement des touristes par pays de nationalité

# Table/Tableau 38

## ARRIVALS OF FOREIGN TOURISTS/VISITORS AT FRONTIERS
## ARRIVÉES DE TOURISTES/VISITEURS ÉTRANGERS AUX FRONTIÈRES

From Italy — *En provenance de l'Italie*
1984=100

| Country | T/V | Volume 1978 | 1979 | 1980 | 1981 | 1982 | 1983 | Volume 1984 | 1985 | 1986 | 1987 | 1988 | 1989 | Volume 1989 | T/V | |
|---|---|---|---|---|---|---|---|---|---|---|---|---|---|---|---|---|
| Finland (R) | V | 6 438 | | | | | | | | | | | | | V | Finlande (R) |
| France (R) | T | 1 295 000 | 55.9 | 61.3 | 54.6 | 78.6 | 86.2 | 2 544 000 | 104.0 | 110.0 | 124.1 | 135.3 | 173.2 | 569 000 | T | France (R) |
| Greece (N) | T | 214 678 | 80.5 | 60.0 | 68.6 | 68.1 | 99.7 | 328 598 | 110.8 | 133.9 | 141.5 | 165.6 | | | T | Grèce (N) |
| Iceland (N) | T | 715 | 78.2 | 90.2 | 79.2 | 87.1 | 101.5 | 1 037 | 112.8 | 204.3 | 260.3 | 272.1 | | | T | Islande (N) |
| Norway (N) | V | 7 126 | | | | | | | | | | | | | V | Norvège (N) |
| Portugal (N) | T | 38 700 | 76.0 | 76.1 | 79.0 | 91.8 | 90.8 | 59 443 | 139.2 | 152.5 | 202.4 | 233.5 | 281.2 | 167 179 | T | Portugal (N) |
| | V | 72 396 | 97.7 | 101.3 | 95.2 | 101.0 | 92.1 | 71 760 | 130.2 | 151.3 | 187.3 | 215.6 | 258.0 | 185 154 | V | |
| Spain (N) | V | 477 711 | 54.3 | 59.3 | 68.6 | 80.8 | 82.2 | 814 303 | 125.5 | 133.9 | 146.5 | 163.7 | 185.6 | 1 511 618 | V | Espagne (N) |
| Turkey (N) | V | 88 494 | 122.9 | 96.0 | 102.8 | 67.7 | 87.4 | 65 856 | 113.6 | 133.1 | 155.4 | 219.1 | 234.0 | 154 083 | V | Turquie (N) |
| United Kingdom (R) | V | 358 000 | 85.8 | 86.0 | 86.2 | 83.7 | 96.5 | 474 900 | 104.1 | 104.0 | 143.8 | 139.2 | 147.4 | 700 100 | V | Royaume-Uni (R) |
| Canada (R) | T | 43 100 | 85.7 | 93.2 | 95.9 | 88.5 | 85.9 | 53 200 | 103.8 | 122.6 | 144.9 | 162.2 | 170.1 | 90 500 | T | Canada (R) |
| | V | 54 100 | 93.6 | 100.3 | 100.3 | 94.8 | 87.8 | 65 600 | 99.4 | 122.7 | 157.8 | 164.0 | 163.7 | 107 400 | V | |
| United States (R) | V | 153 002 | 81.7 | 93.3 | 105.0 | 106.4 | 90.9 | 218 379 / | 100.9 | 122.8 | 146.0 | 163.3 | 162.5 | 354 920 | T | États-Unis (R) |
| Australia (R) | V | 9 100 | 79.1 | 91.7 | 90.7 | 90.2 | 89.6 | 13 400 | 108.2 | 129.1 | 144.0 | 188.1 | 153.0 | 20 500 | V | Australie (R) |
| Japan (N) | V | 11 883 | 67.8 | 79.2 | 93.3 | 87.2 | 90.6 | 15 706 | 137.4 | 119.8 | 132.9 | 149.4 | 176.1 | 27 665 | V | Japon (N) |
| New Zealand (R) | T | 740 | 98.3 | 117.2 | 105.0 | 95.8 | 90.4 | 956 | 131.8 | 179.1 | 273.1 | 294.5 | 274.9 | 2 628 | T | Nouvelle-Zélande (R) |

V    Visitors (travellers in Turkey)    Visiteurs (voyageurs en Turquie)
T    Tourists    Touristes
(R)    Tourist count by country of residence    Recensement des touristes par pays de résidence
(N)    Tourist count by country of nationality    Recensement des touristes par pays de nationalité

# Table/Tableau 39

## ARRIVALS AND NIGHTS OF FOREIGN TOURISTS AT/IN HOTELS
## ARRIVÉES ET NUITÉES DE TOURISTES ÉTRANGERS DANS L'HÔTELLERIE

*From Italy* 1984=100      *En provenance de l'Italie* 1984=100

| | AH/NH | Volume 1978 | 1979 | 1980 | 1981 | 1982 | 1983 | Volume 1984 | 1985 | 1986 | 1987 | 1988 | 1989 | Volume 1989 | AH/NH | |
|---|---|---|---|---|---|---|---|---|---|---|---|---|---|---|---|---|
| Austria (R) | NH | 428 478 | 47.2 | 57.8 | 68.4 | 77.1 | 83.4 | 1 018 728 | 106.5 | 129.6 | 143.5 | 181.0 | 239.5 | 2 440 075 | NH | Autriche (R) |
| | AH | 204 434 | 51.1 | 62.2 | 71.2 | 77.7 | 83.2 | 451 187 | 104.7 | 127.1 | 140.5 | 173.8 | 220.3 | 994 132 | AH | |
| Belgium (R) | NH | 170 400 | 83.4 | 89.2 | 88.5 | 88.6 | 95.5 | 208 770 | 105.3 | 104.4 | 114.8 | 127.5 | 137.9 | 287 863 | NH | Belgique (R) |
| Denmark (N) | NH | 58 200 | 81.3 | 95.0 | 107.3 | 103.7 | 101.1 | 81 200 | 96.8 | 96.6 | 109.1 | 128.0 | 141.9 | 115 200 | NH | Danemark (N) |
| Finland (R) | NH | 20 962 | 53.4 | 67.4 | 68.6 | 84.1 | 88.4 | 44 950 | 104.6 | 112.5 | 149.7 | 182.1 | 193.3 | 86 910 | NH | Finlande (R) |
| France (R) | NH | 970 020 | 75.3 | 89.3 | 95.8 | 91.4 | 94.0 | 1 365 991 | 97.9 | 265.0 | 289.7 | 361.8 | 473.1 | 6 462 006 | NH | France (R) |
| | AH | 365 681 | 79.1 | 87.5 | 99.9 | 94.0 | 93.2 | 476 743 | 102.3 | 338.6 | 370.2 | 443.1 | 594.6 | 2 834 665 | AH | |
| Germany (R) | NH | 657 250 | 74.5 | 79.2 | 82.9 | 87.2 | 91.3 | 956 473 | 105.2 | 115.0 | 123.0 | 139.1 | 164.7 | 1 575 388 | NH | Allemagne (R) |
| | AH | 341 987 | 73.6 | 78.7 | 81.7 | 87.0 | 90.9 | 497 798 | 105.4 | 113.8 | 122.7 | 139.7 | 164.4 | 818 386 | AH | |
| Greece (N) | NH | 762 574 | 70.6 | 75.5 | 76.5 | 80.7 | 87.8 | 1 125 024 | 122.9 | 119.6 | 123.2 | 146.7 | | | NH | Grèce (N) |
| | AH | 257 689 | 67.1 | 70.9 | 72.7 | 78.4 | 89.8 | 388 525 | 113.8 | 111.9 | 128.6 | 128.1 | | | AH | |
| Luxembourg (R) | NH | | | | | | | | | | | | | | NH | Luxembourg (R) |
| | AH | | | | | | | | | | | | | | AH | |
| Netherlands (R) | NH | 149 711 | 81.5 | 92.8 | 97.2 | 99.5 | 90.5 | 212 230 | 104.9 | 126.7 | 146.6 | 170.4 | 193.8 | 411 200 | NH | Pays-Bas (R) |
| | AH | 72 161 | 77.6 | 83.0 | 90.4 | 93.9 | 89.0 | 100 723 | 108.2 | 124.6 | 141.7 | 163.7 | 207.4 | 208 900 | AH | |
| Portugal (N) | NH | 139 365 | 86.1 | 84.7 | 76.4 | 87.6 | 89.6 | 168 860 | 125.8 | 145.9 | 179.9 | 207.8 | 224.4 | 379 000 | NH | Portugal (N) |
| | AH | 43 003 | 68.8 | 74.0 | 70.1 | 81.5 | 89.3 | 64 342 | 125.9 | 147.2 | 184.4 | 209.5 | 228.9 | 147 306 | AH | |
| Spain (N) | NH | 1 489 293 | 28.3 | 30.4 | 40.1 | 50.8 | 66.2 | 3 585 835 | 114.1 | 108.6 | 120.3 | 129.7 | 127.9 | 4 587 802 | NH | Espagne (N) |
| | AH | 480 216 | 36.0 | 37.8 | 48.0 | 59.5 | 71.8 | 951 931 | 111.9 | 116.1 | 114.1 | 118.3 | 125.9 | 1 198 243 | AH | |
| Sweden (N) | NH | 52 002 | 76.3 | 83.0 | 86.4 | 93.6 | 89.4 | 70 115 | 108.5 | 112.6 | 136.6 | 136.8 | 168.1 | 117 855 | NH | Suède (N) |
| | AH | | | | | | | | | | | | | | AH | |
| Switzerland (R) | NH | 668 897 | 76.7 | 88.1 | 98.5 | 97.1 | 94.4 | 892 055 | 102.3 | 109.6 | 116.3 | 122.9 | 142.2 | 1 268 227 | NH | Suisse (R) |
| | AH | 328 454 | 75.9 | 87.5 | 96.2 | 94.8 | 94.3 | 442 321 | 102.5 | 110.0 | 115.5 | 121.0 | 138.9 | 614 178 | AH | |
| Turkey (N) | NH | | | | | 55.7 | 93.7 | 190 200 | 114.1 | 126.0 | 165.3 | 205.7 | 199.0 | 378 578 | NH | Turquie (N) |
| | AH | | | | | 55.9 | 91.5 | 89 444 | 118.6 | 127.9 | 170.5 | 209.3 | 220.8 | 197 465 | AH | |
| Australia (R) | NH | | 95.4 | | 103.6 | | 66.3 | 71 800 | 130.1 | 181.6 | 202.6 | 264.5 | | | NH | Australie (R) |
| Japan (N) | NH | 58 734 | | | | | | | | | | | | | NH | Japon (N) |
| | AH | 18 943 | | | | | | | | | | | | | AH | |
| Yugoslavia (N) | NH | | | | | | | | | | | | | 2 628 237 | NH | Yougoslavie (N) |
| | AH | | | | | | | | | | | | | 875 132 | AH | |

AH   Arrivals at hotels and similar establishments
NH   Nights in hotels and similar establishments
(R)   Tourist count by country of residence
(N)   Tourist count by country of nationality

AH   Arrivées dans les hôtels et les établissements assimilés
NH   Nuitées dans les hôtels et établissements assimilés
(R)   Recensement des touristes par pays de résidence
(N)   Recensement des touristes par pays de nationalité

## Table/Tableau 40

## ARRIVALS AND NIGHTS OF FOREIGN TOURISTS AT/IN ALL MEANS OF ACCOMMODATION
## ARRIVÉES ET NUITÉES DE TOURISTES ÉTRANGERS DANS L'ENSEMBLE DES MOYENS D'HÉBERGEMENT

*From Italy* — 1984=100   *En provenance de l'Italie* — 1984=100

| Country | AAA/NAA | Volume 1978 | 1979 | 1980 | 1981 | 1982 | 1983 | Volume 1984 | 1985 | 1986 | 1987 | 1988 | 1989 | Volume 1989 | AEH/NEH | |
|---|---|---|---|---|---|---|---|---|---|---|---|---|---|---|---|---|
| Austria (R) | NAA | 516 862 | 47.5 | 56.4 | 66.7 | 74.6 | 84.4 | 1 245 719 | 101.5 | 121.9 | 135.7 | 167.9 | 223.7 | 2 786 978 | NEH | Autriche (R) |
| | AAA | 231 820 | 49.0 | 58.7 | 66.8 | 73.7 | 80.4 | 540 344 | 99.0 | 118.7 | 131.0 | 160.3 | 203.8 | 1 101 380 | AEH | |
| Belgium (R) | NAA | 199 361 | 83.4 | 88.0 | 89.4 | 88.9 | 95.2 | 239 640 | 104.3 | 103.4 | 112.5 | 127.0 | 136.1 | 326 226 | NEH | Belgique (R) |
| Denmark (N) | AAA | 75 673 | 74.4 | 86.8 | 98.1 | 98.9 | 100.8 | 119 973 | 100.7 | 98.1 | 114.8 | 127.9 | 145.8 | 174 917 | AEH | Danemark (N) |
| France (R) | NAA | 8 030 000 | 40.9 | 46.2 | 41.2 | 83.4 | 89.3 | 20 255 000 | 102.3 | 114.3 | 131.6 | 139.2 | 139.2 | 28 200 000 | NEH | France (R) |
| | AAA | 1 295 000 | 55.9 | 61.3 | 54.6 | 78.6 | 86.2 | 2 544 000 | 104.0 | 110.0 | 124.1 | 135.3 | | | AEH | |
| Germany (R) | NAA | 699 175 | 75.9 | 79.5 | 81.0 | 85.3 | 89.1 | 998 288 | 106.0 | 116.7 | 124.9 | 141.6 | 166.8 | 1 664 890 | NEH | Allemagne (R) |
| | AAA | 349 913 | 72.9 | 77.6 | 79.7 | 85.0 | 88.6 | 512 886 | 105.7 | 114.8 | 124.0 | 141.3 | 165.8 | 850 151 | AEH | |
| Greece (N) | NAA | 1 001 539 | 67.3 | 75.1 | 75.0 | 78.6 | 82.8 | 1 470 827 | 106.9 | 103.2 | 119.4 | 121.9 | 122.4 | 1 800 000 | NEH | Grèce (N) |
| | AAA | 335 496 | 69.1 | 74.6 | 73.7 | 80.1 | 90.4 | 478 830 | 106.2 | 103.5 | 74.8 | 114.4 | | | AEH | |
| Luxembourg (R) | NAA | | | | | | | | | | | | | | NEH | Luxembourg (R) |
| | AAA | | | | | | | | | | | | | | AEH | |
| Netherlands (R) | NAA | 189 992 | 76.1 | 85.6 | 88.8 | 92.8 | 89.9 | 298 128 | 99.8 | 112.2 | | 155.0 | 179.1 | 533 800 | NEH | Pays-Bas (R) |
| | AAA | 89 442 | 72.3 | 78.3 | 84.4 | 89.4 | 87.8 | 140 334 | 103.8 | 112.0 | | 152.4 | 184.8 | 259 300 | AEH | |
| Portugal (N) | NAA | 163 659 | 87.3 | 96.5 | 96.3 | 106.5 | 97.9 | 202 192 | 132.9 | 159.1 | 184.1 | 211.0 | 229.3 | 463 722 | NEH | Portugal (N) |
| | AAA | 52 939 | 72.9 | 79.8 | 74.8 | 86.1 | 93.3 | 76 372 | 133.3 | 160.0 | 188.1 | 211.7 | 233.1 | 178 013 | AEH | |
| Spain (N) | NAA | 1 489 293 | 28.3 | 30.4 | 40.1 | 50.8 | 66.2 | 3 585 835 | 114.1 | | | | | | NEH | Espagne (N) |
| | AAA | 480 216 | 36.0 | 37.8 | 48.0 | 59.5 | 71.8 | 951 931 | 111.9 | | | | | | AEH | |
| Sweden (N) | NAA | 53 705 | 73.1 | 79.4 | 84.1 | 91.0 | 88.2 | 78 415 | 105.8 | 111.8 | 138.0 | 140.6 | 173.2 | 135 843 | NEH | Suède (N) |
| Switzerland (R) | NAA | 1 002 900 | 72.6 | 82.7 | 93.8 | 94.3 | 94.6 | 1 205 400 | 101.8 | 109.6 | 116.9 | 126.2 | 145.0 | 1 748 400 | NEH | Suisse (R) |
| | AAA | 373 500 | 72.5 | 84.4 | 93.5 | 93.3 | 93.9 | 516 700 | 102.6 | 110.2 | 115.2 | 121.4 | 138.1 | 713 700 | AEH | |
| Turkey (N) | NAA | 154 074 | 48.9 | 35.3 | 52.8 | 52.8 | 92.4 | 206 545 | 114.3 | 128.0 | 183.5 | 238.2 | 237.1 | 489 819 | NEH | Turquie (N) |
| | AAA | 50 945 | 43.5 | 32.8 | 49.4 | 54.8 | 90.4 | 92 024 | 118.0 | 127.2 | 187.2 | 232.0 | 244.9 | 225 353 | AEH | |
| United Kingdom (R) | NAA | 5 177 000 | 99.4 | 104.6 | 91.0 | 84.1 | 102.5 | 6 211 000 | 112.1 | 98.7 | 148.7 | 137.0 | 132.0 | 8 198 000 | NEH | Royaume-Uni (R) |
| Canada (R) | NAA | 559 800 | 91.8 | 80.7 | 92.2 | 100.4 | 74.2 | 731 400 | 103.3 | 114.4 | 136.7 | 146.4 | 137.6 | 1 006 700 | NEH | Canada (R) |
| Australia (R) | NAA | | 84.9 | | 108.8 | 100.2 | 100.2 | 132 400 | 108.1 | 228.1 | 254.5 | 332.3 | | | NEH | Australie (R) |
| Yugoslavia (N) | NAA | 2 518 842 | 56.3 | 64.8 | 69.0 | 71.6 | 77.6 | 4 160 557 | 119.4 | 111.7 | 119.7 | 129.0 | 147.7 | 6 144 277 | NEH | Yougoslavie (N) |
| | AAA | 667 574 | 61.2 | 69.5 | 71.3 | 69.5 | 74.9 | 958 847 | 115.6 | 111.9 | 123.6 | 129.1 | 148.5 | 1 424 021 | AEH | |

AAA  Arrivals in all means of accommodation
NAA  Nights in all means of accommodation
(R)  Tourist count by country of residence
(N)  Tourist count by country of nationality

AEH  Arrivées dans l'ensemble des moyens d'hébergement
NEH  Nuitées dans l'ensemble des moyens d'hébergement
(R)  Recensement des touristes par pays de résidence
(N)  Recensement des touristes par pays de nationalité

## Table/Tableau 41

### ARRIVALS OF FOREIGN TOURISTS/VISITORS AT FRONTIERS
### ARRIVÉES DE TOURISTES/VISITEURS ÉTRANGERS AUX FRONTIÈRES

**From Japan** *1984=100* — **En provenance du Japon** *1984=100*

| | T/V | Volume 1978 | 1979 | 1980 | 1981 | 1982 | 1983 | Volume 1984 | 1985 | 1986 | 1987 | 1988 | 1989 | Volume 1989 | T/V | |
|---|---|---|---|---|---|---|---|---|---|---|---|---|---|---|---|---|
| Finland (R) | V | 4 953 | 82.7 | 78.4 | 87.3 | | | | 103.5 | 99.6 | 112.2 | 129.8 | | | V | Finlande (R) |
| France (R) | T | 360 000 | | | | | | 510 000 | | | | | | | T | France (R) |
| Greece (N) | T | 61 451 | 149.2 | 87.5 | 86.9 | 86.5 | 94.9 | 86 476 | 107.3 | 98.4 | 106.4 | 121.4 | 120.3 | 104 000 | T | Grèce (N) |
| Iceland (N) | T | 323 | 69.9 | 67.9 | 62.9 | 71.6 | 84.0 | 539 | 132.8 | 159.0 | 185.5 | 184.2 | | | T | Islande (N) |
| Italy (N) | V | 333 900 | 112.6 | 102.5 | 77.3 | 89.2 | 96.2 | 340 209 | 98.5 | 118.0 | 113.1 | 113.1 | 134.2 | 456 700 | V | Italie (N) |
| Norway (N) | V | 9 300 | 67.1 | 63.3 | 80.7 | 73.1 | 81.5 | 16 100 | 114.2 | 136.7 | 171.3 | 175.1 | 187.0 | 30 101 | V | Norvège (N) |
| Portugal (N) | T | 12 306 | 65.6 | 65.9 | 75.8 | 70.9 | 73.6 | 19 514 | 102.4 | 119.1 | 146.5 | 152.0 | 164.6 | 32 121 | T | Portugal (N) |
| Spain (N) | V | 70 211 | 65.4 | 81.1 | 79.9 | 73.9 | 87.5 | 108 563 | 116.7 | 111.5 | 120.2 | 156.8 | 199.5 | 216 535 | V | Espagne (N) |
| Turkey (N) | V | 4 615 | 56.6 | 52.6 | 53.2 | 48.0 | 59.6 | 13 060 | 128.7 | 128.2 | 161.3 | 214.5 | 247.3 | 32 298 | V | Turquie (N) |
| United Kingdom (R) | V | 132 000 | 69.5 | 81.0 | 81.7 | 79.5 | 84.9 | 200 600 | 105.0 | 102.4 | 148.2 | 193.5 | 249.0 | 499 500 | V | Royaume-Uni (R) |
| Canada (R) | T | 102 200 | 89.3 | 90.8 | 84.0 | 85.0 | 86.3 | 135 200 | 107.8 | 145.8 | 184.3 | 239.7 | 286.2 | 387 000 | T | Canada (R) |
| United States (R) | V | 127 800 | 97.7 | 100.0 | 90.3 | 86.0 | 85.5 | 162 300 | 107.5 | 144.9 | 192.1 | 249.3 | 285.1 | 462 700 | V | États-Unis (R) |
| United States (R) | T | 886 447 | 73.7 | 84.7 | 95.7 | 101.5 | 90.7 | 1 414 909 | 105.7 | 118.8 | 150.4 | 179.1 | 217.7 | 3 080 396 | T | États-Unis (R) |
| Australia (R) | V | 34 000 | 47.3 | 55.5 | 61.1 | 68.7 | 81.7 | 87 900 | 122.4 | 165.6 | 245.3 | 400.8 | 397.6 | 349 500 | V | Australie (R) |
| New Zealand (R) | T | 13 288 | 37.5 | 45.8 | 61.4 | 65.3 | 77.5 | 41 888 | 120.0 | 149.6 | 181.8 | 223.9 | 232.3 | 97 322 | T | Nouvelle-Zélande (R) |

V  Visitors (travellers in Austria, Germany and Turkey)  
T  Tourists  
(R)  Tourist count by country of residence  
(N)  Tourist count by country of nationality  
1.  Estimates

V  Visiteurs (voyageurs en Allemagne, en Autriche et en Turquie)  
T  Touristes  
(R)  Recensement des touristes par pays de résidence  
(N)  Recensement des touristes par pays de nationalité  
1.  Estimations

## Table/Tableau 42

## ARRIVALS AND NIGHTS OF FOREIGN TOURISTS AT/IN HOTELS
## ARRIVÉES ET NUITÉES DE TOURISTES ÉTRANGERS DANS L'HÔTELLERIE

From Japan — En provenance du Japon — 1984=100

| Country | AH/NH | Volume 1978 | 1979 | 1980 | 1981 | 1982 | 1983 | Volume 1984 | 1985 | 1986 | 1987 | 1988 | 1989 | Volume 1989 | AH/NH | Pays |
|---|---|---|---|---|---|---|---|---|---|---|---|---|---|---|---|---|
| Austria (R) | NH | 119 225 | 65.6 | 64.4 | 78.8 | 84.0 | 91.9 | 197 654 | 118.4 | 116.5 | 156.0 | 162.2 | 187.5 | 370 537 | NH | Autriche (R) |
|  | AH | 55 770 | 61.7 | 57.7 | 68.7 | 79.0 | 85.3 | 106 355 | 118.1 | 111.5 | 153.2 | 156.3 | 180.5 | 191 980 | AH |  |
| Belgium (R) | NH | 79 600 | 107.9 | 79.7 | 95.7 | 93.0 | 85.0 | 85 085 | 110.7 | 112.0 | 125.0 | 141.7 | 179.8 | 153 011 | NH | Belgique (R) |
| Denmark (N) | NH | 20 382 | 53.9 | 103.1 | 100.3 | 93.5 | 103.3 | 79 500 | 98.1 | 92.1 | 104.3 | 135.5 | 149.3 | 118 700 | NH | Danemark (N) |
| Finland (R) | NH |  | 109.5 | 54.0 | 54.4 | 57.5 | 87.9 | 41 872 | 105.5 | 92.1 | 122.6 | 133.2 | 145.3 | 60 855 | NH | Finlande (R) |
| France (R) | NH | 1 135 432 | 99.5 | 112.7 | 107.8 | 104.6 | 106.7 | 1 073 741 | 95.9 | 111.3 | 127.5 | 158.6 | 267.6 | 2 873 372 | NH | France (R) |
|  | AH | 418 112 | 76.6 | 96.6 | 99.4 | 104.9 | 102.1 | 447 843 | 105.0 | 121.4 | 136.7 | 172.4 | 280.6 | 1 256 481 | AH |  |
| Germany (R) | NH | 460 060 | 75.2 | 75.9 | 86.3 | 90.5 | 91.7 | 696 173 | 118.6 | 120.6 | 135.1 | 145.1 | 174.7 | 1 216 423 | NH | Allemagne (R) |
|  | AH | 250 011 | 98.0 | 72.2 | 82.0 | 87.4 | 89.0 | 397 840 | 119.2 | 120.4 | 143.1 | 150.5 | 184.9 | 735 657 | AH |  |
| Greece (N) | NH | 174 182 | 101.4 | 87.6 | 85.8 | 90.7 | 92.5 | 237 199 | 108.4 | 87.4 | 100.5 | 110.2 |  |  | NH | Grèce (N) |
|  | AH | 68 440 |  | 87.5 | 87.5 | 89.5 | 93.3 | 98 665 | 112.7 | 93.1 | 107.0 | 121.5 |  |  | AH |  |
| Italy (N) | NH | 441 402 | 89.5 | 75.5 | 80.2 | 91.4 | 97.7 | 591 790 | 98.5 | 110.7 | 159.2 | 194.3 |  |  | NH | Italie (N) |
|  | AH | 209 240 | 90.0 | 78.8 | 78.3 | 88.3 | 92.9 | 282 319 | 98.4 | 114.4 | 167.7 | 202.7 |  |  | AH |  |
| Luxembourg (R) | NH |  |  |  |  |  |  |  |  |  |  |  |  |  | NH | Luxembourg (R) |
|  | AH |  |  |  |  |  |  |  |  |  |  |  |  |  | AH |  |
| Netherlands (R) | NH | 114 719 | 98.2 | 100.1 | 102.3 | 118.0 | 105.3 | 126 498 | 121.1 | 123.2 | 117.6 | 126.6 | 128.5 | 162 600 | NH | Pays-Bas (R) |
|  | AH | 60 974 | 90.3 | 86.1 | 92.4 | 109.1 | 93.4 | 70 799 | 108.8 | 104.1 | 111.9 | 118.5 | 119.2 | 84 400 | AH |  |
| Norway (N) | NH | 29 370 | 61.6 | 64.9 | 62.7 | 66.1 | 84.2 | 62 958 | 102.2 | 73.1 | 119.3 | 106.0 | 127.2 | 80 093 | NH | Norvège (N) |
| Portugal (N) | NH | 27 185 | 56.4 | 62.2 | 68.0 | 66.2 | 72.3 | 50 000 | 99.2 | 106.4 | 129.3 | 144.4 | 146.6 | 73 312 | NH | Portugal (N) |
|  | AH | 11 188 | 48.4 | 50.6 | 58.0 | 59.8 | 69.2 | 22 991 | 100.5 | 106.8 | 132.3 | 140.5 | 144.3 | 33 170 | AH |  |
| Spain (N) | NH | 299 569 | 81.7 | 75.4 | 91.7 | 91.0 | 92.4 | 338 978 | 115.3 | 124.4 | 174.2 | 188.6 | 252.8 | 857 065 | NH | Espagne (N) |
|  | AH | 129 655 | 72.7 | 68.6 | 81.6 | 79.2 | 83.8 | 170 704 | 120.3 | 136.1 | 191.9 | 208.8 | 276.4 | 471 807 | AH |  |
| Sweden (N) | NH | 44 818 | 91.2 | 95.1 | 86.5 | 95.2 | 89.1 | 58 480 | 98.8 | 91.3 | 106.3 | 127.0 | 139.5 | 81 581 | NH | Suède (N) |
| Switzerland (R) | NH | 354 019 | 82.6 | 81.1 | 84.8 | 90.6 | 97.9 | 496 904 | 103.8 | 108.1 | 125.7 | 131.4 | 157.4 | 782 234 | NH | Suisse (R) |
|  | AH | 197 871 | 81.9 | 77.0 | 80.8 | 87.0 | 95.2 | 280 931 | 104.9 | 111.5 | 131.4 | 141.6 | 168.1 | 472 268 | AH |  |
| Turkey (N) | NH |  |  |  |  | 73.0 | 105.1 | 44 744 | 160.2 | 199.3 | 219.7 | 261.6 | 301.1 | 134 742 | NH | Turquie (N) |
|  | AH |  |  |  |  | 63.2 | 103.5 | 22 047 | 149.5 | 195.4 | 236.3 | 285.9 | 336.4 | 74 163 | AH |  |
| Australia (R) | NH |  | 33.9 |  | 36.7 |  | 69.1 | 545 000 | 116.7 | 133.0 | 197.0 | 321.9 |  |  | NH | Australie (R) |
| Yugoslavia (N) | NH |  |  |  |  |  |  |  |  |  |  |  |  | 31 175 | NH | Yougoslavie (N) |
|  | AH |  |  |  |  |  |  |  |  |  |  |  |  | 15 005 | AH |  |

AH   Arrivals at hotels and similar establishments  
NH   Nights in hotels and similar establishments  
(R)   Tourist count by country of residence  
(N)   Tourist count by country of nationality  

AH   Arrivées dans les hôtels et les établissements assimilés  
NH   Nuitées dans les hôtels et établissements assimilés  
(R)   Recensement des touristes par pays de résidence  
(N)   Recensement des touristes par pays de nationalité

## Table/Tableau 43

### ARRIVALS AND NIGHTS OF FOREIGN TOURISTS AT/IN ALL MEANS OF ACCOMMODATION
### ARRIVÉES ET NUITÉES DE TOURISTES ÉTRANGERS DANS L'ENSEMBLE DES MOYENS D'HÉBERGEMENT

*From Japan* — 1984=100  
*En provenance du Japon* — 1984=100

| Country | AAA/NAA | Volume 1978 | 1979 | 1980 | 1981 | 1982 | 1983 | Volume 1984 | 1985 | 1986 | 1987 | 1988 | 1989 | Volume 1989 | AEH/NEH | Pays |
|---|---|---|---|---|---|---|---|---|---|---|---|---|---|---|---|---|
| Austria (R) | NAA | 119 225 | 65.6 | 64.4 | 78.8 | 84.0 | 91.9 | 197 654 | 118.4 | 116.5 | 156.0 | 162.2 | 187.5 | 370 537 | NEH | Autriche (R) |
| | AAA | 55 770 | 61.7 | 57.7 | 68.7 | 79.0 | 85.3 | 106 355 | 118.1 | 111.5 | 153.2 | 156.3 | 180.5 | 191 980 | AEH | |
| Belgium (R) | NAA | | | 81.0 | 94.8 | 91.3 | 84.4 | 88 665 | 110.8 | 111.6 | 124.2 | 141.4 | 178.8 | 158 573 | NEH | Belgique (R) |
| | AAA | | | | | | | | | | | | | | AEH | |
| France (R) | NAA | 1 700 000 | 51.3 | 44.4 | 86.8 | | 89.2 | 3 605 000 | 103.0 | 102.5 | 117.8 | 125.9 | 124.8 | 4 500 000 | NEH | France (R) |
| | AAA | 360 000 | 82.7 | 78.4 | 87.3 | 87.8 | 86.5 | 510 000 | 103.5 | 99.6 | 112.2 | 129.8 | | | AEH | |
| Germany (R) | NAA | 475 599 | 76.6 | 75.3 | 83.7 | 84.9 | 92.7 | 722 428 | 118.1 | 120.2 | 135.3 | 146.0 | 175.1 | 1 265 140 | NEH | Allemagne (R) |
| | AAA | 252 518 | 73.8 | 70.5 | 79.7 | | 93.1 | 410 296 | 119.1 | 120.5 | 143.5 | 151.8 | 185.9 | 762 554 | AEH | |
| Greece (N) | NAA | 178 363 | 98.4 | 88.0 | 86.0 | 92.4 | | 240 604 | 107.0 | 86.3 | 99.2 | 108.7 | 108.1 | 260 000 | NEH | Grèce (N) |
| | AAA | 69 903 | 101.5 | 87.7 | 87.8 | | | 100 126 | 111.2 | 91.9 | 105.5 | 119.8 | | | AEH | |
| Italy (N) | NAA | 484 910 | 90.3 | 77.7 | 81.8 | 90.4 | 97.3 | 635 436 | 98.9 | 111.9 | 153.8 | 187.2 | 188.8 | 1 200 000 | NEH | Italie (N) |
| | AAA | 216 917 | 90.0 | 79.0 | 78.4 | | 92.9 | 288 851 | 98.8 | 115.0 | 167.1 | 201.9 | | | AEH | |
| Luxembourg (R) | NAA | | | | | | | | | | | | | | NEH | Luxembourg (R) |
| | AAA | | | | | | | | | | | | | | AEH | |
| Netherlands (R) | NAA | 120 159 | 98.0 | 99.8 | 101.7 | 116.0 | 105.4 | 132 577 | 119.2 | 112.3 | | 124.5 | 126.4 | 167 600 | NEH | Pays-Bas (R) |
| | AAA | 64 123 | 91.0 | 86.7 | 92.6 | 107.8 | 93.0 | 74 537 | 107.8 | 95.8 | | 117.5 | 116.9 | 87 100 | AEH | |
| Portugal (N) | NAA | 27 834 | 58.3 | 63.3 | 69.0 | 67.8 | 72.9 | 50 857 | 99.5 | 106.2 | 129.2 | 145.1 | 146.9 | 74 727 | NEH | Portugal (N) |
| | AAA | 11 510 | 50.3 | 51.8 | 59.0 | 60.7 | 69.6 | 23 383 | 100.5 | 106.7 | 132.0 | 141.9 | 144.6 | 33 822 | AEH | |
| Spain (N) | NAA | 299 569 | 81.7 | 75.4 | 91.7 | 91.0 | 92.4 | 338 978 | 115.3 | | | | | | NEH | Espagne (N) |
| | AAA | 129 655 | 72.7 | 68.6 | 81.6 | 79.2 | 83.8 | 170 704 | 120.3 | | | | | | AEH | |
| Sweden (N) | NAA | 45 966 | 91.4 | 94.5 | 86.3 | 94.8 | 90.3 | 60 148 | 99.6 | 90.9 | 106.9 | 127.3 | 139.4 | 83 817 | NEH | Suède (N) |
| | AAA | | | | | | | | | | | | | | AEH | |
| Switzerland (R) | NAA | 373 800 | 83.3 | 82.2 | 85.6 | 90.5 | 97.6 | 516 700 | 104.1 | 108.7 | 126.1 | 131.4 | 157.5 | 813 600 | NEH | Suisse (R) |
| | AAA | 208 900 | 82.1 | 77.8 | 81.3 | 86.8 | 95.1 | 291 500 | 105.3 | 111.9 | 131.3 | 141.6 | 168.0 | 489 700 | AEH | |
| Turkey (N) | NAA | 15 672 | 32.6 | 39.3 | 46.9 | 72.8 | 104.8 | 45 027 | 159.8 | 198.8 | 222.8 | 261.1 | 300.5 | 135 295 | NEH | Turquie (N) |
| | AAA | 7 613 | 30.6 | 35.2 | 39.1 | 63.2 | 103.3 | 22 120 | 149.6 | 195.5 | 239.7 | 285.8 | 336.4 | 74 421 | AEH | |
| United Kingdom (R) | NAA | 1 246 000 | 110.7 | 73.6 | 79.5 | 71.7 | 64.3 | 1 533 000 | 156.4 | 114.4 | 152.1 | 192.0 | 212.8 | 3 262 000 | NEH | Royaume-Uni (R) |
| | AAA | | | | | | | | | | | | | | AEH | |
| Canada (R) | NAA | 781 000 | 85.8 | 87.1 | 89.1 | 84.5 | 73.0 | 1 015 000 | 91.5 | 150.5 | 173.5 | 219.6 | 250.1 | 2 538 300 | NEH | Canada (R) |
| Australia (R) | NAA | | 37.0 | | 50.7 | | 76.7 | 647 900 | 141.4 | 147.6 | 218.6 | 357.3 | | | NEH | Australie (R) |
| Yugoslavia (N) | NAA | 32 271 | 102.6 | 106.1 | 107.1 | 103.9 | 104.1 | 26 352 | 76.2 | 93.3 | 114.5 | 116.7 | 124.9 | 32 917 | NEH | Yougoslavie (N) |
| | AAA | 12 151 | 121.5 | 127.1 | 110.5 | 100.3 | 93.6 | 9 346 | 107.4 | 124.4 | 146.8 | 162.9 | 167.4 | 15 641 | AEH | |

AAA   Arrivals in all means of accommodation  
NAA   Nights in all means of accommodation  
(R)   Tourist count by country of residence  
(N)   Tourist count by country of nationality

AEH   Arrivées dans l'ensemble des moyens d'hébergement  
NEH   Nuitées dans l'ensemble des moyens d'hébergement  
(R)   Recensement des touristes par pays de résidence  
(N)   Recensement des touristes par pays de nationalité

119

## Table/Tableau 44
## ARRIVALS OF FOREIGN TOURISTS/VISITORS AT FRONTIERS
## ARRIVÉES DE TOURISTES/VISITEURS ÉTRANGERS AUX FRONTIÈRES

*From the Netherlands* — *En provenance des Pays-Bas*

1984 = 100

| Country | T/V | Volume 1978 | 1979 | 1980 | 1981 | 1982 | 1983 | Volume 1984 | 1985 | 1986 | 1987 | 1988 | 1989 | Volume 1989 | T/V | Pays |
|---|---|---|---|---|---|---|---|---|---|---|---|---|---|---|---|---|
| Finland (R) | V | 14 165 | 86.9 | 90.8 | 77.8 | 103.2 | 101.0 | | 97.0 | 106.5 | 104.5 | 107.4 | | | V | Finlande (R) |
| France (R) | T | 3 000 000 | 73.1 | 93.2 | 88.1 | 72.2 | 79.7 | 3 768 000 | 145.3 | 171.1 | 178.9 | 201.7 | | | T | France (R) |
| Greece (N) | T | 122 054 | 105.3 | 114.9 | 97.5 | 106.0 | 93.5 | 192 879 | 102.7 | 143.4 | 150.2 | 175.9 | 221.9 | 428 000 | T | Grèce (N) |
| Iceland (N) | T | 1 994 | 114.2 | 104.2 | 87.4 | 100.6 | 96.7 | 1 610 | | | | | | | T | Islande (N) |
| Ireland (R) | V | 1 703 200 | | | | | | 1 763 087 | 94.2 | 98.9 | 78.8 | 102.2 | 104.4 | 1 840 844 | V | Irlande (R) |
| Italy (N) | V | 36 831 | 81.5 | 80.0 | 82.7 | 80.0 | 102.5 | 142 619 | 106.1 | 114.5 | 143.8 | 193.1 | 222.1 | 316 747 | V | Italie (N) |
| Norway (N) | V | 99 400 | 85.5 | 84.1 | 84.7 | 82.1 | 102.9 | 151 887 | 107.8 | 113.1 | 141.0 | 187.8 | 219.1 | 332 797 | V | Norvège (N) |
| Portugal (N) | T | 111 067 | 99.7 | 98.8 | 99.7 | 97.9 | 95.0 | 1 385 031 | 115.2 | 112.4 | 121.6 | 144.7 | 146.9 | 2 034 717 | T | Portugal (N) |
| Spain (N) | V | 1 527 134 | 91.8 | 70.3 | 85.0 | 82.2 | 97.0 | 27 098 | 145.6 | 184.2 | 299.1 | | 393.8 | 106 709 | V | Espagne (N) |
| Turkey (N) | V | 30 107 | | | | | | | | | | | | | V | Turquie (N) |
| United Kingdom (R) | V | 1 003 000 | 131.7 | 122.9 | 100.6 | 94.7 | 99.1 | 740 900 | 102.9 | 103.8 | 115.4 | 118.9 | 127.6 | 945 200 | V | Royaume-Uni (R) |
| Canada (R) | T | 74 300 | 145.9 | 143.1 | 130.1 | 117.8 | 104.1 | 60 800 | 96.1 | 112.8 | 128.1 | 144.7 | 143.7 | 87 400 | T | Canada (R) |
| | V | 84 900 | 151.2 | 146.7 | 131.6 | 118.6 | 103.3 | 66 800 | 95.7 | 113.3 | 132.5 | 148.1 | 144.9 | 96 800 | V | |
| United States (R) | T | 141 021 | 119.1 | 133.1 | 147.1 | 141.5 | 108.1 | 134 192 | 97.9 | 121.3 | 150.3 | 184.7 | 194.4 | 260 840 | T | États-Unis (R) |
| Australia (R) | V | 11 500 | 115.6 | 129.5 | 127.7 | 118.9 | 105.7 | 14 100 | 109.2 | 112.8 | 122.7 | 158.9 | 142.6 | 20 100 | V | Australie (R) |
| Japan (N) | V | 10 600 | 68.9 | 77.0 | 85.6 | 80.9 | 90.5 | 14 162 | 108.8 | 102.3 | 112.3 | 111.9 | 116.0 | 16 432 | V | Japon (N) |
| New Zealand (R) | T | 3 336 | 77.6 | 96.3 | 100.3 | 99.7 | 93.4 | 5 164 | 104.8 | 112.1 | 122.4 | 136.8 | 138.0 | 7 126 | T | Nouvelle-Zélande (R) |

V  Visitors (travellers in Turkey)
T  Tourists
(R)  Tourist count by country of residence
(N)  Tourist count by country of nationality

V  Visiteurs (voyageurs en Turquie)
T  Touristes
(R)  Recensement des touristes par pays de résidence
(N)  Recensement des touristes par pays de nationalité

Table/Tableau 45

## ARRIVALS AND NIGHTS OF FOREIGN TOURISTS AT/IN HOTELS
## ARRIVÉES ET NUITÉES DE TOURISTES ÉTRANGERS DANS L'HÔTELLERIE

From the Netherlands / En provenance des Pays-Bas  
1984=100

| Country | AH/NH | Volume 1978 | 1979 | 1980 | 1981 | 1982 | 1983 | Volume 1984 | 1985 | 1986 | 1987 | 1988 | 1989 | Volume 1989 |
|---|---|---|---|---|---|---|---|---|---|---|---|---|---|---|
| Austria (R) / Autriche (R) | NH | 5 128 330 | 103.5 | 108.7 | 111.5 | 104.6 | 97.4 | 5 306 708 | 95.7 | 94.9 | 96.3 | 94.2 | 99.0 | 5 254 985 |
| | AH | 705 522 | 99.2 | 104.0 | 107.9 | 102.0 | 97.2 | 754 410 | 97.9 | 97.1 | 101.2 | 102.9 | 108.5 | 818 385 |
| Belgium (R) / Belgique (R) | NH | 488 005 | 75.4 | 73.6 | 68.9 | 78.7 | 92.2 | 661 794 | 99.5 | 102.3 | 107.8 | 111.9 | 130.0 | 860 505 |
| Denmark (N) / Danemark (N) | NH | 128 100 | 112.4 | 111.8 | 110.3 | 106.1 | 111.3 | 108 300 | 90.5 | 86.6 | 92.8 | 94.3 | 113.9 | 123 400 |
| Finland (R) / Finlande (R) | NH | 39 416 | 113.4 | 109.5 | 95.9 | 81.7 | 83.3 | 44 140 | 91.5 | 83.8 | 94.6 | 104.8 | 118.2 | 52 189 |
| France (R) / France (R) | NH | 991 114 | 146.3 | 126.3 | 109.2 | 96.0 | 94.7 | 843 017 | 89.7 | 229.4 | 242.9 | 259.5 | 285.0 | 2 402 703 |
| | AH | 411 953 | 144.7 | 135.2 | 115.8 | 103.4 | 101.2 | 313 282 | 94.9 | 330.3 | 353.0 | 381.1 | 401.7 | 1 258 486 |
| Germany (R) / Allemagne (R) | NH | 3 128 821 | 102.6 | 104.5 | 108.8 | 103.4 | 95.8 | 3 123 439 | 100.9 | 106.2 | 110.3 | 110.0 | 116.0 | 3 621 722 |
| | AH | 1 381 970 | 98.3 | 101.4 | 105.4 | 100.1 | 95.5 | 1 435 657 | 100.5 | 101.8 | 107.1 | 108.5 | 111.9 | 1 606 800 |
| Greece (N) / Grèce (N) | NH | 800 724 | 89.4 | 83.1 | 83.3 | 77.1 | 71.2 | 1 275 323 | 147.9 | 152.9 | 129.3 | 130.0 | | |
| | AH | 152 609 | 93.0 | 86.7 | 86.4 | 81.1 | 76.5 | 213 986 | 131.8 | 128.3 | 121.1 | 120.4 | | |
| Ireland (R) / Irlande (R) | NH | | | | | | | | | | | | | 200 000 |
| | AH | | | | | | | | | | | | | 33 000 |
| Italy (N) / Italie (N) | NH | 1 746 926 | 189.1 | 182.7 | 131.6 | 135.1 | 122.7 | 1 039 721 | 108.5 | 123.4 | 177.1 | 144.9 | | |
| | AH | 298 573 | 139.2 | 141.3 | 108.9 | 119.0 | 112.4 | 240 861 | 108.9 | 115.3 | 127.7 | 141.4 | | |
| Luxembourg (R) / Luxembourg (R) | NH | | | | | | | | | | | | | |
| | AH | | | | | | | | | | | | | |
| Norway (N) / Norvège (N) | NH | 164 071 | 127.0 | 134.0 | 121.5 | 85.8 | 79.2 | 137 704 | 96.5 | 80.5 | 87.6 | 78.3 | 85.9 | 118 262 |
| Portugal (N) / Portugal (N) | NH | 620 092 | 139.6 | 135.7 | 112.3 | 105.8 | 88.8 | 725 530 | 102.8 | 112.4 | 120.8 | 164.8 | 177.7 | 1 289 410 |
| | AH | 81 474 | 106.6 | 101.7 | 91.9 | 92.3 | 92.4 | 102 719 | 103.7 | 107.1 | 126.1 | 165.1 | 178.8 | 183 682 |
| Spain (N) / Espagne (N) | NH | 4 102 924 | 88.6 | 74.0 | 91.9 | 92.3 | 87.1 | 3 920 373 | 87.4 | 99.4 | 86.5 | 84.8 | 71.7 | 2 810 356 |
| | AH | | 101.7 | 94.9 | 102.6 | 100.3 | 96.7 | 430 398 | 101.1 | 101.1 | 103.7 | 103.5 | 95.3 | 410 149 |
| Sweden (N) / Suède (N) | NH | 150 173 | 169.7 | 151.0 | 151.1 | 123.3 | 143.7 | 83 868 | 91.9 | 87.4 | 83.5 | 82.6 | 90.7 | 76 064 |
| Switzerland (R) / Suisse (R) | NH | 1 294 106 | 128.4 | 152.8 | 153.0 | 126.3 | 114.6 | 822 955 | 97.3 | 102.9 | 100.4 | 97.4 | 104.4 | 859 552 |
| | AH | 328 846 | 121.1 | 140.1 | 134.7 | 119.1 | 111.0 | 248 906 | 95.9 | 101.8 | 99.8 | 99.4 | 107.1 | 266 645 |
| Australia (R) / Australie (R) | NH | | 130.2 | | 134.0 | | 102.4 | 53 600 | 135.8 | 113.2 | 123.3 | 159.5 | | |
| Japan (N) / Japon (N) | NH | 51 844 | | | | | | | | | | | | |
| | AH | 18 247 | | | | | | | | | | | | |
| Yugoslavia (N) / Yougoslavie (N) | NH | | | | | | | | | | | | | 1 766 036 |
| | AH | | | | | | | | | | | | | 252 120 |

AH  Arrivals at hotels and similar establishments  
NH  Nights in hotels and similar establishments  
(R) Tourist count by country of residence  
(N) Tourist count by country of nationality

AH  Arrivées dans les hôtels et les établissements assimilés  
NH  Nuitées dans les hôtels et établissements assimilés  
(R) Recensement des touristes par pays de résidence  
(N) Recensement des touristes par pays de nationalité

## Table/Tableau 46

## ARRIVALS AND NIGHTS OF FOREIGN TOURISTS AT/IN ALL MEANS OF ACCOMMODATION
## ARRIVÉES ET NUITÉES DE TOURISTES ÉTRANGERS DANS L'ENSEMBLE DES MOYENS D'HÉBERGEMENT

From the Netherlands — En provenance des Pays-Bas

1984=100

| | AAA/NAA | Volume 1978 | 1979 | 1980 | 1981 | 1982 | 1983 | Volume 1984 | 1985 | 1986 | 1987 | 1988 | 1989 | Volume 1989 | AEH/NEH | |
|---|---|---|---|---|---|---|---|---|---|---|---|---|---|---|---|---|
| Austria (R) | NAA | 8 297 331 | 97.5 | 104.4 | 110.5 | 103.9 | 96.7 | 9 354 457 | 98.1 | 98.1 | 99.6 | 99.1 | 103.3 | 9 658 807 | NEH | Autriche (R) |
| | AAA | 1 085 967 | 94.1 | 100.2 | 107.4 | 101.2 | 96.1 | 1 251 737 | 99.7 | 99.3 | 103.8 | 106.3 | 112.1 | 1 403 383 | AEH | |
| Belgium (R) | NAA | 1 951 422 | 64.2 | 62.2 | 62.7 | 90.5 | 99.9 | 3 078 313 | 102.9 | 108.0 | 116.7 | 132.2 | 136.5 | 4 201 445 | NEH | Belgique (R) |
| Denmark (N) | NAA | 640 296 | 85.6 | 80.6 | 94.7 | 106.6 | 122.6 | 724 805 | 92.5 | 82.5 | 74.5 | 70.3 | 83.1 | 602 626 | NEH | Danemark (N) |
| France (R) | NAA | 23 990 000 | 73.9 | 71.4 | 61.1 | 99.9 | 98.0 | 33 541 000 | 93.3 | 103.1 | 98.2 | 99.6 | 99.6 | 33 400 000 | NEH | France (R) |
| | AAA | 3 000 000 | 86.9 | 90.8 | 77.8 | 103.2 | 101.0 | 3 768 000 | 97.0 | 106.5 | 104.5 | 107.4 | | | AEH | |
| Germany (R) | NAA | 5 035 963 | 102.9 | 108.3 | 92.7 | 88.8 | 89.8 | 4 983 625 | 101.4 | 107.1 | 113.2 | 114.2 | 119.7 | 5 963 364 | NEH | Allemagne (R) |
| | AAA | 1 629 481 | 97.8 | 101.6 | 97.3 | 92.6 | 91.7 | 1 699 965 | 100.4 | 102.9 | 109.2 | 110.5 | 115.0 | 1 954 574 | AEH | |
| Greece (N) | NAA | 940 970 | 85.9 | 79.8 | 81.7 | 76.2 | 69.5 | 1 544 269 | 129.7 | 133.5 | 113.8 | 113.5 | 113.3 | 1 750 000 | NEH | Grèce (N) |
| | AAA | 192 618 | 92.9 | 87.0 | 86.1 | 82.6 | 75.5 | 268 741 | 118.8 | 116.1 | 108.7 | 107.5 | | | AEH | |
| Italy (N) | NAA | 4 471 356 | 172.2 | 175.3 | 138.4 | 140.8 | 115.6 | 3 081 711 | 107.8 | 118.8 | 110.4 | 115.4 | 116.8 | 3 600 000 | NEH | Italie (N) |
| | AAA | 525 824 | 134.7 | 142.3 | 115.6 | 123.4 | 110.0 | 445 936 | 108.5 | 117.7 | 124.3 | 131.7 | | | AEH | |
| Luxembourg (R) | NAA | | | | | | | | | | | | | | NEH | Luxembourg (R) |
| | AAA | | | | | | | | | | | | | | AEH | |
| Portugal (N) | NAA | 741 559 | 127.1 | 128.6 | 116.7 | 110.8 | 92.5 | 950 694 | 106.5 | 119.1 | 128.5 | 173.5 | 183.4 | 1 743 792 | NEH | Portugal (N) |
| | AAA | 114 081 | 98.7 | 100.9 | 96.2 | 98.2 | 94.1 | 153 972 | 114.6 | 127.2 | 141.7 | 181.7 | 191.8 | 295 265 | AEH | |
| Sweden (N) | NAA | 422 180 | 93.7 | 81.0 | 106.5 | 90.9 | 137.7 | 520 711 | 90.5 | 72.6 | 72.0 | 66.1 | 76.7 | 399 479 | NEH | Suède (N) |
| Switzerland (R) | NAA | 3 507 300 | 110.4 | 135.3 | 147.1 | 124.5 | 113.1 | 2 961 300 | 93.8 | 103.3 | 100.6 | 100.1 | 104.8 | 3 102 000 | NEH | Suisse (R) |
| | AAA | 582 300 | 108.2 | 130.0 | 133.7 | 118.9 | 110.8 | 519 400 | 91.5 | 100.1 | 98.6 | 99.5 | 106.3 | 552 100 | AEH | |
| United Kingdom (R) | NAA | 7 015 000 | 159.0 | 139.2 | 117.0 | 96.8 | 103.9 | 4 563 000 | 117.8 | 95.8 | 113.1 | 122.0 | 114.1 | 5 206 000 | NEH | Royaume-Uni (R) |
| Canada (R) | NAA | 1 088 900 | 141.9 | 132.2 | 128.2 | 120.6 | 104.8 | 960 600 | 95.4 | 100.9 | 114.3 | 125.6 | 119.6 | 1 148 800 | NEH | Canada (R) |
| Australia (R) | NAA | | 95.1 | | 108.3 | | 144.7 | 161 900 | 90.8 | 91.7 | 99.8 | 129.2 | | | NEH | Australie (R) |
| Yugoslavia (N) | NAA | 1 680 687 | 80.7 | 90.3 | 113.9 | 79.7 | 68.2 | 2 270 268 | 127.7 | 133.3 | 126.6 | 159.1 | 153.5 | 3 485 615 | NEH | Yougoslavie (N) |
| | AAA | 295 755 | 85.4 | 93.1 | 110.8 | 78.7 | 67.6 | 356 808 | 117.4 | 119.7 | 124.3 | 146.8 | 137.5 | 490 541 | AEH | |

AAA  Arrivals in all means of accommodation
NAA  Nights in all means of accommodation
(R)  Tourist count by country of residence
(N)  Tourist count by country of nationality

AEH  Arrivées dans l'ensemble des moyens d'hébergement
NEH  Nuitées dans l'ensemble des moyens d'hébergement
(R)  Recensement des touristes par pays de résidence
(N)  Recensement des touristes par pays de nationalité

122

## Table/Tableau 47

## ARRIVALS OF FOREIGN TOURISTS/VISITORS AT FRONTIERS
## ARRIVÉES DE TOURISTES/VISITEURS ÉTRANGERS AUX FRONTIÈRES

*From the United Kingdom*  
1984=100

*En provenance du Royaume-Uni*  
1984=100

| | T/V | Volume 1978 | 1979 | 1980 | 1981 | 1982 | 1983 | Volume 1984 | 1985 | 1986 | 1987 | 1988 | 1989 | Volume 1989 | T/V | |
|---|---|---|---|---|---|---|---|---|---|---|---|---|---|---|---|---|
| Finland (R) | V | 26 308 | | | | | | | | | | | | | V | Finlande (R) |
| France (R) | T | 2 950 000 | 59.7 | 63.1 | 66.0 | 109.8 | 108.3 | 5 481 000 | 107.0 | 114.9 | 116.2 | 121.2 | 156.5 | 1 632 582 | T | France (R) |
| Greece (N) | T | 514 485 | 53.6 | 73.6 | 92.5 | 98.0 | 85.2 | 1 043 363 | 127.4 | 163.9 | 189.8 | 171.6 | | | T | Grèce (N) |
| Iceland (N) | T | 5 529 | 71.9 | 89.0 | 83.8 | 77.4 | 94.4 | 9 398 | 103.4 | 109.2 | 112.6 | 112.0 | 127.6 | 11 990 | T | Islande (N) |
| Ireland (R) | V | 1 798 200 | | | 86.4 | 90.6 | 95.0 | 1 188 000 | 92.9 | 91.2 | 101.8 | 123.3 | 140.4 | 1 668 000 | V | Irlande (R) |
| Italy (N) | V | 122 974 | 111.8 | 114.4 | 101.0 | 103.2 | 105.7 | 1 788 371 | 99.0 | 114.5 | 111.8 | 101.7 | 106.6 | 1 906 236 | V | Italie (N) |
| Norway (N) | V | 242 100 | 48.1 | 58.0 | 69.6 | 79.7 | 86.7 | 638 641 | 118.3 | 155.4 | 178.1 | 166.7 | 160.9 | 1 027 281 | V | Norvège (N) |
| Portugal (N) | T | 327 872 | 56.3 | 68.2 | 77.3 | 80.4 | 88.7 | 709 724 | 124.0 | 150.6 | 170.0 | 160.6 | 160.3 | 1 137 481 | T | Portugal (N) |
| Spain (N) | V | 3 428 049 | 56.9 | 59.6 | 67.4 | 80.5 | 86.1 | 6 026 612 | 83.5 | 106.7 | 125.3 | 126.9 | 121.9 | 7 345 831 | V | Espagne (N) |
| Turkey (N) | V | 92 365 | 78.1 | 69.3 | 67.2 | 66.4 | 94.1 | 89 709 | 139.0 | 171.9 | 297.5 | 518.5 | 452.5 | 405 943 | V | Turquie (N) |
| Canada (R) | T | 387 200 | 130.0 | 139.8 | 138.6 | 121.6 | 103.8 | 350 000 | 89.7 | 114.1 | 125.5 | 150.6 | 160.3 | 561 200 | T | Canada (R) |
| United States (R) | V | 436 000 | 134.0 | 143.6 | 140.3 | 123.0 | 104.0 | 385 300 | 89.6 | 114.0 | 131.5 | 152.0 | 159.6 | 614 800 | V | États-Unis (R) |
| | T | 1 029 697 | 111.0 | 140.4 | 169.8 | 139.5 | 109.6 | 927 574 | 92.8 | 122.2 | 146.9 | 196.0 | 239.5 | 2 221 871 | T | |
| Australia (R) | V | 89 500 | 78.7 | 87.6 | 97.7 | 119.0 | 101.5 | 145 500 | 105.4 | 121.0 | 136.7 | 178.9 | 187.6 | 272 900 | V | Australie (R) |
| Japan (N) | V | 65 754 | 43.2 | 54.4 | 72.7 | 91.4 | 104.5 | 167 070 | 109.4 | 85.1 | 88.8 | 92.5 | 106.1 | 177 259 | V | Japon (N) |
| New Zealand (R) | T | 28 012 | 80.5 | 84.8 | 94.7 | 94.3 | 97.2 | 40 209 | 108.5 | 123.5 | 151.8 | 180.8 | 184.9 | 74 337 | T | Nouvelle-Zélande (R) |

V   Visitors (travellers in Turkey)  
T   Tourists  
(R)   Tourist count by country of residence  
(N)   Tourist count by country of nationality

V   Visiteurs (voyageurs en Turquie)  
T   Touristes  
(R)   Recensement des touristes par pays de résidence  
(N)   Recensement des touristes par pays de nationalité

## Table/Tableau 48

## ARRIVALS AND NIGHTS OF FOREIGN TOURISTS AT/IN HOTELS
## ARRIVÉES ET NUITÉES DE TOURISTES ÉTRANGERS DANS L'HÔTELLERIE

*From the United Kingdom* — *En provenance du Royaume-Uni*

1984=100

| Country / Pays | AH/NH | Volume 1978 | 1979 | 1980 | 1981 | 1982 | 1983 | Volume 1984 | 1985 | 1986 | 1987 | 1988 | 1989 | Volume 1989 |
|---|---|---|---|---|---|---|---|---|---|---|---|---|---|---|
| Austria (R) / Autriche (R) | NH | 1 237 086 | 34.6 | 50.7 | 60.3 | 81.2 | 92.4 | 3 907 860 | 95.8 | 97.9 | 96.6 | 95.3 | 106.9 | 4 177 673 |
| | AH | 292 628 | 43.2 | 61.1 | 65.1 | 81.6 | 90.4 | 732 403 | 95.2 | 92.0 | 91.2 | 89.5 | 102.6 | 751 581 |
| Belgium (R) / Belgique (R) | NH | 783 177 | 76.3 | 81.8 | 85.4 | 91.7 | 101.0 | 1 050 746 | 100.0 | 92.9 | 101.3 | 81.5 | 90.1 | 947 234 |
| | AH | 274 400 | 97.3 | 105.1 | 112.0 | 120.9 | 113.4 | 300 500 | 110.9 | 103.7 | 107.8 | 96.5 | 106.3 | 319 300 |
| Denmark (N) / Danemark (N) | NH | | | | | | | | | | | | | |
| | AH | | | | | | | | | | | | | |
| Finland (R) / Finlande (R) | NH | 73 290 | 72.6 | 76.4 | 86.6 | 88.9 | 96.3 | 108 073 | 100.2 | 95.6 | 107.8 | 121.9 | 130.7 | 141 265 |
| | AH | | | | | | | | | | | | | |
| France (R) | NH | 1 422 404 | 76.8 | 83.2 | 88.1 | 89.4 | 92.5 | 2 098 601 | 103.5 | 281.1 | 272.6 | 310.8 | 420.5 | 8 824 594 |
| | AH | 583 891 | 81.0 | 87.0 | 96.0 | 96.4 | 97.3 | 812 045 | 108.4 | 382.0 | 379.1 | 411.8 | 566.2 | 4 597 529 |
| Germany (R) / Allemagne (R) | NH | 1 400 275 | 78.3 | 93.3 | 87.4 | 86.4 | 87.5 | 2 182 950 | 104.3 | 109.0 | 104.9 | 106.3 | 123.7 | 2 700 956 |
| | AH | 700 031 | 73.1 | 86.6 | 84.4 | 88.1 | 89.1 | 1 078 733 | 102.9 | 104.0 | 101.9 | 103.5 | 118.3 | 1 276 221 |
| Greece (N) / Grèce (N) | NH | 3 020 432 | 69.5 | 90.2 | 109.7 | 100.0 | 83.0 | 6 231 862 | 121.1 | 138.1 | 135.2 | 115.9 | | 2 901 000 |
| | AH | | | | | | | | | | | | | |
| Ireland (R) / Irlande (R) | NH | 505 006 | 84.3 | 101.1 | 114.3 | 103.1 | 86.4 | 777 348 | 118.4 | 126.6 | 126.8 | 112.8 | | 678 000 |
| | AH | | | | | | | | | | | | | |
| Italy (N) / Italie (N) | NH | 4 420 995 | 101.7 | 122.1 | 103.0 | 113.5 | 114.8 | 5 129 884 | 95.7 | 113.1 | 107.9 | 101.0 | | |
| | AH | 890 060 | 94.9 | 111.6 | 98.5 | 106.8 | 108.6 | 1 083 216 | 97.4 | 107.9 | 109.0 | 107.3 | | |
| Luxembourg (R) | NH | | | | | | 104.3 | 42 630 | 107.3 | 118.1 | 120.7 | 130.6 | | |
| | AH | | | | | | 107.1 | 22 761 | 115.5 | 110.0 | 112.6 | 123.8 | | |
| Netherlands (R) / Pays-Bas (R) | NH | 883 778 | 83.2 | 87.0 | 93.7 | 101.5 | 92.0 | 1 213 926 | 106.4 | 110.6 | 103.0 | 101.3 | 111.9 | 1 358 600 |
| | AH | 403 688 | 80.1 | 82.4 | 92.9 | 101.1 | 93.2 | 559 675 | 106.0 | 85.4 | 107.3 | 107.9 | 116.0 | 649 100 |
| Norway (N) / Norvège (N) | NH | 252 084 | 65.6 | 72.6 | 79.1 | 75.3 | 69.9 | 427 604 | 105.2 | 148.9 | 81.1 | 77.9 | 78.9 | 337 364 |
| | AH | | | | | | | | | | | | | |
| Portugal (N) | NH | 1 420 702 | 54.9 | 68.5 | 76.6 | 84.0 | 91.4 | 3 915 939 | 126.5 | 138.5 | 142.3 | 134.5 | 130.2 | 5 096 614 |
| | AH | 184 427 | 51.8 | 63.8 | 71.0 | 76.7 | 87.8 | 510 246 | 126.1 | 96.2 | 135.4 | 128.2 | 127.0 | 647 775 |
| Spain (N) / Espagne (N) | NH | 21 831 177 | 59.9 | 51.5 | 67.7 | 79.6 | 85.4 | 35 159 463 | 71.2 | 101.2 | 96.0 | 89.0 | 71.8 | 25 253 002 |
| | AH | 2 488 023 | 64.8 | 59.0 | 72.3 | 84.5 | 87.5 | 3 709 606 | 74.9 | 96.4 | 100.9 | 93.2 | 80.5 | 2 984 820 |
| Sweden (N) / Suède (N) | NH | 230 902 | 91.1 | 92.5 | 96.4 | 96.0 | 99.6 | 255 674 | 101.3 | 103.2 | 88.3 | 93.6 | 104.0 | 265 884 |
| | AH | | | | | | | | | | | | | |
| Switzerland (R) / Suisse (R) | NH | 1 081 263 | 53.7 | 69.2 | 89.8 | 100.7 | 103.3 | 1 954 476 | 98.9 | 98.3 | 93.1 | 90.8 | 98.4 | 1 923 820 |
| | AH | 348 699 | 64.4 | 77.7 | 93.9 | 99.2 | 100.1 | 549 095 | 96.8 | | 94.8 | 95.5 | 102.9 | 565 255 |
| Turkey (N) / Turquie (N) | NH | | | | | 52.1 | 91.1 | 165 437 | 153.4 | 198.4 | 307.4 | 538.6 | 467.9 | 774 132 |
| | AH | | | | | 53.9 | 81.4 | 63 802 | 132.6 | 161.8 | 223.2 | 345.7 | 319.4 | 203 779 |
| Australia (R) / Australie (R) | NH | | 62.6 | | 57.6 | | 99.9 | 590 300 | 126.7 | 189.2 | 213.9 | 279.9 | | |
| Japan (N) / Japon (N) | NH | 199 479 | 78.8 | 79.3 | 92.3 | 99.7 | 46.7 | 259 647 | 131.8 | | | | | |
| | AH | 77 102 | 82.4 | 78.4 | 89.7 | 96.3 | 45.5 | 96 014 | | | | | | |
| Yugoslavia (N) / Yougoslavie (N) | NH | | | | | | | | | | | | | 5 300 494 |
| | AH | | | | | | | | | | | | | 571 042 |

AH Arrivals at hotels and similar establishments  
NH Nights in hotels and similar establishments  
(R) Tourist count by country of residence  
(N) Tourist count by country of nationality  

AH Arrivées dans les hôtels et les établissements assimilés  
NH Nuitées dans les hôtels et établissements assimilés  
(R) Recensement des touristes par pays de résidence  
(N) Recensement des touristes par pays de nationalité

Table/Tableau 49

## ARRIVALS AND NIGHTS OF FOREIGN TOURISTS AT/IN ALL MEANS OF ACCOMMODATION
## ARRIVÉES ET NUITÉES DE TOURISTES ÉTRANGERS DANS L'ENSEMBLE DES MOYENS D'HÉBERGEMENT

From the United Kingdom
En provenance du Royaume-Uni

1984=100

| Country | AAA/NAA | Volume 1978 | 1979 | 1980 | 1981 | 1982 | 1983 | Volume 1984 | 1985 | 1986 | 1987 | 1988 | 1989 | AEH/NEH | Volume 1989 | |
|---|---|---|---|---|---|---|---|---|---|---|---|---|---|---|---|---|
| Austria (R) | NAA | 1 439 215 | 35.5 | 50.9 | 61.8 | 82.0 | 93.6 | 4 338 545 | 97.6 | 99.1 | 98.0 | 97.1 | 108.8 | NEH | 4 720 360 | Autriche (R) |
| | AAA | 343 016 | 44.6 | 61.7 | 67.2 | 82.7 | 91.9 | 821 998 | 96.8 | 94.0 | 93.1 | 91.6 | 105.1 | AEH | 863 534 | |
| Belgium (R) | NAA | 1 019 736 | 78.0 | 88.4 | 88.6 | 92.5 | 100.6 | 1 257 111 | 98.2 | 91.5 | 86.0 | 77.5 | 84.9 | NEH | 1 067 821 | Belgique (R) |
| Denmark (N) | NAA | 329 960 | 93.9 | 103.0 | 111.8 | 119.0 | 112.9 | 380 574 | 107.0 | 98.6 | 94.2 | 91.4 | 98.9 | NEH | 376 546 | Danemark (N) |
| France (R) | NAA | 26 850 000 | 56.6 | 62.3 | 65.1 | 103.1 | 104.0 | 50 009 000 | 106.1 | 117.2 | 121.1 | 125.4 | | NEH | | France (R) |
| | AAA | 2 950 000 | 59.7 | 63.1 | 66.0 | 109.8 | 108.3 | 5 481 000 | 107.0 | 114.9 | 116.2 | 121.2 | | AEH | | |
| Germany (R) | NAA | 1 499 356 | 77.8 | 86.3 | 82.8 | 82.2 | 83.5 | 2 359 646 | 105.1 | 109.2 | 107.9 | 108.4 | 125.6 | NEH | 2 963 561 | Allemagne (R) |
| | AAA | 720 522 | 71.1 | 87.6 | 80.4 | 83.9 | 84.9 | 1 142 233 | 103.2 | 103.7 | 102.8 | 103.8 | 118.7 | AEH | 1 355 507 | |
| Greece (N) | NAA | 3 214 299 | 67.5 | 98.9 | 106.9 | 96.9 | 80.8 | 6 803 916 | 112.1 | 127.8 | 122.1 | 107.1 | | NEH | | Grèce (N) |
| | AAA | 557 719 | 82.7 | 103.0 | 110.7 | 87.0 | 84.0 | 864 708 | 108.9 | 116.4 | 116.4 | 103.3 | | AEH | | |
| Ireland (R) | NAA | 11 922 600 | 103.4 | 95.4 | 87.2 | 98.0 | 92.8 | 10 832 300 | 88.4 | 90.0 | 111.2 | 127.4 | 148.9 | NEH | 16 129 000 | Irlande (R) |
| | AAA | 1 055 100 | 96.2 | | 90.0 | 92.1 | 93.7 | 1 120 000 | 99.9 | 100.6 | 110.9 | 135.5 | 153.2 | AEH | 1 716 000 | |
| Italy (N) | NAA | 5 518 843 | 102.5 | 120.3 | 107.2 | 115.4 | 116.1 | 6 220 248 | 96.3 | 114.5 | 142.4 | 135.5 | | NEH | | Italie (N) |
| | AAA | 1 025 793 | 95.6 | 111.1 | 100.9 | 107.4 | 108.9 | 1 228 746 | 97.1 | 109.1 | 109.1 | 107.6 | | AEH | | |
| Luxembourg (R) | NAA | 69 125 | 94.8 | | | | | 70 845 | 95.6 | 102.2 | 102.9 | 109.4 | | NEH | | Luxembourg (R) |
| | AAA | 37 212 | 102.7 | | | | | 34 806 | 99.4 | 100.7 | 99.8 | 107.0 | | AEH | | |
| Netherlands (R) | NAA | 1 093 749 | 82.1 | 85.8 | 91.5 | 99.8 | 90.6 | 1 524 782 | 103.7 | 100.7 | 99.8 | 99.1 | 110.9 | NEH | 1 690 300 | Pays-Bas (R) |
| | AAA | 487 275 | 80.2 | 83.4 | 92.8 | 100.5 | 92.4 | 683 497 | 103.8 | 100.7 | | 104.1 | 109.8 | AEH | 750 800 | |
| Portugal (N) | NAA | 1 469 668 | 55.0 | 68.8 | 78.1 | 85.3 | 92.1 | 4 047 009 | 125.7 | 148.1 | 141.9 | 133.8 | 129.5 | NEH | 5 239 541 | Portugal (N) |
| | AAA | 197 823 | 52.8 | 65.3 | 73.1 | 78.5 | 88.7 | 536 563 | 125.3 | 137.9 | 135.1 | 127.3 | 126.3 | AEH | 677 812 | |
| Spain (N) | NAA | 22 194 464 | 60.1 | 51.8 | 68.0 | 79.9 | 85.6 | 35 541 439 | 71.4 | | | | | NEH | | Espagne (N) |
| | AAA | 2 544 479 | 65.2 | 59.5 | 72.8 | 84.8 | 87.8 | 3 764 913 | 75.2 | | | | | AEH | | |
| Sweden (N) | NAA | 313 848 | 100.4 | 98.0 | 119.0 | 102.1 | 101.4 | 348 159 | 99.4 | 95.7 | 86.6 | 89.5 | 98.0 | NEH | 341 204 | Suède (N) |
| Switzerland (R) | NAA | 1 469 300 | 52.9 | 68.4 | 90.2 | 97.6 | 102.7 | 2 734 900 | 100.0 | 106.1 | 97.5 | 94.0 | 95.3 | NEH | 2 606 200 | Suisse (R) |
| | AAA | 449 400 | 65.2 | 80.0 | 97.5 | 100.2 | 101.3 | 699 000 | 96.7 | 99.3 | 95.6 | 95.4 | 100.9 | AEH | 705 200 | |
| Turkey (N) | NAA | 130 031 | 58.4 | 35.9 | 50.0 | 52.1 | 93.1 | 169 797 | 156.5 | 207.9 | 350.2 | 577.4 | 495.7 | NEH | 841 727 | Turquie (N) |
| | AAA | 51 270 | 53.2 | 31.5 | 51.0 | 53.6 | 81.8 | 64 720 | 133.2 | 165.2 | 234.9 | 358.2 | 330.8 | AEH | 214 096 | |
| Canada (R) | NAA | 5 612 000 | 124.5 | 129.8 | 129.8 | 119.2 | 103.5 | 5 188 300 | 88.8 | 110.6 | 109.8 | 131.3 | 131.7 | NEH | 6 831 200 | Canada (R) |
| | AAA | 387 200 | 130.0 | 139.8 | 138.6 | 121.6 | 103.8 | 350 000 | 89.7 | 114.1 | 125.5 | 150.6 | 160.2 | AEH | 560 600 | |
| Australia (R) | NAA | | 47.1 | | 60.5 | | 160.2 | 1 495 100 | 91.4 | 178.9 | 202.2 | 264.6 | | NEH | | Australie (R) |
| New Zealand (R) | NAA | | | | | | | 1 740 000 | 108.6 | 122.9 | 147.6 | 167.2 | 164.3 | NEH | 2 859 680 | Nouvelle-Zélande (R) |
| Yugoslavia (N) | NAA | 2 062 386 | 70.0 | 60.4 | 74.5 | 74.7 | 77.2 | 3 570 724 | 139.0 | 149.1 | 169.6 | 164.1 | 164.7 | NEH | 5 879 335 | Yougoslavie (N) |
| | AAA | 303 484 | 76.4 | 69.7 | 78.4 | 76.6 | 79.6 | 445 076 | 133.7 | 140.4 | 157.2 | 151.3 | 146.0 | AEH | 649 875 | |

AAA  Arrivals in all means of accommodation
NAA  Nights in all means of accommodation
(R)  Tourist count by country of residence
(N)  Tourist count by country of nationality

AEH  Arrivées dans l'ensemble des moyens d'hébergement
NEH  Nuitées dans l'ensemble des moyens d'hébergement
(R)  Recensement des touristes par pays de résidence
(N)  Recensement des touristes par pays de nationalité

# AUSTRALIA

*ARRIVALS OF FOREIGN VISITORS AT FRONTIERS[1]*

*(by country of residence)*

| | 1988 | Relative share | 1989 | Relative share | % Variation over 1988 |
|---|---|---|---|---|---|
| Austria | 9 100 | 0.4 | 9 200 | 0.4 | 1.1 |
| Belgium | 4 300 | 0.2 | 3 700 | 0.2 | −14.0 |
| Denmark | 11 400 | 0.5 | 10 200 | 0.5 | −10.5 |
| Finland | 5 700 | 0.3 | 5 200 | 0.2 | −8.8 |
| France | 21 000 | 0.9 | 20 100 | 1.0 | −4.3 |
| Germany[2] | 65 900 | 2.9 | 68 100 | 3.3 | 3.3 |
| Greece | 8 100 | 0.4 | 7 400 | 0.4 | −8.6 |
| Iceland | 200 | 0.0 | 100 | 0.0 | −50.0 |
| Ireland | 13 000 | 0.6 | 12 200 | 0.6 | −6.2 |
| Italy | 25 200 | 1.1 | 20 500 | 1.0 | −18.7 |
| Luxembourg | 300 | 0.0 | 300 | 0.0 | 0.0 |
| Netherlands | 22 400 | 1.0 | 20 100 | 1.0 | −10.3 |
| Norway | 5 200 | 0.2 | 3 700 | 0.2 | −28.8 |
| Portugal | 1 500 | 0.1 | 1 100 | 0.1 | −26.7 |
| Spain | 3 800 | 0.2 | 3 300 | 0.2 | −13.2 |
| Sweden | 26 900 | 1.2 | 24 100 | 1.2 | −10.4 |
| Switzerland | 26 000 | 1.2 | 27 400 | 1.3 | 5.4 |
| Turkey | 1 200 | 0.1 | 1 300 | 0.1 | 8.3 |
| United Kingdom | 260 300 | 11.6 | 272 900 | 13.1 | 4.8 |
| Other OECD-Europe | .. | .. | .. | .. | .. |
| **Total Europe** | 511 500 | 22.7 | 510 900 | 24.6 | −0.1 |
| Canada | 66 700 | 3.0 | 54 200 | 2.6 | −18.7 |
| United States | 322 300 | 14.3 | 260 700 | 12.5 | −19.1 |
| **Total North America** | 389 000 | 17.3 | 314 900 | 15.1 | −19.0 |
| Australia | .. | .. | .. | .. | .. |
| New Zealand | 534 300 | 23.8 | 449 300 | 21.6 | −15.9 |
| Japan | 352 300 | 15.7 | 349 500 | 16.8 | −0.8 |
| **Total Australasia and Japan** | 886 600 | 39.4 | 798 800 | 38.4 | −9.9 |
| **Total OECD Countries** | 1 787 100 | 79.4 | 1 624 600 | 78.1 | −9.1 |
| Yugoslavia | 6 800 | 0.3 | 6 400 | 0.3 | −5.9 |
| Other European countries | 26 600 | 1.2 | 29 100 | 1.4 | 9.4 |
| Bulgaria | 200 | 0.0 | 400 | 0.0 | 100.0 |
| Czechoslovakia | 1 100 | 0.0 | 1 100 | 0.1 | 0.0 |
| Germany (D. R.) | 400 | 0.0 | 200 | 0.0 | −50.0 |
| Hungary | 2 100 | 0.1 | 1 700 | 0.1 | −19.0 |
| Poland | 4 100 | 0.2 | 4 400 | 0.2 | 7.3 |
| Rumania | 400 | 0.0 | 200 | 0.0 | −50.0 |
| USSR | 2 900 | 0.1 | 5 200 | 0.2 | 79.3 |
| Latin America | 15 400 | 0.7 | 11 700 | 0.6 | −24.0 |
| Argentina | 2 000 | 0.1 | 2 300 | 0.1 | 15.0 |
| Brazil | 2 600 | 0.1 | 2 500 | 0.1 | −3.8 |
| Chile | 1 400 | 0.1 | 1 700 | 0.1 | 21.4 |
| Colombia | 500 | 0.0 | 400 | 0.0 | −20.0 |
| Mexico | 1 200 | 0.1 | 1 200 | 0.1 | 0.0 |
| Venezuela | 300 | 0.0 | 300 | 0.0 | 0.0 |
| Asia-Oceania | 386 600 | 17.2 | 389 500 | 18.7 | 0.8 |
| China | 18 000 | 0.8 | 29 100 | 1.4 | 61.7 |
| Hong Kong | 49 400 | 2.2 | 54 100 | 2.6 | 9.5 |
| India | 10 700 | 0.5 | 10 900 | 0.5 | 1.9 |
| Iran | 1 600 | 0.1 | 900 | 0.0 | −43.8 |
| Israel | 5 200 | 0.2 | 5 400 | 0.3 | 3.8 |
| Republic of Korea | 9 200 | 0.4 | 10 400 | 0.5 | 13.0 |
| Lebanon | 1 400 | 0.1 | 1 700 | 0.1 | 21.4 |
| Malaysia | 52 100 | 2.3 | 44 300 | 2.1 | −15.0 |
| Pakistan | 2 300 | 0.1 | 2 100 | 0.1 | −8.7 |
| Philippines | 13 400 | 0.6 | 11 000 | 0.5 | −17.9 |
| Saudi Arabia | 1 900 | 0.1 | 1 700 | 0.1 | −10.5 |
| Singapore | 63 500 | 2.8 | 65 200 | 3.1 | 2.7 |
| Taiwan | 19 200 | 0.9 | 21 500 | 1.0 | 12.0 |
| Thailand | 15 800 | 0.7 | 17 300 | 0.8 | 9.5 |
| Africa | 20 300 | 0.9 | 17 300 | 0.8 | −14.8 |
| Algeria | 200 | 0.0 | 200 | 0.0 | 0.0 |
| Egypt | 1 300 | 0.1 | 1 100 | 0.1 | −15.4 |
| Morocco | .. | .. | 100 | 0.0 | .. |
| South Africa | 9 300 | 0.4 | 8 000 | 0.4 | −14.0 |
| Origin country undetermined | 6 600 | 0.3 | 1 700 | 0.1 | −74.2 |
| **Total non-OECD Countries** | 462 300 | 20.6 | 455 700 | 21.9 | −1.4 |
| **TOTAL** | 2 249 400 | 100.0 | 2 080 300 | 100.0 | −7.5 |

1. Includes a small number of "in transit" passengers who leave the port or airport, but do not necessarily stay overnight in Australia.
2. Germany includes Federal and Democratic Republics.

# AUSTRALIA

## NIGHTS SPENT BY FOREIGN TOURISTS IN HOTELS
### (by country of residence)

| | 1987 | Relative share | 1988 | Relative share | % Variation over 1987 |
|---|---|---|---|---|---|
| Austria | 51 000 | 0.5 | 72 500 | 0.5 | 42.2 |
| Belgium | 11 500 | 0.1 | 16 400 | 0.1 | 42.6 |
| Denmark | 69 300 | 0.6 | 90 800 | 0.6 | 31.0 |
| Finland | 33 500 | 0.3 | 45 400 | 0.3 | 35.5 |
| France | 104 500 | 0.9 | 128 400 | 0.9 | 22.9 |
| Germany | 424 800 | 3.8 | 525 200 | 3.7 | 23.6 |
| Greece | 40 700 | 0.4 | 46 400 | 0.3 | 14.0 |
| Iceland | 1 600 | 0.0 | 1 600 | 0.0 | 0.0 |
| Ireland | 62 200 | 0.6 | 82 500 | 0.6 | 32.6 |
| Italy | 145 500 | 1.3 | 189 900 | 1.3 | 30.5 |
| Luxembourg | 1 100 | 0.0 | 1 100 | 0.0 | 0.0 |
| Netherlands | 66 100 | 0.6 | 85 500 | 0.6 | 29.3 |
| Norway | 34 300 | 0.3 | 41 400 | 0.3 | 20.7 |
| Portugal | 6 100 | 0.1 | 9 200 | 0.1 | 50.8 |
| Spain | 16 500 | 0.1 | 23 200 | 0.2 | 40.6 |
| Sweden | 174 500 | 1.6 | 214 300 | 1.5 | 22.8 |
| Switzerland | 209 400 | 1.9 | 255 600 | 1.8 | 22.1 |
| Turkey | 5 200 | 0.0 | 6 900 | 0.0 | 32.7 |
| United Kingdom | 1 262 500 | 11.4 | 1 652 200 | 11.7 | 30.9 |
| Other OECD-Europe | .. | .. | .. | .. | .. |
| **Total Europe** | 2 720 300 | 24.6 | 3 488 500 | 24.6 | 28.2 |
| Canada | 470 300 | 4.3 | 595 300 | 4.2 | 26.6 |
| United States | 2 716 500 | 24.6 | 2 833 400 | 20.0 | 4.3 |
| **Total North America** | 3 186 800 | 28.8 | 3 428 700 | 24.2 | 7.6 |
| Australia | .. | .. | .. | .. | .. |
| New Zealand | 2 104 200 | 19.0 | 2 631 200 | 18.6 | 25.0 |
| Japan | 1 073 700 | 9.7 | 1 754 500 | 12.4 | 63.4 |
| **Total Australasia and Japan** | 3 177 900 | 28.8 | 4 385 700 | 31.0 | 38.0 |
| **Total OECD Countries** | 9 085 000 | 82.2 | 11 302 900 | 79.9 | 24.4 |
| Yugoslavia | 36 100 | 0.3 | 39 000 | 0.3 | 8.0 |
| Other European countries | 126 100 | 1.1 | 352 100 | 2.5 | 179.2 |
| Latin America | 43 200 | 0.4 | 68 500 | 0.5 | 58.6 |
| Asia-Oceania | 1 679 800 | 15.2 | 2 272 200 | 16.1 | 35.3 |
| Hong Kong | 221 900 | 2.0 | 256 700 | 1.8 | 15.7 |
| Malaysia | 184 300 | 1.7 | 203 800 | 1.4 | 10.6 |
| Singapore | 291 600 | 2.6 | 324 800 | 2.3 | 11.4 |
| Africa | 77 900 | 0.7 | 90 300 | 0.6 | 15.9 |
| Origin country undetermined | .. | .. | 29 400 | 0.2 | .. |
| **Total non-OECD Countries** | 1 963 100 | 17.8 | 2 851 500 | 20.1 | 45.3 |
| **TOTAL** | 11 048 100 | 100.0 | 14 154 400 | 100.0 | 28.1 |

# AUSTRALIA

*NIGHTS SPENT BY FOREIGN TOURISTS IN REGISTERED TOURIST ACCOMMODATION*[1]
*(by country of residence)*

| | 1987 | Relative share | 1988 | Relative share | % Variation over 1987 |
|---|---|---|---|---|---|
| Austria | 120 000 | 0.5 | 170 600 | 0.6 | 42.2 |
| Belgium | 28 000 | 0.1 | 40 200 | 0.1 | 43.6 |
| Denmark | 215 800 | 1.0 | 282 800 | 1.0 | 31.0 |
| Finland | 104 200 | 0.5 | 141 400 | 0.5 | 35.7 |
| France | 237 000 | 1.1 | 291 100 | 1.0 | 22.8 |
| Germany | 999 100 | 4.4 | 1 235 300 | 4.3 | 23.6 |
| Greece | 94 000 | 0.4 | 107 200 | 0.4 | 14.0 |
| Iceland | 5 000 | 0.0 | 4 900 | 0.0 | –2.0 |
| Ireland | 148 900 | 0.7 | 197 600 | 0.7 | 32.7 |
| Italy | 336 900 | 1.5 | 439 900 | 1.5 | 30.6 |
| Luxembourg | 2 800 | 0.0 | 2 800 | 0.0 | 0.0 |
| Netherlands | 161 500 | 0.7 | 209 200 | 0.7 | 29.5 |
| Norway | 106 700 | 0.5 | 129 000 | 0.5 | 20.9 |
| Portugal | 13 900 | 0.1 | 20 800 | 0.1 | 49.6 |
| Spain | 37 400 | 0.2 | 52 700 | 0.2 | 40.9 |
| Sweden | 543 200 | 2.4 | 667 200 | 2.3 | 22.8 |
| Switzerland | 502 300 | 2.2 | 613 100 | 2.2 | 22.1 |
| Turkey | 11 900 | 0.1 | 15 900 | 0.1 | 33.6 |
| United Kingdom | 3 022 900 | 13.4 | 3 956 000 | 13.9 | 30.9 |
| Other OECD-Europe | .. | .. | .. | .. | .. |
| **Total Europe** | 6 691 500 | 29.6 | 8 577 700 | 30.2 | 28.2 |
| | | | | | |
| Canada | 967 000 | 4.3 | 1 223 900 | 4.3 | 26.6 |
| United States | 4 215 400 | 18.7 | 4 396 900 | 15.5 | 4.3 |
| **Total North America** | 5 182 400 | 23.0 | 5 620 800 | 19.8 | 8.5 |
| | | | | | |
| Australia | .. | .. | .. | .. | .. |
| New Zealand | 4 620 700 | 20.5 | 5 777 800 | 20.3 | 25.0 |
| Japan | 1 416 500 | 6.3 | 2 314 700 | 8.1 | 63.4 |
| **Total Australasia and Japan** | 6 037 200 | 26.7 | 8 092 500 | 28.5 | 34.0 |
| | | | | | |
| **Total OECD Countries** | 17 911 100 | 79.4 | 22 291 000 | 78.4 | 24.5 |
| | | | | | |
| Yugoslavia | 83 400 | 0.4 | 90 000 | 0.3 | 7.9 |
| Other European countries | 291 200 | 1.3 | 352 100 | 1.2 | 20.9 |
| Latin America | 95 700 | 0.4 | 151 900 | 0.5 | 58.7 |
| Asia-Oceania | 3 960 900 | 17.5 | 5 293 400 | 18.6 | 33.6 |
|   Hong Kong | 341 200 | 1.5 | 394 700 | 1.4 | 15.7 |
|   Malaysia | 1 121 500 | 5.0 | 1 240 600 | 4.4 | 10.6 |
|   Singapore | 481 400 | 2.1 | 536 300 | 1.9 | 11.4 |
| Africa | 172 600 | 0.8 | 200 200 | 0.7 | 16.0 |
| Origin country undetermined | 56 200 | 0.2 | 65 100 | 0.2 | 15.8 |
| | | | | | |
| **Total non-OECD Countries** | 4 660 000 | 20.6 | 6 152 700 | 21.6 | 32.0 |
| | | | | | |
| **TOTAL** | 22 571 100 | 100.0 | 28 443 700 | 100.0 | 26.0 |

1. Covers only commercial accommodation (ie excluding stays with friends/relatives).

# AUSTRIA

## ARRIVALS OF FOREIGN TOURISTS AT HOTELS
### (by country of residence)

| | 1988 | Relative share | 1989 | Relative share | % Variation over 1988 |
|---|---|---|---|---|---|
| Austria | .. | .. | .. | .. | .. |
| Belgium[1] | 265 750 | 2.2 | 299 497 | 2.3 | 12.7 |
| Denmark | 127 952 | 1.1 | 131 820 | 1.0 | 3.0 |
| Finland | 52 933 | 0.4 | 59 347 | 0.5 | 12.1 |
| France | 560 006 | 4.7 | 620 227 | 4.7 | 10.8 |
| Germany | 5 947 865 | 49.9 | 6 362 138 | 48.5 | 7.0 |
| Greece | 62 022 | 0.5 | 71 365 | 0.5 | 15.1 |
| Iceland[2] | .. | .. | .. | .. | .. |
| Ireland | 7 821 | 0.1 | 11 363 | 0.1 | 45.3 |
| Italy | 784 077 | 6.6 | 994 132 | 7.6 | 26.8 |
| Luxembourg[1] | .. | .. | .. | .. | .. |
| Netherlands | 776 351 | 6.5 | 818 385 | 6.2 | 5.4 |
| Norway | 61 298 | 0.5 | 59 890 | 0.5 | −2.3 |
| Portugal | 12 634 | 0.1 | 11 612 | 0.1 | −8.1 |
| Spain | 174 020 | 1.5 | 226 304 | 1.7 | 30.0 |
| Sweden | 259 541 | 2.2 | 272 574 | 2.1 | 5.0 |
| Switzerland | 556 489 | 4.7 | 641 679 | 4.9 | 15.3 |
| Turkey | 29 032 | 0.2 | 48 823 | 0.4 | 68.2 |
| United Kingdom | 655 460 | 5.5 | 751 581 | 5.7 | 14.7 |
| Other OECD-Europe | .. | .. | .. | .. | .. |
| **Total Europe** | 10 333 251 | 86.7 | 11 380 737 | 86.7 | 10.1 |
| Canada | 67 350 | 0.6 | 72 314 | 0.6 | 7.4 |
| United States | 562 655 | 4.7 | 613 624 | 4.7 | 9.1 |
| **Total North America** | 630 005 | 5.3 | 685 938 | 5.2 | 8.9 |
| Australia[3] | 79 419 | 0.7 | 101 996 | 0.8 | 28.4 |
| New Zealand[3] | .. | .. | .. | .. | .. |
| Japan | 166 215 | 1.4 | 191 980 | 1.5 | 15.5 |
| **Total Australasia and Japan** | 245 634 | 2.1 | 293 976 | 2.2 | 19.7 |
| **Total OECD Countries** | 11 208 890 | 94.0 | 12 360 651 | 94.2 | 10.3 |
| Yugoslavia | 94 425 | 0.8 | 112 026 | 0.9 | 18.6 |
| Other European countries[2] | 292 906 | 2.5 | 314 089 | 2.4 | 7.2 |
| Bulgaria | 7 659 | 0.1 | 11 520 | 0.1 | 50.4 |
| Czechoslovakia | 37 170 | 0.3 | 54 487 | 0.4 | 46.6 |
| Hungary | 197 015 | 1.7 | 159 303 | 1.2 | −19.1 |
| Poland | 31 826 | 0.3 | 49 882 | 0.4 | 56.7 |
| Rumania | 5 657 | 0.0 | 4 587 | 0.0 | −18.9 |
| USSR | 13 579 | 0.1 | 34 310 | 0.3 | 152.7 |
| Latin America | 69 469 | 0.6 | 44 814 | 0.3 | −35.5 |
| Asia-Oceania | 149 341 | 1.3 | 168 178 | 1.3 | 12.6 |
| Africa | 25 576 | 0.2 | 25 628 | 0.2 | 0.2 |
| Origin country undetermined | 81 018 | 0.7 | 95 254 | 0.7 | 17.6 |
| **Total non-OECD Countries** | 712 735 | 6.0 | 759 989 | 5.8 | 6.6 |
| **TOTAL** | 11 921 625 | 100.0 | 13 120 640 | 100.0 | 10.1 |

1. Belgium includes Luxembourg.
2. "Other European countries" includes Iceland.
3. Australia includes New Zealand.

# AUSTRIA

## ARRIVALS OF FOREIGN TOURISTS AT REGISTERED TOURIST ACCOMMODATION
### (by country of residence)

| | 1988 | Relative share | 1989 | Relative share | % Variation over 1988 |
|---|---|---|---|---|---|
| Austria | .. | .. | .. | .. | .. |
| Belgium[1] | 378 080 | 2.3 | 422 431 | 2.3 | 11.7 |
| Denmark | 197 538 | 1.2 | 203 524 | 1.1 | 3.0 |
| Finland | 52 933 | 0.3 | 59 347 | 0.3 | 12.1 |
| France | 701 455 | 4.2 | 778 415 | 4.3 | 11.0 |
| Germany | 8 996 778 | 54.3 | 9 666 493 | 53.1 | 7.4 |
| Greece | 66 724 | 0.4 | 76 802 | 0.4 | 15.1 |
| Iceland[2] | .. | .. | .. | .. | .. |
| Ireland | 7 821 | 0.0 | 11 363 | 0.1 | 45.3 |
| Italy | 866 122 | 5.2 | 1 101 380 | 6.1 | 27.2 |
| Luxembourg[1] | .. | .. | .. | .. | .. |
| Netherlands | 1 331 165 | 8.0 | 1 403 383 | 7.7 | 5.4 |
| Norway | 61 298 | 0.4 | 59 890 | 0.3 | −2.3 |
| Portugal | 12 634 | 0.1 | 11 612 | 0.1 | −8.1 |
| Spain | 174 020 | 1.1 | 226 304 | 1.2 | 30.0 |
| Sweden | 336 390 | 2.0 | 350 512 | 1.9 | 4.2 |
| Switzerland | 641 456 | 3.9 | 744 672 | 4.1 | 16.1 |
| Turkey | 29 032 | 0.2 | 48 823 | 0.3 | 68.2 |
| United Kingdom | 753 230 | 4.5 | 863 534 | 4.7 | 14.6 |
| Other OECD-Europe | .. | .. | .. | .. | .. |
| **Total Europe** | 14 606 676 | 88.1 | 16 028 485 | 88.1 | 9.7 |
| | | | | | |
| Canada | 84 614 | 0.5 | 89 938 | 0.5 | 6.3 |
| United States | 620 078 | 3.7 | 676 085 | 3.7 | 9.0 |
| **Total North America** | 704 692 | 4.3 | 766 023 | 4.2 | 8.7 |
| | | | | | |
| Australia[3] | 79 419 | 0.5 | 101 996 | 0.6 | 28.4 |
| New Zealand[3] | .. | .. | .. | .. | .. |
| Japan | 166 215 | 1.0 | 191 980 | 1.1 | 15.5 |
| **Total Australasia and Japan** | 245 634 | 1.5 | 293 976 | 1.6 | 19.7 |
| | | | | | |
| **Total OECD Countries** | 15 557 002 | 93.9 | 17 088 484 | 93.9 | 9.8 |
| | | | | | |
| Yugoslavia | 112 976 | 0.7 | 131 241 | 0.7 | 16.2 |
| Other European countries[2] | 416 662 | 2.5 | 443 689 | 2.4 | 6.5 |
| Bulgaria | 8 972 | 0.1 | 14 034 | 0.1 | 56.4 |
| Czechoslovakia | 49 128 | 0.3 | 76 862 | 0.4 | 56.5 |
| Hungary | 279 368 | 1.7 | 229 795 | 1.3 | −17.7 |
| Poland | 57 538 | 0.3 | 82 539 | 0.5 | 43.5 |
| Rumania | 8 077 | 0.0 | 6 149 | 0.0 | −23.9 |
| USSR | 13 579 | 0.1 | 34 310 | 0.2 | 152.7 |
| Latin America | 69 469 | 0.4 | 77 872 | 0.4 | 12.1 |
| Asia-Oceania | 155 018 | 0.9 | 174 915 | 1.0 | 12.8 |
| Africa | 25 576 | 0.2 | 25 628 | 0.1 | 0.2 |
| Origin country undetermined | 234 586 | 1.4 | 259 934 | 1.4 | 10.8 |
| | | | | | |
| **Total non-OECD Countries** | 1 014 287 | 6.1 | 1 113 279 | 6.1 | 9.8 |
| | | | | | |
| **TOTAL** | 16 571 289 | 100.0 | 18 201 763 | 100.0 | 9.8 |

1. Belgium includes Luxembourg.
2. "Other European countries" includes Iceland.
3. Australia includes New Zealand.

# AUSTRIA

## NIGHTS SPENT BY FOREIGN TOURISTS IN HOTELS
### (by country of residence)

| | 1988 | Relative share | 1989 | Relative share | % Variation over 1988 |
|---|---|---|---|---|---|
| Austria | .. | .. | .. | .. | .. |
| Belgium[1] | 1 538 699 | 2.7 | 1 768 233 | 2.9 | 14.9 |
| Denmark | 632 840 | 1.1 | 670 669 | 1.1 | 6.0 |
| Finland | 206 669 | 0.4 | 226 838 | 0.4 | 9.8 |
| France | 2 074 545 | 3.7 | 2 269 067 | 3.7 | 9.4 |
| Germany | 33 421 932 | 59.3 | 35 648 584 | 58.0 | 6.7 |
| Greece | 160 610 | 0.3 | 170 843 | 0.3 | 6.4 |
| Iceland[2] | .. | .. | .. | .. | .. |
| Ireland | 33 141 | 0.1 | 58 004 | 0.1 | 75.0 |
| Italy | 1 844 312 | 3.3 | 2 440 075 | 4.0 | 32.3 |
| Luxembourg[1] | .. | .. | .. | .. | .. |
| Netherlands | 4 999 132 | 8.9 | 5 254 985 | 8.6 | 5.1 |
| Norway | 206 501 | 0.4 | 194 790 | 0.3 | −5.7 |
| Portugal | 26 661 | 0.0 | 24 185 | 0.0 | −9.3 |
| Spain | 364 711 | 0.6 | 456 040 | 0.7 | 25.0 |
| Sweden | 1 054 355 | 1.9 | 1 077 227 | 1.8 | 2.2 |
| Switzerland | 2 034 966 | 3.6 | 2 394 604 | 3.9 | 17.7 |
| Turkey | 65 530 | 0.1 | 108 755 | 0.2 | 66.0 |
| United Kingdom | 3 722 901 | 6.6 | 4 177 673 | 6.8 | 12.2 |
| Other OECD-Europe | .. | .. | .. | .. | .. |
| Total Europe | 52 387 505 | 93.0 | 56 940 572 | 92.7 | 8.7 |
| Canada | 168 266 | 0.3 | 173 757 | 0.3 | 3.3 |
| United States | 1 428 035 | 2.5 | 1 531 322 | 2.5 | 7.2 |
| Total North America | 1 596 301 | 2.8 | 1 705 079 | 2.8 | 6.8 |
| Australia[3] | 188 485 | 0.3 | 237 527 | 0.4 | 26.0 |
| New Zealand[3] | .. | .. | .. | .. | .. |
| Japan | 320 548 | 0.6 | 370 537 | 0.6 | 15.6 |
| Total Australasia and Japan | 509 033 | 0.9 | 608 064 | 1.0 | 19.5 |
| **Total OECD Countries** | 54 492 839 | 96.7 | 59 253 715 | 96.5 | 8.7 |
| Yugoslavia | 267 722 | 0.5 | 296 273 | 0.5 | 10.7 |
| Other European countries[2] | 731 267 | 1.3 | 936 486 | 1.5 | 28.1 |
|     Bulgaria | 22 694 | 0.0 | 30 126 | 0.0 | 32.7 |
|     Czechoslovakia | 106 597 | 0.2 | 131 312 | 0.2 | 23.2 |
|     Hungary | 397 494 | 0.7 | 360 425 | 0.6 | −9.3 |
|     Poland | 96 438 | 0.2 | 140 764 | 0.2 | 46.0 |
|     Rumania | 17 961 | 0.0 | 18 209 | 0.0 | 1.4 |
|     USSR | 72 083 | 0.1 | 255 650 | 0.4 | 254.7 |
| Latin America | 149 157 | 0.3 | 162 815 | 0.3 | 9.2 |
| Asia-Oceania | 391 435 | 0.7 | 430 319 | 0.7 | 9.9 |
| Africa | 102 138 | 0.2 | 102 717 | 0.2 | 0.6 |
| Origin country undetermined | 223 269 | 0.4 | 246 084 | 0.4 | 10.2 |
| **Total non-OECD Countries** | 1 864 988 | 3.3 | 2 174 694 | 3.5 | 16.6 |
| **TOTAL** | 56 357 827 | 100.0 | 61 428 409 | 100.0 | 9.0 |

1. Belgium includes Luxembourg.
2. "Other European countries" includes Iceland.
3. Australia includes New Zealand.

# AUSTRIA

## NIGHTS SPENT BY FOREIGN TOURISTS IN REGISTERED TOURIST ACCOMMODATION
### (by country of residence)

| | 1988 | Relative share | 1989 | Relative share | % Variation over 1988 |
|---|---|---|---|---|---|
| Austria | .. | .. | .. | .. | .. |
| Belgium[1] | 2 348 352 | 2.7 | 2 656 856 | 2.8 | 13.1 |
| Denmark | 952 164 | 1.1 | 1 014 646 | 1.1 | 6.6 |
| Finland | 206 669 | 0.2 | 226 838 | 0.2 | 9.8 |
| France | 2 651 607 | 3.0 | 2 897 071 | 3.1 | 9.3 |
| Germany | 56 058 730 | 64.0 | 59 921 841 | 63.1 | 6.9 |
| Greece | 174 498 | 0.2 | 188 901 | 0.2 | 8.3 |
| Iceland[2] | .. | .. | .. | .. | .. |
| Ireland | 33 141 | 0.0 | 58 004 | 0.1 | 75.0 |
| Italy | 2 091 245 | 2.4 | 2 786 978 | 2.9 | 33.3 |
| Luxembourg[1] | .. | .. | .. | .. | .. |
| Netherlands | 9 268 514 | 10.6 | 9 658 807 | 10.2 | 4.2 |
| Norway | 206 501 | 0.2 | 194 790 | 0.2 | −5.7 |
| Portugal | 26 661 | 0.0 | 24 185 | 0.0 | −9.3 |
| Spain | 364 711 | 0.4 | 456 040 | 0.5 | 25.0 |
| Sweden | 1 374 559 | 1.6 | 1 416 555 | 1.5 | 3.1 |
| Switzerland | 2 490 755 | 2.8 | 2 940 566 | 3.1 | 18.1 |
| Turkey | 65 530 | 0.1 | 108 755 | 0.1 | 66.0 |
| United Kingdom | 4 213 101 | 4.8 | 4 720 360 | 5.0 | 12.0 |
| Other OECD-Europe | .. | .. | .. | .. | .. |
| **Total Europe** | 82 526 738 | 94.2 | 89 271 193 | 94.0 | 8.2 |
| Canada | 223 492 | 0.3 | 220 697 | 0.2 | −1.3 |
| United States | 1 591 663 | 1.8 | 1 697 928 | 1.8 | 6.7 |
| **Total North America** | 1 815 155 | 2.1 | 1 918 625 | 2.0 | 5.7 |
| Australia[3] | 188 485 | 0.2 | 237 527 | 0.3 | 26.0 |
| New Zealand[3] | .. | .. | .. | .. | .. |
| Japan | 320 548 | 0.4 | 370 537 | 0.4 | 15.6 |
| **Total Australasia and Japan** | 509 033 | 0.6 | 608 064 | 0.6 | 19.5 |
| **Total OECD Countries** | 84 850 926 | 96.9 | 91 797 882 | 96.7 | 8.2 |
| Yugoslavia | 382 639 | 0.4 | 408 548 | 0.4 | 6.8 |
| Other European countries[2] | 1 038 063 | 1.2 | 1 305 333 | 1.4 | 25.7 |
| Bulgaria | 29 485 | 0.0 | 42 859 | 0.0 | 45.4 |
| Czechoslovakia | 137 437 | 0.2 | 182 672 | 0.2 | 32.9 |
| Hungary | 606 689 | 0.7 | 573 604 | 0.6 | −5.5 |
| Poland | 168 562 | 0.2 | 227 449 | 0.2 | 34.9 |
| Rumania | 23 807 | 0.0 | 23 099 | 0.0 | −3.0 |
| USSR | 72 083 | 0.1 | 255 650 | 0.3 | 254.7 |
| Latin America | 149 157 | 0.2 | 162 815 | 0.2 | 9.2 |
| Asia-Oceania | 411 212 | 0.5 | 453 683 | 0.5 | 10.3 |
| Africa | 102 138 | 0.1 | 102 717 | 0.1 | 0.6 |
| Origin country undetermined | 641 012 | 0.7 | 737 523 | 0.8 | 15.1 |
| **Total non-OECD Countries** | 2 724 221 | 3.1 | 3 170 619 | 3.3 | 16.4 |
| **TOTAL** | 87 575 147 | 100.0 | 94 968 501 | 100.0 | 8.4 |

1. Belgium includes Luxembourg.
2. "Other European countries" includes Iceland.
3. Australia includes New Zealand.

# BELGIUM

### NIGHTS SPENT BY FOREIGN TOURISTS IN HOTELS[1]
*(by country of residence)*

| | 1988 | Relative share | 1989 | Relative share | % Variation over 1988 |
|---|---|---|---|---|---|
| Austria | 50 087 | 0.9 | 49 727 | 0.8 | −0.7 |
| Belgium | .. | | .. | | |
| Denmark | 66 986 | 1.2 | 73 439 | 1.2 | 9.6 |
| Finland[2] | .. | | .. | | |
| France | 657 214 | 12.1 | 711 885 | 11.9 | 8.3 |
| Germany | 801 827 | 14.8 | 866 682 | 14.5 | 8.1 |
| Greece | 74 103 | 1.4 | 68 590 | 1.1 | −7.4 |
| Iceland[2] | .. | | .. | | |
| Ireland | 32 407 | 0.6 | 37 573 | 0.6 | 15.9 |
| Italy | 266 212 | 4.9 | 287 863 | 4.8 | 8.1 |
| Luxembourg | 80 793 | 1.5 | 78 639 | 1.3 | −2.7 |
| Netherlands | 740 873 | 13.7 | 860 505 | 14.4 | 16.1 |
| Norway | 48 867 | 0.9 | 46 431 | 0.8 | −5.0 |
| Portugal | 58 341 | 1.1 | 66 355 | 1.1 | 13.7 |
| Spain | 179 629 | 3.3 | 214 498 | 3.6 | 19.4 |
| Sweden | 97 748 | 1.8 | 117 789 | 2.0 | 20.5 |
| Switzerland | 88 178 | 1.6 | 92 525 | 1.6 | 4.9 |
| Turkey | 16 942 | 0.3 | 17 842 | 0.3 | 5.3 |
| United Kingdom | 856 412 | 15.8 | 947 234 | 15.9 | 10.6 |
| Other OECD-Europe | .. | | .. | | .. |
| **Total Europe** | 4 116 619 | 75.9 | 4 537 577 | 76.0 | 10.2 |
| | | | | | |
| Canada | 79 376 | 1.5 | 86 146 | 1.4 | 8.5 |
| United States | 463 917 | 8.6 | 511 738 | 8.6 | 10.3 |
| **Total North America** | 543 293 | 10.0 | 597 884 | 10.0 | 10.0 |
| | | | | | |
| Australia[3] | .. | | .. | | .. |
| New Zealand[3] | .. | | .. | | .. |
| Japan | 120 540 | 2.2 | 153 011 | 2.6 | 26.9 |
| **Total Australasia and Japan** | 120 540 | 2.2 | 153 011 | 2.6 | 26.9 |
| | | | | | |
| **Total OECD Countries** | 4 780 452 | 88.1 | 5 288 472 | 88.6 | 10.6 |
| | | | | | |
| Yugoslavia | .. | | .. | | .. |
| Other European countries[2] | 163 675 | 3.0 | 179 372 | 3.0 | 9.6 |
| USSR | 13 087 | 0.2 | 21 542 | 0.4 | 64.6 |
| Latin America | 72 950 | 1.3 | 82 750 | 1.4 | 13.4 |
| Mexico[4] | 24 626 | 0.5 | 30 568 | 0.5 | 24.1 |
| Asia-Oceania[3] | 198 113 | 3.7 | 204 819 | 3.4 | 3.4 |
| Africa | 208 950 | 3.9 | 212 914 | 3.6 | 1.9 |
| | | | | | |
| **Total non-OECD Countries** | 643 688 | 11.9 | 679 855 | 11.4 | 5.6 |
| | | | | | |
| **TOTAL** | 5 424 140 | 100.0 | 5 968 327 | 100.0 | 10.0 |

1. Preliminary data for 1989.
2. "Other European countries" includes Finland and Iceland.
3. "Asia-Oceania" includes Australia and New Zealand.
4. Mexico includes Central America.

# BELGIUM

## NIGHTS SPENT BY FOREIGN TOURISTS IN REGISTERED TOURIST ACCOMMODATION[1]
### (by country of residence)

| | 1988 | Relative share | 1989 | Relative share | % Variation over 1988 |
|---|---|---|---|---|---|
| Austria | 60 028 | 0.6 | 59 081 | 0.5 | −1.6 |
| Belgium | .. | .. | .. | .. | .. |
| Denmark | 90 042 | 0.9 | 98 432 | 0.9 | 9.3 |
| Finland[2] | .. | .. | .. | .. | .. |
| France | 1 010 799 | 9.6 | 939 061 | 8.7 | −7.1 |
| Germany | 1 691 014 | 16.0 | 1 636 191 | 15.2 | −3.2 |
| Greece | 77 410 | 0.7 | 71 137 | 0.7 | −8.1 |
| Iceland[2] | .. | .. | .. | .. | .. |
| Ireland | 37 500 | 0.4 | 45 287 | 0.4 | 20.8 |
| Italy | 304 331 | 2.9 | 326 226 | 3.0 | 7.2 |
| Luxembourg | 167 430 | 1.6 | 130 774 | 1.2 | −21.9 |
| Netherlands | 4 069 115 | 38.5 | 4 201 445 | 39.0 | 3.3 |
| Norway | 58 086 | 0.5 | 52 806 | 0.5 | −9.1 |
| Portugal | 69 378 | 0.7 | 75 593 | 0.7 | 9.0 |
| Spain | 213 848 | 2.0 | 248 468 | 2.3 | 16.2 |
| Sweden | 108 774 | 1.0 | 132 847 | 1.2 | 22.1 |
| Switzerland | 95 554 | 0.9 | 99 998 | 0.9 | 4.7 |
| Turkey | 18 653 | 0.2 | 20 226 | 0.2 | 8.4 |
| United Kingdom | 974 784 | 9.2 | 1 067 821 | 9.9 | 9.5 |
| Other OECD-Europe | .. | .. | .. | .. | .. |
| **Total Europe** | 9 046 746 | 85.5 | 9 205 393 | 85.4 | 1.8 |
| | | | | | |
| Canada | 90 735 | 0.9 | 97 631 | 0.9 | 7.6 |
| United States | 572 837 | 5.4 | 546 129 | 5.1 | −4.7 |
| **Total North America** | 663 572 | 6.3 | 643 760 | 6.0 | −3.0 |
| | | | | | |
| Australia[3] | .. | .. | .. | .. | .. |
| New Zealand[3] | .. | .. | .. | .. | .. |
| Japan | 125 375 | 1.2 | 158 573 | 1.5 | 26.5 |
| **Total Australasia and Japan** | 125 375 | 1.2 | 158 573 | 1.5 | 26.5 |
| | | | | | |
| **Total OECD Countries** | 9 835 693 | 93.0 | 10 007 726 | 92.9 | 1.7 |
| | | | | | |
| Yugoslavia | .. | .. | .. | .. | .. |
| Other European countries[2] | 202 882 | 1.9 | 209 315 | 1.9 | 3.2 |
| USSR | 13 930 | 0.1 | 23 887 | 0.2 | 71.5 |
| Latin America | 82 024 | 0.8 | 93 237 | 0.9 | 13.7 |
| Mexico[4] | 27 545 | 0.3 | 34 650 | 0.3 | 25.8 |
| Asia-Oceania[3] | 220 033 | 2.1 | 226 778 | 2.1 | 3.1 |
| Africa | 234 881 | 2.2 | 237 722 | 2.2 | 1.2 |
| Origin country undetermined | 1 512 | 0.0 | .. | .. | .. |
| | | | | | |
| **Total non-OECD Countries** | 741 332 | 7.0 | 767 052 | 7.1 | 3.5 |
| | | | | | |
| **TOTAL** | 10 577 025 | 100.0 | 10 774 778 | 100.0 | 1.9 |

1. Preliminary data for 1989.
2. "Other European countries" includes Finland and Iceland.
3. "Asia-Oceania" includes Australia and New Zealand.
4. Mexico includes Central America.

# CANADA

## ARRIVALS OF FOREIGN TOURISTS AT FRONTIERS

*(by country of residence)*

| | 1988 | Relative share | 1989 | Relative share | % Variation over 1988 |
|---|---|---|---|---|---|
| Austria | 23 400 | 0.2 | 21 100 | 0.1 | −9.8 |
| Belgium[1] | 28 600 | 0.2 | 27 600 | 0.2 | −3.5 |
| Denmark | 20 700 | 0.1 | 21 300 | 0.1 | 2.9 |
| Finland | 14 800 | 0.1 | 17 400 | 0.1 | 17.6 |
| France[2] | 229 700 | 1.5 | 242 900 | 1.6 | 5.7 |
| Germany | 263 000 | 1.7 | 262 700 | 1.7 | −0.1 |
| Greece | 18 100 | 0.1 | 17 600 | 0.1 | −2.8 |
| Iceland | 1 300 | 0.0 | 1 200 | 0.0 | −7.7 |
| Ireland | 17 700 | 0.1 | 17 700 | 0.1 | 0.0 |
| Italy | 86 300 | 0.6 | 90 500 | 0.6 | 4.9 |
| Luxembourg[1] | 1 600 | 0.0 | 1 600 | 0.0 | 0.0 |
| Netherlands | 88 000 | 0.6 | 87 400 | 0.6 | −0.7 |
| Norway | 13 800 | 0.1 | 12 200 | 0.1 | −11.6 |
| Portugal | 17 300 | 0.1 | 18 800 | 0.1 | 8.7 |
| Spain | 19 300 | 0.1 | 20 000 | 0.1 | 3.6 |
| Sweden | 30 000 | 0.2 | 30 900 | 0.2 | 3.0 |
| Switzerland | 75 200 | 0.5 | 73 800 | 0.5 | −1.9 |
| Turkey | 3 500 | 0.0 | 2 900 | 0.0 | −17.1 |
| United Kingdom | 527 200 | 3.4 | 561 200 | 3.7 | 6.4 |
| Other OECD-Europe | .. | .. | .. | .. | .. |
| **Total Europe** | 1 479 500 | 9.6 | 1 528 800 | 10.1 | 3.3 |
| Canada | .. | .. | .. | .. | .. |
| United States | 12 763 100 | 82.4 | 12 195 400 | 80.6 | −4.4 |
| **Total North America** | 12 763 100 | 82.4 | 12 195 400 | 80.6 | −4.4 |
| Australia[4] | 90 900 | 0.6 | 109 700 | 0.7 | 20.7 |
| New Zealand | 35 800 | 0.2 | 39 300 | 0.3 | 9.8 |
| Japan | 324 100 | 2.1 | 387 000 | 2.6 | 19.4 |
| **Total Australasia and Japan** | 450 800 | 2.9 | 536 000 | 3.5 | 18.9 |
| **Total OECD Countries** | 14 693 400 | 94.9 | 14 260 200 | 94.3 | −2.9 |
| Yugoslavia | 14 800 | 0.1 | 15 300 | 0.1 | 3.4 |
| Other European countries | 60 200 | 0.4 | 75 100 | 0.5 | 24.8 |
| Bulgaria[1] | 800 | 0.0 | 1 000 | 0.0 | 25.0 |
| Czechoslovakia | 6 400 | 0.0 | 8 200 | 0.1 | 28.1 |
| Germany (D. R.) | 2 100 | 0.0 | 1 600 | 0.0 | −23.8 |
| Hungary | 9 400 | 0.1 | 9 200 | 0.1 | −2.1 |
| Poland | 29 200 | 0.2 | 33 200 | 0.2 | 13.7 |
| Rumania[1] | 1 700 | 0.0 | 1 500 | 0.0 | −11.8 |
| USSR | 9 600 | 0.1 | 19 000 | 0.1 | 97.9 |
| Latin America[3] | 163 500 | 1.1 | 168 600 | 1.1 | 3.1 |
| Argentina | 30 700 | 0.2 | 28 700 | 0.2 | −6.5 |
| Brazil | 29 500 | 0.2 | 32 100 | 0.2 | 8.8 |
| Chile | 5 800 | 0.0 | 6 700 | 0.0 | 15.5 |
| Colombia | 7 000 | 0.0 | 7 000 | 0.0 | 0.0 |
| Mexico | 57 700 | 0.4 | 63 200 | 0.4 | 9.5 |
| Venezuela | 8 200 | 0.1 | 8 700 | 0.1 | 6.1 |
| Asia-Oceania | 377 500 | 2.4 | 443 300 | 2.9 | 17.4 |
| China[6] | 26 600 | 0.2 | 27 900 | 0.2 | 4.9 |
| Hong Kong | 82 500 | 0.5 | 117 900 | 0.8 | 42.9 |
| India[1] | 69 300 | 0.4 | 66 600 | 0.4 | −3.9 |
| Iran[1] | 3 800 | 0.0 | 5 500 | 0.0 | 44.7 |
| Israel | 62 800 | 0.4 | 60 700 | 0.4 | −3.3 |
| Republic of Korea[1] | 20 100 | 0.1 | 30 600 | 0.2 | 52.2 |
| Lebanon | 3 800 | 0.0 | 4 300 | 0.0 | 13.2 |
| Malaysia[1] | 14 300 | 0.1 | 16 500 | 0.1 | 15.4 |
| Pakistan[1] | 9 400 | 0.1 | 9 600 | 0.1 | 2.1 |
| Philippines[1] | 18 500 | 0.1 | 20 100 | 0.1 | 8.6 |
| Saudi Arabia[1] | 9 000 | 0.1 | 8 100 | 0.1 | −10.0 |
| Singapore[1] | 15 000 | 0.1 | 18 300 | 0.1 | 22.0 |
| Taiwan | 21 100 | 0.1 | 33 600 | 0.2 | 59.2 |
| Thailand[1] | 6 400 | 0.0 | 8 300 | 0.1 | 29.7 |
| Africa | 45 500 | 0.3 | 46 900 | 0.3 | 3.1 |
| Algeria[1] | 1 500 | 0.0 | 1 900 | 0.0 | 26.7 |
| Egypt[1] | 5 900 | 0.0 | 5 600 | 0.0 | −5.1 |
| Morocco[1] | 3 700 | 0.0 | 4 600 | 0.0 | 24.3 |
| South Africa | 10 400 | 0.1 | 10 700 | 0.1 | 2.9 |
| Origin country undetermined[5] | 129 900 | 0.8 | 112 900 | 0.7 | −13.1 |
| **Total non-OECD Countries** | 791 400 | 5.1 | 862 100 | 5.7 | 8.9 |
| **TOTAL[1]** | 15 484 800 | 100.0 | 15 122 300 | 100.0 | −2.3 |

1. Estimate.
2. France includes Andorra and Monaco.
3. Latin America includes South America, Central America and Mexico.
4. Australia includes Papua New Guinea, Solomon, Caroline and Christmas islands.
5. Origin country undetermined includes Bermuda, Caribbean, Greenland and St. Pierre and Miquelon.
6. China includes Mongolia and Tibet.

# CANADA

*ARRIVALS OF FOREIGN VISITORS AT FRONTIERS*

*(by country of residence)*

| | 1988 | Relative share | 1989 | Relative share | % Variation over 1988 |
|---|---|---|---|---|---|
| Austria | 27 300 | 0.1 | 24 800 | 0.1 | −9.2 |
| Belgium[1] | 32 200 | 0.1 | 30 500 | 0.1 | −5.3 |
| Denmark | 25 000 | 0.1 | 24 800 | 0.1 | −0.8 |
| Finland[2] | 17 300 | 0.0 | 19 400 | 0.1 | 12.1 |
| France[2] | 250 400 | 0.6 | 262 600 | 0.7 | 4.9 |
| Germany | 321 700 | 0.8 | 308 500 | 0.8 | −4.1 |
| Greece | 20 100 | 0.1 | 19 300 | 0.1 | −4.0 |
| Iceland | 1 500 | 0.0 | 1 500 | 0.0 | 0.0 |
| Ireland | 20 700 | 0.1 | 19 800 | 0.1 | −4.3 |
| Italy | 107 600 | 0.3 | 107 400 | 0.3 | −0.2 |
| Luxembourg[1] | 1 700 | 0.0 | 1 700 | 0.0 | 0.0 |
| Netherlands | 98 900 | 0.3 | 96 800 | 0.3 | −2.1 |
| Norway | 15 700 | 0.0 | 13 600 | 0.0 | −13.4 |
| Portugal | 17 800 | 0.0 | 19 400 | 0.1 | 9.0 |
| Spain | 24 600 | 0.1 | 24 400 | 0.1 | −0.8 |
| Sweden | 36 800 | 0.1 | 35 600 | 0.1 | −3.3 |
| Switzerland | 83 500 | 0.2 | 81 900 | 0.2 | −1.9 |
| Turkey | 3 700 | 0.0 | 3 200 | 0.0 | −13.5 |
| United Kingdom | 585 800 | 1.5 | 614 800 | 1.6 | 5.0 |
| Other OECD-Europe | .. | .. | .. | .. | .. |
| **Total Europe** | 1 692 300 | 4.3 | 1 710 000 | 4.5 | 1.0 |
| | | | | | |
| Canada | .. | .. | .. | .. | |
| United States | 36 147 100 | 92.1 | 34 705 100 | 91.4 | −4.0 |
| **Total North America** | 36 147 100 | 92.1 | 34 705 100 | 91.4 | −4.0 |
| | | | | | |
| Australia[4] | 101 300 | 0.3 | 120 800 | 0.3 | 19.2 |
| New Zealand | 39 500 | 0.1 | 42 600 | 0.1 | 7.8 |
| Japan | 404 600 | 1.0 | 462 700 | 1.2 | 14.4 |
| **Total Australasia and Japan** | 545 400 | 1.4 | 626 100 | 1.6 | 14.8 |
| | | | | | |
| **Total OECD Countries** | 38 384 800 | 97.8 | 37 041 200 | 97.5 | −3.5 |
| | | | | | |
| Yugoslavia | 15 900 | 0.0 | 16 000 | 0.0 | 0.6 |
| Other European countries | 62 800 | 0.2 | 78 800 | 0.2 | 25.5 |
| Bulgaria[1] | 900 | 0.0 | 1 000 | 0.0 | 11.1 |
| Czechoslovakia | 6 900 | 0.0 | 8 700 | 0.0 | 26.1 |
| Germany (D. R.) | 2 100 | 0.0 | 1 600 | 0.0 | −23.8 |
| Hungary | 9 700 | 0.0 | 9 900 | 0.0 | 2.1 |
| Poland | 29 900 | 0.1 | 34 400 | 0.1 | 15.1 |
| Rumania[1] | 1 800 | 0.0 | 1 600 | 0.0 | −11.1 |
| USSR | 9 800 | 0.0 | 20 000 | 0.1 | 104.1 |
| Latin America[3] | 185 300 | 0.5 | 189 900 | 0.5 | 2.5 |
| Argentina | 32 400 | 0.1 | 29 900 | 0.1 | −7.7 |
| Brazil | 31 500 | 0.1 | 34 000 | 0.1 | 7.9 |
| Chile | 6 100 | 0.0 | 7 000 | 0.0 | 14.8 |
| Colombia | 7 900 | 0.0 | 8 000 | 0.0 | 1.3 |
| Mexico | 65 700 | 0.2 | 72 800 | 0.2 | 10.8 |
| Venezuela | 9 100 | 0.0 | 9 500 | 0.0 | 4.4 |
| Asia-Oceania | 422 900 | 1.1 | 490 200 | 1.3 | 15.9 |
| China[6] | 29 400 | 0.1 | 30 900 | 0.1 | 5.1 |
| Hong Kong | 87 800 | 0.2 | 123 100 | 0.3 | 40.2 |
| India[1] | 83 100 | 0.2 | 78 600 | 0.2 | −5.4 |
| Iran[1] | 3 900 | 0.0 | 3 600 | 0.0 | −7.7 |
| Israel | 71 600 | 0.2 | 69 400 | 0.2 | −3.1 |
| Republic of Korea[1] | 23 300 | 0.1 | 35 600 | 0.1 | 52.8 |
| Lebanon | 4 300 | 0.0 | 4 900 | 0.0 | 14.0 |
| Malaysia[1] | 16 500 | 0.0 | 19 100 | 0.1 | 15.8 |
| Pakistan[1] | 10 600 | 0.0 | 10 800 | 0.0 | 1.9 |
| Philippines[1] | 21 000 | 0.1 | 22 200 | 0.1 | 5.7 |
| Saudi Arabia[1] | 9 600 | 0.0 | 8 600 | 0.0 | −10.4 |
| Singapore[1] | 16 200 | 0.0 | 19 500 | 0.1 | 20.4 |
| Taiwan | 22 900 | 0.1 | 33 900 | 0.1 | 48.0 |
| Thailand[1] | 7 500 | 0.0 | 7 300 | 0.0 | −2.7 |
| Africa | 47 100 | 0.1 | 48 500 | 0.1 | 3.0 |
| Algeria[1] | 1 600 | 0.0 | 1 900 | 0.0 | 18.8 |
| Egypt[1] | 6 200 | 0.0 | 5 900 | 0.0 | −4.8 |
| Morocco[1] | 3 800 | 0.0 | 4 700 | 0.0 | 23.7 |
| South Africa | 11 000 | 0.0 | 11 100 | 0.0 | 0.9 |
| Origin country undetermined[5] | 134 300 | 0.3 | 117 500 | 0.3 | −12.5 |
| | | | | | |
| **Total non-OECD Countries** | 868 300 | 2.2 | 940 900 | 2.5 | 8.4 |
| | | | | | |
| **TOTAL[1]** | 39 253 100 | 100.0 | 37 982 100 | 100.0 | −3.2 |

1. Estimate.
2. France includes Andorra and Monaco.
3. Latin America includes South America, Central America and Mexico.
4. Australia includes Papua New Guinea, Solomon, Caroline and Christmas islands.
5. Origin country undetermined includes Bermuda, Caribbean, Greenland and St. Pierre and Miquelon.
6. China includes Mongolia and Tibet.

# CANADA

*NIGHTS SPENT BY FOREIGN TOURISTS IN TOURIST ACCOMMODATION[1]*
*(by country of residence)*

|  | 1988 | Relative share | 1989 | Relative share | % Variation over 1988 |
|---|---|---|---|---|---|
| Austria | 308 600 | 0.3 | 240 700 | 0.3 | −22.0 |
| Belgium | 311 200 | 0.3 | 342 500 | 0.4 | 10.1 |
| Denmark | 233 100 | 0.3 | 268 100 | 0.3 | 15.0 |
| Finland | 141 300 | 0.2 | 163 400 | 0.2 | 15.6 |
| France | 2 841 800 | 3.1 | 2 922 100 | 3.2 | 2.8 |
| Germany | 3 580 900 | 3.9 | 3 247 300 | 3.6 | −9.3 |
| Greece | 382 500 | 0.4 | 352 100 | 0.4 | −7.9 |
| Iceland | 17 700 | 0.0 | 10 700 | 0.0 | −39.5 |
| Ireland | 239 000 | 0.3 | 261 400 | 0.3 | 9.4 |
| Italy | 1 070 600 | 1.2 | 1 006 700 | 1.1 | −6.0 |
| Luxembourg | 17 400 | 0.0 | 20 500 | 0.0 | 17.8 |
| Netherlands | 1 206 600 | 1.3 | 1 148 800 | 1.3 | −4.8 |
| Norway | 143 500 | 0.2 | 119 400 | 0.1 | −16.8 |
| Portugal | 356 700 | 0.4 | 329 700 | 0.4 | −7.6 |
| Spain | 248 000 | 0.3 | 203 200 | 0.2 | −18.1 |
| Sweden | 277 400 | 0.3 | 259 400 | 0.3 | −6.5 |
| Switzerland | 929 600 | 1.0 | 923 300 | 1.0 | −0.7 |
| Turkey | 64 500 | 0.1 | 67 600 | 0.1 | 4.8 |
| United Kingdom | 6 813 500 | 7.4 | 6 831 200 | 7.6 | 0.3 |
| Other OECD-Europe | .. | .. | .. | .. | .. |
| **Total Europe** | 19 183 900 | 20.9 | 18 718 100 | 20.8 | −2.4 |
| Canada | .. | .. | .. | .. | .. |
| United States | 56 201 900 | 61.1 | 53 598 000 | 59.5 | −4.6 |
| **Total North America** | 56 201 900 | 61.1 | 53 598 000 | 59.5 | −4.6 |
| Australia | 1 154 000 | 1.3 | 1 269 600 | 1.4 | 10.0 |
| New Zealand | 427 600 | 0.5 | 420 100 | 0.5 | −1.8 |
| Japan | 2 229 000 | 2.4 | 2 538 300 | 2.8 | 13.9 |
| **Total Australasia and Japan** | 3 810 600 | 4.1 | 4 228 000 | 4.7 | 11.0 |
| **Total OECD Countries** | 79 196 400 | 86.2 | 76 544 100 | 85.0 | −3.3 |
| Yugoslavia | 458 300 | 0.5 | 349 200 | 0.4 | −23.8 |
| Other European countries | 3 107 100 | 3.4 | 3 253 000 | 3.6 | 4.7 |
| Bulgaria | 18 200 | 0.0 | 25 800 | 0.0 | 41.8 |
| Czechoslovakia | 295 700 | 0.3 | 250 200 | 0.3 | −15.4 |
| Germany (D. R.) | 49 900 | 0.1 | 31 200 | 0.0 | −37.5 |
| Hungary | 234 100 | 0.3 | 198 800 | 0.2 | −15.1 |
| Poland | 2 050 900 | 2.2 | 2 081 300 | 2.3 | 1.5 |
| Rumania | 38 800 | 0.0 | 17 100 | 0.0 | −55.9 |
| USSR | 386 900 | 0.4 | 617 100 | 0.7 | 59.5 |
| Latin America[2] | 1 820 800 | 2.0 | 1 857 200 | 2.1 | 2.0 |
| Mexico[2] | 513 600 | 0.6 | 626 800 | 0.7 | 22.0 |
| Asia-Oceania | 4 760 300 | 5.2 | 5 620 600 | 6.2 | 18.1 |
| China | 564 900 | 0.6 | 913 800 | 1.0 | 61.8 |
| Hong Kong | 1 047 400 | 1.1 | 1 509 100 | 1.7 | 44.1 |
| India | 942 400 | 1.0 | 823 700 | 0.9 | −12.6 |
| Israel | 508 000 | 0.6 | 593 200 | 0.7 | 16.8 |
| Lebanon | 61 300 | 0.1 | 65 300 | 0.1 | 6.5 |
| Taiwan | 205 800 | 0.2 | 260 600 | 0.3 | 26.6 |
| Africa | 785 600 | 0.9 | 795 500 | 0.9 | 1.3 |
| South Africa | 168 600 | 0.2 | 127 600 | 0.1 | −24.3 |
| Origin country undetermined | 1 783 400 | 1.9 | 1 612 000 | 1.8 | −9.6 |
| **Total non-OECD Countries** | 12 715 500 | 13.8 | 13 487 500 | 15.0 | 6.1 |
| **TOTAL** | 91 911 900 | 100.0 | 90 031 600 | 100.0 | −2.0 |

1. Covers all forms of accommodation, including homes of friends or relatives.
2. Latin America includes Mexico.

# DENMARK

## NIGHTS SPENT BY FOREIGN TOURISTS IN HOTELS
### (by country of nationality)

| | 1988 | Relative share | 1989 | Relative share | % Variation over 1988 |
|---|---|---|---|---|---|
| Austria[1] | .. | .. | .. | .. | .. |
| Belgium[1] | .. | .. | .. | .. | .. |
| Denmark | .. | .. | .. | .. | .. |
| Finland | 112 500 | 2.6 | 125 100 | 2.4 | 11.2 |
| France | 75 800 | 1.7 | 82 700 | 1.6 | 9.1 |
| Germany | 929 200 | 21.2 | 1 147 200 | 22.4 | 23.5 |
| Greece[1] | .. | .. | .. | .. | .. |
| Iceland[1] | .. | .. | .. | .. | .. |
| Ireland[1] | .. | .. | .. | .. | .. |
| Italy | 103 900 | 2.4 | 115 200 | 2.2 | 10.9 |
| Luxembourg[1] | .. | .. | .. | .. | .. |
| Netherlands | 102 100 | 2.3 | 123 400 | 2.4 | 20.9 |
| Norway | 677 100 | 15.5 | 718 500 | 14.0 | 6.1 |
| Portugal[1] | .. | .. | .. | .. | .. |
| Spain[1] | .. | .. | .. | .. | .. |
| Sweden | 1 053 500 | 24.1 | 1 319 600 | 25.7 | 25.3 |
| Switzerland[1] | .. | .. | .. | .. | .. |
| Turkey[1] | .. | .. | .. | .. | .. |
| United Kingdom | 290 000 | 6.6 | 319 300 | 6.2 | 10.1 |
| Other OECD-Europe | .. | .. | .. | .. | .. |
| **Total Europe** | 3 344 100 | 76.4 | 3 951 000 | 77.0 | 18.1 |
| | | | | | |
| Canada[2] | .. | | .. | | .. |
| United States | 378 200 | 8.6 | 425 200 | 8.3 | 12.4 |
| **Total North America** | 378 200 | 8.6 | 425 200 | 8.3 | 12.4 |
| | | | | | |
| Australia[2] | .. | | .. | | .. |
| New Zealand[2] | .. | | .. | | .. |
| Japan | 107 700 | 2.5 | 118 700 | 2.3 | 10.2 |
| **Total Australasia and Japan** | 107 700 | 2.5 | 118 700 | 2.3 | 10.2 |
| | | | | | |
| **Total OECD Countries** | 3 830 000 | 87.5 | 4 494 900 | 87.6 | 17.4 |
| | | | | | |
| Yugoslavia | .. | | .. | | .. |
| Other European countries[1] | 240 100 | 5.5 | 269 100 | 5.2 | 12.1 |
| Origin country undetermined[2] | 307 700 | 7.0 | 368 000 | 7.2 | 19.6 |
| | | | | | |
| **Total non-OECD Countries** | 547 800 | 12.5 | 637 100 | 12.4 | 16.3 |
| | | | | | |
| **TOTAL** | 4 377 800 | 100.0 | 5 132 000 | 100.0 | 17.2 |

1. Included in "Other European countries".
2. Included in "Origin country undetermined".

# DENMARK

## NIGHTS SPENT BY FOREIGN TOURISTS IN REGISTERED TOURIST ACCOMMODATION
### (by country of nationality)

| | 1988 | Relative share | 1989 | Relative share | % Variation over 1988 |
|---|---|---|---|---|---|
| Austria | .. | .. | .. | .. | .. |
| Belgium | .. | .. | .. | .. | .. |
| Denmark | .. | .. | .. | .. | .. |
| Finland | 203 937 | 2.5 | 215 038 | 2.4 | 5.4 |
| France | 138 810 | 1.7 | 154 036 | 1.7 | 11.0 |
| Germany | 2 818 399 | 35.2 | 3 210 790 | 35.3 | 13.9 |
| Greece | .. | .. | .. | .. | .. |
| Iceland | .. | .. | .. | .. | .. |
| Ireland | .. | .. | .. | .. | .. |
| Italy | 153 449 | 1.9 | 174 917 | 1.9 | 14.0 |
| Luxembourg | .. | .. | .. | .. | .. |
| Netherlands | 509 366 | 6.4 | 602 626 | 6.6 | 18.3 |
| Norway | 985 947 | 12.3 | 1 039 698 | 11.4 | 5.5 |
| Portugal | .. | .. | .. | .. | .. |
| Spain | .. | .. | .. | .. | .. |
| Sweden | 1 657 356 | 20.7 | 1 935 911 | 21.3 | 16.8 |
| Switzerland | .. | .. | .. | .. | .. |
| Turkey | .. | .. | .. | .. | .. |
| United Kingdom | 347 978 | 4.3 | 376 546 | 4.1 | 8.2 |
| Other OECD-Europe | .. | .. | .. | .. | .. |
| **Total Europe** | 6 815 242 | 85.1 | 7 709 562 | 84.8 | 13.1 |
| Canada[2] | .. | .. | .. | .. | .. |
| United States | 398 777 | 5.0 | 447 229 | 4.9 | 12.2 |
| **Total North America** | 398 777 | 5.0 | 447 229 | 4.9 | 12.2 |
| Australia[2] | .. | .. | .. | .. | .. |
| New Zealand[2] | .. | .. | .. | .. | .. |
| Japan | .. | .. | .. | .. | .. |
| **Total Australasia and Japan** | .. | .. | .. | .. | .. |
| **Total OECD Countries** | 7 214 019 | 90.1 | 8 156 791 | 89.8 | 13.1 |
| Yugoslavia | .. | .. | .. | .. | .. |
| Other European countries | 328 973 | 4.1 | 375 108 | 4.1 | 14.0 |
| Origin country undetermined[2] | 468 014 | 5.8 | 555 884 | 6.1 | 18.8 |
| **Total non-OECD Countries[1]** | 796 987 | 9.9 | 930 992 | 10.2 | 16.8 |
| **TOTAL** | 8 011 006 | 100.0 | 9 087 783 | 100.0 | 13.4 |

1. Includes nights spent by foreign tourists from Member countries.
2. Included in "Origin country undetermined".

# FINLAND

## NIGHTS SPENT BY FOREIGN TOURISTS IN HOTELS
### (by country of residence)

| | 1988 | Relative share | 1989 | Relative share | % Variation over 1988 |
|---|---|---|---|---|---|
| Austria | 24 626 | 1.1 | 26 239 | 1.0 | 6.5 |
| Belgium | 16 018 | 0.7 | 17 080 | 0.7 | 6.6 |
| Denmark | 69 569 | 3.0 | 77 147 | 3.1 | 10.9 |
| Finland | .. | | .. | | .. |
| France | 66 433 | 2.9 | 71 269 | 2.8 | 7.3 |
| Germany | 321 592 | 14.0 | 353 506 | 14.0 | 9.9 |
| Greece[1] | .. | | .. | | .. |
| Iceland | 6 855 | 0.3 | 6 325 | 0.3 | −7.7 |
| Ireland[2] | .. | | .. | | .. |
| Italy | 81 838 | 3.6 | 86 910 | 3.5 | 6.2 |
| Luxembourg[1] | .. | | .. | | .. |
| Netherlands | 46 266 | 2.0 | 52 189 | 2.1 | 12.8 |
| Norway | 122 201 | 5.3 | 115 563 | 4.6 | −5.4 |
| Portugal[3] | .. | | .. | | .. |
| Spain[3] | 29 079 | 1.3 | 32 510 | 1.3 | 11.8 |
| Sweden | 557 463 | 24.3 | 584 866 | 23.2 | 4.9 |
| Switzerland | 73 365 | 3.2 | 76 152 | 3.0 | 3.8 |
| Turkey[1] | .. | | .. | | .. |
| United Kingdom[2] | 131 711 | 5.7 | 141 265 | 5.6 | 7.3 |
| Other OECD-Europe | .. | | .. | | .. |
| **Total Europe** | 1 547 016 | 67.3 | 1 641 021 | 65.2 | 6.1 |
| | | | | | |
| Canada | 30 427 | 1.3 | 33 223 | 1.3 | 9.2 |
| United States | 203 202 | 8.8 | 202 452 | 8.0 | −0.4 |
| **Total North America** | 233 629 | 10.2 | 235 675 | 9.4 | 0.9 |
| | | | | | |
| Australia | .. | .. | .. | .. | .. |
| New Zealand | .. | .. | .. | .. | .. |
| Japan | 55 766 | 2.4 | 60 855 | 2.4 | 9.1 |
| **Total Australasia and Japan** | 55 766 | 2.4 | 60 855 | 2.4 | 9.1 |
| | | | | | |
| **Total OECD Countries** | 1 836 411 | 79.9 | 1 937 551 | 77.0 | 5.5 |
| | | | | | |
| Yugoslavia | .. | | .. | | .. |
| Other European countries[1] | 332 300 | 14.5 | 438 185 | 17.4 | 31.9 |
|   Bulgaria[4] | 9 328 | 0.4 | 12 788 | 0.5 | 37.1 |
|   Czechoslovakia | 15 049 | 0.7 | 15 224 | 0.6 | 1.2 |
|   Germany (D. R.) | 19 229 | 0.8 | 22 813 | 0.9 | 18.6 |
|   Hungary | 18 397 | 0.8 | 20 450 | 0.8 | 11.2 |
|   Poland | 21 149 | 0.9 | 22 453 | 0.9 | 6.2 |
|   USSR | 214 487 | 9.3 | 313 549 | 12.5 | 46.2 |
| Origin country undetermined[5] | 129 589 | 5.6 | 141 564 | 5.6 | 9.2 |
| | | | | | |
| **Total non-OECD Countries** | 461 889 | 20.1 | 579 749 | 23.0 | 25.5 |
| | | | | | |
| **TOTAL** | 2 298 300 | 100.0 | 2 517 300 | 100.0 | 9.5 |

1. "Other European countries" includes Greece, Luxembourg and Turkey.
2. United Kingdom includes Ireland.
3. Spain includes Portugal.
4. Bulgaria includes Rumania.
5. "Origin country undetermined" includes Latin America, Asia-Oceania and Africa.

# FRANCE

## ARRIVALS OF FOREIGN TOURISTS AT FRONTIERS[1]
### (by country of residence)

| | 1987 | Relative share | 1988 | Relative share | % Variation over 1987 |
|---|---|---|---|---|---|
| Austria | 312 000 | 0.8 | 317 000 | 0.8 | 1.6 |
| Belgium[3] | 3 111 000 | 8.4 | 3 146 000 | 8.2 | 1.1 |
| Denmark | 355 000 | 1.0 | 361 000 | 0.9 | 1.7 |
| Finland[2] | .. | .. | .. | .. | .. |
| France | .. | .. | .. | .. | .. |
| Germany | 8 915 000 | 24.1 | 9 113 000 | 23.8 | 2.2 |
| Greece[5] | .. | .. | .. | .. | .. |
| Iceland[2] | .. | .. | .. | .. | .. |
| Ireland[4] | .. | .. | .. | .. | .. |
| Italy | 3 157 000 | 8.5 | 3 441 000 | 9.0 | 9.0 |
| Luxembourg[3] | .. | .. | .. | .. | .. |
| Netherlands | 3 936 000 | 10.6 | 4 047 000 | 10.6 | 2.8 |
| Norway[2] | .. | .. | .. | .. | .. |
| Portugal[5] | .. | .. | .. | .. | .. |
| Spain | 1 223 000 | 3.3 | 1 310 000 | 3.4 | 7.1 |
| Sweden[2] | 390 000 | 1.1 | 403 000 | 1.1 | 3.3 |
| Switzerland | 3 372 000 | 9.1 | 3 378 000 | 8.8 | 0.2 |
| Turkey[5] | .. | .. | .. | .. | .. |
| United Kingdom[4] | 6 368 000 | 17.2 | 6 645 000 | 17.4 | 4.3 |
| Other OECD-Europe[5] | 430 000 | 1.2 | 444 000 | 1.2 | 3.3 |
| **Total Europe** | 31 569 000 | 85.4 | 32 605 000 | 85.2 | 3.3 |
| Canada | 349 000 | 0.9 | 344 000 | 0.9 | −1.4 |
| United States | 1 802 000 | 4.9 | 1 950 000 | 5.1 | 8.2 |
| **Total North America** | 2 151 000 | 5.8 | 2 294 000 | 6.0 | 6.6 |
| Australia[6] | 281 000 | 0.8 | 288 000 | 0.8 | 2.5 |
| New Zealand[6] | .. | .. | .. | .. | .. |
| Japan | 572 000 | 1.5 | 662 000 | 1.7 | 15.7 |
| **Total Australasia and Japan** | 853 000 | 2.3 | 950 000 | 2.5 | 11.4 |
| **Total OECD Countries** | 34 573 000 | 93.5 | 35 849 000 | 93.6 | 3.7 |
| Yugoslavia[7] | .. | .. | .. | .. | .. |
| Other European countries[7] | 180 000 | 0.5 | 173 000 | 0.5 | −3.9 |
| Latin America[8] | 780 000 | 2.1 | 751 000 | 2.0 | −3.7 |
| Argentina | 111 000 | 0.3 | 80 000 | 0.2 | −27.9 |
| Brazil | 291 000 | 0.8 | 310 000 | 0.8 | 6.5 |
| Mexico | 165 000 | 0.4 | 170 000 | 0.4 | 3.0 |
| Asia-Oceania[9] | 405 000 | 1.1 | 449 000 | 1.2 | 10.9 |
| Africa | 1 036 000 | 2.8 | 1 066 000 | 2.8 | 2.9 |
| **Total non-OECD Countries** | 2 401 000 | 6.5 | 2 439 000 | 6.4 | 1.6 |
| **TOTAL** | 36 974 000 | 100.0 | 38 288 000 | 100.0 | 3.6 |

1. Estimates of number of "trips", the same person coming perhaps several times in one year.
2. Sweden includes Iceland, Finland and Norway.
3. Belgium includes Luxembourg.
4. United Kingdom includes Ireland.
5. "Other OECD-Europe" includes Cyprus, Greece, Portugal and Turkey.
6. Australia includes New Zealand and Oceania.
7. "Other European countries" includes Yugoslavia.
8. Latin America includes Central America.
9. Asia only.

# FRANCE[1]

## ARRIVALS OF FOREIGN TOURISTS AT HOTELS
### (by country of residence)

| | 1988 | Relative share | 1989 | Relative share | % Variation over 1988 |
|---|---|---|---|---|---|
| Austria[4] | .. | .. | .. | .. | .. |
| Belgium[2] | 1 484 149 | 7.8 | 1 598 434 | 6.6 | 7.7 |
| Denmark[4] | .. | .. | .. | .. | .. |
| Finland[4] | .. | .. | .. | .. | .. |
| France | .. | .. | .. | .. | .. |
| Germany | 3 253 113 | 17.2 | 3 745 116 | 15.6 | 15.1 |
| Greece[4] | .. | .. | .. | .. | .. |
| Iceland[4] | .. | .. | .. | .. | .. |
| Ireland[3] | .. | .. | .. | .. | .. |
| Italy | 2 112 322 | 11.2 | 2 834 665 | 11.8 | 34.2 |
| Luxembourg[2] | .. | .. | .. | .. | .. |
| Netherlands | 1 194 026 | 6.3 | 1 258 486 | 5.2 | 5.4 |
| Norway[4] | .. | .. | .. | .. | .. |
| Portugal[4] | .. | .. | .. | .. | .. |
| Spain | 959 993 | 5.1 | 1 298 484 | 5.4 | 35.3 |
| Sweden[4] | .. | .. | .. | .. | .. |
| Switzerland | 940 387 | 5.0 | 1 066 092 | 4.4 | 13.4 |
| Turkey[4] | .. | .. | .. | .. | .. |
| United Kingdom[3] | 3 343 738 | 17.7 | 4 597 529 | 19.1 | 37.5 |
| Other OECD-Europe[4] | 946 368 | 5.0 | 1 276 525 | 5.3 | 34.9 |
| **Total Europe** | 14 234 096 | 75.1 | 17 675 331 | 73.5 | 24.2 |
| | | | | | |
| Canada | 328 519 | 1.7 | 429 411 | 1.8 | 30.7 |
| United States | 1 744 901 | 9.2 | 2 308 421 | 9.6 | 32.3 |
| **Total North America** | 2 073 420 | 10.9 | 2 737 832 | 11.4 | 32.0 |
| | | | | | |
| Australia[5] | 131 203 | 0.7 | 173 346 | 0.7 | 32.1 |
| New Zealand[5] | | | | | |
| Japan | 772 227 | 4.1 | 1 256 481 | 5.2 | 62.7 |
| **Total Australasia and Japan** | 903 430 | 4.8 | 1 429 827 | 5.9 | 58.3 |
| | | | | | |
| **Total OECD Countries** | 17 210 946 | 90.9 | 21 842 990 | 90.8 | 26.9 |
| | | | | | |
| Yugoslavia | | | | | |
| Latin America[6] | 253 347 | 1.3 | 341 686 | 1.4 | 34.9 |
| Asia-Oceania[7] | 499 209 | 2.6 | 558 009 | 2.3 | 11.8 |
| Africa | 520 819 | 2.7 | 526 716 | 2.2 | 1.1 |
| Origin country undetermined | 458 606 | 2.4 | 776 829 | 3.2 | 69.4 |
| | | | | | |
| **Total non-OECD Countries** | 1 731 981 | 9.1 | 2 203 240 | 9.2 | 27.2 |
| | | | | | |
| **TOTAL** | 18 942 927 | 100.0 | 24 046 230 | 100.0 | 26.9 |

1. Data covering all France except 3 regions(Pays de la Loire, Champagne-Ardennes and Corse).
2. Belgium includes Luxembourg.
3. United Kingdom includes Ireland.
4. "Other OECD-Europe" includes Austria, Denmark, Greece, Iceland, Finland, Norway, Portugal, Sweden , Turkey, USSR and Socialist countries of Eastern Europe.
5. Australia includes New Zealand and Oceania.
6. Latin America includes Central America.
7. Asia only.

# FRANCE[1]

### NIGHTS SPENT BY FOREIGN TOURISTS IN HOTELS
*(by country of residence)*

| | 1988 | Relative share | 1989 | Relative share | % Variation over 1988 |
|---|---|---|---|---|---|
| Austria[4] | .. | .. | .. | .. | .. |
| Belgium[2] | 3 176 564 | 7.9 | 3 391 061 | 6.7 | 6.8 |
| Denmark[4] | .. | .. | .. | .. | .. |
| Finland[4] | .. | .. | .. | .. | .. |
| France | .. | .. | .. | .. | .. |
| Germany | 6 442 371 | 16.0 | 7 410 610 | 14.5 | 15.0 |
| Greece[4] | .. | .. | .. | .. | .. |
| Iceland[4] | .. | .. | .. | .. | .. |
| Ireland[3] | .. | .. | .. | .. | .. |
| Italy | 4 941 706 | 12.2 | 6 462 006 | 12.7 | 30.8 |
| Luxembourg[2] | .. | .. | .. | .. | .. |
| Netherlands | 2 187 936 | 5.4 | 2 402 703 | 4.7 | 9.8 |
| Norway[4] | .. | .. | .. | .. | .. |
| Portugal[4] | .. | .. | .. | .. | .. |
| Spain | 1 812 806 | 4.5 | 2 426 353 | 4.8 | 33.8 |
| Sweden[4] | .. | .. | .. | .. | .. |
| Switzerland | 1 955 993 | 4.8 | 2 223 616 | 4.4 | 13.7 |
| Turkey[4] | .. | .. | .. | .. | .. |
| United Kingdom[3] | 6 521 759 | 16.2 | 8 824 594 | 17.3 | 35.3 |
| Other OECD-Europe[4] | 2 339 979 | 5.8 | 3 120 718 | 6.1 | 33.4 |
| Total Europe | 29 379 114 | 72.8 | 36 261 661 | 71.2 | 23.4 |
| | | | | | |
| Canada | 746 105 | 1.8 | 952 905 | 1.9 | 27.7 |
| United States | 3 934 837 | 9.7 | 5 231 991 | 10.3 | 33.0 |
| Total North America | 4 680 942 | 11.6 | 6 184 896 | 12.1 | 32.1 |
| | | | | | |
| Australia[5] | 296 819 | 0.7 | 381 732 | 0.7 | 28.6 |
| New Zealand[5] | .. | .. | .. | .. | .. |
| Japan | 1 703 448 | 4.2 | 2 873 372 | 5.6 | 68.7 |
| Total Australasia and Japan | 2 000 267 | 5.0 | 3 255 104 | 6.4 | 62.7 |
| | | | | | |
| **Total OECD Countries** | 36 060 323 | 89.3 | 45 701 661 | 89.7 | 26.7 |
| | | | | | |
| Yugoslavia | .. | .. | .. | .. | .. |
| Latin America[6] | 683 982 | 1.7 | 894 214 | 1.8 | 30.7 |
| Asia-Oceania[7] | 1 185 957 | 2.9 | 1 410 480 | 2.8 | 18.9 |
| Africa | 1 318 655 | 3.3 | 1 424 661 | 2.8 | 8.0 |
| Origin country undetermined | 1 129 001 | 2.8 | 1 522 291 | 3.0 | 34.8 |
| | | | | | |
| **Total non-OECD Countries** | 4 317 595 | 10.7 | 5 251 646 | 10.3 | 21.6 |
| | | | | | |
| **TOTAL** | 40 377 918 | 100.0 | 50 953 307 | 100.0 | 26.2 |

1. Data covering all France except 3 regions(Pays de la Loire, Champagne-Ardennes and Corse).
2. Belgium includes Luxembourg.
3. United Kingdom includes Ireland.
4. "Other OECD-Europe" includes Austria, Denmark, Finland, Greece, Iceland, Norway, Portugal, Sweden , Turkey, USSR and Socialist countries of Eastern Europe.
5. Australia includes New Zealand and Oceania.
6. Latin America includes Central America.
7. Asia only.

# FRANCE

## NIGHTS SPENT BY FOREIGN TOURISTS IN TOURIST ACCOMMODATION[1]
### (by country of residence)

| | 1987 | Relative share | 1988 | Relative share | % Variation over 1987 |
|---|---|---|---|---|---|
| Austria | 2 301 000 | 0.7 | 2 334 000 | 0.7 | 1.4 |
| Belgium[3] | 26 423 000 | 7.8 | 26 640 000 | 7.7 | 0.8 |
| Denmark | 4 999 000 | 1.5 | 5 080 000 | 1.5 | 1.6 |
| Finland[2] | .. | .. | .. | .. | .. |
| France | .. | .. | .. | .. | .. |
| Germany | 78 836 000 | 23.2 | 80 201 000 | 23.1 | 1.7 |
| Greece[5] | .. | .. | .. | .. | .. |
| Iceland[2] | .. | .. | .. | .. | .. |
| Ireland[4] | .. | .. | .. | .. | .. |
| Italy | 26 655 000 | 7.8 | 28 198 000 | 8.1 | 5.8 |
| Luxembourg[3] | .. | .. | .. | .. | .. |
| Netherlands | 32 923 000 | 9.7 | 33 411 000 | 9.6 | 1.5 |
| Norway[2] | .. | .. | .. | .. | .. |
| Portugal[5] | .. | .. | .. | .. | .. |
| Spain | 7 435 000 | 2.2 | 7 785 000 | 2.2 | 4.7 |
| Sweden[2] | 4 005 000 | 1.2 | 4 136 000 | 1.2 | 3.3 |
| Switzerland | 17 854 000 | 5.3 | 17 749 000 | 5.1 | −0.6 |
| Turkey[5] | .. | .. | .. | .. | .. |
| United Kingdom[4] | 60 553 000 | 17.8 | 62 711 000 | 18.1 | 3.6 |
| Other OECD-Europe[5] | 4 329 000 | 1.3 | 4 349 000 | 1.3 | 0.5 |
| Total Europe | 266 313 000 | 78.3 | 272 594 000 | 78.5 | 2.4 |
| | | | | | |
| Canada | 5 683 000 | 1.7 | 5 687 000 | 1.6 | 0.1 |
| United States | 25 477 000 | 7.5 | 26 300 000 | 7.6 | 3.2 |
| Total North America | 31 160 000 | 9.2 | 31 987 000 | 9.2 | 2.7 |
| | | | | | |
| Australia[6] | 1 952 000 | 0.6 | 1 926 000 | 0.6 | −1.3 |
| New Zealand[6] | .. | .. | .. | .. | .. |
| Japan | 4 248 000 | 1.2 | 4 540 000 | 1.3 | 6.9 |
| Total Australasia and Japan | 6 200 000 | 1.8 | 6 466 000 | 1.9 | 4.3 |
| | | | | | |
| **Total OECD Countries** | 303 673 000 | 89.3 | 311 047 000 | 89.6 | 2.4 |
| | | | | | |
| Yugoslavia[7] | .. | .. | .. | .. | .. |
| Other European countries[7] | 3 290 000 | 1.0 | 3 162 000 | 0.9 | −3.9 |
| Latin America[8] | 7 860 000 | 2.3 | 7 470 000 | 2.2 | −5.0 |
| Argentina | 1 265 000 | 0.4 | 912 000 | 0.3 | −27.9 |
| Brazil | 3 107 000 | 0.9 | 3 306 000 | 1.0 | 6.4 |
| Mexico | 955 000 | 0.3 | 982 000 | 0.3 | 2.8 |
| Asia-Oceania[9] | 4 495 000 | 1.3 | 4 595 000 | 1.3 | 2.2 |
| Africa | 20 604 000 | 6.1 | 20 834 000 | 6.0 | 1.1 |
| | | | | | |
| **Total non-OECD Countries** | 36 249 000 | 10.7 | 36 061 000 | 10.4 | −0.5 |
| | | | | | |
| **TOTAL** | 339 922 000 | 100.0 | 347 108 000 | 100.0 | 2.1 |

1. Based on an update of the findings of the 1982 frontier survey.
2. Sweden includes Finland, Iceland and Norway.
3. Belgium includes Luxembourg.
4. United Kingdom includes Ireland.
5. "Other OECD-Europe" includes Cyprus, Greece, Portugal and Turkey.
6. Australia includes New Zealand and Oceania.
7. "Other European countries" includes Yugoslavia.
8. Latin America includes Central America.
9. Asia only.

# GERMANY (F.R.)[1]

## ARRIVALS OF FOREIGN TOURISTS AT HOTELS[2]

### (by country of residence)

| | 1988 | Relative share | 1989 | Relative share | % Variation over 1988 |
|---|---|---|---|---|---|
| Austria | 488 131 | 4.0 | 524 250 | 3.9 | 7.4 |
| Belgium | 417 935 | 3.5 | 449 240 | 3.3 | 7.5 |
| Denmark | 591 592 | 4.9 | 610 795 | 4.5 | 3.2 |
| Finland | 154 157 | 1.3 | 178 531 | 1.3 | 15.8 |
| France | 639 893 | 5.3 | 725 665 | 5.4 | 13.4 |
| Germany | .. | .. | .. | .. | .. |
| Greece | 107 052 | 0.9 | 117 415 | 0.9 | 9.7 |
| Iceland | 21 694 | 0.2 | 23 633 | 0.2 | 8.9 |
| Ireland | 33 987 | 0.3 | 31 977 | 0.2 | −5.9 |
| Italy | 695 591 | 5.8 | 818 386 | 6.1 | 17.7 |
| Luxembourg | 62 444 | 0.5 | 62 948 | 0.5 | 0.8 |
| Netherlands | 1 557 603 | 12.9 | 1 606 800 | 11.9 | 3.2 |
| Norway | 276 853 | 2.3 | 298 117 | 2.2 | 7.7 |
| Portugal | 43 908 | 0.4 | 43 409 | 0.3 | −1.1 |
| Spain | 242 945 | 2.0 | 282 019 | 2.1 | 16.1 |
| Sweden | 779 765 | 6.5 | 905 677 | 6.7 | 16.1 |
| Switzerland | 604 647 | 5.0 | 675 360 | 5.0 | 11.7 |
| Turkey | 75 592 | 0.6 | 82 704 | 0.6 | 9.4 |
| United Kingdom | 1 116 501 | 9.3 | 1 276 221 | 9.5 | 14.3 |
| Other OECD-Europe | .. | .. | .. | .. | .. |
| **Total Europe** | 7 910 290 | 65.6 | 8 713 147 | 64.7 | 10.1 |
| Canada | 148 974 | 1.2 | 171 013 | 1.3 | 14.8 |
| United States | 1 785 005 | 14.8 | 1 963 587 | 14.6 | 10.0 |
| **Total North America** | 1 933 979 | 16.0 | 2 134 600 | 15.9 | 10.4 |
| Australia | 78 217 | 0.6 | 96 694 | 0.7 | 23.6 |
| New Zealand | 11 624 | 0.1 | 14 212 | 0.1 | 22.3 |
| Japan | 598 784 | 5.0 | 735 657 | 5.5 | 22.9 |
| **Total Australasia and Japan** | 688 625 | 5.7 | 846 563 | 6.3 | 22.9 |
| **Total OECD Countries** | 10 532 894 | 87.3 | 11 694 310 | 86.8 | 11.0 |
| Yugoslavia | 160 096 | 1.3 | 184 336 | 1.4 | 15.1 |
| Other European countries | 367 809 | 3.0 | 500 771 | 3.7 | 36.1 |
| Bulgaria | 16 232 | 0.1 | 19 363 | 0.1 | 19.3 |
| Czechoslovakia | 51 868 | 0.4 | 68 525 | 0.5 | 32.1 |
| Germany (D. R.) | 70 179 | 0.6 | 117 001 | 0.9 | 66.7 |
| Hungary | 77 783 | 0.6 | 92 788 | 0.7 | 19.3 |
| Poland | 103 976 | 0.9 | 122 419 | 0.9 | 17.7 |
| Rumania | 12 127 | 0.1 | 12 238 | 0.1 | 0.9 |
| USSR | 35 644 | 0.3 | 68 437 | 0.5 | 92.0 |
| Latin America | 115 137 | 1.0 | 135 051 | 1.0 | 17.3 |
| Argentina | 24 213 | 0.2 | 23 927 | 0.2 | −1.2 |
| Brazil | 56 495 | 0.5 | 70 637 | 0.5 | 25.0 |
| Chile | 6 752 | 0.1 | 8 607 | 0.1 | 27.5 |
| Mexico | 27 677 | 0.2 | 31 880 | 0.2 | 15.2 |
| Asia-Oceania | 114 119 | 0.9 | 119 061 | 0.9 | 4.3 |
| Israel | 114 119 | 0.9 | 119 061 | 0.9 | 4.3 |
| Africa | 41 284 | 0.3 | 43 994 | 0.3 | 6.6 |
| South Africa | 41 284 | 0.3 | 43 994 | 0.3 | 6.6 |
| Origin country undetermined | 730 234 | 6.1 | 789 261 | 5.9 | 8.1 |
| **Total non-OECD Countries** | 1 528 679 | 12.7 | 1 772 474 | 13.2 | 15.9 |
| **TOTAL** | 12 061 573 | 100.0 | 13 466 784 | 100.0 | 11.7 |

1. Includes West Berlin.
2. Arrivals at hotels (including "bed and breakfast"), boarding houses and inns.

# GERMANY (F.R.)[1]

## ARRIVALS OF FOREIGN TOURISTS AT REGISTERED TOURIST ACCOMMODATION[2]

### (by country of residence)

| | 1988 | Relative share | 1989 | Relative share | % Variation over 1988 |
|---|---|---|---|---|---|
| Austria | 506 274 | 3.9 | 545 392 | 3.7 | 7.7 |
| Belgium | 451 786 | 3.4 | 488 986 | 3.3 | 8.2 |
| Denmark | 657 699 | 5.0 | 680 758 | 4.6 | 3.5 |
| Finland | 168 221 | 1.3 | 192 145 | 1.3 | 14.2 |
| France | 714 545 | 5.4 | 808 102 | 5.5 | 13.1 |
| Germany | .. | .. | .. | .. | .. |
| Greece | 110 238 | 0.8 | 121 274 | 0.8 | 10.0 |
| Iceland | 25 029 | 0.2 | 27 525 | 0.2 | 10.0 |
| Ireland | 40 260 | 0.3 | 41 063 | 0.3 | 2.0 |
| Italy | 724 486 | 5.5 | 850 151 | 5.8 | 17.3 |
| Luxembourg | 66 070 | 0.5 | 67 242 | 0.5 | 1.8 |
| Netherlands | 1 878 699 | 14.3 | 1 954 574 | 13.3 | 4.0 |
| Norway | 288 737 | 2.2 | 311 482 | 2.1 | 7.9 |
| Portugal | 47 228 | 0.4 | 46 647 | 0.3 | -1.2 |
| Spain | 258 323 | 2.0 | 298 568 | 2.0 | 15.6 |
| Sweden | 818 923 | 6.2 | 942 251 | 6.4 | 15.1 |
| Switzerland | 633 258 | 4.8 | 706 668 | 4.8 | 11.6 |
| Turkey | 79 109 | 0.6 | 87 912 | 0.6 | 11.1 |
| United Kingdom | 1 186 131 | 9.0 | 1 355 507 | 9.3 | 14.3 |
| Other OECD-Europe | .. | .. | .. | .. | .. |
| **Total Europe** | 8 655 016 | 66.0 | 9 526 247 | 65.0 | 10.1 |
| | | | | | |
| Canada | 169 977 | 1.3 | 195 312 | 1.3 | 14.9 |
| United States | 1 878 557 | 14.3 | 2 067 317 | 14.1 | 10.0 |
| **Total North America** | 2 048 534 | 15.6 | 2 262 629 | 15.4 | 10.5 |
| | | | | | |
| Australia | 107 336 | 0.8 | 132 574 | 0.9 | 23.5 |
| New Zealand | 17 725 | 0.1 | 21 614 | 0.1 | 21.9 |
| Japan | 622 770 | 4.7 | 762 554 | 5.2 | 22.4 |
| **Total Australasia and Japan** | 747 831 | 5.7 | 916 742 | 6.3 | 22.6 |
| | | | | | |
| **Total OECD Countries** | 11 451 381 | 87.3 | 12 705 618 | 86.7 | 11.0 |
| | | | | | |
| Yugoslavia | 165 659 | 1.3 | 193 807 | 1.3 | 17.0 |
| Other European countries | 430 599 | 3.3 | 590 990 | 4.0 | 37.2 |
| Bulgaria | 17 216 | 0.1 | 20 437 | 0.1 | 18.7 |
| Czechoslovakia | 59 013 | 0.5 | 78 141 | 0.5 | 32.4 |
| Germany (D. R.) | 87 572 | 0.7 | 150 675 | 1.0 | 72.1 |
| Hungary | 88 411 | 0.7 | 105 873 | 0.7 | 19.8 |
| Poland | 128 100 | 1.0 | 149 405 | 1.0 | 16.6 |
| Rumania | 12 566 | 0.1 | 12 597 | 0.1 | 0.2 |
| USSR | 37 721 | 0.3 | 73 862 | 0.5 | 95.8 |
| Latin America | 126 232 | 1.0 | 151 114 | 1.0 | 19.7 |
| Argentina | 26 376 | 0.2 | 27 076 | 0.2 | 2.7 |
| Brazil | 62 506 | 0.5 | 78 720 | 0.5 | 25.9 |
| Chile | 7 738 | 0.1 | 10 697 | 0.1 | 38.2 |
| Mexico | 29 612 | 0.2 | 34 621 | 0.2 | 16.9 |
| Asia-Oceania | 121 855 | 0.9 | 126 107 | 0.9 | 3.5 |
| Israel | 121 855 | 0.9 | 126 107 | 0.9 | 3.5 |
| Africa | 45 349 | 0.3 | 48 001 | 0.3 | 5.8 |
| South Africa | 45 349 | 0.3 | 48 001 | 0.3 | 5.8 |
| Origin country undetermined | 771 942 | 5.9 | 837 564 | 5.7 | 8.5 |
| | | | | | |
| **Total non-OECD Countries** | 1 661 636 | 12.7 | 1 947 583 | 13.3 | 17.2 |
| | | | | | |
| **TOTAL** | 13 113 017 | 100.0 | 14 653 201 | 100.0 | 11.7 |

1. Includes West Berlin.
2. Arrivals at hotels and similar establishments, holiday villages, sanatoria and recreation and holiday homes.

# GERMANY (F.R.)[1]

### NIGHTS SPENT BY FOREIGN TOURISTS IN HOTELS[2]
*(by country of residence)*

| | 1988 | Relative share | 1989 | Relative share | % Variation over 1988 |
|---|---|---|---|---|---|
| Austria | 974 047 | 3.9 | 1 067 356 | 3.8 | 9.6 |
| Belgium | 913 867 | 3.6 | 1 014 032 | 3.6 | 11.0 |
| Denmark | 1 062 862 | 4.2 | 1 106 644 | 3.9 | 4.1 |
| Finland | 275 540 | 1.1 | 323 638 | 1.1 | 17.5 |
| France | 1 222 269 | 4.8 | 1 393 211 | 4.9 | 14.0 |
| Germany | .. | .. | .. | .. | .. |
| Greece | 253 368 | 1.0 | 279 034 | 1.0 | 10.1 |
| Iceland | 48 768 | 0.2 | 52 988 | 0.2 | 8.7 |
| Ireland | 83 342 | 0.3 | 78 038 | 0.3 | −6.4 |
| Italy | 1 330 648 | 5.3 | 1 575 388 | 5.5 | 18.4 |
| Luxembourg | 161 853 | 0.6 | 172 057 | 0.6 | 6.3 |
| Netherlands | 3 436 766 | 13.6 | 3 621 722 | 12.8 | 5.4 |
| Norway | 454 344 | 1.8 | 502 629 | 1.8 | 10.6 |
| Portugal | 97 376 | 0.4 | 104 335 | 0.4 | 7.1 |
| Spain | 483 840 | 1.9 | 569 378 | 2.0 | 17.7 |
| Sweden | 1 212 509 | 4.8 | 1 405 096 | 4.9 | 15.9 |
| Switzerland | 1 249 005 | 5.0 | 1 389 021 | 4.9 | 11.2 |
| Turkey | 209 314 | 0.8 | 221 728 | 0.8 | 5.9 |
| United Kingdom | 2 320 020 | 9.2 | 2 700 956 | 9.5 | 16.4 |
| Other OECD-Europe | .. | .. | .. | .. | .. |
| **Total Europe** | 15 789 738 | 62.6 | 17 577 251 | 61.9 | 11.3 |
| | | | | | |
| Canada | 308 906 | 1.2 | 356 156 | 1.3 | 15.3 |
| United States | 3 654 158 | 14.5 | 3 982 998 | 14.0 | 9.0 |
| **Total North America** | 3 963 064 | 15.7 | 4 339 154 | 15.3 | 9.5 |
| | | | | | |
| Australia | 157 447 | 0.6 | 193 181 | 0.7 | 22.7 |
| New Zealand | 23 781 | 0.1 | 29 824 | 0.1 | 25.4 |
| Japan | 1 009 960 | 4.0 | 1 216 423 | 4.3 | 20.4 |
| **Total Australasia and Japan** | 1 191 188 | 4.7 | 1 439 428 | 5.1 | 20.8 |
| | | | | | |
| **Total OECD Countries** | 20 943 990 | 83.0 | 23 355 833 | 82.3 | 11.5 |
| | | | | | |
| Yugoslavia | 396 772 | 1.6 | 461 009 | 1.6 | 16.2 |
| Other European countries | 1 335 914 | 5.3 | 1 750 682 | 6.2 | 31.0 |
| Bulgaria | 47 540 | 0.2 | 57 907 | 0.2 | 21.8 |
| Czechoslovakia | 136 460 | 0.5 | 172 654 | 0.6 | 26.5 |
| Germany (D. R.) | 231 052 | 0.9 | 376 971 | 1.3 | 63.2 |
| Hungary | 206 848 | 0.8 | 244 851 | 0.9 | 18.4 |
| Poland | 546 840 | 2.2 | 617 665 | 2.2 | 13.0 |
| Rumania | 47 700 | 0.2 | 40 016 | 0.1 | −16.1 |
| USSR | 119 474 | 0.5 | 240 618 | 0.8 | 101.4 |
| Latin America | 266 624 | 1.1 | 325 352 | 1.1 | 22.0 |
| Argentina | 54 967 | 0.2 | 60 020 | 0.2 | 9.2 |
| Brazil | 136 046 | 0.5 | 169 503 | 0.6 | 24.6 |
| Chile | 17 325 | 0.1 | 23 030 | 0.1 | 32.9 |
| Mexico | 58 286 | 0.2 | 72 799 | 0.3 | 24.9 |
| Asia-Oceania | 324 881 | 1.3 | 338 622 | 1.2 | 4.2 |
| Israel | 324 881 | 1.3 | 338 622 | 1.2 | 4.2 |
| Africa | 101 484 | 0.4 | 105 914 | 0.4 | 4.4 |
| South Africa | 101 484 | 0.4 | 105 914 | 0.4 | 4.4 |
| Origin country undetermined | 1 856 476 | 7.4 | 2 051 321 | 7.2 | 10.5 |
| | | | | | |
| **Total non-OECD Countries** | 4 282 151 | 17.0 | 5 032 900 | 17.7 | 17.5 |
| | | | | | |
| **TOTAL** | 25 226 141 | 100.0 | 28 388 733 | 100.0 | 12.5 |

1. Includes West Berlin.
2. Nights spent in hotels (including "bed and breakfast"), boarding houses and inns.

# GERMANY (F.R.)[1]

## NIGHTS SPENT BY FOREIGN TOURISTS IN REGISTERED TOURIST ACCOMMODATION[2]
### *(by country of residence)*

| | 1988 | Relative share | 1989 | Relative share | % Variation over 1988 |
|---|---|---|---|---|---|
| Austria | 1 040 039 | 3.5 | 1 138 589 | 3.4 | 9.5 |
| Belgium | 1 080 110 | 3.6 | 1 208 753 | 3.6 | 11.9 |
| Denmark | 1 359 130 | 4.5 | 1 404 417 | 4.2 | 3.3 |
| Finland | 303 745 | 1.0 | 354 274 | 1.1 | 16.6 |
| France | 1 466 820 | 4.9 | 1 657 966 | 4.9 | 13.0 |
| Germany | .. | .. | .. | .. | .. |
| Greece | 264 454 | 0.9 | 291 574 | 0.9 | 10.3 |
| Iceland | 79 286 | 0.3 | 82 718 | 0.2 | 4.3 |
| Ireland | 98 131 | 0.3 | 96 854 | 0.3 | −1.3 |
| Italy | 1 413 465 | 4.7 | 1 664 890 | 5.0 | 17.8 |
| Luxembourg | 184 543 | 0.6 | 196 940 | 0.6 | 6.7 |
| Netherlands | 5 690 235 | 18.9 | 5 963 364 | 17.8 | 4.8 |
| Norway | 481 775 | 1.6 | 530 269 | 1.6 | 10.1 |
| Portugal | 115 063 | 0.4 | 118 387 | 0.4 | 2.9 |
| Spain | 536 014 | 1.8 | 620 440 | 1.8 | 15.8 |
| Sweden | 1 296 419 | 4.3 | 1 499 421 | 4.5 | 15.7 |
| Switzerland | 1 365 079 | 4.5 | 1 513 276 | 4.5 | 10.9 |
| Turkey | 229 889 | 0.8 | 240 380 | 0.7 | 4.6 |
| United Kingdom | 2 558 954 | 8.5 | 2 963 561 | 8.8 | 15.8 |
| Other OECD-Europe | .. | .. | .. | .. | .. |
| **Total Europe** | 19 563 151 | 65.0 | 21 546 073 | 64.2 | 10.1 |
| | | | | | |
| Canada | 350 624 | 1.2 | 404 892 | 1.2 | 15.5 |
| United States | 3 874 820 | 12.9 | 4 230 468 | 12.6 | 9.2 |
| **Total North America** | 4 225 444 | 14.0 | 4 635 360 | 13.8 | 9.7 |
| | | | | | |
| Australia | 204 636 | 0.7 | 249 411 | 0.7 | 21.9 |
| New Zealand | 32 944 | 0.1 | 40 971 | 0.1 | 24.4 |
| Japan | 1 054 941 | 3.5 | 1 265 140 | 3.8 | 19.9 |
| **Total Australasia and Japan** | 1 292 521 | 4.3 | 1 555 522 | 4.6 | 20.3 |
| | | | | | |
| **Total OECD Countries** | 25 081 116 | 83.3 | 27 736 955 | 82.6 | 10.6 |
| | | | | | |
| Yugoslavia | 421 500 | 1.4 | 496 349 | 1.5 | 17.8 |
| Other European countries | 1 813 114 | 6.0 | 2 274 906 | 6.8 | 25.5 |
|   Bulgaria | 50 063 | 0.2 | 61 017 | 0.2 | 21.9 |
|   Czechoslovakia | 154 085 | 0.5 | 194 084 | 0.6 | 26.0 |
|   Germany (D. R.) | 337 336 | 1.1 | 523 749 | 1.6 | 55.3 |
|   Hungary | 235 741 | 0.8 | 276 507 | 0.8 | 17.3 |
|   Poland | 853 774 | 2.8 | 911 084 | 2.7 | 6.7 |
|   Rumania | 51 234 | 0.2 | 43 378 | 0.1 | −15.3 |
|   USSR | 130 881 | 0.4 | 265 087 | 0.8 | 102.5 |
| Latin America | 298 304 | 1.0 | 362 851 | 1.1 | 21.6 |
|   Argentina | 61 543 | 0.2 | 67 050 | 0.2 | 8.9 |
|   Brazil | 153 485 | 0.5 | 189 329 | 0.6 | 23.4 |
|   Chile | 20 365 | 0.1 | 28 211 | 0.1 | 38.5 |
|   Mexico | 62 911 | 0.2 | 78 261 | 0.2 | 24.4 |
| Asia-Oceania | 353 938 | 1.2 | 367 848 | 1.1 | 3.9 |
|   Israel | 353 938 | 1.2 | 367 848 | 1.1 | 3.9 |
| Africa | 111 981 | 0.4 | 116 331 | 0.3 | 3.9 |
|   South Africa | 111 981 | 0.4 | 116 331 | 0.3 | 3.9 |
| Origin country undetermined | 2 036 791 | 6.8 | 2 222 315 | 6.6 | 9.1 |
| | | | | | |
| **Total non-OECD Countries** | 5 035 628 | 16.7 | 5 840 600 | 17.4 | 16.0 |
| | | | | | |
| **TOTAL** | 30 116 744 | 100.0 | 33 577 555 | 100.0 | 11.5 |

1. Includes West Berlin.
2. Nights spent in hotels and similar establishments, holiday villages, sanatoria, and recreation and holiday homes.

# GREECE

## ARRIVALS OF FOREIGN TOURISTS AT FRONTIERS[1]
### (by country of nationality)

| | 1988 | Relative share | 1989 | Relative share | % Variation over 1988 |
|---|---|---|---|---|---|
| Austria | 311 000 | 4.0 | 268 000 | 3.3 | −13.8 |
| Belgium[2] | 175 000 | 2.2 | 163 000 | 2.0 | −6.9 |
| Denmark | 235 000 | 3.0 | 316 000 | 3.9 | 34.5 |
| Finland | 198 000 | 2.5 | 255 000 | 3.2 | 28.8 |
| France | 469 000 | 6.0 | 478 000 | 5.9 | 1.9 |
| Germany | 1 382 000 | 17.8 | 1 655 000 | 20.5 | 19.8 |
| Greece | .. | .. | .. | .. | .. |
| Iceland[3] | .. | .. | .. | .. | .. |
| Ireland | 49 000 | 0.6 | 63 000 | 0.8 | 28.6 |
| Italy | 544 000 | 7.0 | 569 000 | 7.0 | 4.6 |
| Luxembourg[2] | .. | .. | .. | .. | .. |
| Netherlands | 389 000 | 5.0 | 428 000 | 5.3 | 10.0 |
| Norway | 107 000 | 1.4 | 69 000 | 0.9 | −35.5 |
| Portugal | 12 000 | 0.2 | 36 000 | 0.4 | 200.0 |
| Spain | 62 000 | 0.8 | 103 000 | 1.3 | 66.1 |
| Sweden | 262 000 | 3.4 | 261 000 | 3.2 | −0.4 |
| Switzerland | 175 000 | 2.2 | 139 000 | 1.7 | −20.6 |
| Turkey | 58 000 | 0.7 | 43 000 | 0.5 | −25.9 |
| United Kingdom | 1 790 000 | 23.0 | 1 632 000 | 20.2 | −8.8 |
| Other OECD-Europe | .. | .. | .. | .. | .. |
| **Total Europe** | 6 218 000 | 79.9 | 6 478 000 | 80.2 | 4.2 |
| | | | | | |
| Canada | 107 000 | 1.4 | 79 000 | 1.0 | −26.2 |
| United States | 295 000 | 3.8 | 279 000 | 3.5 | −5.4 |
| **Total North America** | 402 000 | 5.2 | 358 000 | 4.4 | −10.9 |
| | | | | | |
| Australia | 102 000 | 1.3 | 114 000 | 1.4 | 11.8 |
| New Zealand[4] | 15 000 | 0.2 | 14 000 | 0.2 | −6.7 |
| Japan | 105 000 | 1.3 | 104 000 | 1.3 | −1.0 |
| **Total Australasia and Japan** | 222 000 | 2.9 | 232 000 | 2.9 | 4.5 |
| | | | | | |
| **Total OECD Countries** | 6 842 000 | 88.0 | 7 068 000 | 87.5 | 3.3 |
| | | | | | |
| Yugoslavia | 388 000 | 5.0 | 369 000 | 4.6 | −4.9 |
| Other European countries[3] | 293 000 | 3.8 | 314 317 | 3.9 | 7.3 |
| Bulgaria | 47 198 | 0.6 | 73 622 | 0.9 | 56.0 |
| Czechoslovakia | 15 608 | 0.2 | 18 445 | 0.2 | 18.2 |
| Hungary | 30 082 | 0.4 | 54 167 | 0.7 | 80.1 |
| Poland | 85 711 | 1.1 | 67 770 | 0.8 | −20.9 |
| Rumania | 9 383 | 0.1 | 6 853 | 0.1 | −27.0 |
| USSR | 13 169 | 0.2 | 23 996 | 0.3 | 82.2 |
| Latin America | 42 000 | 0.5 | 69 210 | 0.9 | 64.8 |
| Argentina | 5 088 | 0.1 | 6 105 | 0.1 | 20.0 |
| Brazil | 13 229 | 0.2 | 15 348 | 0.2 | 16.0 |
| Mexico | 6 953 | 0.1 | 8 482 | 0.1 | 22.0 |
| Asia-Oceania[4] | 118 000 | 1.5 | 160 790 | 2.0 | 36.3 |
| Iran | 4 670 | 0.1 | 5 007 | 0.1 | 7.2 |
| Israel | 34 000 | 0.4 | 36 338 | 0.4 | 6.9 |
| Lebanon | 31 100 | 0.4 | 33 931 | 0.4 | 9.1 |
| Africa | 95 000 | 1.2 | 100 534 | 1.2 | 5.8 |
| Egypt | 32 000 | 0.4 | 30 419 | 0.4 | −4.9 |
| South Africa | 22 350 | 0.3 | 20 274 | 0.3 | −9.3 |
| | | | | | |
| **Total non-OECD Countries** | 936 000 | 12.0 | 1 013 851 | 12.5 | 8.3 |
| | | | | | |
| **TOTAL** | 7 778 000 | 100.0 | 8 081 851 | 100.0 | 3.9 |

1. Excluding Greek nationals residing abroad and cruise passengers.
2. Belgium includes Luxembourg.
3. "Other European countries" includes Iceland.
4. "Asia-Oceania" includes New Zealand.

# GREECE

## ARRIVALS OF FOREIGN TOURISTS AT HOTELS
### (by country of residence)

| | 1987 | Relative share | 1988 | Relative share | % Variation over 1987 |
|---|---|---|---|---|---|
| Austria | 206 320 | 3.3 | 224 852 | 3.7 | 9.0 |
| Belgium | 141 632 | 2.3 | 149 926 | 2.5 | 5.9 |
| Denmark | 170 132 | 2.8 | 160 274 | 2.7 | −5.8 |
| Finland | 161 026 | 2.6 | 166 266 | 2.8 | 3.3 |
| France | 778 404 | 12.6 | 722 049 | 12.0 | −7.2 |
| Germany | 1 032 837 | 16.7 | 1 061 566 | 17.7 | 2.8 |
| Greece | .. | .. | .. | .. | .. |
| Iceland | .. | .. | .. | .. | .. |
| Ireland | .. | .. | .. | .. | .. |
| Italy | 499 607 | 8.1 | 497 727 | 8.3 | −0.4 |
| Luxembourg | .. | .. | .. | .. | .. |
| Netherlands | 259 145 | 4.2 | 257 698 | 4.3 | −0.6 |
| Norway | 108 889 | 1.8 | 80 723 | 1.3 | −25.9 |
| Portugal | .. | .. | .. | .. | .. |
| Spain | 109 870 | 1.8 | 126 663 | 2.1 | 15.3 |
| Sweden | 231 968 | 3.8 | 227 019 | 3.8 | −2.1 |
| Switzerland | 167 426 | 2.7 | 162 354 | 2.7 | −3.0 |
| Turkey | 21 915 | 0.4 | 25 484 | 0.4 | 16.3 |
| United Kingdom | 985 904 | 16.0 | 876 995 | 14.6 | −11.0 |
| Other OECD-Europe | .. | .. | .. | .. | .. |
| **Total Europe** | 4 875 075 | 79.1 | 4 739 596 | 78.9 | −2.8 |
| Canada | 88 682 | 1.4 | 91 304 | 1.5 | 3.0 |
| United States | 323 903 | 5.3 | 357 240 | 5.9 | 10.3 |
| **Total North America** | 412 585 | 6.7 | 448 544 | 7.5 | 8.7 |
| Australia | .. | .. | .. | .. | .. |
| New Zealand | 119 211 | 1.9 | 109 879 | 1.8 | −7.8 |
| Japan | 105 583 | 1.7 | 119 831 | 2.0 | 13.5 |
| **Total Australasia and Japan** | 224 794 | 3.6 | 229 710 | 3.8 | 2.2 |
| **Total OECD Countries** | 5 512 454 | 89.4 | 5 417 850 | 90.2 | −1.7 |
| Yugoslavia | 103 529 | 1.7 | 75 943 | 1.3 | −26.6 |
| Other European countries | 149 972 | 2.4 | 154 352 | 2.6 | 2.9 |
| Latin America | 52 507 | 0.9 | 52 915 | 0.9 | 0.8 |
| Mexico | 7 933 | 0.1 | 8 081 | 0.1 | 1.9 |
| Asia-Oceania | 145 477 | 2.4 | 127 474 | 2.1 | −12.4 |
| Israel | 34 525 | 0.6 | 27 037 | 0.5 | −21.7 |
| Lebanon | 25 124 | 0.4 | 26 859 | 0.4 | 6.9 |
| Africa | 100 348 | 1.6 | 105 039 | 1.7 | 4.7 |
| Egypt | 37 463 | 0.6 | 39 319 | 0.7 | 5.0 |
| South Africa | 22 427 | 0.4 | 25 274 | 0.4 | 12.7 |
| Origin country undetermined | 102 371 | 1.7 | 73 186 | 1.2 | −28.5 |
| **Total non-OECD Countries** | 654 204 | 10.6 | 588 909 | 9.8 | −10.0 |
| **TOTAL** | 6 166 658 | 100.0 | 6 006 759 | 100.0 | −2.6 |

# GREECE

### ARRIVALS OF FOREIGN TOURISTS AT REGISTERED TOURIST ACCOMMODATION
*(by country of residence)*

| | 1987 | Relative share | 1988 | Relative share | % Variation over 1987 |
|---|---|---|---|---|---|
| Austria | 242 154 | 3.6 | 255 673 | 3.9 | 5.6 |
| Belgium | 151 385 | 2.3 | 158 275 | 2.4 | 4.6 |
| Denmark | 177 332 | 2.7 | 167 381 | 2.6 | −5.6 |
| Finland | 162 654 | 2.4 | 167 742 | 2.6 | 3.1 |
| France | 851 363 | 12.7 | 792 487 | 12.2 | −6.9 |
| Germany | 1 193 510 | 17.8 | 1 209 492 | 18.6 | 1.3 |
| Greece | .. | .. | .. | .. | .. |
| Iceland | .. | .. | .. | .. | .. |
| Ireland | .. | .. | .. | .. | .. |
| Italy | 358 261 | 5.4 | 548 002 | 8.4 | 53.0 |
| Luxembourg | .. | .. | .. | .. | .. |
| Netherlands | 292 234 | 4.4 | 288 995 | 4.4 | −1.1 |
| Norway | 110 104 | 1.6 | 82 833 | 1.3 | −24.8 |
| Portugal | .. | .. | .. | .. | .. |
| Spain | 116 163 | 1.7 | 131 778 | 2.0 | 13.4 |
| Sweden | 234 662 | 3.5 | 229 329 | 3.5 | −2.3 |
| Switzerland | 174 793 | 2.6 | 169 145 | 2.6 | −3.2 |
| Turkey | 22 155 | 0.3 | 25 762 | 0.4 | 16.3 |
| United Kingdom | 1 006 878 | 15.0 | 892 953 | 13.7 | −11.3 |
| Other OECD-Europe | .. | .. | .. | .. | .. |
| **Total Europe** | 5 093 648 | 76.1 | 5 119 847 | 78.8 | 0.5 |
| Canada | 91 022 | 1.4 | 93 197 | 1.4 | 2.4 |
| United States | 327 799 | 4.9 | 360 204 | 5.5 | 9.9 |
| **Total North America** | 418 821 | 6.3 | 453 401 | 7.0 | 8.3 |
| Australia | .. | .. | .. | .. | .. |
| New Zealand | 129 836 | 1.9 | 119 466 | 1.8 | −8.0 |
| Japan | 105 671 | 1.6 | 119 921 | 1.8 | 13.5 |
| **Total Australasia and Japan** | 235 507 | 3.5 | 239 387 | 3.7 | 1.6 |
| **Total OECD Countries** | 5 747 976 | 85.9 | 5 812 635 | 89.4 | 1.1 |
| Yugoslavia | 123 943 | 1.9 | 85 717 | 1.3 | −30.8 |
| Other European countries | 213 226 | 3.2 | 200 516 | 3.1 | −6.0 |
| Latin America | 53 033 | 0.8 | 53 533 | 0.8 | 0.9 |
| Mexico | 8 012 | 0.1 | 8 144 | 0.1 | 1.6 |
| Asia-Oceania | 147 045 | 2.2 | 129 359 | 2.0 | −12.0 |
| Israel | 35 415 | 0.5 | 28 132 | 0.4 | −20.6 |
| Lebanon | 25 286 | 0.4 | 26 975 | 0.4 | 6.7 |
| Africa | 101 452 | 1.5 | 106 096 | 1.6 | 4.6 |
| Egypt | 37 607 | 0.6 | 39 373 | 0.6 | 4.7 |
| South Africa | 23 177 | 0.3 | 25 554 | 0.4 | 10.3 |
| Origin country undetermined | 304 000 | 4.5 | 112 485 | 1.7 | −63.0 |
| **Total non-OECD Countries** | 942 699 | 14.1 | 687 706 | 10.6 | −27.0 |
| **TOTAL** | 6 690 675 | 100.0 | 6 500 341 | 100.0 | −2.8 |

# GREECE

*NIGHTS SPENT BY FOREIGN TOURISTS IN HOTELS*
*(by country of residence)*

| | 1987 | Relative share | 1988 | Relative share | % Variation over 1987 |
|---|---|---|---|---|---|
| Austria | 1 526 361 | 4.5 | 1 814 014 | 5.4 | 18.8 |
| Belgium | 712 823 | 2.1 | 803 378 | 2.4 | 12.7 |
| Denmark | 1 310 311 | 3.9 | 1 186 017 | 3.6 | −9.5 |
| Finland | 1 303 839 | 3.9 | 1 340 445 | 4.0 | 2.8 |
| France | 2 550 897 | 7.6 | 2 445 075 | 7.3 | −4.1 |
| Germany | 7 201 113 | 21.3 | 7 868 225 | 23.6 | 9.3 |
| Greece | .. | .. | .. | .. | .. |
| Iceland | .. | .. | .. | .. | .. |
| Ireland | .. | .. | .. | .. | .. |
| Italy | 1 386 069 | 4.1 | 1 649 934 | 4.9 | 19.0 |
| Luxembourg | .. | .. | .. | .. | .. |
| Netherlands | 1 648 814 | 4.9 | 1 657 731 | 5.0 | 0.5 |
| Norway | 1 012 266 | 3.0 | 715 206 | 2.1 | −29.3 |
| Portugal | .. | .. | .. | .. | .. |
| Spain | 269 577 | 0.8 | 310 435 | 0.9 | 15.2 |
| Sweden | 1 695 366 | 5.0 | 1 694 839 | 5.1 | −0.0 |
| Switzerland | 962 557 | 2.9 | 961 306 | 2.9 | −0.1 |
| Turkey | 63 235 | 0.2 | 80 917 | 0.2 | 28.0 |
| United Kingdom | 8 423 975 | 25.0 | 7 222 144 | 21.7 | −14.3 |
| Other OECD-Europe | .. | .. | .. | .. | .. |
| Total Europe | 30 067 203 | 89.1 | 29 749 666 | 89.2 | −1.1 |
| Canada | 229 838 | 0.7 | 236 549 | 0.7 | 2.9 |
| United States | 790 346 | 2.3 | 828 553 | 2.5 | 4.8 |
| Total North America | 1 020 184 | 3.0 | 1 065 102 | 3.2 | 4.4 |
| Australia | .. | .. | .. | .. | .. |
| New Zealand | 299 294 | 0.9 | 254 886 | 0.8 | −14.8 |
| Japan | 238 414 | 0.7 | 261 343 | 0.8 | 9.6 |
| Total Australasia and Japan | 537 708 | 1.6 | 516 229 | 1.5 | −4.0 |
| **Total OECD Countries** | 31 625 095 | 93.7 | 31 330 997 | 94.0 | −0.9 |
| Yugoslavia | 280 483 | 0.8 | 203 183 | 0.6 | −27.6 |
| Other European countries | 521 237 | 1.5 | 561 582 | 1.7 | 7.7 |
| Latin America | 180 306 | 0.5 | 175 219 | 0.5 | −2.8 |
| Mexico | 18 041 | 0.1 | 21 020 | 0.1 | 16.5 |
| Asia-Oceania | 489 146 | 1.4 | 411 669 | 1.2 | −15.8 |
| Israel | 102 151 | 0.3 | 75 495 | 0.2 | −26.1 |
| Lebanon | 92 610 | 0.3 | 102 179 | 0.3 | 10.3 |
| Africa | 381 229 | 1.1 | 360 592 | 1.1 | −5.4 |
| Egypt | 139 717 | 0.4 | 134 432 | 0.4 | −3.8 |
| South Africa | 64 482 | 0.2 | 72 596 | 0.2 | 12.6 |
| Origin country undetermined | 280 070 | 0.8 | 297 882 | 0.9 | 6.4 |
| **Total non-OECD Countries** | 2 132 471 | 6.3 | 2 010 127 | 6.0 | −5.7 |
| **TOTAL** | 33 757 566 | 100.0 | 33 341 124 | 100.0 | −1.2 |

# GREECE

## NIGHTS SPENT BY FOREIGN TOURISTS IN REGISTERED TOURIST ACCOMMODATION

### *(by country of residence)*

| | 1987 | Relative share | 1988 | Relative share | % Variation over 1987 |
|---|---|---|---|---|---|
| Austria | 1 685 395 | 4.7 | 1 942 491 | 5.6 | 15.3 |
| Belgium | 738 402 | 2.1 | 825 747 | 2.4 | 11.8 |
| Denmark | 1 336 630 | 3.7 | 1 213 588 | 3.5 | −9.2 |
| Finland | 1 311 314 | 3.7 | 1 345 398 | 3.9 | 2.6 |
| France | 2 729 910 | 7.6 | 2 594 230 | 7.5 | −5.0 |
| Germany | 7 715 103 | 21.6 | 8 315 638 | 23.9 | 7.8 |
| Greece | .. | .. | .. | .. | .. |
| Iceland | .. | .. | .. | .. | .. |
| Ireland | .. | .. | .. | .. | .. |
| Italy | 1 756 643 | 4.9 | 1 792 673 | 5.2 | 2.1 |
| Luxembourg | .. | .. | .. | .. | .. |
| Netherlands | 1 756 987 | 4.9 | 1 752 071 | 5.0 | −0.3 |
| Norway | 1 013 864 | 2.8 | 724 370 | 2.1 | −28.6 |
| Portugal | .. | .. | .. | .. | .. |
| Spain | 282 731 | 0.8 | 321 224 | 0.9 | 13.6 |
| Sweden | 1 704 107 | 4.8 | 1 703 850 | 4.9 | −0.0 |
| Switzerland | 981 790 | 2.7 | 979 064 | 2.8 | −0.3 |
| Turkey | 63 848 | 0.2 | 81 550 | 0.2 | 27.7 |
| United Kingdom | 8 307 877 | 23.2 | 7 284 895 | 20.9 | −12.3 |
| Other OECD-Europe | .. | .. | .. | .. | .. |
| **Total Europe** | 31 384 601 | 87.8 | 30 876 789 | 88.8 | −1.6 |
| Canada | 235 251 | 0.7 | 240 936 | 0.7 | 2.4 |
| United States | 799 345 | 2.2 | 836 234 | 2.4 | 4.6 |
| **Total North America** | 1 034 596 | 2.9 | 1 077 170 | 3.1 | 4.1 |
| Australia | .. | .. | .. | .. | .. |
| New Zealand | 323 990 | 0.9 | 276 520 | 0.8 | −14.7 |
| Japan | 238 613 | 0.7 | 261 527 | 0.8 | 9.6 |
| **Total Australasia and Japan** | 562 603 | 1.6 | 538 047 | 1.5 | −4.4 |
| **Total OECD Countries** | 32 981 800 | 92.2 | 32 492 006 | 93.4 | −1.5 |
| Yugoslavia | 430 854 | 1.2 | 272 127 | 0.8 | −36.8 |
| Other European countries | 796 224 | 2.2 | 744 752 | 2.1 | −6.5 |
| Latin America | 182 214 | 0.5 | 176 544 | 0.5 | −3.1 |
| Mexico | 18 252 | 0.1 | 21 153 | 0.1 | 15.9 |
| Asia-Oceania | 493 280 | 1.4 | 415 593 | 1.2 | −15.7 |
| Israel | 103 581 | 0.3 | 77 127 | 0.2 | −25.5 |
| Lebanon | 93 019 | 0.3 | 102 453 | 0.3 | 10.1 |
| Africa | 384 401 | 1.1 | 363 178 | 1.0 | −5.5 |
| Egypt | 140 156 | 0.4 | 134 609 | 0.4 | −4.0 |
| South Africa | 66 585 | 0.2 | 74 360 | 0.2 | 11.7 |
| Origin country undetermined | 486 535 | 1.4 | 314 883 | 0.9 | −35.3 |
| **Total non-OECD Countries** | 2 773 508 | 7.8 | 2 287 077 | 6.6 | −17.5 |
| **TOTAL** | 35 755 308 | 100.0 | 34 779 083 | 100.0 | −2.7 |

# ICELAND

*ARRIVALS OF FOREIGN TOURISTS AT FRONTIERS[1]*

*(by country of nationality)*

| | 1987 | Relative share | 1988 | Relative share | % Variation over 1987 |
|---|---|---|---|---|---|
| Austria | 2 359 | 1.8 | 2 142 | 1.7 | −9.2 |
| Belgium | 841 | 0.6 | 742 | 0.6 | −11.8 |
| Denmark | 16 191 | 12.5 | 16 398 | 12.7 | 1.3 |
| Finland | 3 103 | 2.4 | 3 676 | 2.9 | 18.5 |
| France | 5 311 | 4.1 | 6 141 | 4.8 | 15.6 |
| Germany | 14 011 | 10.8 | 15 894 | 12.3 | 13.4 |
| Greece | 126 | 0.1 | 189 | 0.1 | 50.0 |
| Iceland | .. | .. | .. | .. | .. |
| Ireland | 325 | 0.3 | 425 | 0.3 | 30.8 |
| Italy | 2 699 | 2.1 | 2 822 | 2.2 | 4.6 |
| Luxembourg | 383 | 0.3 | 353 | 0.3 | −7.8 |
| Netherlands | 2 419 | 1.9 | 2 832 | 2.2 | 17.1 |
| Norway | 10 165 | 7.8 | 9 767 | 7.6 | −3.9 |
| Portugal | 276 | 0.2 | 170 | 0.1 | −38.4 |
| Spain | 524 | 0.4 | 841 | 0.7 | 60.5 |
| Sweden | 15 614 | 12.1 | 17 322 | 13.4 | 10.9 |
| Switzerland | 2 993 | 2.3 | 3 817 | 3.0 | 27.5 |
| Turkey | 57 | 0.0 | 42 | 0.0 | −26.3 |
| United Kingdom | 10 579 | 8.2 | 10 525 | 8.2 | −0.5 |
| Other OECD-Europe | .. | .. | .. | .. | .. |
| **Total Europe** | 87 976 | 67.9 | 94 098 | 73.0 | 7.0 |
| | | | | | |
| Canada | 1 286 | 1.0 | 1 277 | 1.0 | −0.7 |
| United States | 35 669 | 27.5 | 28 724 | 22.3 | −19.5 |
| **Total North America** | 36 955 | 28.5 | 30 001 | 23.3 | −18.8 |
| | | | | | |
| Australia | 432 | 0.3 | 504 | 0.4 | 16.7 |
| New Zealand | 192 | 0.1 | 203 | 0.2 | 5.7 |
| Japan | 1 000 | 0.8 | 993 | 0.8 | −0.7 |
| **Total Australasia and Japan** | 1 624 | 1.3 | 1 700 | 1.3 | 4.7 |
| | | | | | |
| **Total OECD Countries** | 126 555 | 97.7 | 125 799 | 97.6 | −0.6 |
| | | | | | |
| Yugoslavia | 250 | 0.2 | 258 | 0.2 | 3.2 |
| Other European countries | 900 | 0.7 | 1 220 | 0.9 | 35.6 |
| Bulgaria | 18 | 0.0 | 44 | 0.0 | 144.4 |
| Czechoslovakia | 122 | 0.1 | 93 | 0.1 | −23.8 |
| Germany (D. R.) | 174 | 0.1 | 53 | 0.0 | −69.5 |
| Hungary | 58 | 0.0 | 157 | 0.1 | 170.7 |
| Poland | 287 | 0.2 | 505 | 0.4 | 76.0 |
| Rumania | 1 | 0.0 | 26 | 0.0 | 2500.0 |
| USSR | 240 | 0.2 | 342 | 0.3 | 42.5 |
| Latin America | 307 | 0.2 | 431 | 0.3 | 40.4 |
| Argentina | 31 | 0.0 | 24 | 0.0 | −22.6 |
| Brazil | 69 | 0.1 | 69 | 0.1 | 0.0 |
| Chile | 38 | 0.0 | 24 | 0.0 | −36.8 |
| Colombia | 20 | 0.0 | 30 | 0.0 | 50.0 |
| Mexico | 46 | 0.0 | 70 | 0.1 | 52.2 |
| Venezuela | 9 | 0.0 | 26 | 0.0 | 188.9 |
| Asia-Oceania | 915 | 0.7 | 710 | 0.6 | −22.4 |
| China | 87 | 0.1 | 83 | 0.1 | −4.6 |
| Hong Kong | 5 | 0.0 | 10 | 0.0 | 100.0 |
| India | 97 | 0.1 | 80 | 0.1 | −17.5 |
| Iran | 35 | 0.0 | 35 | 0.0 | 0.0 |
| Israel | 321 | 0.2 | 124 | 0.1 | −61.4 |
| Republic of Korea | 42 | 0.0 | 60 | 0.0 | 42.9 |
| Lebanon | 18 | 0.0 | 26 | 0.0 | 44.4 |
| Malaysia | 45 | 0.0 | 28 | 0.0 | −37.8 |
| Pakistan | 13 | 0.0 | 15 | 0.0 | 15.4 |
| Philippines | 117 | 0.1 | 95 | 0.1 | −18.8 |
| Saudi Arabia | 2 | 0.0 | 9 | 0.0 | 350.0 |
| Singapore | 34 | 0.0 | 22 | 0.0 | −35.3 |
| Thailand | 37 | 0.0 | 55 | 0.0 | 48.6 |
| Africa | 313 | 0.2 | 341 | 0.3 | 8.9 |
| Algeria | 37 | 0.0 | 11 | 0.0 | −70.3 |
| Egypt | 14 | 0.0 | 17 | 0.0 | 21.4 |
| Morocco | .. | .. | 37 | 0.0 | .. |
| South Africa | 119 | 0.1 | 122 | 0.1 | 2.5 |
| Origin country undetermined | 325 | 0.3 | 71 | 0.1 | −78.2 |
| | | | | | |
| **Total non-OECD Countries** | 3 010 | 2.3 | 3 031 | 2.4 | 0.7 |
| | | | | | |
| **TOTAL** | 129 565 | 100.0 | 128 830 | 100.0 | −0.6 |

1. Excluding shore excursionists.

# IRELAND

## ARRIVALS OF FOREIGN VISITORS AT FRONTIERS[1]

*(by country of residence)*

| | 1988 | Relative share | 1989 | Relative share | % Variation over 1988 |
|---|---|---|---|---|---|
| Austria | .. | .. | .. | .. | .. |
| Belgium | .. | .. | .. | .. | .. |
| Denmark | .. | .. | .. | .. | .. |
| Finland | .. | .. | .. | .. | .. |
| France | 107 000 | 4.6 | 136 000 | 5.0 | 27.1 |
| Germany | 112 000 | 4.8 | 151 000 | 5.5 | 34.8 |
| Greece | .. | .. | .. | .. | .. |
| Iceland | .. | .. | .. | .. | .. |
| Ireland | .. | .. | .. | .. | .. |
| Italy | .. | .. | .. | .. | .. |
| Luxembourg | .. | .. | .. | .. | .. |
| Netherlands | .. | .. | .. | .. | .. |
| Norway | .. | .. | .. | .. | .. |
| Portugal | .. | .. | .. | .. | .. |
| Spain | .. | .. | .. | .. | .. |
| Sweden | .. | .. | .. | .. | .. |
| Switzerland | .. | .. | .. | .. | .. |
| Turkey | .. | .. | .. | .. | .. |
| United Kingdom | 1 465 000 | 62.4 | 1 668 000 | 61.1 | 13.9 |
| Other OECD-Europe | 179 000 | 7.6 | 251 000 | 9.2 | 40.2 |
| Total Europe | 1 863 000 | 79.4 | 2 206 000 | 80.7 | 18.4 |
| Canada | 28 000 | 1.2 | 37 000 | 1.4 | 32.1 |
| United States | 373 000 | 15.9 | 380 000 | 13.9 | 1.9 |
| Total North America | 401 000 | 17.1 | 417 000 | 15.3 | 4.0 |
| Australia[2] | 42 000 | 1.8 | 59 000 | 2.2 | 40.5 |
| New Zealand[2] | .. | .. | .. | .. | .. |
| Japan[3] | .. | .. | .. | .. | .. |
| Total Australasia and Japan | 42 000 | 1.8 | 59 000 | 2.2 | 40.5 |
| **Total OECD Countries** | 2 306 000 | 98.3 | 2 682 000 | 98.2 | 16.3 |
| Yugoslavia | .. | .. | .. | .. | .. |
| Origin country unspecified[3] | 40 000 | 1.7 | 50 000 | 1.8 | 25.0 |
| **Total non-OECD Countries** | 40 000 | 1.7 | 50 000 | 1.8 | 25.0 |
| **TOTAL** | 2 346 000 | 100.0 | 2 732 000 | 100.0 | 16.5 |

1. Visitors arrivals on overseas routes only.
2. Australia includes New Zealand.
3. Origin country unspecified includes Japan.

# IRELAND

## ARRIVALS OF FOREIGN TOURISTS AT HOTELS
### *(by country of residence)*

| | 1988 | Relative share | 1989 | Relative share | % Variation over 1988 |
|---|---|---|---|---|---|
| Austria | .. | .. | .. | .. | .. |
| Belgium | .. | .. | .. | .. | .. |
| Denmark | 13 000 | 1.1 | 17 000 | 1.1 | 30.8 |
| Finland | .. | .. | .. | .. | .. |
| France | 67 000 | 5.4 | 77 000 | 5.1 | 14.9 |
| Germany | 67 000 | 5.4 | 87 000 | 5.8 | 29.9 |
| Greece | .. | .. | .. | .. | .. |
| Iceland | .. | .. | .. | .. | .. |
| Ireland | .. | .. | .. | .. | .. |
| Italy | .. | .. | .. | .. | .. |
| Luxembourg | .. | .. | .. | .. | .. |
| Netherlands | 25 000 | 2.0 | 33 000 | 2.2 | 32.0 |
| Norway | .. | .. | .. | .. | .. |
| Portugal | .. | .. | .. | .. | .. |
| Spain | .. | .. | .. | .. | .. |
| Sweden | .. | .. | .. | .. | .. |
| Switzerland | .. | .. | .. | .. | .. |
| Turkey | .. | .. | .. | .. | .. |
| United Kingdom[1] | 529 000 | 42.8 | 678 000 | 45.0 | 28.2 |
| Other OECD-Europe | .. | .. | .. | .. | .. |
| Total Europe | 701 000 | 56.8 | 892 000 | 59.3 | 27.2 |
| | | | | | |
| Canada | 24 000 | 1.9 | 37 000 | 2.5 | 54.2 |
| United States | 380 000 | 30.8 | 378 000 | 25.1 | –0.5 |
| Total North America | 404 000 | 32.7 | 415 000 | 27.6 | 2.7 |
| | | | | | |
| Australia | .. | .. | .. | .. | .. |
| New Zealand[2] | 130 000 | 10.5 | 198 000 | 13.2 | 52.3 |
| Japan | .. | .. | .. | .. | .. |
| Total Australasia and Japan | 130 000 | 10.5 | 198 000 | 13.2 | 52.3 |
| | | | | | |
| **Total OECD Countries** | 1 235 000 | 100.0 | 1 505 000 | 100.0 | 21.9 |
| | | | | | |
| Yugoslavia | .. | .. | .. | .. | .. |
| | | | | | |
| **TOTAL** | 1 235 000 | 100.0 | 1 505 000 | 100.0 | 21.9 |

1. Excludes Northern Ireland.
2. New Zealand includes all others countries not specified.

# IRELAND

## NIGHTS SPENT BY FOREIGN TOURISTS IN HOTELS
### (by country of residence)

| | 1988 | Relative share | 1989 | Relative share | % Variation over 1988 |
|---|---|---|---|---|---|
| Austria | .. | .. | .. | .. | .. |
| Belgium | .. | .. | .. | .. | .. |
| Denmark | 75 000 | 1.2 | 86 000 | 1.2 | 14.7 |
| Finland | .. | .. | .. | .. | .. |
| France | 447 000 | 7.2 | 470 000 | 6.3 | 5.1 |
| Germany | 514 000 | 8.3 | 564 000 | 7.6 | 9.7 |
| Greece | .. | .. | .. | .. | .. |
| Iceland | .. | .. | .. | .. | .. |
| Ireland | .. | .. | .. | .. | .. |
| Italy | .. | .. | .. | .. | .. |
| Luxembourg | .. | .. | .. | .. | .. |
| Netherlands | 125 000 | 2.0 | 200 000 | 2.7 | 60.0 |
| Norway | .. | .. | .. | .. | .. |
| Portugal | .. | .. | .. | .. | .. |
| Spain | .. | .. | .. | .. | .. |
| Sweden | .. | .. | .. | .. | .. |
| Switzerland | .. | .. | .. | .. | .. |
| Turkey | .. | .. | .. | .. | .. |
| United Kingdom[1] | 2 098 000 | 33.9 | 2 901 000 | 39.0 | 38.3 |
| Other OECD-Europe | .. | .. | .. | .. | .. |
| Total Europe | 3 259 000 | 52.7 | 4 221 000 | 56.8 | 29.5 |
| Canada | 115 000 | 1.9 | 254 000 | 3.4 | 120.9 |
| United States | 2 133 000 | 34.5 | 1 948 000 | 26.2 | -8.7 |
| Total North America | 2 248 000 | 36.4 | 2 202 000 | 29.6 | -2.0 |
| Australia | .. | .. | .. | .. | .. |
| New Zealand[2] | 677 000 | 10.9 | 1 011 000 | 13.6 | 49.3 |
| Japan | .. | .. | .. | .. | .. |
| Total Australasia and Japan | 677 000 | 10.9 | 1 011 000 | 13.6 | 49.3 |
| **Total OECD Countries** | 6 184 000 | 100.0 | 7 434 000 | 100.0 | 20.2 |
| Yugoslavia | .. | .. | .. | .. | .. |
| **TOTAL** | 6 184 000 | 100.0 | 7 434 000 | 100.0 | 20.2 |

1. Excludes Northern Ireland.
2. New Zealand includes all other countries not specified.

# ITALY

## ARRIVALS OF FOREIGN VISITORS AT FRONTIERS[1]
### (by country of nationality)

| | 1988 | Relative share | 1989 | Relative share | % Variation over 1988 |
|---|---|---|---|---|---|
| Austria | 6 174 611 | 11.1 | 6 083 370 | 11.0 | −1.5 |
| Belgium | 1 005 567 | 1.8 | 1 048 930 | 1.9 | 4.3 |
| Denmark | 628 357 | 1.1 | 646 335 | 1.2 | 2.9 |
| Finland | 283 943 | 0.5 | 311 448 | 0.6 | 9.7 |
| France | 8 975 273 | 16.1 | 9 390 152 | 17.0 | 4.6 |
| Germany | 10 479 061 | 18.8 | 10 134 213 | 18.4 | −3.3 |
| Greece | 422 530 | 0.8 | 508 838 | 0.9 | 20.4 |
| Iceland[2] | .. | .. | .. | .. | .. |
| Ireland | 96 472 | 0.2 | 130 922 | 0.2 | 35.7 |
| Italy | .. | .. | .. | .. | .. |
| Luxembourg | 164 248 | 0.3 | 193 983 | 0.4 | 18.1 |
| Netherlands | 1 802 684 | 3.2 | 1 840 844 | 3.3 | 2.1 |
| Norway | 259 409 | 0.5 | 301 341 | 0.5 | 16.2 |
| Portugal | 239 809 | 0.4 | 226 102 | 0.4 | −5.7 |
| Spain | 642 681 | 1.2 | 700 609 | 1.3 | 9.0 |
| Sweden | 580 071 | 1.0 | 597 104 | 1.1 | 2.9 |
| Switzerland | 11 754 847 | 21.1 | 10 190 559 | 18.5 | −13.3 |
| Turkey | 249 251 | 0.4 | 193 036 | 0.4 | −22.6 |
| United Kingdom | 1 819 232 | 3.3 | 1 906 236 | 3.5 | 4.8 |
| Other OECD-Europe | .. | .. | .. | .. | .. |
| **Total Europe** | 45 578 046 | 81.8 | 44 404 022 | 80.5 | −2.6 |
| Canada | 354 258 | 0.6 | 422 939 | 0.8 | 19.4 |
| United States | 1 351 257 | 2.4 | 1 356 662 | 2.5 | 0.4 |
| **Total North America** | 1 705 515 | 3.1 | 1 779 601 | 3.2 | 4.3 |
| Australia | 227 371 | 0.4 | 274 271 | 0.5 | 20.6 |
| New Zealand | .. | .. | .. | .. | .. |
| Japan | 384 850 | 0.7 | 456 700 | 0.8 | 18.7 |
| **Total Australasia and Japan** | 612 221 | 1.1 | 730 971 | 1.3 | 19.4 |
| **Total OECD Countries** | 47 895 782 | 86.0 | 46 914 594 | 85.1 | −2.0 |
| Yugoslavia | 5 467 441 | 9.8 | 5 909 741 | 10.7 | 8.1 |
| Other European countries[2] | 677 641 | 1.2 | 806 804 | 1.5 | 19.1 |
| USSR | 50 305 | 0.1 | 93 092 | 0.2 | 85.1 |
| Latin America | 330 428 | 0.6 | 493 425 | 0.9 | 49.3 |
| Argentina | 85 610 | 0.2 | 112 185 | 0.2 | 31.0 |
| Brazil | 88 770 | 0.2 | 121 368 | 0.2 | 36.7 |
| Mexico | 58 163 | 0.1 | 89 359 | 0.2 | 53.6 |
| Venezuela | 41 966 | 0.1 | 66 409 | 0.1 | 58.2 |
| Asia-Oceania | 97 923 | 0.2 | 166 460 | 0.3 | 70.0 |
| Israel | 62 050 | 0.1 | 91 084 | 0.2 | 46.8 |
| Africa | 60 820 | 0.1 | 86 911 | 0.2 | 42.9 |
| Egypt | 30 161 | 0.1 | 39 807 | 0.1 | 32.0 |
| South Africa | 30 659 | 0.1 | 47 104 | 0.1 | 53.6 |
| Origin country undetermined | 1 160 399 | 2.1 | 753 163 | 1.4 | −35.1 |
| **Total non-OECD Countries** | 7 794 652 | 14.0 | 8 216 504 | 14.9 | 5.4 |
| **TOTAL** | 55 690 434 | 100.0 | 55 131 098 | 100.0 | −1.0 |

1. Includes about 53% of excursionists.
2. "Other European countries" includes Iceland.

# ITALY

## ARRIVALS OF FOREIGN TOURISTS AT HOTELS
### (by country of nationality)

| | 1987 | Relative share | 1988 | Relative share | % Variation over 1987 |
|---|---|---|---|---|---|
| Austria | 980 306 | 5.8 | 932 883 | 5.4 | −4.8 |
| Belgium | 371 332 | 2.2 | 405 362 | 2.3 | 9.2 |
| Denmark | 139 122 | 0.8 | 139 357 | 0.8 | 0.2 |
| Finland | 111 771 | 0.7 | 112 746 | 0.6 | 0.9 |
| France | 1 802 788 | 10.6 | 1 795 569 | 10.3 | −0.4 |
| Germany | 4 933 170 | 29.0 | 5 046 194 | 28.9 | 2.3 |
| Greece | 149 985 | 0.9 | 175 782 | 1.0 | 17.2 |
| Iceland[1] | .. | .. | .. | .. | .. |
| Ireland | 50 747 | 0.3 | 50 321 | 0.3 | −0.8 |
| Italy | .. | .. | .. | .. | .. |
| Luxembourg | 32 987 | 0.2 | 36 377 | 0.2 | 10.3 |
| Netherlands | 307 468 | 1.8 | 340 605 | 2.0 | 10.8 |
| Norway | 84 707 | 0.5 | 78 443 | 0.4 | −7.4 |
| Portugal | 59 321 | 0.3 | 71 949 | 0.4 | 21.3 |
| Spain | 710 065 | 4.2 | 808 996 | 4.6 | 13.9 |
| Sweden | 251 338 | 1.5 | 245 237 | 1.4 | −2.4 |
| Switzerland | 1 036 010 | 6.1 | 1 076 175 | 6.2 | 3.9 |
| Turkey | 62 182 | 0.4 | 66 094 | 0.4 | 6.3 |
| United Kingdom | 1 180 489 | 6.9 | 1 162 034 | 6.7 | −1.6 |
| Other OECD-Europe | .. | .. | .. | .. | .. |
| **Total Europe** | 12 263 788 | 72.0 | 12 544 124 | 71.9 | 2.3 |
| Canada | 237 070 | 1.4 | 231 982 | 1.3 | −2.1 |
| United States | 1 885 168 | 11.1 | 1 864 011 | 10.7 | −1.1 |
| **Total North America** | 2 122 238 | 12.5 | 2 095 993 | 12.0 | −1.2 |
| Australia | 214 684 | 1.3 | 204 372 | 1.2 | −4.8 |
| New Zealand | .. | .. | .. | .. | .. |
| Japan | 473 362 | 2.8 | 572 236 | 3.3 | 20.9 |
| **Total Australasia and Japan** | 688 046 | 4.0 | 776 608 | 4.5 | 12.9 |
| **Total OECD Countries** | 15 074 072 | 88.5 | 15 416 725 | 88.4 | 2.3 |
| Yugoslavia | 162 364 | 1.0 | 168 440 | 1.0 | 3.7 |
| Other European countries[1] | 252 302 | 1.5 | 314 983 | 1.8 | 24.8 |
| USSR | 32 714 | 0.2 | 46 824 | 0.3 | 43.1 |
| Latin America | 500 679 | 2.9 | 485 762 | 2.8 | −3.0 |
| Argentina | 140 497 | 0.8 | 97 062 | 0.6 | −30.9 |
| Brazil | 149 518 | 0.9 | 169 698 | 1.0 | 13.5 |
| Mexico | 81 222 | 0.5 | 85 560 | 0.5 | 5.3 |
| Venezuela | 28 550 | 0.2 | 33 215 | 0.2 | 16.3 |
| Asia-Oceania | 230 921 | 1.4 | 213 768 | 1.2 | −7.4 |
| Israel | 156 049 | 0.9 | 138 482 | 0.8 | −11.3 |
| Africa | 57 677 | 0.3 | 61 804 | 0.4 | 7.2 |
| Egypt | 22 948 | 0.1 | 24 870 | 0.1 | 8.4 |
| South Africa | 34 729 | 0.2 | 36 934 | 0.2 | 6.3 |
| Origin country undetermined | 747 530 | 4.4 | 775 241 | 4.4 | 3.7 |
| **Total non-OECD Countries** | 1 951 473 | 11.5 | 2 019 998 | 11.6 | 3.5 |
| **TOTAL** | 17 025 545 | 100.0 | 17 436 723 | 100.0 | 2.4 |

1. "Other European countries" includes Iceland.

# ITALY

## ARRIVALS OF FOREIGN TOURISTS AT REGISTERED TOURIST ACCOMMODATION
### (by country of nationality)

| | 1987 | Relative share | 1988 | Relative share | % Variation over 1987 |
|---|---|---|---|---|---|
| Austria | 1 175 573 | 5.8 | 1 119 539 | 5.4 | −4.8 |
| Belgium | 441 427 | 2.2 | 476 000 | 2.3 | 7.8 |
| Denmark | 216 455 | 1.1 | 217 786 | 1.1 | 0.6 |
| Finland | 126 222 | 0.6 | 128 299 | 0.6 | 1.6 |
| France | 2 104 321 | 10.4 | 2 085 589 | 10.1 | −0.9 |
| Germany | 6 362 305 | 31.5 | 6 487 347 | 31.5 | 2.0 |
| Greece | 157 326 | 0.8 | 182 854 | 0.9 | 16.2 |
| Iceland[1] | .. | .. | .. | .. | .. |
| Ireland | 59 281 | 0.3 | 58 458 | 0.3 | −1.4 |
| Italy | .. | .. | .. | .. | .. |
| Luxembourg | 37 142 | 0.2 | 40 316 | 0.2 | 8.5 |
| Netherlands | 554 293 | 2.7 | 587 287 | 2.8 | 6.0 |
| Norway | 101 511 | 0.5 | 94 405 | 0.5 | −7.0 |
| Portugal | 70 879 | 0.4 | 83 479 | 0.4 | 17.8 |
| Spain | 783 836 | 3.9 | 877 663 | 4.3 | 12.0 |
| Sweden | 313 986 | 1.6 | 308 747 | 1.5 | −1.7 |
| Switzerland | 1 188 000 | 5.9 | 1 225 998 | 5.9 | 3.2 |
| Turkey | 66 739 | 0.3 | 71 833 | 0.3 | 7.6 |
| United Kingdom | 1 340 781 | 6.6 | 1 322 407 | 6.4 | −1.4 |
| Other OECD-Europe | .. | .. | .. | .. | .. |
| **Total Europe** | 15 100 077 | 74.8 | 15 368 007 | 74.5 | 1.8 |
| | | | | | |
| Canada | 261 245 | 1.3 | 259 056 | 1.3 | −0.8 |
| United States | 1 956 153 | 9.7 | 1 936 456 | 9.4 | −1.0 |
| **Total North America** | 2 217 398 | 11.0 | 2 195 512 | 10.6 | −1.0 |
| | | | | | |
| Australia | 255 831 | 1.3 | 249 520 | 1.2 | −2.5 |
| New Zealand | .. | .. | .. | .. | .. |
| Japan | 482 629 | 2.4 | 583 158 | 2.8 | 20.8 |
| **Total Australasia and Japan** | 738 460 | 3.7 | 832 678 | 4.0 | 12.8 |
| | | | | | |
| **Total OECD Countries** | 18 055 935 | 89.4 | 18 396 197 | 89.2 | 1.9 |
| | | | | | |
| Yugoslavia | 171 876 | 0.9 | 178 265 | 0.9 | 3.7 |
| Other European countries[1] | 325 306 | 1.6 | 403 876 | 2.0 | 24.2 |
| USSR | 33 128 | 0.2 | 47 953 | 0.2 | 44.8 |
| Latin America | 530 552 | 2.6 | 520 963 | 2.5 | −1.8 |
| Argentina | 149 202 | 0.7 | 106 110 | 0.5 | −28.9 |
| Brazil | 158 129 | 0.8 | 180 823 | 0.9 | 14.4 |
| Mexico | 87 334 | 0.4 | 90 975 | 0.4 | 4.2 |
| Venezuela | 29 983 | 0.1 | 35 248 | 0.2 | 17.6 |
| Asia-Oceania | 241 855 | 1.2 | 225 385 | 1.1 | −6.8 |
| Israel | 164 255 | 0.8 | 147 236 | 0.7 | −10.4 |
| Africa | 63 513 | 0.3 | 69 379 | 0.3 | 9.2 |
| Egypt | 23 967 | 0.1 | 25 912 | 0.1 | 8.1 |
| South Africa | 39 546 | 0.2 | 43 467 | 0.2 | 9.9 |
| Origin country undetermined | 798 549 | 4.0 | 826 125 | 4.0 | 3.5 |
| | | | | | |
| **Total non-OECD Countries** | 2 131 651 | 10.6 | 2 223 993 | 10.8 | 4.3 |
| | | | | | |
| **TOTAL** | 20 187 586 | 100.0 | 20 620 190 | 100.0 | 2.1 |

1. "Other European countries" includes Iceland.

# ITALY

## NIGHTS SPENT BY FOREIGN TOURISTS IN HOTELS
### (by country of nationality)

| | 1987 | Relative share | 1988 | Relative share | % Variation over 1987 |
|---|---|---|---|---|---|
| Austria | 4 384 450 | 6.2 | 4 202 789 | 6.0 | −4.1 |
| Belgium | 1 804 351 | 2.6 | 1 968 229 | 2.8 | 9.1 |
| Denmark | 678 687 | 1.0 | 652 947 | 0.9 | −3.8 |
| Finland | 662 635 | 0.9 | 622 553 | 0.9 | −6.0 |
| France | 5 743 428 | 8.1 | 5 530 553 | 7.9 | −3.7 |
| Germany | 28 309 774 | 40.0 | 28 396 344 | 40.3 | 0.3 |
| Greece | 344 457 | 0.5 | 395 477 | 0.6 | 14.8 |
| Iceland[1] | .. | .. | .. | .. | .. |
| Ireland | 193 758 | 0.3 | 211 709 | 0.3 | 9.3 |
| Italy | .. | .. | .. | .. | .. |
| Luxembourg | 225 854 | 0.3 | 246 713 | 0.4 | 9.2 |
| Netherlands | 1 840 833 | 2.6 | 1 506 585 | 2.1 | −18.2 |
| Norway | 366 436 | 0.5 | 306 094 | 0.4 | −16.5 |
| Portugal | 147 900 | 0.2 | 177 911 | 0.3 | 20.3 |
| Spain | 1 441 354 | 2.0 | 1 701 352 | 2.4 | 18.0 |
| Sweden | 1 021 582 | 1.4 | 991 887 | 1.4 | −2.9 |
| Switzerland | 4 836 926 | 6.8 | 5 054 499 | 7.2 | 4.5 |
| Turkey | 161 683 | 0.2 | 169 690 | 0.2 | 5.0 |
| United Kingdom | 5 537 159 | 7.8 | 5 183 734 | 7.4 | −6.4 |
| Other OECD-Europe | .. | .. | .. | .. | .. |
| **Total Europe** | 57 701 267 | 81.6 | 57 319 066 | 81.4 | −0.7 |
| Canada | 606 738 | 0.9 | 573 385 | 0.8 | −5.5 |
| United States | 4 760 100 | 6.7 | 4 590 361 | 6.5 | −3.6 |
| **Total North America** | 5 366 838 | 7.6 | 5 163 746 | 7.3 | −3.8 |
| Australia | 494 528 | 0.7 | 467 305 | 0.7 | −5.5 |
| New Zealand | .. | .. | .. | .. | .. |
| Japan | 941 896 | 1.3 | 1 149 702 | 1.6 | 22.1 |
| **Total Australasia and Japan** | 1 436 424 | 2.0 | 1 617 007 | 2.3 | 12.6 |
| **Total OECD Countries** | 64 504 529 | 91.2 | 64 099 819 | 91.0 | −0.6 |
| Yugoslavia | 428 097 | 0.6 | 448 736 | 0.6 | 4.8 |
| Other European countries[1] | 1 281 709 | 1.8 | 1 456 648 | 2.1 | 13.6 |
| USSR | 120 852 | 0.2 | 163 000 | 0.2 | 34.9 |
| Latin America | 1 334 621 | 1.9 | 1 322 955 | 1.9 | −0.9 |
| Argentina | 273 912 | 0.4 | 279 684 | 0.4 | 2.1 |
| Brazil | 406 908 | 0.6 | 458 793 | 0.7 | 12.8 |
| Mexico | 185 263 | 0.3 | 195 615 | 0.3 | 5.6 |
| Venezuela | 86 184 | 0.1 | 96 321 | 0.1 | 11.8 |
| Asia-Oceania | 610 330 | 0.9 | 551 506 | 0.8 | −9.6 |
| Israel | 345 633 | 0.5 | 306 622 | 0.4 | −11.3 |
| Africa | 170 694 | 0.2 | 181 233 | 0.3 | 6.2 |
| Egypt | 79 540 | 0.1 | 82 876 | 0.1 | 4.2 |
| South Africa | 91 154 | 0.1 | 98 357 | 0.1 | 7.9 |
| Origin country undetermined | 2 364 854 | 3.3 | 2 344 919 | 3.3 | −0.8 |
| **Total non-OECD Countries** | 6 190 305 | 8.8 | 6 305 997 | 9.0 | 1.9 |
| **TOTAL** | 70 694 834 | 100.0 | 70 405 816 | 100.0 | −0.4 |

1. "Other European countries" includes Iceland.

# ITALY

## NIGHTS SPENT BY FOREIGN TOURISTS IN REGISTERED TOURIST ACCOMMODATION
### (by country of nationality)

| | 1987 | Relative share | 1988 | Relative share | % Variation over 1987 |
|---|---|---|---|---|---|
| Austria | 5 805 497 | 6.3 | 5 572 391 | 6.0 | –4.0 |
| Belgium | 2 407 846 | 2.6 | 2 574 321 | 2.8 | 6.9 |
| Denmark | 1 262 596 | 1.4 | 1 253 253 | 1.4 | –0.7 |
| Finland | 731 973 | 0.8 | 697 599 | 0.8 | –4.7 |
| France | 7 162 935 | 7.8 | 6 838 470 | 7.4 | –4.5 |
| Germany | 39 242 604 | 42.5 | 39 498 355 | 42.7 | 0.7 |
| Greece | 411 888 | 0.4 | 447 791 | 0.5 | 8.7 |
| Iceland[1] | .. | .. | .. | .. | .. |
| Ireland | 230 195 | 0.2 | 246 039 | 0.3 | 6.9 |
| Italy | .. | .. | .. | .. | .. |
| Luxembourg | 261 911 | 0.3 | 281 222 | 0.3 | 7.4 |
| Netherlands | 3 403 175 | 3.7 | 3 556 767 | 3.8 | 4.5 |
| Norway | 475 646 | 0.5 | 413 120 | 0.4 | –13.1 |
| Portugal | 180 078 | 0.2 | 210 734 | 0.2 | 17.0 |
| Spain | 1 652 304 | 1.8 | 1 896 142 | 2.1 | 14.8 |
| Sweden | 1 441 198 | 1.6 | 1 433 974 | 1.6 | –0.5 |
| Switzerland | 6 089 212 | 6.6 | 6 296 880 | 6.8 | 3.4 |
| Turkey | 184 068 | 0.2 | 201 021 | 0.2 | 9.2 |
| United Kingdom | 6 513 692 | 7.1 | 6 131 890 | 6.6 | –5.9 |
| Other OECD-Europe | .. | .. | .. | .. | .. |
| **Total Europe** | 77 456 818 | 84.0 | 77 549 969 | 83.9 | 0.1 |
| | | | | | |
| Canada | 704 207 | 0.8 | 675 189 | 0.7 | –4.1 |
| United States | 5 164 996 | 5.6 | 4 923 551 | 5.3 | –4.7 |
| **Total North America** | 5 869 203 | 6.4 | 5 598 740 | 6.1 | –4.6 |
| | | | | | |
| Australia | 598 393 | 0.6 | 574 932 | 0.6 | –3.9 |
| New Zealand | .. | .. | .. | .. | .. |
| Japan | 977 382 | 1.1 | 1 189 552 | 1.3 | 21.7 |
| **Total Australasia and Japan** | 1 575 775 | 1.7 | 1 764 484 | 1.9 | 12.0 |
| | | | | | |
| **Total OECD Countries** | 84 901 796 | 92.1 | 84 913 193 | 91.8 | 0.0 |
| | | | | | |
| Yugoslavia | 493 738 | 0.5 | 508 184 | 0.5 | 2.9 |
| Other European countries[1] | 1 589 950 | 1.7 | 1 866 138 | 2.0 | 17.4 |
| USSR | 123 518 | 0.1 | 168 931 | 0.2 | 36.8 |
| Latin America | 1 488 575 | 1.6 | 1 505 289 | 1.6 | 1.1 |
| Argentina | 409 730 | 0.4 | 331 396 | 0.4 | –19.1 |
| Brazil | 445 518 | 0.5 | 506 109 | 0.5 | 13.6 |
| Mexico | 226 241 | 0.2 | 215 360 | 0.2 | –4.8 |
| Venezuela | 100 881 | 0.1 | 115 725 | 0.1 | 14.7 |
| Asia-Oceania | 652 604 | 0.7 | 594 837 | 0.6 | –8.9 |
| Israel | 367 354 | 0.4 | 329 351 | 0.4 | –10.3 |
| Africa | 200 358 | 0.2 | 220 061 | 0.2 | 9.8 |
| Egypt | 86 814 | 0.1 | 90 408 | 0.1 | 4.1 |
| South Africa | 113 544 | 0.1 | 129 653 | 0.1 | 14.2 |
| Origin country undetermined | 2 901 068 | 3.1 | 2 859 794 | 3.1 | –1.4 |
| | | | | | |
| **Total non-OECD Countries** | 7 326 293 | 7.9 | 7 554 303 | 8.2 | 3.1 |
| | | | | | |
| **TOTAL** | 92 228 089 | 100.0 | 92 467 496 | 100.0 | 0.3 |

1. "Other European countries" includes Iceland.

# JAPAN

*ARRIVALS OF FOREIGN VISITORS AT FRONTIERS*

*(by country of nationality)*

| | 1988 | Relative share | 1989 | Relative share | % Variation over 1988 |
|---|---|---|---|---|---|
| Austria | 6 673 | 0.3 | 8 684 | 0.3 | 30.1 |
| Belgium | 6 483 | 0.3 | 7 606 | 0.3 | 17.3 |
| Denmark | 7 587 | 0.3 | 7 813 | 0.3 | 3.0 |
| Finland | 8 955 | 0.4 | 9 271 | 0.3 | 3.5 |
| France | 40 455 | 1.7 | 47 261 | 1.7 | 16.8 |
| Germany | 56 941 | 2.4 | 61 580 | 2.2 | 8.1 |
| Greece | 2 467 | 0.1 | 2 641 | 0.1 | 7.1 |
| Iceland | 453 | 0.0 | 546 | 0.0 | 20.5 |
| Ireland | 3 303 | 0.1 | 4 034 | 0.1 | 22.1 |
| Italy | 23 462 | 1.0 | 27 665 | 1.0 | 17.9 |
| Luxembourg | 336 | 0.0 | 442 | 0.0 | 31.5 |
| Netherlands | 15 852 | 0.7 | 16 432 | 0.6 | 3.7 |
| Norway | 5 086 | 0.2 | 4 604 | 0.2 | −9.5 |
| Portugal | 4 193 | 0.2 | 4 448 | 0.2 | 6.1 |
| Spain | 11 133 | 0.5 | 12 877 | 0.5 | 15.7 |
| Sweden | 15 271 | 0.6 | 15 198 | 0.5 | −0.5 |
| Switzerland | 16 433 | 0.7 | 17 286 | 0.6 | 5.2 |
| Turkey | 2 152 | 0.1 | 2 642 | 0.1 | 22.8 |
| United Kingdom | 154 582 | 6.6 | 177 259 | 6.3 | 14.7 |
| Other OECD-Europe | .. | .. | .. | .. | .. |
| **Total Europe** | 381 817 | 16.2 | 428 289 | 15.1 | 12.2 |
| Canada | 58 164 | 2.5 | 59 754 | 2.1 | 2.7 |
| United States | 516 259 | 21.9 | 531 625 | 18.8 | 3.0 |
| **Total North America** | 574 423 | 24.4 | 591 379 | 20.9 | 3.0 |
| Australia | 45 572 | 1.9 | 55 586 | 2.0 | 22.0 |
| New Zealand | 14 811 | 0.6 | 15 564 | 0.5 | 5.1 |
| Japan | .. | .. | .. | .. | .. |
| **Total Australasia and Japan** | 60 383 | 2.6 | 71 150 | 2.5 | 17.8 |
| **Total OECD Countries** | 1 016 623 | 43.2 | 1 090 818 | 38.5 | 7.3 |
| Yugoslavia | 1 156 | 0.0 | 1 360 | 0.0 | 17.6 |
| Other European countries | 19 975 | 0.8 | 28 221 | 1.0 | 41.3 |
| Bulgaria | 961 | 0.0 | 929 | 0.0 | −3.3 |
| Czechoslovakia | 1 256 | 0.1 | .. | .. | .. |
| Hungary | 1 984 | 0.1 | 1 880 | 0.1 | −5.2 |
| Poland | 2 087 | 0.1 | 3 176 | 0.1 | 52.2 |
| Rumania | 299 | 0.0 | 294 | 0.0 | −1.7 |
| USSR | 9 868 | 0.4 | 18 745 | 0.7 | 90.0 |
| Latin America | 47 139 | 2.0 | 62 414 | 2.2 | 32.4 |
| Argentina | 4 493 | 0.2 | 5 278 | 0.2 | 17.5 |
| Brazil | 16 011 | 0.7 | 27 521 | 1.0 | 71.9 |
| Chile | 1 432 | 0.1 | 1 611 | 0.1 | 12.5 |
| Colombia | 2 455 | 0.1 | 2 666 | 0.1 | 8.6 |
| Mexico | 10 977 | 0.5 | 9 053 | 0.3 | −17.5 |
| Venezuela | 1 653 | 0.1 | 1 197 | 0.0 | −27.6 |
| Asia-Oceania | 1 256 913 | 53.4 | 1 637 612 | 57.8 | 30.3 |
| China | 108 930 | 4.6 | 98 255 | 3.5 | −9.8 |
| Hong Kong | 30 927 | 1.3 | 34 259 | 1.2 | 10.8 |
| India | 29 780 | 1.3 | 30 877 | 1.1 | 3.7 |
| Iran | 14 504 | 0.6 | 16 798 | 0.6 | 15.8 |
| Israel | 6 505 | 0.3 | 6 784 | 0.2 | 4.3 |
| Republic of Korea | 341 278 | 14.5 | 609 984 | 21.5 | 78.7 |
| Lebanon | 421 | 0.0 | 388 | 0.0 | −7.8 |
| Malaysia | 46 033 | 2.0 | 54 397 | 1.9 | 18.2 |
| Pakistan | 19 660 | 0.8 | 7 115 | 0.3 | −63.8 |
| Philippines | 102 418 | 4.3 | 96 624 | 3.4 | −5.7 |
| Singapore | 32 480 | 1.4 | 37 822 | 1.3 | 16.4 |
| Taiwan | 411 314 | 17.5 | 527 969 | 18.6 | 28.4 |
| Thailand | 46 949 | 2.0 | 53 288 | 1.9 | 13.5 |
| Africa | 10 510 | 0.4 | 11 883 | 0.4 | 13.1 |
| Egypt | 1 716 | 0.1 | 1 818 | 0.1 | 5.9 |
| South Africa | 1 799 | 0.1 | 1 696 | 0.1 | −5.7 |
| Origin country undetermined | 3 096 | 0.1 | 2 756 | 0.1 | −11.0 |
| **Total non-OECD Countries** | 1 338 789 | 56.8 | 1 744 246 | 61.5 | 30.3 |
| **TOTAL** | 2 355 412 | 100.0 | 2 835 064 | 100.0 | 20.4 |

# NETHERLANDS

## ARRIVALS OF FOREIGN TOURISTS AT HOTELS

### (by country of residence)

| | 1988 | Relative share | 1989 | Relative share | % Variation over 1988 |
|---|---|---|---|---|---|
| Austria[3] | .. | .. | .. | .. | .. |
| Belgium | 140 200 | 4.2 | 143 800 | 4.1 | 2.6 |
| Denmark | 67 200 | 2.0 | 72 100 | 2.1 | 7.3 |
| Finland | 29 300 | 0.9 | 32 600 | 0.9 | 11.3 |
| France | 257 700 | 7.8 | 259 100 | 7.4 | 0.5 |
| Germany | 664 800 | 20.0 | 675 000 | 19.4 | 1.5 |
| Greece[3] | .. | .. | .. | .. | .. |
| Iceland[3] | .. | .. | .. | .. | .. |
| Ireland | 18 900 | 0.6 | 20 000 | 0.6 | 5.8 |
| Italy | 164 900 | 5.0 | 208 900 | 6.0 | 26.7 |
| Luxembourg | 11 400 | 0.3 | 11 500 | 0.3 | 0.9 |
| Netherlands | .. | | .. | | |
| Norway | 46 700 | 1.4 | 53 900 | 1.5 | 15.4 |
| Portugal[1] | .. | .. | .. | .. | .. |
| Spain[1] | 112 100 | 3.4 | 127 600 | 3.7 | 13.8 |
| Sweden | 102 400 | 3.1 | 109 600 | 3.1 | 7.0 |
| Switzerland | 80 100 | 2.4 | 91 500 | 2.6 | 14.2 |
| Turkey | .. | .. | .. | .. | .. |
| United Kingdom | 603 800 | 18.2 | 649 100 | 18.6 | 7.5 |
| Other OECD-Europe[3] | 112 500 | 3.4 | 127 600 | 3.7 | 13.4 |
| Total Europe | 2 412 000 | 72.6 | 2 582 300 | 74.1 | 7.1 |
| | | | | | |
| Canada | 102 900 | 3.1 | 93 900 | 2.7 | −8.7 |
| United States | 381 000 | 11.5 | 412 400 | 11.8 | 8.2 |
| Total North America | 483 900 | 14.6 | 506 300 | 14.5 | 4.6 |
| | | | | | |
| Australia[2] | 46 000 | 1.4 | 50 200 | 1.4 | 9.1 |
| New Zealand[2] | .. | .. | .. | .. | .. |
| Japan | 83 900 | 2.5 | 84 400 | 2.4 | 0.6 |
| Total Australasia and Japan | 129 900 | 3.9 | 134 600 | 3.9 | 3.6 |
| | | | | | |
| **Total OECD Countries** | 3 025 800 | 91.1 | 3 223 200 | 92.4 | 6.5 |
| | | | | | |
| Yugoslavia | .. | .. | .. | .. | .. |
| Latin America | 62 500 | 1.9 | 64 300 | 1.8 | 2.9 |
| Asia-Oceania | 171 800 | 5.2 | 147 900 | 4.2 | −13.9 |
| Africa | 61 600 | 1.9 | 51 600 | 1.5 | −16.2 |
| | | | | | |
| **Total non-OECD Countries** | 295 900 | 8.9 | 263 800 | 7.6 | −10.8 |
| | | | | | |
| **TOTAL** | 3 321 700 | 100.0 | 3 487 000 | 100.0 | 5.0 |

1. Spain includes Portugal.
2. Australia includes New Zealand.
3. Other OECD-Europe includes Austria, Greece, Iceland and all non-OECD European countries.

# NETHERLANDS

## ARRIVALS OF FOREIGN TOURISTS AT REGISTERED TOURIST ACCOMMODATION
### (by country of residence)

| | 1988 | Relative share | 1989 | Relative share | % Variation over 1988 |
|---|---|---|---|---|---|
| Austria[3] | .. | .. | .. | .. | .. |
| Belgium | 272 000 | 5.6 | 298 000 | 5.8 | 9.6 |
| Denmark | 101 100 | 2.1 | 110 000 | 2.1 | 8.8 |
| Finland | 37 300 | 0.8 | 40 700 | 0.8 | 9.1 |
| France | 363 500 | 7.5 | 349 500 | 6.8 | -3.9 |
| Germany | 1 530 600 | 31.4 | 1 650 400 | 32.0 | 7.8 |
| Greece[3] | .. | .. | .. | .. | .. |
| Iceland[3] | .. | .. | .. | .. | .. |
| Ireland | 24 300 | 0.5 | 25 600 | 0.5 | 5.3 |
| Italy | 213 800 | 4.4 | 259 300 | 5.0 | 21.3 |
| Luxembourg | 12 600 | 0.3 | 12 700 | 0.2 | 0.8 |
| Netherlands | | | | | |
| Norway | 56 300 | 1.2 | 64 100 | 1.2 | 13.9 |
| Portugal[1] | .. | .. | .. | .. | .. |
| Spain[1] | 148 100 | 3.0 | 163 400 | 3.2 | 10.3 |
| Sweden | 125 300 | 2.6 | 137 800 | 2.7 | 10.0 |
| Switzerland | 97 900 | 2.0 | 110 200 | 2.1 | 12.6 |
| Turkey | .. | .. | .. | .. | .. |
| United Kingdom | 711 200 | 14.6 | 750 800 | 14.6 | 5.6 |
| Other OECD-Europe[3] | 134 600 | 2.8 | 152 800 | 3.0 | 13.5 |
| Total Europe | 3 828 600 | 78.5 | 4 125 300 | 80.1 | 7.7 |
| Canada | 122 800 | 2.5 | 108 700 | 2.1 | -11.5 |
| United States | 433 000 | 8.9 | 454 600 | 8.8 | 5.0 |
| Total North America | 555 800 | 11.4 | 563 300 | 10.9 | 1.3 |
| Australia[2] | 75 800 | 1.6 | 76 900 | 1.5 | 1.5 |
| New Zealand[2] | .. | .. | .. | .. | .. |
| Japan | 87 600 | 1.8 | 87 100 | 1.7 | -0.6 |
| Total Australasia and Japan | 163 400 | 3.4 | 164 000 | 3.2 | 0.4 |
| **Total OECD Countries** | 4 547 800 | 93.3 | 4 852 600 | 94.2 | 6.7 |
| Yugoslavia | .. | .. | .. | .. | .. |
| Latin America | 73 800 | 1.5 | 74 000 | 1.4 | 0.3 |
| Asia-Oceania | 184 600 | 3.8 | 164 100 | 3.2 | -11.1 |
| Africa | 69 900 | 1.4 | 59 400 | 1.2 | -15.0 |
| **Total non-OECD Countries** | 328 300 | 6.7 | 297 500 | 5.8 | -9.4 |
| **TOTAL** | 4 876 100 | 100.0 | 5 150 100 | 100.0 | 5.6 |

1. Spain includes Portugal.
2. Australia includes New Zealand.
3. Other OECD-Europe includes Austria, Greece, Iceland and non-OECD European countries.

# NETHERLANDS

## NIGHTS SPENT BY FOREIGN TOURISTS IN HOTELS
### (by country of residence)

| | 1988 | Relative share | 1989 | Relative share | % Variation over 1988 |
|---|---|---|---|---|---|
| Austria[3] | .. | .. | .. | .. | .. |
| Belgium | 245 600 | 3.6 | 264 400 | 3.7 | 7.7 |
| Denmark | 139 900 | 2.1 | 143 600 | 2.0 | 2.6 |
| Finland | 56 800 | 0.8 | 65 700 | 0.9 | 15.7 |
| France | 444 800 | 6.6 | 464 700 | 6.5 | 4.5 |
| Germany | 1 474 200 | 21.8 | 1 523 100 | 21.2 | 3.3 |
| Greece[3] | .. | .. | .. | .. | .. |
| Iceland[3] | .. | .. | .. | .. | |
| Ireland | 41 100 | 0.6 | 44 400 | 0.6 | 8.0 |
| Italy | 361 600 | 5.3 | 411 200 | 5.7 | 13.7 |
| Luxembourg | 21 300 | 0.3 | 22 500 | 0.3 | 5.6 |
| Netherlands | | | | | |
| Norway | 99 800 | 1.5 | 113 200 | 1.6 | 13.4 |
| Portugal[1] | .. | | .. | | |
| Spain[1] | 239 500 | 3.5 | 261 200 | 3.6 | 9.1 |
| Sweden | 194 100 | 2.9 | 214 400 | 3.0 | 10.5 |
| Switzerland | 170 100 | 2.5 | 185 800 | 2.6 | 9.2 |
| Turkey | .. | | .. | | |
| United Kingdom | 1 229 800 | 18.2 | 1 358 600 | 18.9 | 10.5 |
| Other OECD-Europe[3] | 256 800 | 3.8 | 284 000 | 4.0 | 10.6 |
| **Total Europe** | 4 975 400 | 73.6 | 5 356 800 | 74.6 | 7.7 |
| Canada | 175 400 | 2.6 | 180 200 | 2.5 | 2.7 |
| United States | 756 100 | 11.2 | 819 400 | 11.4 | 8.4 |
| **Total North America** | 931 500 | 13.8 | 999 600 | 13.9 | 7.3 |
| Australia[2] | 90 700 | 1.3 | 102 500 | 1.4 | 13.0 |
| New Zealand[2] | .. | | .. | | |
| Japan | 160 100 | 2.4 | 162 600 | 2.3 | 1.6 |
| **Total Australasia and Japan** | 250 800 | 3.7 | 265 100 | 3.7 | 5.7 |
| **Total OECD Countries** | 6 157 700 | 91.1 | 6 621 500 | 92.2 | 7.5 |
| Yugoslavia | | | | | |
| Latin America | 129 500 | 1.9 | 132 000 | 1.8 | 1.9 |
| Asia-Oceania | 357 100 | 5.3 | 317 300 | 4.4 | −11.1 |
| Africa | 117 200 | 1.7 | 107 600 | 1.5 | −8.2 |
| **Total non-OECD Countries** | 603 800 | 8.9 | 556 900 | 7.8 | −7.8 |
| **TOTAL** | 6 761 500 | 100.0 | 7 178 400 | 100.0 | 6.2 |

1. Spain includes Portugal.
2. Australia includes New Zealand.
3. Other OECD-Europe includes Austria, Greece, Iceland and all non-OECD European countries.

# NETHERLANDS

*NIGHTS SPENT BY FOREIGN TOURISTS IN REGISTERED TOURIST ACCOMMODATION*

*(by country of residence)*

| | 1988 | Relative share | 1989 | Relative share | % Variation over 1988 |
|---|---|---|---|---|---|
| Austria[3] | .. | | .. | | .. |
| Belgium | 864 700 | 6.8 | 1 001 600 | 7.1 | 15.8 |
| Denmark | 217 100 | 1.7 | 274 000 | 1.9 | 26.2 |
| Finland | 72 400 | 0.6 | 86 100 | 0.6 | 18.9 |
| France | 618 700 | 4.9 | 672 800 | 4.7 | 8.7 |
| Germany | 5 638 200 | 44.6 | 6 379 400 | 45.0 | 13.1 |
| Greece[3] | .. | | .. | | .. |
| Iceland[3] | .. | | .. | | .. |
| Ireland | 54 100 | 0.4 | 59 500 | 0.4 | 10.0 |
| Italy | 462 200 | 3.7 | 533 800 | 3.8 | 15.5 |
| Luxembourg | 25 000 | 0.2 | 27 100 | 0.2 | 8.4 |
| Netherlands | | | | | |
| Norway | 119 000 | 0.9 | 140 400 | 1.0 | 18.0 |
| Portugal[1] | .. | | .. | | .. |
| Spain[1] | 309 900 | 2.5 | 351 400 | 2.5 | 13.4 |
| Sweden | 244 700 | 1.9 | 288 300 | 2.0 | 17.8 |
| Switzerland | 208 900 | 1.7 | 241 900 | 1.7 | 15.8 |
| Turkey | .. | | .. | | .. |
| United Kingdom | 1 510 800 | 11.9 | 1 690 300 | 11.9 | 11.9 |
| Other OECD-Europe[3] | 303 700 | 2.4 | 360 500 | 2.5 | 18.7 |
| Total Europe | 10 649 400 | 84.2 | 12 107 100 | 85.4 | 13.7 |
| Canada | 204 400 | 1.6 | 210 900 | 1.5 | 3.2 |
| United States | 830 800 | 6.6 | 909 400 | 6.4 | 9.5 |
| Total North America | 1 035 200 | 8.2 | 1 120 300 | 7.9 | 8.2 |
| Australia[2] | 140 500 | 1.1 | 161 000 | 1.1 | 14.6 |
| New Zealand[2] | .. | | .. | | |
| Japan | 165 000 | 1.3 | 167 600 | 1.2 | 1.6 |
| Total Australasia and Japan | 305 500 | 2.4 | 328 600 | 2.3 | 7.6 |
| **Total OECD Countries** | 11 990 100 | 94.8 | 13 556 000 | 95.7 | 13.1 |
| Yugoslavia | .. | | .. | | .. |
| Latin America | 144 400 | 1.1 | 147 900 | 1.0 | 2.4 |
| Asia-Oceania | 378 600 | 3.0 | 342 500 | 2.4 | –9.5 |
| Africa | 133 000 | 1.1 | 125 300 | 0.9 | –5.8 |
| **Total non-OECD Countries** | 656 000 | 5.2 | 615 700 | 4.3 | –6.1 |
| **TOTAL** | 12 646 100 | 100.0 | 14 171 700 | 100.0 | 12.1 |

1. Spain includes Portugal.
2. Australia includes New Zealand.
3. Other OECD-Europe includes Austria, Greece, Iceland and non-OECD European countries.

# NEW ZEALAND

## ARRIVALS OF FOREIGN TOURISTS AT FRONTIERS
### (by country of residence)

| | 1988 | Relative share | 1989 | Relative share | % Variation over 1988 |
|---|---|---|---|---|---|
| Austria | 2 045 | 0.2 | 2 083 | 0.2 | 1.9 |
| Belgium | 1 014 | 0.1 | 706 | 0.1 | −30.4 |
| Denmark | 3 184 | 0.4 | 3 195 | 0.4 | 0.3 |
| Finland | 982 | 0.1 | 1 197 | 0.1 | 21.9 |
| France | 3 437 | 0.4 | 4 074 | 0.5 | 18.5 |
| Germany | 20 111 | 2.3 | 23 768 | 2.6 | 18.2 |
| Greece | 374 | 0.0 | 326 | 0.0 | −12.8 |
| Iceland | 173 | 0.0 | 116 | 0.0 | −32.9 |
| Ireland | 1 440 | 0.2 | 1 443 | 0.2 | 0.2 |
| Italy | 2 815 | 0.3 | 2 628 | 0.3 | −6.6 |
| Luxembourg | 103 | 0.0 | 100 | 0.0 | −2.9 |
| Netherlands | 7 063 | 0.8 | 7 126 | 0.8 | 0.9 |
| Norway | 1 484 | 0.2 | 1 275 | 0.1 | −14.1 |
| Portugal | 355 | 0.0 | 132 | 0.0 | −62.8 |
| Spain | 802 | 0.1 | 837 | 0.1 | 4.4 |
| Sweden | 8 623 | 1.0 | 9 071 | 1.0 | 5.2 |
| Switzerland | 8 635 | 1.0 | 9 638 | 1.1 | 11.6 |
| Turkey | 86 | 0.0 | 148 | 0.0 | 72.1 |
| United Kingdom | 72 704 | 8.4 | 74 337 | 8.2 | 2.2 |
| Other OECD-Europe | .. | .. | .. | .. | .. |
| **Total Europe** | 135 430 | 15.7 | 142 200 | 15.8 | 5.0 |
| | | | | | |
| Canada | 37 137 | 4.3 | 30 919 | 3.4 | −16.7 |
| United States | 167 525 | 19.4 | 137 509 | 15.3 | −17.9 |
| **Total North America** | 204 662 | 23.7 | 168 428 | 18.7 | −17.7 |
| | | | | | |
| Australia | 266 414 | 30.8 | 312 217 | 34.6 | 17.2 |
| New Zealand[1] | 16 503 | 1.9 | 19 605 | 2.2 | 18.8 |
| Japan | 93 789 | 10.8 | 97 322 | 10.8 | 3.8 |
| **Total Australasia and Japan** | 376 706 | 43.6 | 429 144 | 47.6 | 13.9 |
| | | | | | |
| **Total OECD Countries** | 716 798 | 82.9 | 739 772 | 82.1 | 3.2 |
| | | | | | |
| Yugoslavia | 266 | 0.0 | 208 | 0.0 | −21.8 |
| Bulgaria | .. | .. | 54 | 0.0 | |
| Czechoslovakia | 80 | 0.0 | 40 | 0.0 | −50.0 |
| Germany (D. R.) | 49 | 0.0 | 11 | 0.0 | −77.6 |
| Hungary | 126 | 0.0 | 116 | 0.0 | −7.9 |
| Poland | 91 | 0.0 | 160 | 0.0 | 75.8 |
| Rumania | 20 | 0.0 | 20 | 0.0 | 0.0 |
| USSR | 1 255 | 0.1 | 1 933 | 0.2 | 54.0 |
| Latin America | 6 049 | 0.7 | 5 083 | 0.6 | −16.0 |
| Argentina | 2 090 | 0.2 | 1 472 | 0.2 | −29.6 |
| Brazil | 1 303 | 0.2 | 1 073 | 0.1 | −17.7 |
| Chile | 461 | 0.1 | 485 | 0.1 | 5.2 |
| Colombia | 165 | 0.0 | 173 | 0.0 | 4.8 |
| Mexico | 623 | 0.1 | 730 | 0.1 | 17.2 |
| Venezuela | 96 | 0.0 | 100 | 0.0 | 4.2 |
| China | 2 882 | 0.3 | 2 513 | 0.3 | −12.8 |
| Hong Kong | 8 730 | 1.0 | 15 474 | 1.7 | 77.3 |
| India | 2 035 | 0.2 | 3 078 | 0.3 | 51.3 |
| Iran | 160 | 0.0 | 186 | 0.0 | 16.3 |
| Israel | 795 | 0.1 | 937 | 0.1 | 17.9 |
| Republic of Korea | 2 473 | 0.3 | 2 845 | 0.3 | 15.0 |
| Lebanon | 19 | 0.0 | 79 | 0.0 | 315.8 |
| Malaysia | 9 664 | 1.1 | 7 457 | 0.8 | −22.8 |
| Pakistan | 278 | 0.0 | 352 | 0.0 | 26.6 |
| Philippines | 2 698 | 0.3 | 2 462 | 0.3 | −8.7 |
| Saudi Arabia | 993 | 0.1 | 755 | 0.1 | −24.0 |
| Singapore | 14 679 | 1.7 | 14 808 | 1.6 | 0.9 |
| Taiwan | 8 421 | 1.0 | 13 828 | 1.5 | 64.2 |
| Thailand | 3 651 | 0.4 | 3 827 | 0.4 | 4.8 |
| Africa | 3 457 | 0.4 | 3 050 | 0.3 | −11.8 |
| Algeria | 18 | 0.0 | 0 | 0.0 | −100.0 |
| Egypt | 86 | 0.0 | 168 | 0.0 | 95.3 |
| Morocco | 20 | 0.0 | 9 | 0.0 | −55.0 |
| South Africa | 2 012 | 0.2 | 1 737 | 0.2 | −13.7 |
| Origin country undetermined | 138 322 | 16.0 | 152 965 | 17.0 | 10.6 |
| | | | | | |
| **Total non-OECD Countries** | 148 094 | 17.1 | 161 306 | 17.9 | 8.9 |
| | | | | | |
| **TOTAL** | 864 892 | 100.0 | 901 078 | 100.0 | 4.2 |

1. New Zealanders who have lived abroad for less than 12 months and who return for a short stay.

# NORWAY

## NIGHTS SPENT BY FOREIGN TOURISTS IN HOTELS
### (by country of nationality)

| | 1988 | Relative share | 1989 | Relative share | % Variation over 1988 |
|---|---|---|---|---|---|
| Austria[1] | .. | .. | .. | .. | .. |
| Belgium[1] | .. | .. | .. | .. | .. |
| Denmark | 643 096 | 19.2 | 648 444 | 18.9 | 0.8 |
| Finland | 102 887 | 3.1 | 98 583 | 2.9 | −4.2 |
| France | 119 897 | 3.6 | 139 979 | 4.1 | 16.7 |
| Germany | 539 333 | 16.1 | 580 599 | 16.9 | 7.7 |
| Greece[1] | .. | .. | .. | .. | .. |
| Iceland[1] | .. | .. | .. | .. | .. |
| Ireland[1] | .. | .. | .. | .. | .. |
| Italy[1] | .. | .. | .. | .. | .. |
| Luxembourg[1] | .. | .. | .. | .. | .. |
| Netherlands | 107 853 | 3.2 | 118 262 | 3.4 | 9.7 |
| Norway | .. | .. | .. | .. | .. |
| Portugal[1] | .. | .. | .. | .. | .. |
| Spain[1] | .. | .. | .. | .. | .. |
| Sweden | 577 695 | 17.2 | 518 707 | 15.1 | −10.2 |
| Switzerland[1] | .. | .. | .. | .. | .. |
| Turkey[1] | .. | .. | .. | .. | .. |
| United Kingdom | 333 142 | 9.9 | 337 364 | 9.8 | 1.3 |
| Other OECD-Europe | 231 318 | 6.9 | 265 117 | 7.7 | 14.6 |
| Total Europe | 2 655 221 | 79.1 | 2 707 055 | 78.9 | 2.0 |
| Canada[1] | .. | .. | .. | .. | .. |
| United States | 348 049 | 10.4 | 347 258 | 10.1 | −0.2 |
| Total North America | 348 049 | 10.4 | 347 258 | 10.1 | −0.2 |
| Australia[1] | .. | .. | .. | .. | .. |
| New Zealand[1] | .. | .. | .. | .. | .. |
| Japan | 66 715 | 2.0 | 80 093 | 2.3 | 20.1 |
| Total Australasia and Japan | 66 715 | 2.0 | 80 093 | 2.3 | 20.1 |
| **Total OECD Countries** | 3 069 985 | 91.5 | 3 134 406 | 91.3 | 2.1 |
| Yugoslavia (S.F.R.)[1] | .. | .. | .. | .. | .. |
| Origin country undetermined[1] | 286 270 | 8.5 | 296 948 | 8.7 | 3.7 |
| **Total non-OECD Countries** | 286 270 | 8.5 | 296 948 | 8.7 | 3.7 |
| **TOTAL** | 3 356 255 | 100.0 | 3 431 354 | 100.0 | 2.2 |

1. Included in "Origin country undetermined".

# PORTUGAL

*ARRIVALS OF FOREIGN TOURISTS AT FRONTIERS*

*(by country of nationality)*

| | 1988 | Relative share | 1989 | Relative share | % Variation over 1988 |
|---|---|---|---|---|---|
| Austria | 33 508 | 0.5 | 32 730 | 0.5 | -2.3 |
| Belgium | 113 712 | 1.7 | 146 429 | 2.1 | 28.8 |
| Denmark | 77 361 | 1.2 | 83 949 | 1.2 | 8.5 |
| Finland | 39 429 | 0.6 | 64 092 | 0.9 | 62.6 |
| France | 565 440 | 8.5 | 610 896 | 8.6 | 8.0 |
| Germany | 529 569 | 8.0 | 564 726 | 7.9 | 6.6 |
| Greece[1] | .. | .. | .. | .. | .. |
| Iceland[1] | .. | .. | .. | .. | .. |
| Ireland | 54 255 | 0.8 | 59 982 | 0.8 | 10.6 |
| Italy | 138 798 | 2.1 | 167 179 | 2.3 | 20.4 |
| Luxembourg | 5 948 | 0.1 | 7 427 | 0.1 | 24.9 |
| Netherlands | 275 420 | 4.2 | 316 747 | 4.5 | 15.0 |
| Norway | 27 399 | 0.4 | 21 042 | 0.3 | -23.2 |
| Portugal | .. | .. | .. | .. | .. |
| Spain | 2 985 615 | 45.1 | 3 246 826 | 45.6 | 8.7 |
| Sweden | 80 241 | 1.2 | 81 771 | 1.1 | 1.9 |
| Switzerland | 63 632 | 1.0 | 68 135 | 1.0 | 7.1 |
| Turkey[1] | .. | .. | .. | .. | .. |
| United Kingdom | 1 064 571 | 16.1 | 1 027 281 | 14.4 | -3.5 |
| Other OECD-Europe | .. | .. | .. | .. | .. |
| **Total Europe** | 6 054 898 | 91.4 | 6 499 212 | 91.3 | 7.3 |
| Canada | 76 009 | 1.1 | 83 070 | 1.2 | 9.3 |
| United States | 194 206 | 2.9 | 186 736 | 2.6 | -3.8 |
| **Total North America** | 270 215 | 4.1 | 269 806 | 3.8 | -0.2 |
| Australia[2] | 18 064 | 0.3 | 20 044 | 0.3 | 11.0 |
| New-Zealand[2] | .. | .. | .. | .. | .. |
| Japan | 28 189 | 0.4 | 30 101 | 0.4 | 6.8 |
| **Total Australasia and Japan** | 46 253 | 0.7 | 50 145 | 0.7 | 8.4 |
| **Total OECD Countries** | 6 371 366 | 96.2 | 6 819 163 | 95.8 | 7.0 |
| Yugoslavia (S.F.R.)[1] | .. | .. | .. | .. | .. |
| Other European countries[1] | 36 897 | 0.6 | 42 674 | 0.6 | 15.7 |
| Africa | 78 355 | 1.2 | 93 118 | 1.3 | 18.8 |
| Origin country undetermined | 137 249 | 2.1 | 160 945 | 2.3 | 17.3 |
| **Total non-OECD Countries** | 252 501 | 3.8 | 296 737 | 4.2 | 17.5 |
| **TOTAL** | 6 623 867 | 100.0 | 7 115 900 | 100.0 | 7.4 |

1. "Other European countries" includes Greece, Iceland, Turkey and Yugoslavia.
2. Australia includes New Zealand.

# PORTUGAL

*ARRIVALS OF FOREIGN VISITORS AT FRONTIERS*

*(by country of nationality)*

| | 1988 | Relative share | 1989 | Relative share | % Variation over 1988 |
|---|---|---|---|---|---|
| Austria | 35 253 | 0.2 | 35 643 | 0.2 | 1.1 |
| Belgium | 116 937 | 0.7 | 150 731 | 0.9 | 28.9 |
| Denmark | 82 417 | 0.5 | 89 954 | 0.5 | 9.1 |
| Finland | 44 280 | 0.3 | 69 894 | 0.4 | 57.8 |
| France | 593 422 | 3.7 | 646 847 | 3.9 | 9.0 |
| Germany | 568 656 | 3.5 | 611 275 | 3.7 | 7.5 |
| Greece | 12 653 | 0.1 | 16 124 | 0.1 | 27.4 |
| Iceland | 1 973 | 0.0 | 3 098 | 0.0 | 57.0 |
| Ireland | 56 638 | 0.4 | 60 797 | 0.4 | 7.3 |
| Italy | 154 684 | 1.0 | 185 154 | 1.1 | 19.7 |
| Luxembourg | 6 012 | 0.0 | 8 228 | 0.0 | 36.9 |
| Netherlands | 285 199 | 1.8 | 332 797 | 2.0 | 16.7 |
| Norway | 29 202 | 0.2 | 25 481 | 0.2 | −12.7 |
| Portugal | .. | .. | .. | .. | .. |
| Spain | 12 124 419 | 75.4 | 12 187 242 | 74.0 | 0.5 |
| Sweden | 86 463 | 0.5 | 94 752 | 0.6 | 9.6 |
| Switzerland | 73 253 | 0.5 | 77 763 | 0.5 | 6.2 |
| Turkey | 2 725 | 0.0 | 3 215 | 0.0 | 18.0 |
| United Kingdom | 1 139 693 | 7.1 | 1 137 481 | 6.9 | −0.2 |
| Other OECD-Europe | .. | .. | .. | .. | .. |
| **Total Europe** | 15 413 879 | 95.9 | 15 736 476 | 95.5 | 2.1 |
| Canada | 79 069 | 0.5 | 91 126 | 0.6 | 15.2 |
| United States | 223 288 | 1.4 | 235 503 | 1.4 | 5.5 |
| **Total North America** | 302 357 | 1.9 | 326 629 | 2.0 | 8.0 |
| Australia | 14 781 | 0.1 | 16 486 | 0.1 | 11.5 |
| New Zealand | 4 445 | 0.0 | 4 949 | 0.0 | 11.3 |
| Japan | 29 661 | 0.2 | 32 121 | 0.2 | 8.3 |
| **Total Australasia and Japan** | 48 887 | 0.3 | 53 556 | 0.3 | 9.6 |
| **Total OECD Countries** | 15 765 123 | 98.1 | 16 116 661 | 97.8 | 2.2 |
| Yugoslavia | 5 433 | 0.0 | 7 662 | 0.0 | 41.0 |
| Other European countries | 41 657 | 0.3 | 50 657 | 0.3 | 21.6 |
| Bulgaria | .. | .. | 2 177 | 0.0 | .. |
| Czechoslovakia | 2 463 | 0.0 | 2 984 | 0.0 | 21.2 |
| Germany (D. R.) | 1 209 | 0.0 | 3 737 | 0.0 | 209.1 |
| Hungary | 1 671 | 0.0 | 2 024 | 0.0 | 21.1 |
| Poland | 6 787 | 0.0 | 7 877 | 0.0 | 16.1 |
| Rumania | 737 | 0.0 | 971 | 0.0 | 31.8 |
| USSR | 24 536 | 0.2 | 28 864 | 0.2 | 17.6 |
| Latin America | 138 777 | 0.9 | 155 131 | 0.9 | 11.8 |
| Argentina | 8 377 | 0.1 | 9 594 | 0.1 | 14.5 |
| Brazil | 92 123 | 0.6 | 102 990 | 0.6 | 11.8 |
| Chile | 2 671 | 0.0 | 2 990 | 0.0 | 11.9 |
| Colombia | 3 260 | 0.0 | 2 995 | 0.0 | −8.1 |
| Mexico | 5 852 | 0.0 | 7 152 | 0.0 | 22.2 |
| Venezuela | 17 448 | 0.1 | 18 935 | 0.1 | 8.5 |
| Asia-Oceania | 41 190 | 0.3 | 46 752 | 0.3 | 13.5 |
| China | .. | .. | 2 252 | 0.0 | .. |
| Hong Kong | .. | .. | 786 | 0.0 | .. |
| India | .. | .. | 8 144 | 0.0 | .. |
| Iran | .. | .. | 627 | 0.0 | .. |
| Israel | .. | .. | 7 810 | 0.0 | .. |
| Republic of Korea | .. | .. | 4 703 | 0.0 | .. |
| Lebanon | .. | .. | 579 | 0.0 | .. |
| Malaysia | .. | .. | 837 | 0.0 | .. |
| Pakistan | .. | .. | 1 372 | 0.0 | .. |
| Philippines | .. | .. | 12 463 | 0.1 | .. |
| Saudi Arabia | .. | .. | 568 | 0.0 | .. |
| Singapore | .. | .. | 949 | 0.0 | .. |
| Thailand | .. | .. | 983 | 0.0 | .. |
| Africa | 82 522 | 0.5 | 97 461 | 0.6 | 18.1 |
| Algeria | .. | .. | 1 533 | 0.0 | .. |
| Egypt | .. | .. | 1 046 | 0.0 | .. |
| Morocco | .. | .. | 7 657 | 0.0 | .. |
| South Africa | .. | .. | 12 232 | 0.1 | .. |
| Origin country undetermined | 1 979 | 0.0 | 1 475 | 0.0 | −25.5 |
| **Total non-OECD Countries** | 311 558 | 1.9 | 359 138 | 2.2 | 15.3 |
| **TOTAL** | 16 076 681 | 100.0 | 16 475 799 | 100.0 | 2.5 |

# PORTUGAL

## ARRIVALS OF FOREIGN TOURISTS AT HOTELS[1]
### (by country of residence)

| | 1988 | Relative share | 1989 | Relative share | % Variation over 1988 |
|---|---|---|---|---|---|
| Austria | 28 968 | 0.9 | 30 948 | 0.9 | 6.8 |
| Belgium | 74 752 | 2.3 | 87 362 | 2.6 | 16.9 |
| Denmark | 58 227 | 1.8 | 57 947 | 1.7 | −0.5 |
| Finland | 41 302 | 1.3 | 62 852 | 1.9 | 52.2 |
| France | 280 101 | 8.8 | 297 166 | 8.9 | 6.1 |
| Germany | 375 576 | 11.8 | 376 477 | 11.2 | 0.2 |
| Greece | 6 927 | 0.2 | 8 728 | 0.3 | 26.0 |
| Iceland | 1 528 | 0.0 | 2 272 | 0.1 | 48.7 |
| Ireland | 30 230 | 0.9 | 32 990 | 1.0 | 9.1 |
| Italy | 134 794 | 4.2 | 147 306 | 4.4 | 9.3 |
| Luxembourg | 3 797 | 0.1 | 3 870 | 0.1 | 1.9 |
| Netherlands | 169 588 | 5.3 | 183 682 | 5.5 | 8.3 |
| Norway | 30 589 | 1.0 | 25 413 | 0.8 | −16.9 |
| Portugal | .. | .. | .. | .. | .. |
| Spain | 553 831 | 17.3 | 612 036 | 18.2 | 10.5 |
| Sweden | 85 693 | 2.7 | 91 861 | 2.7 | 7.2 |
| Switzerland | 95 918 | 3.0 | 96 843 | 2.9 | 1.0 |
| Turkey | 1 159 | 0.0 | 1 103 | 0.0 | −4.8 |
| United Kingdom | 654 178 | 20.5 | 647 775 | 19.3 | −1.0 |
| Other OECD-Europe | .. | .. | .. | .. | .. |
| **Total Europe** | 2 627 158 | 82.3 | 2 766 631 | 82.5 | 5.3 |
| Canada | 91 731 | 2.9 | 99 598 | 3.0 | 8.6 |
| United States | 239 623 | 7.5 | 254 047 | 7.6 | 6.0 |
| **Total North America** | 331 354 | 10.4 | 353 645 | 10.5 | 6.7 |
| Australia | 8 615 | 0.3 | 9 484 | 0.3 | 10.1 |
| New Zealand | 1 638 | 0.1 | 1 687 | 0.1 | 3.0 |
| Japan | 32 309 | 1.0 | 33 170 | 1.0 | 2.7 |
| **Total Australasia and Japan** | 42 562 | 1.3 | 44 341 | 1.3 | 4.2 |
| **Total OECD Countries** | 3 001 074 | 94.0 | 3 164 617 | 94.3 | 5.4 |
| Yugoslavia | 1 718 | 0.1 | 1 695 | 0.1 | −1.3 |
| Other European countries | 10 457 | 0.3 | 14 002 | 0.4 | 33.9 |
| Bulgaria | 529 | 0.0 | 755 | 0.0 | 42.7 |
| Czechoslovakia | 1 588 | 0.0 | 2 153 | 0.1 | 35.6 |
| Hungary | 688 | 0.0 | 918 | 0.0 | 33.4 |
| Poland | 1 516 | 0.0 | 1 968 | 0.1 | 29.8 |
| Rumania | 227 | 0.0 | 158 | 0.0 | −30.4 |
| USSR | 5 266 | 0.2 | 6 726 | 0.2 | 27.7 |
| Latin America | 106 235 | 3.3 | 103 221 | 3.1 | −2.8 |
| Argentina | 5 040 | 0.2 | 4 849 | 0.1 | −3.8 |
| Brazil | 83 176 | 2.6 | 82 885 | 2.5 | −0.3 |
| Chile | 1 100 | 0.0 | 1 000 | 0.0 | −9.1 |
| Colombia | 1 339 | 0.0 | 1 293 | 0.0 | −3.4 |
| Mexico | 3 822 | 0.1 | 3 294 | 0.1 | −13.8 |
| Venezuela | 8 296 | 0.3 | 6 306 | 0.2 | −24.0 |
| Asia-Oceania | 20 841 | 0.7 | 21 515 | 0.6 | 3.2 |
| China | 1 019 | 0.0 | 1 168 | 0.0 | 14.6 |
| Iran | 560 | 0.0 | 400 | 0.0 | −28.6 |
| Iraq | 718 | 0.0 | .. | .. | .. |
| Israel | 10 684 | 0.3 | 10 459 | 0.3 | −2.1 |
| Lebanon | 215 | 0.0 | 351 | 0.0 | 63.3 |
| Philippines | 1 105 | 0.0 | 989 | 0.0 | −10.5 |
| Saudi Arabia | 970 | 0.0 | 1 178 | 0.0 | 21.4 |
| Africa | 52 630 | 1.6 | 49 551 | 1.5 | −5.9 |
| Egypt | 488 | 0.0 | 434 | 0.0 | −11.1 |
| Morocco | 3 051 | 0.1 | 4 500 | 0.1 | 47.5 |
| South Africa | 17 203 | 0.5 | 15 358 | 0.5 | −10.7 |
| **Total non-OECD Countries** | 191 881 | 6.0 | 189 984 | 5.7 | −1.0 |
| **TOTAL** | 3 192 955 | 100.0 | 3 354 601 | 100.0 | 5.1 |

1. Includes arrivals at hotels, studio-hotels, holiday-flats, villages, motels, inns and boarding-houses.

# PORTUGAL

*ARRIVALS OF FOREIGN TOURISTS AT REGISTERED TOURIST ACCOMMODATION[1]*

*(by country of residence)*

| | 1988 | Relative share | 1989 | Relative share | % Variation over 1988 |
|---|---|---|---|---|---|
| Austria | 37 967 | 1.0 | 41 364 | 1.0 | 8.9 |
| Belgium | 104 413 | 2.6 | 121 429 | 2.9 | 16.3 |
| Denmark | 76 282 | 1.9 | 76 888 | 1.8 | 0.8 |
| Finland | 42 867 | 1.1 | 64 603 | 1.6 | 50.7 |
| France | 457 459 | 11.5 | 482 700 | 11.6 | 5.5 |
| Germany | 573 400 | 14.4 | 561 958 | 13.5 | −2.0 |
| Greece | 7 333 | 0.2 | 9 065 | 0.2 | 23.6 |
| Iceland | 1 541 | 0.0 | 2 275 | 0.1 | 47.6 |
| Ireland | 31 457 | 0.8 | 34 775 | 0.8 | 10.5 |
| Italy | 161 651 | 4.1 | 178 013 | 4.3 | 10.1 |
| Luxembourg | 4 641 | 0.1 | 4 597 | 0.1 | −0.9 |
| Netherlands | 279 737 | 7.0 | 295 265 | 7.1 | 5.6 |
| Norway | 31 506 | 0.8 | 26 531 | 0.6 | −15.8 |
| Portugal | .. | .. | .. | .. | .. |
| Spain | 694 868 | 17.4 | 756 639 | 18.2 | 8.9 |
| Sweden | 89 032 | 2.2 | 95 008 | 2.3 | 6.7 |
| Switzerland | 107 251 | 2.7 | 108 546 | 2.6 | 1.2 |
| Turkey | 1 292 | 0.0 | 1 267 | 0.0 | −1.9 |
| United Kingdom | 683 221 | 17.1 | 677 812 | 16.3 | −0.8 |
| Other OECD-Europe | .. | .. | .. | .. | .. |
| **Total Europe** | **3 385 918** | **84.9** | **3 538 735** | **85.0** | **4.5** |
| Canada | 95 940 | 2.4 | 104 219 | 2.5 | 8.6 |
| United States | 245 967 | 6.2 | 260 107 | 6.2 | 5.7 |
| **Total North America** | **341 907** | **8.6** | **364 326** | **8.8** | **6.6** |
| Australia | 15 850 | 0.4 | 16 905 | 0.4 | 6.7 |
| New Zealand | 5 988 | 0.2 | 6 328 | 0.2 | 5.7 |
| Japan | 33 190 | 0.8 | 33 822 | 0.8 | 1.9 |
| **Total Australasia and Japan** | **55 028** | **1.4** | **57 055** | **1.4** | **3.7** |
| **Total OECD Countries** | **3 782 853** | **94.9** | **3 960 116** | **95.1** | **4.7** |
| Yugoslavia | 2 436 | 0.1 | 2 591 | 0.1 | 6.4 |
| Other European countries | 13 359 | 0.3 | 16 752 | 0.4 | 25.4 |
| Bulgaria | 591 | 0.0 | 787 | 0.0 | 33.2 |
| Czechoslovakia | 1 807 | 0.0 | 2 356 | 0.1 | 30.4 |
| Hungary | 1 894 | 0.0 | 2 107 | 0.1 | 11.2 |
| Poland | 2 735 | 0.1 | 3 189 | 0.1 | 16.6 |
| Rumania | 299 | 0.0 | 172 | 0.0 | −42.5 |
| USSR | 5 268 | 0.1 | 6 769 | 0.2 | 28.5 |
| Latin America | 110 687 | 2.8 | 107 235 | 2.6 | −3.1 |
| Argentina | 5 404 | 0.1 | 5 279 | 0.1 | −2.3 |
| Brazil | 86 467 | 2.2 | 85 510 | 2.1 | −1.1 |
| Chile | 1 252 | 0.0 | 1 178 | 0.0 | −5.9 |
| Colombia | 1 385 | 0.0 | 1 375 | 0.0 | −0.7 |
| Mexico | 4 034 | 0.1 | 3 451 | 0.1 | −14.5 |
| Venezuela | 8 408 | 0.2 | 6 450 | 0.2 | −23.3 |
| Asia-Oceania | 21 406 | 0.5 | 22 244 | 0.5 | 3.9 |
| China | 1 046 | 0.0 | 1 199 | 0.0 | 14.6 |
| Iran | 602 | 0.0 | 429 | 0.0 | −28.7 |
| Iraq | 724 | 0.0 | .. | .. | .. |
| Israel | 10 929 | 0.3 | 10 775 | 0.3 | −1.4 |
| Lebanon | 223 | 0.0 | 359 | 0.0 | 61.0 |
| Philippines | 1 125 | 0.0 | 997 | 0.0 | −11.4 |
| Saudi Arabia | 970 | 0.0 | 1 178 | 0.0 | 21.4 |
| Africa | 57 221 | 1.4 | 53 909 | 1.3 | −5.8 |
| Egypt | 491 | 0.0 | 447 | 0.0 | −9.0 |
| Morocco | 4 288 | 0.1 | 6 046 | 0.1 | 41.0 |
| South Africa | 18 094 | 0.5 | 16 223 | 0.4 | −10.3 |
| **Total non-OECD Countries** | **205 109** | **5.1** | **202 731** | **4.9** | **−1.2** |
| **TOTAL** | **3 987 962** | **100.0** | **4 162 847** | **100.0** | **4.4** |

1. Includes arrivals at hotels, studio-hotels, holiday-flats, villages, motels, inns, boarding-houses, recreation centres for children and camping-sites.

# PORTUGAL

### NIGHTS SPENT BY FOREIGN TOURISTS IN HOTELS[1]
*(by country of residence)*

| | 1988 | Relative share | 1989 | Relative share | % Variation over 1988 |
|---|---|---|---|---|---|
| Austria | 134 171 | 0.9 | 132 738 | 0.9 | −1.1 |
| Belgium | 306 459 | 2.0 | 375 944 | 2.4 | 22.7 |
| Denmark | 355 448 | 2.4 | 362 462 | 2.3 | 2.0 |
| Finland | 299 772 | 2.0 | 448 780 | 2.9 | 49.7 |
| France | 740 838 | 4.9 | 799 573 | 5.2 | 7.9 |
| Germany | 2 056 623 | 13.7 | 2 081 997 | 13.5 | 1.2 |
| Greece | 20 384 | 0.1 | 25 118 | 0.2 | 23.2 |
| Iceland | 15 382 | 0.1 | 22 109 | 0.1 | 43.7 |
| Ireland | 254 577 | 1.7 | 242 192 | 1.6 | −4.9 |
| Italy | 350 827 | 2.3 | 379 000 | 2.5 | 8.0 |
| Luxembourg | 18 651 | 0.1 | 14 673 | 0.1 | −21.3 |
| Netherlands | 1 195 354 | 8.0 | 1 289 410 | 8.3 | 7.9 |
| Norway | 196 632 | 1.3 | 139 886 | 0.9 | −28.9 |
| Portugal | .. | .. | .. | .. | .. |
| Spain | 1 275 914 | 8.5 | 1 458 325 | 9.4 | 14.3 |
| Sweden | 557 182 | 3.7 | 560 968 | 3.6 | 0.7 |
| Switzerland | 337 589 | 2.2 | 349 125 | 2.3 | 3.4 |
| Turkey | 3 873 | 0.0 | 4 153 | 0.0 | 7.2 |
| United Kingdom | 5 268 854 | 35.1 | 5 096 614 | 33.0 | −3.3 |
| Other OECD-Europe | .. | .. | .. | .. | .. |
| **Total Europe** | 13 388 530 | 89.2 | 13 783 067 | 89.1 | 2.9 |
| Canada | 311 957 | 2.1 | 340 529 | 2.2 | 9.2 |
| United States | 649 983 | 4.3 | 677 442 | 4.4 | 4.2 |
| **Total North America** | 961 940 | 6.4 | 1 017 971 | 6.6 | 5.8 |
| Australia | 22 117 | 0.1 | 23 581 | 0.2 | 6.6 |
| New Zealand | 3 856 | 0.0 | 4 185 | 0.0 | 8.5 |
| Japan | 72 195 | 0.5 | 73 312 | 0.5 | 1.5 |
| **Total Australasia and Japan** | 98 168 | 0.7 | 101 078 | 0.7 | 3.0 |
| **Total OECD Countries** | 14 448 638 | 96.3 | 14 902 116 | 96.3 | 3.1 |
| Yugoslavia | 5 213 | 0.0 | 5 172 | 0.0 | −0.8 |
| Other European countries | 31 697 | 0.2 | 40 823 | 0.3 | 28.8 |
| Bulgaria | 2 397 | 0.0 | 4 421 | 0.0 | 84.4 |
| Czechoslovakia | 4 651 | 0.0 | 5 609 | 0.0 | 20.6 |
| Hungary | 2 755 | 0.0 | 2 980 | 0.0 | 8.2 |
| Poland | 5 355 | 0.0 | 8 311 | 0.1 | 55.2 |
| Rumania | 616 | 0.0 | 427 | 0.0 | −30.7 |
| USSR | 13 795 | 0.1 | 14 887 | 0.1 | 7.9 |
| Latin America | 268 205 | 1.8 | 272 897 | 1.8 | 1.7 |
| Argentina | 11 917 | 0.1 | 12 164 | 0.1 | 2.1 |
| Brazil | 215 385 | 1.4 | 220 424 | 1.4 | 2.3 |
| Chile | 2 549 | 0.0 | 3 007 | 0.0 | 18.0 |
| Colombia | 3 218 | 0.0 | 3 138 | 0.0 | −2.5 |
| Mexico | 8 575 | 0.1 | 7 105 | 0.0 | −17.1 |
| Venezuela | 17 167 | 0.1 | 17 767 | 0.1 | 3.5 |
| Asia-Oceania | 63 330 | 0.4 | 60 874 | 0.4 | −3.9 |
| China | 2 541 | 0.0 | 3 569 | 0.0 | 40.5 |
| Iran | 7 191 | 0.0 | 3 466 | 0.0 | −51.8 |
| Iraq | 2 127 | 0.0 | .. | .. | .. |
| Israel | 23 951 | 0.2 | 22 219 | 0.1 | −7.2 |
| Lebanon | 839 | 0.0 | 1 343 | 0.0 | 60.1 |
| Philippines | 2 989 | 0.0 | 3 534 | 0.0 | 18.2 |
| Saudi Arabia | 5 914 | 0.0 | 6 399 | 0.0 | 8.2 |
| Africa | 188 235 | 1.3 | 185 606 | 1.2 | −1.4 |
| Egypt | 1 631 | 0.0 | 1 712 | 0.0 | 5.0 |
| Morocco | 8 761 | 0.1 | 14 603 | 0.1 | 66.7 |
| South Africa | 57 828 | 0.4 | 47 464 | 0.3 | −17.9 |
| **Total non-OECD Countries** | 556 680 | 3.7 | 565 372 | 3.7 | 1.6 |
| **TOTAL** | 15 005 318 | 100.0 | 15 467 488 | 100.0 | 3.1 |

1. Includes nights spent at hotels, studio-hotels, holiday-flats, villages, motels, inns and boarding-houses.

# PORTUGAL

## NIGHTS SPENT BY FOREIGN TOURISTS IN REGISTERED TOURIST ACCOMMODATION[1]

### (by country of residence)

| | 1988 | Relative share | 1989 | Relative share | % Variation over 1988 |
|---|---|---|---|---|---|
| Austria | 160 741 | 0.9 | 162 388 | 0.9 | 1.0 |
| Belgium | 410 818 | 2.3 | 504 272 | 2.8 | 22.7 |
| Denmark | 425 278 | 2.4 | 435 519 | 2.4 | 2.4 |
| Finland | 304 763 | 1.7 | 455 568 | 2.5 | 49.5 |
| France | 1 254 330 | 7.1 | 1 329 929 | 7.3 | 6.0 |
| Germany | 2 781 176 | 15.6 | 2 752 402 | 15.1 | −1.0 |
| Greece | 21 657 | 0.1 | 26 136 | 0.1 | 20.7 |
| Iceland | 15 403 | 0.1 | 22 116 | 0.1 | 43.6 |
| Ireland | 259 347 | 1.5 | 248 838 | 1.4 | −4.1 |
| Italy | 426 693 | 2.4 | 463 722 | 2.5 | 8.7 |
| Luxembourg | 20 861 | 0.1 | 16 834 | 0.1 | −19.3 |
| Netherlands | 1 649 848 | 9.3 | 1 743 792 | 9.6 | 5.7 |
| Norway | 199 717 | 1.1 | 144 401 | 0.8 | −27.7 |
| Portugal | .. | .. | .. | .. | .. |
| Spain | 1 767 077 | 9.9 | 1 931 155 | 10.6 | 9.3 |
| Sweden | 570 097 | 3.2 | 572 111 | 3.1 | 0.4 |
| Switzerland | 370 759 | 2.1 | 383 391 | 2.1 | 3.4 |
| Turkey | 4 310 | 0.0 | 4 670 | 0.0 | 8.4 |
| United Kingdom | 5 414 867 | 30.4 | 5 239 541 | 28.7 | −3.2 |
| Other OECD-Europe | .. | .. | .. | .. | .. |
| **Total Europe** | 16 057 742 | 90.3 | 16 436 785 | 90.2 | 2.4 |
| | | | | | |
| Canada | 323 486 | 1.8 | 351 615 | 1.9 | 8.7 |
| United States | 667 041 | 3.8 | 692 615 | 3.8 | 3.8 |
| **Total North America** | 990 527 | 5.6 | 1 044 230 | 5.7 | 5.4 |
| | | | | | |
| Australia | 40 564 | 0.2 | 41 232 | 0.2 | 1.6 |
| New Zealand | 14 589 | 0.1 | 14 681 | 0.1 | 0.6 |
| Japan | 73 801 | 0.4 | 74 727 | 0.4 | 1.3 |
| **Total Australasia and Japan** | 128 954 | 0.7 | 130 640 | 0.7 | 1.3 |
| | | | | | |
| **Total OECD Countries** | 17 177 223 | 96.6 | 17 611 655 | 96.6 | 2.5 |
| | | | | | |
| Yugoslavia | 6 866 | 0.0 | 7 037 | 0.0 | 2.5 |
| Other European countries | 39 665 | 0.2 | 49 369 | 0.3 | 24.5 |
| Bulgaria | 2 534 | 0.0 | 4 574 | 0.0 | 80.5 |
| Czechoslovakia | 5 300 | 0.0 | 6 197 | 0.0 | 16.9 |
| Hungary | 6 826 | 0.0 | 7 234 | 0.0 | 6.0 |
| Poland | 7 768 | 0.0 | 11 050 | 0.1 | 42.3 |
| Rumania | 715 | 0.0 | 801 | 0.0 | 12.0 |
| USSR | 13 799 | 0.1 | 15 150 | 0.1 | 9.8 |
| Latin America | 279 836 | 1.6 | 285 929 | 1.6 | 2.2 |
| Argentina | 12 820 | 0.1 | 13 370 | 0.1 | 4.3 |
| Brazil | 223 706 | 1.3 | 229 863 | 1.3 | 2.8 |
| Chile | 3 287 | 0.0 | 3 607 | 0.0 | 9.7 |
| Colombia | 3 307 | 0.0 | 3 315 | 0.0 | 0.2 |
| Mexico | 9 081 | 0.1 | 7 421 | 0.0 | −18.3 |
| Venezuela | 17 582 | 0.1 | 18 189 | 0.1 | 3.5 |
| Asia-Oceania | 64 744 | 0.4 | 63 105 | 0.3 | −2.5 |
| China | 2 602 | 0.0 | 3 622 | 0.0 | 39.2 |
| Iran | 7 360 | 0.0 | 3 597 | 0.0 | −51.1 |
| Iraq | 2 136 | 0.0 | .. | .. | .. |
| Israel | 24 703 | 0.1 | 22 931 | 0.1 | −7.2 |
| Lebanon | 847 | 0.0 | 1 357 | 0.0 | 60.2 |
| Philippines | 3 048 | 0.0 | 3 551 | 0.0 | 16.5 |
| Saudi Arabia | 5 914 | 0.0 | 6 399 | 0.0 | 8.2 |
| Africa | 218 234 | 1.2 | 212 690 | 1.2 | −2.5 |
| Egypt | 1 634 | 0.0 | 1 736 | 0.0 | 6.2 |
| Morocco | 14 633 | 0.1 | 21 118 | 0.1 | 44.3 |
| South Africa | 60 104 | 0.3 | 49 593 | 0.3 | −17.5 |
| | | | | | |
| **Total non-OECD Countries** | 609 345 | 3.4 | 618 130 | 3.4 | 1.4 |
| | | | | | |
| **TOTAL** | 17 786 568 | 100.0 | 18 229 785 | 100.0 | 2.5 |

1. Includes nights spent at hotels, studio-hotels, holiday-flats, villages, motels, inns, boarding-houses, recreation centres for children and camping-sites.

# SPAIN

## ARRIVALS OF FOREIGN VISITORS AT FRONTIERS[1]
### (by country of nationality)

| | 1988 | Relative share | 1989 | Relative share | % Variation over 1988 |
|---|---|---|---|---|---|
| Austria | 280 699 | 0.5 | 306 073 | 0.6 | 9.0 |
| Belgium | 1 383 086 | 2.6 | 1 374 776 | 2.5 | −0.6 |
| Denmark | 609 382 | 1.1 | 537 332 | 1.0 | −11.8 |
| Finland | 445 017 | 0.8 | 487 824 | 0.9 | 9.6 |
| France | 12 085 584 | 22.3 | 11 994 421 | 22.2 | −0.8 |
| Germany | 6 904 418 | 12.7 | 6 783 753 | 12.5 | −1.7 |
| Greece | 75 057 | 0.1 | 67 951 | 0.1 | −9.5 |
| Iceland | 22 683 | 0.0 | 23 044 | 0.0 | 1.6 |
| Ireland | 296 267 | 0.5 | 232 617 | 0.4 | −21.5 |
| Italy | 1 333 055 | 2.5 | 1 511 618 | 2.8 | 13.4 |
| Luxembourg | 84 544 | 0.2 | 88 262 | 0.2 | 4.4 |
| Netherlands | 2 004 455 | 3.7 | 2 034 717 | 3.8 | 1.5 |
| Norway | 491 177 | 0.9 | 346 083 | 0.6 | −29.5 |
| Portugal | 10 065 026 | 18.6 | 10 044 244 | 18.6 | −0.2 |
| Spain[2] | 2 867 812 | 5.3 | 3 144 905 | 5.8 | 9.7 |
| Sweden | 844 418 | 1.6 | 857 997 | 1.6 | 1.6 |
| Switzerland | 1 124 233 | 2.1 | 1 138 923 | 2.1 | 1.3 |
| Turkey | 15 962 | 0.0 | 16 659 | 0.0 | 4.4 |
| United Kingdom | 7 645 598 | 14.1 | 7 345 831 | 13.6 | −3.9 |
| Other OECD-Europe[3] | 233 050 | 0.4 | 261 829 | 0.5 | 12.3 |
| Total Europe | 48 811 523 | 90.1 | 48 598 859 | 89.9 | −0.4 |
| | | | | | |
| Canada | 167 972 | 0.3 | 172 357 | 0.3 | 2.6 |
| United States | 858 894 | 1.6 | 953 782 | 1.8 | 11.0 |
| Total North America | 1 026 866 | 1.9 | 1 126 139 | 2.1 | 9.7 |
| | | | | | |
| Australia | 47 432 | 0.1 | 53 940 | 0.1 | 13.7 |
| New Zealand | 19 548 | 0.0 | 16 971 | 0.0 | −13.2 |
| Japan | 170 281 | 0.3 | 216 535 | 0.4 | 27.2 |
| Total Australasia and Japan | 237 261 | 0.4 | 287 446 | 0.5 | 21.2 |
| | | | | | |
| **Total OECD Countries** | 50 075 650 | 92.4 | 50 012 444 | 92.5 | −0.1 |
| | | | | | |
| Yugoslavia | 38 117 | 0.1 | 43 679 | 0.1 | 14.6 |
| Other European countries | 281 557 | 0.5 | 345 034 | 0.6 | 22.5 |
| Bulgaria | 5 288 | 0.0 | 8 136 | 0.0 | 53.9 |
| Czechoslovakia | 10 162 | 0.0 | 9 218 | 0.0 | −9.3 |
| Germany (D. R.) | 7 039 | 0.0 | 7 792 | 0.0 | 10.7 |
| Hungary | 11 622 | 0.0 | 11 797 | 0.0 | 1.5 |
| Poland | 32 749 | 0.1 | 36 529 | 0.1 | 11.5 |
| Rumania | 9 107 | 0.0 | 17 344 | 0.0 | 90.4 |
| USSR | 205 590 | 0.4 | 254 218 | 0.5 | 23.7 |
| Latin America | 527 261 | 1.0 | 550 630 | 1.0 | 4.4 |
| Argentina | 108 787 | 0.2 | 112 629 | 0.2 | 3.5 |
| Brazil | 103 092 | 0.2 | 118 661 | 0.2 | 15.1 |
| Chile | 27 385 | 0.1 | 28 722 | 0.1 | 4.9 |
| Colombia | 33 424 | 0.1 | 39 145 | 0.1 | 17.1 |
| Mexico | 82 812 | 0.2 | 80 283 | 0.1 | −3.1 |
| Venezuela | 58 876 | 0.1 | 55 976 | 0.1 | −4.9 |
| Asia-Oceania | 197 416 | 0.4 | 208 140 | 0.4 | 5.4 |
| Africa | 3 046 819 | 5.6 | 2 887 026 | 5.3 | −5.2 |
| Origin country undetermined | 11 327 | 0.0 | 10 609 | 0.0 | −6.3 |
| | | | | | |
| **Total non-OECD Countries** | 4 102 497 | 7.6 | 4 045 118 | 7.5 | −1.4 |
| | | | | | |
| **TOTAL** | 54 178 147 | 100.0 | 54 057 562 | 100.0 | −0.2 |

1. Includes about 34% of arrivals of excursionists.
2. Spanish nationals residing abroad.
3. "Other OECD-Europe" includes Andorra, Cyprus, Malta, Monaco, and the Vatican States.

# SPAIN

### *ARRIVALS OF FOREIGN TOURISTS AT HOTELS[1]*
*(by country of nationality)*

| | 1988 | Relative share | 1989 | Relative share | % Variation over 1988 |
|---|---|---|---|---|---|
| Austria | .. | .. | .. | .. | .. |
| Belgium | 487 495 | 3.6 | 468 090 | 3.6 | –4.0 |
| Denmark | 191 212 | 1.4 | 154 917 | 1.2 | –19.0 |
| Finland | .. | .. | .. | .. | .. |
| France | 1 728 250 | 12.7 | 1 745 352 | 13.2 | 1.0 |
| Germany | 2 692 662 | 19.7 | 2 482 027 | 18.8 | –7.8 |
| Greece | 36 772 | 0.3 | 43 737 | 0.3 | 18.9 |
| Iceland | .. | .. | .. | .. | .. |
| Ireland | 35 594 | 0.3 | 32 701 | 0.2 | –8.1 |
| Italy | 1 125 665 | 8.3 | 1 198 243 | 9.1 | 6.4 |
| Luxembourg | 24 917 | 0.2 | 28 750 | 0.2 | 15.4 |
| Netherlands | 445 589 | 3.3 | 410 149 | 3.1 | –8.0 |
| Norway | 68 942 | 0.5 | 61 639 | 0.5 | –10.6 |
| Portugal | 354 813 | 2.6 | 340 523 | 2.6 | –4.0 |
| Spain | .. | .. | .. | .. | .. |
| Sweden | 193 484 | 1.4 | 205 291 | 1.6 | 6.1 |
| Switzerland | 371 788 | 2.7 | 356 956 | 2.7 | –4.0 |
| Turkey | .. | .. | .. | .. | .. |
| United Kingdom | 3 458 626 | 25.4 | 2 984 820 | 22.6 | –13.7 |
| Other OECD-Europe | .. | .. | .. | .. | .. |
| Total Europe | 11 215 809 | 82.3 | 10 513 195 | 79.7 | –6.3 |
| | | | | | |
| Canada | 78 264 | 0.6 | 75 274 | 0.6 | –3.8 |
| United States | 775 281 | 5.7 | 826 781 | 6.3 | 6.6 |
| Total North America | 853 545 | 6.3 | 902 055 | 6.8 | 5.7 |
| | | | | | |
| Australia | .. | .. | .. | .. | .. |
| New Zealand | .. | .. | .. | .. | .. |
| Japan | 356 506 | 2.6 | 471 807 | 3.6 | 32.3 |
| Total Australasia and Japan | 356 506 | 2.6 | 471 807 | 3.6 | 32.3 |
| | | | | | |
| **Total OECD Countries** | 12 425 860 | 91.1 | 11 887 057 | 90.2 | –4.3 |
| | | | | | |
| Yugoslavia | .. | .. | .. | .. | .. |
| Other European countries | 296 895 | 2.2 | 343 333 | 2.6 | 15.6 |
| Latin America | 478 084 | 3.5 | 499 165 | 3.8 | 4.4 |
| Origin country undetermined | 434 926 | 3.2 | 454 857 | 3.4 | 4.6 |
| | | | | | |
| **Total non-OECD Countries** | 1 209 905 | 8.9 | 1 297 355 | 9.8 | 7.2 |
| | | | | | |
| **TOTAL** | 13 635 765 | 100.0 | 13 184 412 | 100.0 | –3.3 |

1. Arrivals recorded in hotels with "estrellas de oro" (golden stars) and "estrellas de plata" (silver stars).

# SPAIN

## NIGHTS SPENT BY FOREIGN TOURISTS IN HOTELS[1]
### (by country of nationality)

| | 1988 | Relative share | 1989 | Relative share | % Variation over 1988 |
|---|---|---|---|---|---|
| Austria | .. | .. | .. | .. | .. |
| Belgium | 3 698 174 | 4.2 | 3 456 487 | 4.4 | −6.5 |
| Denmark | 1 275 846 | 1.4 | 1 073 560 | 1.4 | −15.9 |
| Finland | .. | .. | .. | .. | .. |
| France | 7 115 042 | 8.1 | 7 049 426 | 9.0 | −0.9 |
| Germany | 24 635 737 | 27.9 | 21 791 970 | 27.8 | −11.5 |
| Greece | 84 078 | 0.1 | 99 195 | 0.1 | 18.0 |
| Iceland | .. | .. | .. | .. | .. |
| Ireland | 196 135 | 0.2 | 150 897 | 0.2 | −23.1 |
| Italy | 4 650 705 | 5.3 | 4 587 802 | 5.9 | −1.4 |
| Luxembourg | 240 737 | 0.3 | 225 199 | 0.3 | −6.5 |
| Netherlands | 3 324 088 | 3.8 | 2 810 356 | 3.6 | −15.5 |
| Norway | 430 624 | 0.5 | 299 475 | 0.4 | −30.5 |
| Portugal | 687 368 | 0.8 | 683 368 | 0.9 | −0.6 |
| Spain | .. | .. | .. | .. | .. |
| Sweden | 1 211 566 | 1.4 | 1 182 807 | 1.5 | −2.4 |
| Switzerland | 2 400 842 | 2.7 | 2 171 330 | 2.8 | −9.6 |
| Turkey | .. | .. | .. | .. | .. |
| United Kingdom | 31 291 489 | 35.4 | 25 253 002 | 32.3 | −19.3 |
| Other OECD-Europe | .. | .. | .. | .. | .. |
| **Total Europe** | 81 242 431 | 92.0 | 70 834 874 | 90.5 | −12.8 |
| | | | | | |
| Canada | 182 900 | 0.2 | 177 846 | 0.2 | −2.8 |
| United States | 1 756 732 | 2.0 | 1 835 837 | 2.3 | 4.5 |
| **Total North America** | 1 939 632 | 2.2 | 2 013 683 | 2.6 | 3.8 |
| | | | | | |
| Australia | .. | .. | .. | .. | .. |
| New Zealand | .. | .. | .. | .. | .. |
| Japan | 639 230 | 0.7 | 857 065 | 1.1 | 34.1 |
| **Total Australasia and Japan** | 639 230 | 0.7 | 857 065 | 1.1 | 34.1 |
| | | | | | |
| **Total OECD Countries** | 83 821 293 | 94.9 | 73 705 622 | 94.1 | −12.1 |
| | | | | | |
| Yugoslavia | .. | .. | .. | .. | .. |
| Other European countries | 2 000 685 | 2.3 | 2 149 697 | 2.7 | 7.4 |
| Latin America | 1 190 002 | 1.3 | 1 164 819 | 1.5 | −2.1 |
| Origin country undetermined | 1 339 017 | 1.5 | 1 281 268 | 1.6 | −4.3 |
| | | | | | |
| **Total non-OECD Countries** | 4 529 704 | 5.1 | 4 595 784 | 5.9 | 1.5 |
| | | | | | |
| **TOTAL** | 88 350 997 | 100.0 | 78 301 406 | 100.0 | −11.4 |

1. Nights recorded in hotels with "estrellas de oro" (golden stars) and "estrellas de plata" (silver stars).

# SWEDEN

## *NIGHTS SPENT BY FOREIGN TOURISTS IN HOTELS*
### *(by country of nationality)*

| | 1988 | Relative share | 1989 | Relative share | % Variation over 1988 |
|---|---|---|---|---|---|
| Austria[1] | .. | .. | .. | .. | .. |
| Belgium[1] | .. | .. | .. | .. | .. |
| Denmark | 202 971 | 6.4 | 218 040 | 6.5 | 7.4 |
| Finland | 361 567 | 11.3 | 399 549 | 11.9 | 10.5 |
| France | 90 889 | 2.8 | 96 153 | 2.9 | 5.8 |
| Germany | 475 778 | 14.9 | 510 670 | 15.2 | 7.3 |
| Greece[1] | .. | .. | .. | .. | .. |
| Iceland[1] | .. | .. | .. | .. | .. |
| Ireland[1] | .. | .. | .. | .. | .. |
| Italy | 95 907 | 3.0 | 117 855 | 3.5 | 22.9 |
| Luxembourg[1] | .. | .. | .. | .. | .. |
| Netherlands | 69 273 | 2.2 | 76 064 | 2.3 | 9.8 |
| Norway | 623 166 | 19.5 | 588 033 | 17.5 | −5.6 |
| Portugal[1] | .. | .. | .. | .. | .. |
| Spain[1] | .. | .. | .. | .. | .. |
| Sweden | .. | .. | .. | .. | .. |
| Switzerland | 59 919 | 1.9 | 72 820 | 2.2 | 21.5 |
| Turkey[1] | .. | .. | .. | .. | .. |
| United Kingdom | 239 379 | 7.5 | 265 884 | 7.9 | 11.1 |
| Other OECD-Europe | .. | .. | .. | .. | .. |
| **Total Europe** | 2 218 849 | 69.5 | 2 345 068 | 69.7 | 5.7 |
| Canada | 22 849 | 0.7 | 25 075 | 0.7 | 9.7 |
| United States | 325 521 | 10.2 | 331 449 | 9.8 | 1.8 |
| **Total North America** | 348 370 | 10.9 | 356 524 | 10.6 | 2.3 |
| Australia[2] | .. | .. | .. | .. | .. |
| New Zealand[2] | .. | .. | .. | .. | .. |
| Japan | 74 298 | 2.3 | 81 581 | 2.4 | 9.8 |
| **Total Australasia and Japan** | 74 298 | 2.3 | 81 581 | 2.4 | 9.8 |
| **Total OECD Countries** | 2 641 517 | 82.8 | 2 783 173 | 82.7 | 5.4 |
| Yugoslavia | .. | .. | .. | .. | .. |
| Other European countries[1] | 210 854 | 6.6 | 251 372 | 7.5 | 19.2 |
| Origin country undetermined[2] | 339 623 | 10.6 | 332 354 | 9.9 | −2.1 |
| **Total non-OECD Countries** | 550 477 | 17.2 | 583 726 | 17.3 | 6.0 |
| **TOTAL** | 3 191 994 | 100.0 | 3 366 899 | 100.0 | 5.5 |

1. Included in "Other European countries".
2. Included in "Origin country undetermined".

# SWEDEN

## NIGHTS SPENT BY FOREIGN TOURISTS IN REGISTERED TOURIST ACCOMMODATION
### (by country of nationality)

| | 1988 | Relative share | 1989 | Relative share | % Variation over 1988 |
|---|---|---|---|---|---|
| Austria[1] | .. | .. | .. | .. | .. |
| Belgium[1] | .. | .. | .. | .. | .. |
| Denmark | 650 231 | 9.1 | 656 744 | 8.7 | 1.0 |
| Finland | 589 276 | 8.3 | 640 910 | 8.5 | 8.8 |
| France | 151 345 | 2.1 | 166 622 | 2.2 | 10.1 |
| Germany | 1 377 213 | 19.4 | 1 514 151 | 20.0 | 9.9 |
| Greece[1] | .. | .. | .. | .. | .. |
| Iceland[1] | .. | .. | .. | .. | .. |
| Ireland[1] | .. | .. | .. | .. | .. |
| Italy | 110 245 | 1.6 | 135 843 | 1.8 | 23.2 |
| Luxembourg[1] | .. | .. | .. | .. | .. |
| Netherlands | 343 965 | 4.8 | 399 479 | 5.3 | 16.1 |
| Norway | 2 283 362 | 32.1 | 2 288 849 | 30.2 | 0.2 |
| Portugal[1] | .. | .. | .. | .. | .. |
| Spain[1] | .. | .. | .. | .. | .. |
| Sweden | .. | .. | .. | .. | .. |
| Switzerland | 73 621 | 1.0 | 88 266 | 1.2 | 19.9 |
| Turkey[1] | .. | .. | .. | .. | .. |
| United Kingdom | 311 699 | 4.4 | 341 204 | 4.5 | 9.5 |
| Other OECD-Europe | .. | .. | .. | .. | .. |
| **Total Europe** | 5 890 957 | 82.8 | 6 232 068 | 82.2 | 5.8 |
| | | | | | |
| Canada | 25 802 | 0.4 | 28 101 | 0.4 | 8.9 |
| United States | 339 886 | 4.8 | 347 643 | 4.6 | 2.3 |
| **Total North America** | 365 688 | 5.1 | 375 744 | 5.0 | 2.7 |
| | | | | | |
| Australia[2] | .. | .. | .. | .. | .. |
| New Zealand[2] | .. | .. | .. | .. | .. |
| Japan | 76 564 | 1.1 | 83 817 | 1.1 | 9.5 |
| **Total Australasia and Japan** | 76 564 | 1.1 | 83 817 | 1.1 | 9.5 |
| | | | | | |
| **Total OECD Countries** | 6 333 209 | 89.0 | 6 691 629 | 88.2 | 5.7 |
| | | | | | |
| Yugoslavia | .. | .. | .. | .. | .. |
| Other European countries[1] | 328 473 | 4.6 | 424 704 | 5.6 | 29.3 |
| Origin country undetermined[2] | 450 735 | 6.3 | 467 688 | 6.2 | 3.8 |
| **Total non-OECD Countries** | 779 208 | 11.0 | 892 392 | 11.8 | 14.5 |
| | | | | | |
| **TOTAL** | 7 112 417 | 100.0 | 7 584 021 | 100.0 | 6.6 |

1. Included in "Other European countries".
2. Included in "Origin country undetermined".

# SWITZERLAND

## ARRIVALS OF FOREIGN TOURISTS AT HOTELS
### (by country of residence)

| | 1988 | Relative share | 1989 | Relative share | % Variation over 1988 |
|---|---|---|---|---|---|
| Austria | 153 854 | 2.2 | 164 695 | 2.1 | 7.0 |
| Belgium | 203 750 | 2.9 | 219 331 | 2.9 | 7.6 |
| Denmark | 42 988 | 0.6 | 44 620 | 0.6 | 3.8 |
| Finland | 31 653 | 0.5 | 34 708 | 0.5 | 9.7 |
| France | 539 767 | 7.7 | 561 007 | 7.3 | 3.9 |
| Germany | 2 016 032 | 28.8 | 2 130 168 | 27.8 | 5.7 |
| Greece | 48 317 | 0.7 | 55 013 | 0.7 | 13.9 |
| Iceland[1] | .. | .. | .. | .. | .. |
| Ireland | 11 332 | 0.2 | 14 206 | 0.2 | 25.4 |
| Italy | 535 132 | 7.6 | 614 178 | 8.0 | 14.8 |
| Luxembourg | 23 690 | 0.3 | 26 401 | 0.3 | 11.4 |
| Netherlands | 247 410 | 3.5 | 266 645 | 3.5 | 7.8 |
| Norway | 32 434 | 0.5 | 34 102 | 0.4 | 5.1 |
| Portugal | 33 765 | 0.5 | 38 083 | 0.5 | 12.8 |
| Spain | 195 342 | 2.8 | 249 237 | 3.2 | 27.6 |
| Sweden | 109 514 | 1.6 | 114 005 | 1.5 | 4.1 |
| Switzerland | .. | .. | .. | .. | .. |
| Turkey | 33 229 | 0.5 | 33 251 | 0.4 | 0.1 |
| United Kingdom | 524 254 | 7.5 | 565 255 | 7.4 | 7.8 |
| Other OECD-Europe | .. | .. | .. | .. | .. |
| **Total Europe** | 4 782 463 | 68.2 | 5 164 905 | 67.3 | 8.0 |
| Canada | 93 386 | 1.3 | 100 031 | 1.3 | 7.1 |
| United States | 927 961 | 13.2 | 1 032 600 | 13.5 | 11.3 |
| **Total North America** | 1 021 347 | 14.6 | 1 132 631 | 14.8 | 10.9 |
| Australia[2] | 76 052 | 1.1 | 95 022 | 1.2 | 24.9 |
| New Zealand[2] | .. | .. | .. | .. | .. |
| Japan | 397 739 | 5.7 | 472 268 | 6.2 | 18.7 |
| **Total Australasia and Japan** | 473 791 | 6.8 | 567 290 | 7.4 | 19.7 |
| **Total OECD Countries** | 6 277 601 | 89.6 | 6 864 826 | 89.5 | 9.4 |
| Yugoslavia | 39 589 | 0.6 | 46 094 | 0.6 | 16.4 |
| Other European countries[1] | 72 270 | 1.0 | 86 533 | 1.1 | 19.7 |
| Germany (D. R.) | 5 901 | 0.1 | 6 440 | 0.1 | 9.1 |
| USSR | 9 323 | 0.1 | 14 138 | 0.2 | 51.6 |
| Latin America | 133 518 | 1.9 | 146 413 | 1.9 | 9.7 |
| Argentina | 18 903 | 0.3 | 19 708 | 0.3 | 4.3 |
| Brazil | 49 980 | 0.7 | 55 604 | 0.7 | 11.3 |
| Mexico | 20 440 | 0.3 | 21 197 | 0.3 | 3.7 |
| Asia-Oceania | 354 635 | 5.1 | 397 900 | 5.2 | 12.2 |
| India | 34 245 | 0.5 | 34 550 | 0.5 | 0.9 |
| Iran | 11 256 | 0.2 | 10 891 | 0.1 | −3.2 |
| Israel | 123 383 | 1.8 | 125 620 | 1.6 | 1.8 |
| Africa | 131 023 | 1.9 | 131 359 | 1.7 | 0.3 |
| Egypt | 23 173 | 0.3 | 22 767 | 0.3 | −1.8 |
| South Africa | 30 205 | 0.4 | 29 683 | 0.4 | −1.7 |
| **Total non-OECD Countries** | 731 035 | 10.4 | 808 299 | 10.5 | 10.6 |
| **TOTAL** | 7 008 636 | 100.0 | 7 673 125 | 100.0 | 9.5 |

1. "Other European countries" includes Iceland.
2. Australia includes New Zealand.

# SWITZERLAND

## ARRIVALS OF FOREIGN TOURISTS AT REGISTERED TOURIST ACCOMMODATION
### (by country of residence)

| | 1988 | Relative share | 1989 | Relative share | % Variation over 1988 |
|---|---|---|---|---|---|
| Austria | 190 300 | 2.0 | 203 100 | 2.0 | 6.7 |
| Belgium | 325 500 | 3.5 | 345 700 | 3.4 | 6.2 |
| Denmark | 62 100 | 0.7 | 63 000 | 0.6 | 1.4 |
| Finland | 41 400 | 0.4 | 44 600 | 0.4 | 7.7 |
| France | 720 000 | 7.7 | 743 300 | 7.4 | 3.2 |
| Germany | 3 130 400 | 33.5 | 3 272 000 | 32.4 | 4.5 |
| Greece | 51 000 | 0.5 | 57 600 | 0.6 | 12.9 |
| Iceland[1] | .. | | .. | | |
| Ireland | 16 000 | 0.2 | 19 000 | 0.2 | 18.8 |
| Italy | 627 400 | 6.7 | 713 700 | 7.1 | 13.8 |
| Luxembourg | 32 200 | 0.3 | 35 800 | 0.4 | 11.2 |
| Netherlands | 516 900 | 5.5 | 552 100 | 5.5 | 6.8 |
| Norway | 38 000 | 0.4 | 39 400 | 0.4 | 3.7 |
| Portugal | 40 400 | 0.4 | 45 400 | 0.4 | 12.4 |
| Spain | 252 600 | 2.7 | 314 600 | 3.1 | 24.5 |
| Sweden | 133 500 | 1.4 | 136 200 | 1.3 | 2.0 |
| Switzerland | .. | | .. | | |
| Turkey | 34 900 | 0.4 | 35 200 | 0.3 | 0.9 |
| United Kingdom | 666 600 | 7.1 | 705 200 | 7.0 | 5.8 |
| Other OECD-Europe | .. | | .. | | |
| **Total Europe** | 6 879 200 | 73.6 | 7 325 900 | 72.5 | 6.5 |
| Canada | 114 100 | 1.2 | 122 500 | 1.2 | 7.4 |
| United States | 1 003 800 | 10.7 | 1 112 700 | 11.0 | 10.8 |
| **Total North America** | 1 117 900 | 12.0 | 1 235 200 | 12.2 | 10.5 |
| Australia[2] | 126 200 | 1.3 | 147 700 | 1.5 | 17.0 |
| New Zealand[2] | .. | | .. | | |
| Japan | 412 900 | 4.4 | 489 700 | 4.8 | 18.6 |
| **Total Australasia and Japan** | 539 100 | 5.8 | 637 400 | 6.3 | 18.2 |
| **Total OECD Countries** | 8 536 200 | 91.3 | 9 198 500 | 91.0 | 7.8 |
| Yugoslavia | 44 100 | 0.5 | 52 600 | 0.5 | 19.3 |
| Other European countries[1] | 89 900 | 1.0 | 104 600 | 1.0 | 16.4 |
| Latin America | 146 900 | 1.6 | 162 000 | 1.6 | 10.3 |
| Argentina | 21 100 | 0.2 | 22 200 | 0.2 | 5.2 |
| Brazil | 55 500 | 0.6 | 62 300 | 0.6 | 12.3 |
| Mexico | 23 000 | 0.2 | 23 600 | 0.2 | 2.6 |
| Asia-Oceania | 387 900 | 4.1 | 434 500 | 4.3 | 12.0 |
| India | 36 900 | 0.4 | 36 400 | 0.4 | −1.4 |
| Iran | 12 000 | 0.1 | 11 700 | 0.1 | −2.5 |
| Israel | 138 200 | 1.5 | 139 100 | 1.4 | 0.7 |
| Africa | 147 900 | 1.6 | 151 200 | 1.5 | 2.2 |
| Egypt | 24 000 | 0.3 | 24 300 | 0.2 | 1.3 |
| South Africa | 37 300 | 0.4 | 35 600 | 0.4 | −4.6 |
| **Total non-OECD Countries** | 816 700 | 8.7 | 904 900 | 9.0 | 10.8 |
| **TOTAL** | 9 352 900 | 100.0 | 10 103 400 | 100.0 | 8.0 |

1. "Other European countries" includes Iceland.
2. Australia includes New Zealand.

# SWITZERLAND

*NIGHTS SPENT BY FOREIGN TOURISTS IN HOTELS*
*(by country of residence)*

| | 1988 | Relative share | 1989 | Relative share | % Variation over 1988 |
|---|---|---|---|---|---|
| Austria | 354 587 | 1.9 | 370 200 | 1.8 | 4.4 |
| Belgium | 822 231 | 4.3 | 858 430 | 4.2 | 4.4 |
| Denmark | 106 990 | 0.6 | 107 467 | 0.5 | 0.4 |
| Finland | 77 447 | 0.4 | 80 599 | 0.4 | 4.1 |
| France | 1 558 541 | 8.2 | 1 576 870 | 7.7 | 1.2 |
| Germany | 6 223 904 | 32.6 | 6 492 704 | 31.7 | 4.3 |
| Greece | 122 061 | 0.6 | 133 050 | 0.6 | 9.0 |
| Iceland[1] | .. | .. | .. | .. | .. |
| Ireland | 29 770 | 0.2 | 35 630 | 0.2 | 19.7 |
| Italy | 1 096 670 | 5.7 | 1 268 227 | 6.2 | 15.6 |
| Luxembourg | 87 670 | 0.5 | 97 245 | 0.5 | 10.9 |
| Netherlands | 801 212 | 4.2 | 859 552 | 4.2 | 7.3 |
| Norway | 72 215 | 0.4 | 73 996 | 0.4 | 2.5 |
| Portugal | 79 172 | 0.4 | 85 948 | 0.4 | 8.6 |
| Spain | 359 949 | 1.9 | 454 118 | 2.2 | 26.2 |
| Sweden | 251 849 | 1.3 | 262 216 | 1.3 | 4.1 |
| Switzerland | .. | .. | .. | .. | .. |
| Turkey | 173 860 | 0.9 | 159 690 | 0.8 | −8.2 |
| United Kingdom | 1 775 380 | 9.3 | 1 923 820 | 9.4 | 8.4 |
| Other OECD-Europe | .. | .. | .. | .. | .. |
| **Total Europe** | 13 993 508 | 73.3 | 14 839 762 | 72.4 | 6.0 |
| Canada | 209 480 | 1.1 | 217 828 | 1.1 | 4.0 |
| United States | 2 038 856 | 10.7 | 2 224 447 | 10.9 | 9.1 |
| **Total North America** | 2 248 336 | 11.8 | 2 442 275 | 11.9 | 8.6 |
| Australia[2] | 167 523 | 0.9 | 208 985 | 1.0 | 24.8 |
| New Zealand[2] | .. | .. | .. | .. | .. |
| Japan | 652 954 | 3.4 | 782 234 | 3.8 | 19.8 |
| **Total Australasia and Japan** | 820 477 | 4.3 | 991 219 | 4.8 | 20.8 |
| **Total OECD Countries** | 17 062 321 | 89.3 | 18 273 256 | 89.2 | 7.1 |
| Yugoslavia | 89 973 | 0.5 | 110 571 | 0.5 | 22.9 |
| Other European countries[1] | 228 595 | 1.2 | 272 931 | 1.3 | 19.4 |
| Germany (D. R.) | 16 834 | 0.1 | 19 405 | 0.1 | 15.3 |
| USSR | 43 782 | 0.2 | 62 200 | 0.3 | 42.1 |
| Latin America | 322 476 | 1.7 | 346 958 | 1.7 | 7.6 |
| Argentina | 50 092 | 0.3 | 51 169 | 0.2 | 2.2 |
| Brazil | 118 321 | 0.6 | 134 777 | 0.7 | 13.9 |
| Mexico | 42 371 | 0.2 | 43 374 | 0.2 | 2.4 |
| Asia-Oceania | 956 932 | 5.0 | 1 060 076 | 5.2 | 10.8 |
| India | 88 315 | 0.5 | 91 541 | 0.4 | 3.7 |
| Iran | 43 406 | 0.2 | 38 919 | 0.2 | −10.3 |
| Israel | 328 742 | 1.7 | 335 419 | 1.6 | 2.0 |
| Africa | 441 002 | 2.3 | 425 619 | 2.1 | −3.5 |
| Egypt | 74 085 | 0.4 | 75 013 | 0.4 | 1.3 |
| South Africa | 81 744 | 0.4 | 80 758 | 0.4 | −1.2 |
| **Total non-OECD Countries** | 2 038 978 | 10.7 | 2 216 155 | 10.8 | 8.7 |
| **TOTAL** | 19 101 299 | 100.0 | 20 489 411 | 100.0 | 7.3 |

1. "Other European countries" includes Iceland.
2. Australia includes New Zealand.

# SWITZERLAND

## NIGHTS SPENT BY FOREIGN TOURISTS IN REGISTERED TOURIST ACCOMMODATION
### (by country of residence)

| | 1988 | Relative share | 1989 | Relative share | % Variation over 1988 |
|---|---|---|---|---|---|
| Austria | 504 600 | 1.5 | 521 500 | 1.5 | 3.3 |
| Belgium | 1 844 600 | 5.4 | 1 937 600 | 5.4 | 5.0 |
| Denmark | 195 600 | 0.6 | 174 500 | 0.5 | −10.8 |
| Finland | 100 900 | 0.3 | 106 200 | 0.3 | 5.3 |
| France | 2 494 600 | 7.2 | 2 498 000 | 6.9 | 0.1 |
| Germany | 14 805 900 | 43.0 | 15 095 500 | 42.0 | 2.0 |
| Greece | 132 800 | 0.4 | 144 000 | 0.4 | 8.4 |
| Iceland[1] | .. | .. | .. | .. | .. |
| Ireland | 44 400 | 0.1 | 49 100 | 0.1 | 10.6 |
| Italy | 1 521 100 | 4.4 | 1 748 400 | 4.9 | 14.9 |
| Luxembourg | 166 700 | 0.5 | 182 400 | 0.5 | 9.4 |
| Netherlands | 2 963 400 | 8.6 | 3 102 000 | 8.6 | 4.7 |
| Norway | 88 500 | 0.3 | 89 300 | 0.2 | 0.9 |
| Portugal | 96 400 | 0.3 | 105 800 | 0.3 | 9.8 |
| Spain | 514 000 | 1.5 | 640 000 | 1.8 | 24.5 |
| Sweden | 363 200 | 1.1 | 339 200 | 0.9 | −6.6 |
| Switzerland | .. | .. | .. | .. | .. |
| Turkey | 187 200 | 0.5 | 187 500 | 0.5 | 0.2 |
| United Kingdom | 2 570 000 | 7.5 | 2 606 200 | 7.3 | 1.4 |
| Other OECD-Europe | .. | .. | .. | .. | .. |
| **Total Europe** | 28 593 900 | 83.0 | 29 527 200 | 82.1 | 3.3 |
| Canada | 255 900 | 0.7 | 269 200 | 0.7 | 5.2 |
| United States | 2 268 500 | 6.6 | 2 465 400 | 6.9 | 8.7 |
| **Total North America** | 2 524 400 | 7.3 | 2 734 600 | 7.6 | 8.3 |
| Australia[2] | 265 600 | 0.8 | 310 100 | 0.9 | 16.8 |
| New Zealand[2] | .. | .. | .. | .. | .. |
| Japan | 679 100 | 2.0 | 813 600 | 2.3 | 19.8 |
| **Total Australasia and Japan** | 944 700 | 2.7 | 1 123 700 | 3.1 | 18.9 |
| **Total OECD Countries** | 32 063 000 | 93.1 | 33 385 500 | 92.9 | 4.1 |
| Yugoslavia | 110 100 | 0.3 | 134 400 | 0.4 | 22.1 |
| Other European countries[1] | 285 300 | 0.8 | 324 400 | 0.9 | 13.7 |
| Latin America | 362 100 | 1.1 | 392 000 | 1.1 | 8.3 |
| Argentina | 55 700 | 0.2 | 57 600 | 0.2 | 3.4 |
| Brazil | 135 000 | 0.4 | 153 400 | 0.4 | 13.6 |
| Mexico | 47 800 | 0.1 | 48 400 | 0.1 | 1.3 |
| Asia-Oceania | 1 108 800 | 3.2 | 1 210 900 | 3.4 | 9.2 |
| India | 96 400 | 0.3 | 96 900 | 0.3 | 0.5 |
| Iran | 50 400 | 0.1 | 42 800 | 0.1 | −15.1 |
| Israel | 412 400 | 1.2 | 416 200 | 1.2 | 0.9 |
| Africa | 517 600 | 1.5 | 499 500 | 1.4 | −3.5 |
| Egypt | 79 400 | 0.2 | 90 300 | 0.3 | 13.7 |
| South Africa | 108 800 | 0.3 | 95 200 | 0.3 | −12.5 |
| **Total non-OECD Countries** | 2 383 900 | 6.9 | 2 561 200 | 7.1 | 7.4 |
| **TOTAL** | 34 446 900 | 100.0 | 35 946 700 | 100.0 | 4.4 |

1. "Other European countries" includes Iceland.
2. Australia includes New Zealand.

# TURKEY

## ARRIVALS OF FOREIGN TRAVELLERS AT FRONTIERS
### (by country of nationality)

| | 1988 | Relative share | 1989 | Relative share | % Variation over 1988 |
|---|---|---|---|---|---|
| Austria | 118 259 | 2.8 | 156 875 | 3.5 | 32.7 |
| Belgium | 39 207 | 0.9 | 47 533 | 1.1 | 21.2 |
| Denmark | 30 517 | 0.7 | 32 362 | 0.7 | 6.0 |
| Finland | 48 710 | 1.2 | 69 626 | 1.6 | 42.9 |
| France | 246 784 | 5.9 | 283 545 | 6.4 | 14.9 |
| Germany | 767 905 | 18.4 | 896 989 | 20.1 | 16.8 |
| Greece | 430 331 | 10.3 | 277 333 | 6.2 | −35.6 |
| Iceland[1] | .. | .. | .. | .. | .. |
| Ireland[1] | .. | .. | .. | .. | .. |
| Italy | 144 322 | 3.5 | 154 083 | 3.5 | 6.8 |
| Luxembourg[1] | .. | .. | .. | .. | .. |
| Netherlands | 81 039 | 1.9 | 106 709 | 2.4 | 31.7 |
| Norway | 21 174 | 0.5 | 25 735 | 0.6 | 21.5 |
| Portugal[1] | .. | .. | .. | .. | .. |
| Spain | 44 283 | 1.1 | 56 176 | 1.3 | 26.9 |
| Sweden | 43 393 | 1.0 | 66 761 | 1.5 | 53.9 |
| Switzerland | 67 662 | 1.6 | 77 945 | 1.7 | 15.2 |
| Turkey | .. | .. | .. | .. | .. |
| United Kingdom | 465 142 | 11.1 | 405 943 | 9.1 | −12.7 |
| Other OECD-Europe[1] | 23 350 | 0.6 | 32 215 | 0.7 | 38.0 |
| Total Europe | 2 572 078 | 61.6 | 2 689 830 | 60.3 | 4.6 |
| Canada | 29 220 | 0.7 | 31 587 | 0.7 | 8.1 |
| United States | 165 401 | 4.0 | 204 502 | 4.6 | 23.6 |
| Total North America | 194 621 | 4.7 | 236 089 | 5.3 | 21.3 |
| Australia | 28 989 | 0.7 | 33 628 | 0.8 | 16.0 |
| New Zealand | 9 655 | 0.2 | 9 584 | 0.2 | −0.7 |
| Japan | 28 008 | 0.7 | 32 298 | 0.7 | 15.3 |
| Total Australasia and Japan | 66 652 | 1.6 | 75 510 | 1.7 | 13.3 |
| **Total OECD Countries** | 2 833 351 | 67.9 | 3 001 429 | 67.3 | 5.9 |
| Yugoslavia | 290 498 | 7.0 | 217 266 | 4.9 | −25.2 |
| Other European countries | 285 426 | 6.8 | 481 178 | 10.8 | 68.6 |
| Bulgaria | 9 098 | 0.2 | 15 626 | 0.4 | 71.8 |
| Czechoslovakia | 8 199 | 0.2 | 11 942 | 0.3 | 45.7 |
| Germany (D. R.) | 689 | 0.0 | 2 719 | 0.1 | 294.6 |
| Hungary | 61 323 | 1.5 | 194 391 | 4.4 | 217.0 |
| Poland | 166 470 | 4.0 | 196 376 | 4.4 | 18.0 |
| Rumania | 16 067 | 0.4 | 13 223 | 0.3 | −17.7 |
| USSR | 22 013 | 0.5 | 43 369 | 1.0 | 97.0 |
| Latin America | 21 471 | 0.5 | 27 158 | 0.6 | 26.5 |
| Argentina | 2 341 | 0.1 | 3 147 | 0.1 | 34.4 |
| Brazil | 6 493 | 0.2 | 7 531 | 0.2 | 16.0 |
| Chile | 928 | 0.0 | 1 236 | 0.0 | 33.2 |
| Mexico | 6 030 | 0.1 | 7 048 | 0.2 | 16.9 |
| Asia-Oceania | 536 171 | 12.8 | 591 049 | 13.3 | 10.2 |
| Iran | 233 838 | 5.6 | 240 972 | 5.4 | 3.1 |
| Israel | 25 076 | 0.6 | 41 058 | 0.9 | 63.7 |
| Lebanon | 12 999 | 0.3 | 16 766 | 0.4 | 29.0 |
| Pakistan | 10 755 | 0.3 | 14 136 | 0.3 | 31.4 |
| Saudi Arabia | 32 708 | 0.8 | 27 338 | 0.6 | −16.4 |
| Africa | 202 008 | 4.8 | 133 912 | 3.0 | −33.7 |
| Algeria | 36 027 | 0.9 | 17 575 | 0.4 | −51.2 |
| Egypt | 15 729 | 0.4 | 15 452 | 0.3 | −1.8 |
| Morocco | 4 472 | 0.1 | 6 074 | 0.1 | 35.8 |
| Origin country undetermined[2] | 3 802 | 0.1 | 7 159 | 0.2 | 88.3 |
| **Total non-OECD Countries** | 1 339 376 | 32.1 | 1 457 722 | 32.7 | 8.8 |
| **TOTAL** | 4 172 727 | 100.0 | 4 459 151 | 100.0 | 6.9 |

1. "Other OECD-Europe" includes Iceland, Ireland, Luxembourg and Portugal.
2. "Origin country undetermined" includes Other North America and Stateless persons.

# TURKEY

## ARRIVALS OF FOREIGN TOURISTS AT HOTELS
### (by country of nationality)

| | 1988 | Relative share | 1989 | Relative share | % Variation over 1988 |
|---|---|---|---|---|---|
| Austria | 94 260 | 3.0 | 101 591 | 2.9 | 7.8 |
| Belgium[1] | 141 467 | 4.6 | 178 147 | 5.1 | 25.9 |
| Denmark[2] | 91 611 | 3.0 | 150 754 | 4.3 | 64.6 |
| Finland[2] | .. | .. | .. | .. | .. |
| France | 542 400 | 17.5 | 655 816 | 18.9 | 20.9 |
| Germany | 896 931 | 28.9 | 950 001 | 27.4 | 5.9 |
| Greece | 110 353 | 3.6 | 65 501 | 1.9 | −40.6 |
| Iceland | .. | .. | .. | .. | .. |
| Ireland | .. | .. | .. | .. | .. |
| Italy | 187 249 | 6.0 | 197 465 | 5.7 | 5.5 |
| Luxembourg[1] | .. | .. | .. | .. | .. |
| Netherlands[1] | .. | .. | .. | .. | .. |
| Norway[2] | .. | .. | .. | .. | .. |
| Portugal | .. | .. | .. | .. | .. |
| Spain | 65 878 | 2.1 | 89 576 | 2.6 | 36.0 |
| Sweden[2] | .. | .. | .. | .. | .. |
| Switzerland | 58 565 | 1.9 | 67 857 | 2.0 | 15.9 |
| Turkey | .. | .. | .. | .. | .. |
| United Kingdom | 220 537 | 7.1 | 203 779 | 5.9 | −7.6 |
| Other OECD-Europe | .. | .. | .. | .. | .. |
| **Total Europe** | 2 409 251 | 77.7 | 2 660 487 | 76.7 | 10.4 |
| Canada | 10 546 | 0.3 | 15 802 | 0.5 | 49.8 |
| United States | 118 080 | 3.8 | 167 555 | 4.8 | 41.9 |
| **Total North America** | 128 626 | 4.1 | 183 357 | 5.3 | 42.6 |
| Australia | 9 090 | 0.3 | 14 905 | 0.4 | 64.0 |
| New Zealand | .. | .. | .. | .. | .. |
| Japan | 63 043 | 2.0 | 74 163 | 2.1 | 17.6 |
| **Total Australasia and Japan** | 72 133 | 2.3 | 89 068 | 2.6 | 23.5 |
| **Total OECD Countries** | 2 610 010 | 84.2 | 2 932 912 | 84.6 | 12.4 |
| Yugoslavia | 29 565 | 1.0 | 22 523 | 0.6 | −23.8 |
| Other European countries | 98 425 | 3.2 | 113 298 | 3.3 | 15.1 |
| Bulgaria | 6 243 | 0.2 | 5 611 | 0.2 | −10.1 |
| Hungary | 26 938 | 0.9 | 55 719 | 1.6 | 106.8 |
| Poland | 58 000 | 1.9 | 32 628 | 0.9 | −43.7 |
| Rumania | 2 579 | 0.1 | 5 101 | 0.1 | 97.8 |
| USSR | 4 665 | 0.2 | 14 239 | 0.4 | 205.2 |
| Asia-Oceania[3] | 151 972 | 4.9 | 157 162 | 4.5 | 3.4 |
| Iran | 62 545 | 2.0 | 54 966 | 1.6 | −12.1 |
| Lebanon | 5 308 | 0.2 | 8 307 | 0.2 | 56.5 |
| Pakistan | 6 706 | 0.2 | 10 297 | 0.3 | 53.5 |
| Saudi Arabia | 31 317 | 1.0 | 32 899 | 0.9 | 5.1 |
| Africa | 20 884 | 0.7 | 18 753 | 0.5 | −10.2 |
| Egypt | 5 966 | 0.2 | 8 671 | 0.3 | 45.3 |
| Origin country undetermined | 189 658 | 6.1 | 223 177 | 6.4 | 17.7 |
| **Total non-OECD Countries** | 490 504 | 15.8 | 534 913 | 15.4 | 9.1 |
| **TOTAL** | 3 100 514 | 100.0 | 3 467 825 | 100.0 | 11.8 |

1. Belgium includes Luxembourg and Netherlands.
2. Denmark includes Finland, Norway and Sweden.
3. Asia-Oceania includes Iraq, Kuwait, Lebanon, Syria, Saudi Arabia, Jordan, Iran and Pakistan.

# TURKEY

*ARRIVALS OF FOREIGN TOURISTS AT REGISTERED TOURIST ACCOMMODATION*

*(by country of nationality)*

|  | 1988 | Relative share | 1989 | Relative share | % Variation over 1988 |
|---|---|---|---|---|---|
| Austria | 121 084 | 3.5 | 128 908 | 3.4 | 6.5 |
| Belgium[1] | 154 929 | 4.5 | 193 948 | 5.1 | 25.2 |
| Denmark[2] | 103 929 | 3.0 | 163 183 | 4.3 | 57.0 |
| Finland[2] | .. | .. | .. | .. | .. |
| France | 594 487 | 17.4 | 709 696 | 18.8 | 19.4 |
| Germany | 1 028 920 | 30.2 | 1 081 801 | 28.6 | 5.1 |
| Greece | 110 681 | 3.2 | 66 457 | 1.8 | –40.0 |
| Iceland | .. | .. | .. | .. | .. |
| Ireland | .. | .. | .. | .. | .. |
| Italy | 213 460 | 6.3 | 225 353 | 6.0 | 5.6 |
| Luxembourg[1] | .. | .. | .. | .. | .. |
| Netherlands[1] | .. | .. | .. | .. | .. |
| Norway[2] | .. | .. | .. | .. | .. |
| Portugal | .. | .. | .. | .. | .. |
| Spain | 67 814 | 2.0 | 90 951 | 2.4 | 34.1 |
| Sweden[2] | .. | .. | .. | .. | .. |
| Switzerland | 69 947 | 2.1 | 80 235 | 2.1 | 14.7 |
| Turkey | .. | .. | .. | .. | .. |
| United Kingdom | 231 857 | 6.8 | 214 096 | 5.7 | –7.7 |
| Other OECD-Europe | .. | .. | .. | .. | .. |
| **Total Europe** | 2 697 108 | 79.0 | 2 954 628 | 78.1 | 9.5 |
| Canada | 11 162 | 0.3 | 16 132 | 0.4 | 44.5 |
| United States | 120 858 | 3.5 | 169 919 | 4.5 | 40.6 |
| **Total North America** | 132 020 | 3.9 | 186 051 | 4.9 | 40.9 |
| Australia | 11 157 | 0.3 | 15 370 | 0.4 | 37.8 |
| New Zealand | .. | .. | .. | .. | .. |
| Japan | 63 212 | 1.9 | 74 421 | 2.0 | 17.7 |
| **Total Australasia and Japan** | 74 369 | 2.2 | 89 791 | 2.4 | 20.7 |
| **Total OECD Countries** | 2 903 497 | 85.1 | 3 230 470 | 85.4 | 11.3 |
| Yugoslavia | 29 981 | 0.9 | 22 933 | 0.6 | –23.5 |
| Other European countries | 104 981 | 3.1 | 116 808 | 3.1 | 11.3 |
| Bulgaria | 6 318 | 0.2 | 5 612 | 0.1 | –11.2 |
| Hungary | 27 601 | 0.8 | 56 456 | 1.5 | 104.5 |
| Poland | 63 549 | 1.9 | 34 157 | 0.9 | –46.3 |
| Rumania | 2 673 | 0.1 | 6 067 | 0.2 | 127.0 |
| USSR | 4 840 | 0.1 | 14 516 | 0.4 | 199.9 |
| Asia-Oceania[3] | 154 369 | 4.5 | 164 731 | 4.4 | 6.7 |
| Iran | 63 098 | 1.8 | 56 062 | 1.5 | –11.2 |
| Lebanon | 5 737 | 0.2 | 8 699 | 0.2 | 51.6 |
| Pakistan | 6 895 | 0.2 | 10 626 | 0.3 | 54.1 |
| Saudi Arabia | 32 123 | 0.9 | 37 191 | 1.0 | 15.8 |
| Africa | 21 049 | 0.6 | 19 144 | 0.5 | –9.1 |
| Egypt | 6 048 | 0.2 | 8 880 | 0.2 | 46.8 |
| Libyan Arab Jamahiriya | 15 001 | 0.4 | .. | .. | .. |
| Origin country undetermined | 198 106 | 5.8 | 229 855 | 6.1 | 16.0 |
| **Total non-OECD Countries** | 508 486 | 14.9 | 553 471 | 14.6 | 8.8 |
| **TOTAL** | 3 411 983 | 100.0 | 3 783 941 | 100.0 | 10.9 |

1. Belgium includes Luxembourg and Netherlands.
2. Denmark includes Finland, Norway and Sweden.
3. Asia-Oceania includes Iraq, Kuwait, Lebanon, Syria, Saudi Arabia, Jordan, Iran and Pakistan.

# TURKEY

## NIGHTS SPENT BY FOREIGN TOURISTS IN HOTELS
### (by country of nationality)

| | 1988 | Relative share | 1989 | Relative share | % Variation over 1988 |
|---|---|---|---|---|---|
| Austria | 384 715 | 4.1 | 380 915 | 3.9 | −1.0 |
| Belgium[1] | 388 517 | 4.1 | 459 583 | 4.7 | 18.3 |
| Denmark[2] | 340 435 | 3.6 | 660 992 | 6.8 | 94.2 |
| Finland[2] | .. | .. | .. | .. | .. |
| France | 1 120 980 | 11.9 | 1 133 899 | 11.6 | 1.2 |
| Germany | 3 519 989 | 37.3 | 3 689 697 | 37.9 | 4.8 |
| Greece | 240 580 | 2.6 | 124 253 | 1.3 | −48.4 |
| Iceland | .. | .. | .. | .. | .. |
| Ireland | .. | .. | .. | .. | .. |
| Italy | 391 230 | 4.1 | 378 578 | 3.9 | −3.2 |
| Luxembourg[1] | .. | .. | .. | .. | .. |
| Netherlands[1] | .. | .. | .. | .. | .. |
| Norway[2] | .. | .. | .. | .. | .. |
| Portugal | .. | .. | .. | .. | .. |
| Spain | 133 843 | 1.4 | 169 652 | 1.7 | 26.8 |
| Sweden[2] | .. | .. | .. | .. | .. |
| Switzerland | 203 894 | 2.2 | 225 407 | 2.3 | 10.6 |
| Turkey | .. | .. | .. | .. | .. |
| United Kingdom | 890 987 | 9.5 | 774 132 | 7.9 | −13.1 |
| Other OECD-Europe | .. | .. | .. | .. | .. |
| **Total Europe** | 7 615 170 | 80.8 | 7 997 108 | 82.1 | 5.0 |
| Canada | 29 606 | 0.3 | 30 801 | 0.3 | 4.0 |
| United States | 314 818 | 3.3 | 380 779 | 3.9 | 21.0 |
| **Total North America** | 344 424 | 3.7 | 411 580 | 4.2 | 19.5 |
| Australia | 26 861 | 0.3 | 28 925 | 0.3 | 7.7 |
| New Zealand | .. | | .. | | |
| Japan | 117 035 | 1.2 | 134 742 | 1.4 | 15.1 |
| **Total Australasia and Japan** | 143 896 | 1.5 | 163 667 | 1.7 | 13.7 |
| **Total OECD Countries** | 8 103 490 | 86.0 | 8 572 355 | 88.0 | 5.8 |
| Yugoslavia | 57 606 | 0.6 | 39 147 | 0.4 | −32.0 |
| Other European countries | 323 578 | 3.4 | 289 634 | 3.0 | −10.5 |
| Bulgaria | 9 120 | 0.1 | 7 635 | 0.1 | −16.3 |
| Hungary | 75 970 | 0.8 | 139 683 | 1.4 | 83.9 |
| Poland | 218 753 | 2.3 | 95 463 | 1.0 | −56.4 |
| Rumania | 9 276 | 0.1 | 14 217 | 0.1 | 53.3 |
| USSR | 10 459 | 0.1 | 32 636 | 0.3 | 212.0 |
| Asia-Oceania[3] | 402 306 | 4.3 | 331 859 | 3.4 | −17.5 |
| Iran | 184 688 | 2.0 | 119 271 | 1.2 | −35.4 |
| Lebanon | 12 499 | 0.1 | 17 643 | 0.2 | 41.2 |
| Pakistan | 16 074 | 0.2 | 16 745 | 0.2 | 4.2 |
| Saudi Arabia | 77 600 | 0.8 | 75 676 | 0.8 | −2.5 |
| Africa | 65 846 | 0.7 | 46 514 | 0.5 | −29.4 |
| Egypt | 19 219 | 0.2 | 21 168 | 0.2 | 10.1 |
| Origin country undetermined | 475 039 | 5.0 | 462 803 | 4.8 | −2.6 |
| **Total non-OECD Countries** | 1 324 375 | 14.0 | 1 169 957 | 12.0 | −11.7 |
| **TOTAL** | 9 427 865 | 100.0 | 9 742 312 | 100.0 | 3.3 |

1. Belgium includes Luxembourg and Netherlands.
2. Denmark includes Finland, Norway and Sweden.
3. Asia-Oceania includes Iraq, Kuwait, Lebanon, Syria, Saudi Arabia, Jordan, Iran and Pakistan.

# TURKEY

## NIGHTS SPENT BY FOREIGN TOURISTS IN REGISTERED TOURIST ACCOMMODATION
### (by country of nationality)

| | 1988 | Relative share | 1989 | Relative share | % Variation over 1988 |
|---|---|---|---|---|---|
| Austria | 570 235 | 4.9 | 594 535 | 5.0 | 4.3 |
| Belgium[1] | 474 107 | 4.1 | 569 652 | 4.8 | 20.2 |
| Denmark[2] | 444 376 | 3.8 | 744 163 | 6.3 | 67.5 |
| Finland[2] | .. | .. | .. | .. | .. |
| France | 1 529 027 | 13.1 | 1 476 849 | 12.4 | −3.4 |
| Germany | 4 593 089 | 39.4 | 4 709 013 | 39.7 | 2.5 |
| Greece | 241 294 | 2.1 | 127 697 | 1.1 | −47.1 |
| Iceland | .. | .. | .. | .. | .. |
| Ireland | .. | .. | .. | .. | .. |
| Italy | 491 999 | 4.2 | 489 819 | 4.1 | −0.4 |
| Luxembourg[1] | .. | .. | .. | .. | .. |
| Netherlands[1] | .. | .. | .. | .. | .. |
| Norway[2] | .. | .. | .. | .. | .. |
| Portugal | .. | .. | .. | .. | .. |
| Spain | 137 688 | 1.2 | 173 057 | 1.5 | 25.7 |
| Sweden[2] | .. | .. | .. | .. | .. |
| Switzerland | 320 510 | 2.7 | 343 405 | 2.9 | 7.1 |
| Turkey | .. | .. | .. | .. | .. |
| United Kingdom | 980 484 | 8.4 | 841 727 | 7.1 | −14.2 |
| Other OECD-Europe | .. | .. | .. | .. | .. |
| **Total Europe** | 9 782 809 | 83.9 | 10 069 917 | 84.9 | 2.9 |
| | | | | | |
| Canada | 31 074 | 0.3 | 31 631 | 0.3 | 1.8 |
| United States | 321 917 | 2.8 | 388 945 | 3.3 | 20.8 |
| **Total North America** | 352 991 | 3.0 | 420 576 | 3.5 | 19.1 |
| | | | | | |
| Australia | 32 662 | 0.3 | 30 819 | 0.3 | −5.6 |
| New Zealand | .. | .. | .. | .. | .. |
| Japan | 117 549 | 1.0 | 135 295 | 1.1 | 15.1 |
| **Total Australasia and Japan** | 150 211 | 1.3 | 166 114 | 1.4 | 10.6 |
| | | | | | |
| **Total OECD Countries** | 10 286 011 | 88.3 | 10 656 607 | 89.8 | 3.6 |
| | | | | | |
| Yugoslavia | 58 925 | 0.5 | 39 956 | 0.3 | −32.2 |
| Other European countries | 342 767 | 2.9 | 296 660 | 2.5 | −13.5 |
| Bulgaria | 9 550 | 0.1 | 7 651 | 0.1 | −19.9 |
| Hungary | 78 186 | 0.7 | 141 550 | 1.2 | 81.0 |
| Poland | 233 843 | 2.0 | 98 388 | 0.8 | −57.9 |
| Rumania | 9 526 | 0.1 | 15 549 | 0.1 | 63.2 |
| USSR | 11 662 | 0.1 | 33 522 | 0.3 | 187.4 |
| Asia-Oceania[3] | 408 438 | 3.5 | 347 236 | 2.9 | −15.0 |
| Iran | 185 841 | 1.6 | 121 363 | 1.0 | −34.7 |
| Lebanon | 13 129 | 0.1 | 18 454 | 0.2 | 40.6 |
| Pakistan | 16 386 | 0.1 | 17 303 | 0.1 | 5.6 |
| Saudi Arabia | 80 453 | 0.7 | 84 779 | 0.7 | 5.4 |
| Africa | 66 185 | 0.6 | 47 218 | 0.4 | −28.7 |
| Egypt | 19 398 | 0.2 | 21 575 | 0.2 | 11.2 |
| Libyan Arab Jamahiriya | 46 787 | 0.4 | 25 643 | 0.2 | −45.2 |
| Origin country undetermined | 492 856 | 4.2 | 477 069 | 4.0 | −3.2 |
| | | | | | |
| **Total non-OECD Countries** | 1 369 171 | 11.7 | 1 208 139 | 10.2 | −11.8 |
| | | | | | |
| **TOTAL** | 11 655 182 | 100.0 | 11 864 746 | 100.0 | 1.8 |

1. Belgium includes Luxembourg and Netherlands.
2. Denmark includes Finland, Norway and Sweden.
3. Asia-Oceania includes Iraq, Kuwait, Lebanon, Syria, Saudi Arabia, Jordan, Iran and Pakistan.

# UNITED KINGDOM

## ARRIVALS OF FOREIGN VISITORS AT FRONTIERS
### (by country of residence)

| | 1988 | Relative share | 1989 | Relative share | % Variation over 1988 |
|---|---|---|---|---|---|
| Austria | 117 300 | 0.7 | 146 300 | 0.9 | 24.7 |
| Belgium | 560 800 | 3.6 | 589 500 | 3.4 | 5.1 |
| Denmark | 248 500 | 1.6 | 256 000 | 1.5 | 3.0 |
| Finland | 113 900 | 0.7 | 164 000 | 1.0 | 44.0 |
| France | 1 969 400 | 12.5 | 2 254 300 | 13.1 | 14.5 |
| Germany | 1 830 200 | 11.6 | 2 011 700 | 11.7 | 9.9 |
| Greece | 122 300 | 0.8 | 126 300 | 0.7 | 3.3 |
| Iceland | 31 900 | 0.2 | 29 900 | 0.2 | −6.3 |
| Ireland | 1 251 700 | 7.9 | 1 301 800 | 7.6 | 4.0 |
| Italy | 660 900 | 4.2 | 700 100 | 4.1 | 5.9 |
| Luxembourg | 25 600 | 0.2 | 26 500 | 0.2 | 3.5 |
| Netherlands | 880 800 | 5.6 | 945 200 | 5.5 | 7.3 |
| Norway | 281 000 | 1.8 | 283 300 | 1.6 | 0.8 |
| Portugal | 88 400 | 0.6 | 93 200 | 0.5 | 5.4 |
| Spain | 509 400 | 3.2 | 613 100 | 3.6 | 20.4 |
| Sweden | 381 500 | 2.4 | 476 200 | 2.8 | 24.8 |
| Switzerland | 420 300 | 2.7 | 418 000 | 2.4 | −0.5 |
| Turkey | 41 000 | 0.3 | 50 300 | 0.3 | 22.7 |
| United Kingdom | .. | .. | .. | .. | .. |
| Other OECD-Europe | .. | .. | .. | .. | .. |
| **Total Europe** | 9 534 900 | 60.4 | 10 485 700 | 60.9 | 10.0 |
| Canada | 651 400 | 4.1 | 633 400 | 3.7 | −2.8 |
| United States | 2 620 100 | 16.6 | 2 814 100 | 16.4 | 7.4 |
| **Total North America** | 3 271 500 | 20.7 | 3 447 500 | 20.0 | 5.4 |
| Australia | 481 500 | 3.0 | 529 400 | 3.1 | 9.9 |
| New Zealand | 129 000 | 0.8 | 122 200 | 0.7 | −5.3 |
| Japan | 388 200 | 2.5 | 499 500 | 2.9 | 28.7 |
| **Total Australasia and Japan** | 998 700 | 6.3 | 1 151 100 | 6.7 | 15.3 |
| **Total OECD Countries** | 13 805 100 | 87.4 | 15 084 300 | 87.7 | 9.3 |
| Yugoslavia | 29 200 | 0.2 | 30 600 | 0.2 | 4.8 |
| Other European countries | 227 800 | 1.4 | 272 500 | 1.6 | 19.6 |
| Latin America | 153 800 | 1.0 | 178 200 | 1.0 | 15.9 |
| Asia-Oceania | 994 700 | 6.3 | 1 023 900 | 6.0 | 2.9 |
| Africa | 522 300 | 3.3 | 539 800 | 3.1 | 3.4 |
| Origin country undetermined | 62 300 | 0.4 | 74 600 | 0.4 | 19.7 |
| **Total non-OECD Countries** | 1 990 100 | 12.6 | 2 119 600 | 12.3 | 6.5 |
| **TOTAL** | 15 795 200 | 100.0 | 17 203 900 | 100.0 | 8.9 |

# UNITED KINGDOM

## NIGHTS SPENT BY FOREIGN TOURISTS IN TOURIST ACCOMMODATION[1]
### (by country of residence)

| | 1988 | Relative share | 1989 | Relative share | % Variation over 1988 |
|---|---|---|---|---|---|
| Austria | 1 195 000 | 0.7 | 2 017 000 | 1.1 | 68.8 |
| Belgium | 2 194 000 | 1.3 | 2 617 000 | 1.4 | 19.3 |
| Denmark | 1 912 000 | 1.1 | 1 901 000 | 1.0 | −0.6 |
| Finland | 775 000 | 0.4 | 1 393 000 | 0.8 | 79.7 |
| France | 14 045 000 | 8.1 | 16 259 000 | 8.8 | 15.8 |
| Germany | 17 226 000 | 10.0 | 17 624 000 | 9.5 | 2.3 |
| Greece | 1 846 000 | 1.1 | 1 870 000 | 1.0 | 1.3 |
| Iceland | 312 000 | 0.2 | 240 000 | 0.1 | −23.1 |
| Ireland | 10 631 000 | 6.1 | 11 117 000 | 6.0 | 4.6 |
| Italy | 8 507 000 | 4.9 | 8 198 000 | 4.4 | −3.6 |
| Luxembourg | 169 000 | 0.1 | 139 000 | 0.1 | −17.8 |
| Netherlands | 5 566 000 | 3.2 | 5 206 000 | 2.8 | −6.5 |
| Norway | 1 882 000 | 1.1 | 2 121 000 | 1.1 | 12.7 |
| Portugal | 874 000 | 0.5 | 990 000 | 0.5 | 13.3 |
| Spain[2] | 7 780 000 | 4.5 | 8 275 000 | 4.5 | 6.4 |
| Sweden | 2 981 000 | 1.7 | 3 286 000 | 1.8 | 10.2 |
| Switzerland | 4 592 000 | 2.7 | 3 801 000 | 2.1 | −17.2 |
| Turkey | 945 000 | 0.5 | 1 175 000 | 0.6 | 24.3 |
| United Kingdom | .. | .. | .. | .. | .. |
| Other OECD-Europe | .. | .. | .. | .. | .. |
| Total Europe | 83 432 000 | 48.3 | 88 229 000 | 47.7 | 5.7 |
| Canada | 8 855 000 | 5.1 | 8 537 000 | 4.6 | −3.6 |
| United States | 25 520 000 | 14.8 | 27 432 000 | 14.8 | 7.5 |
| Total North America | 34 375 000 | 19.9 | 35 969 000 | 19.4 | 4.6 |
| Australia | 10 963 000 | 6.3 | 11 703 000 | 6.3 | 6.7 |
| New Zealand | 3 881 000 | 2.2 | 3 086 000 | 1.7 | −20.5 |
| Japan | 2 944 000 | 1.7 | 3 262 000 | 1.8 | 10.8 |
| Total Australasia and Japan | 17 788 000 | 10.3 | 18 051 000 | 9.8 | 1.5 |
| **Total OECD Countries** | 135 595 000 | 78.4 | 142 249 000 | 76.9 | 4.9 |
| Yugoslavia | 627 000 | 0.4 | 498 000 | 0.3 | −20.6 |
| Other European countries | 4 795 000 | 2.8 | 5 964 000 | 3.2 | 24.4 |
| Latin America | 1 923 000 | 1.1 | 2 538 000 | 1.4 | 32.0 |
| Asia-Oceania | 18 047 000 | 10.4 | 20 459 000 | 11.1 | 13.4 |
| Africa | 10 336 000 | 6.0 | 11 143 000 | 6.0 | 7.8 |
| Origin country undetermined | 1 576 000 | 0.9 | 2 193 000 | 1.2 | 39.1 |
| **Total non-OECD Countries** | 37 304 000 | 21.6 | 42 795 000 | 23.1 | 14.7 |
| **TOTAL** | 172 899 000 | 100.0 | 185 044 000 | 100.0 | 7.0 |

1. Estimates of total number of nights spent in all forms of accommodation, including stays with friends and relatives. Excluding: visitors in transit, visits of merchant seamen, airline personnel and military on duty.
2. Spain includes Canary Islands.

# UNITED STATES

*ARRIVALS OF FOREIGN TOURISTS AT FRONTIERS*

*(by country of residence)*

| | 1988 | Relative share | 1989 | Relative share | % Variation over 1988 |
|---|---|---|---|---|---|
| Austria | 102 649 | 0.3 | 95 760 | 0.3 | -6.7 |
| Belgium | 114 420 | 0.4 | 115 439 | 0.3 | 0.9 |
| Denmark | 100 479 | 0.3 | 107 062 | 0.3 | 6.6 |
| Finland | 73 967 | 0.2 | 92 992 | 0.3 | 25.7 |
| France | 618 439 | 2.0 | 653 685 | 1.9 | 5.7 |
| Germany | 1 153 356 | 3.7 | 1 076 385 | 3.1 | -6.7 |
| Greece | 53 909 | 0.2 | 53 184 | 0.2 | -1.3 |
| Iceland | 15 420 | 0.0 | 13 531 | 0.0 | -12.3 |
| Ireland | 111 135 | 0.4 | 105 429 | 0.3 | -5.1 |
| Italy | 356 528 | 1.1 | 354 920 | 1.0 | -0.5 |
| Luxembourg | 9 680 | 0.0 | 8 752 | 0.0 | -9.6 |
| Netherlands | 247 843 | 0.8 | 260 840 | 0.7 | 5.2 |
| Norway | 107 088 | 0.3 | 105 147 | 0.3 | -1.8 |
| Portugal | 32 487 | 0.1 | 35 468 | 0.1 | 9.2 |
| Spain | 176 757 | 0.6 | 201 947 | 0.6 | 14.3 |
| Sweden | 239 958 | 0.8 | 281 261 | 0.8 | 17.2 |
| Switzerland | 282 588 | 0.9 | 274 885 | 0.8 | -2.7 |
| Turkey | 20 491 | 0.1 | 23 449 | 0.1 | 14.4 |
| United Kingdom | 1 818 029 | 5.8 | 2 221 871 | 6.3 | 22.2 |
| Other OECD-Europe | .. | .. | .. | .. | .. |
| Total Europe | 5 635 223 | 17.9 | 6 082 007 | 17.3 | 7.9 |
| | | | | | |
| Canada | 13 843 106 | 43.9 | 15 365 937 | 43.6 | 11.0 |
| United States | .. | .. | .. | .. | .. |
| Total North America | 13 843 106 | 43.9 | 15 365 937 | 43.6 | 11.0 |
| | | | | | |
| Australia | 336 385 | 1.1 | 406 392 | 1.2 | 20.8 |
| New Zealand | 152 091 | 0.5 | 166 774 | 0.5 | 9.7 |
| Japan | 2 534 084 | 8.0 | 3 080 396 | 8.7 | 21.6 |
| Total Australasia and Japan | 3 022 560 | 9.6 | 3 653 562 | 10.4 | 20.9 |
| | | | | | |
| **Total OECD Countries** | 22 500 889 | 71.3 | 25 101 506 | 71.2 | 11.6 |
| | | | | | |
| Yugoslavia | 28 376 | 0.1 | 28 092 | 0.1 | -1.0 |
| Czechoslovakia | 6 779 | 0.0 | 8 984 | 0.0 | 32.5 |
| Hungary | 17 928 | 0.1 | 18 924 | 0.1 | 5.6 |
| Poland | 48 326 | 0.2 | 63 202 | 0.2 | 30.8 |
| Rumania | 5 741 | 0.0 | 4 776 | 0.0 | -16.8 |
| USSR | 30 388 | 0.1 | 56 818 | 0.2 | 87.0 |
| Latin America[1] | 8 868 710 | 28.1 | .. | .. | .. |
| Argentina | 121 030 | 0.4 | 132 432 | 0.4 | 9.4 |
| Brazil | 298 784 | 0.9 | 333 489 | 0.9 | 11.6 |
| Chile | 62 795 | 0.2 | 70 018 | 0.2 | 11.5 |
| Colombia | 146 742 | 0.5 | 152 319 | 0.4 | 3.8 |
| Cuba | .. | .. | 26 069 | 0.1 | .. |
| Mexico | 7 505 000 | 23.8 | 1 241 376 | 3.5 | -83.5 |
| Venezuela | 183 850 | 0.6 | 219 345 | 0.6 | 19.3 |
| China | 23 080 | 0.1 | 239 955 | 0.7 | 939.7 |
| Hong Kong | 125 796 | 0.4 | 142 911 | 0.4 | 13.6 |
| India | 109 501 | 0.3 | 106 908 | 0.3 | -2.4 |
| Iran | 12 827 | 0.0 | 15 625 | 0.0 | 21.8 |
| Iraq | .. | .. | 2 712 | 0.0 | .. |
| Israel | 150 655 | 0.5 | 156 289 | 0.4 | 3.7 |
| Jordan | .. | .. | 17 209 | 0.0 | .. |
| Republic of Korea | 92 426 | 0.3 | 149 323 | 0.4 | 61.6 |
| Kuwait | .. | .. | 19 843 | 0.1 | .. |
| Lebanon | 19 509 | 0.1 | 14 767 | 0.0 | -24.3 |
| Malaysia | 39 024 | 0.1 | 40 472 | 0.1 | 3.7 |
| Oman | .. | .. | 2 047 | 0.0 | .. |
| Pakistan | 32 923 | 0.1 | 31 364 | 0.1 | -4.7 |
| Philippines | 94 568 | 0.3 | 89 155 | 0.3 | -5.7 |
| Saudi Arabia | 48 638 | 0.2 | 48 526 | 0.1 | -0.2 |
| Singapore | 45 115 | 0.1 | 48 567 | 0.1 | 7.7 |
| Syrian Arab Republic | .. | .. | 7 768 | 0.0 | .. |
| Taiwan | 183 402 | 0.6 | .. | .. | .. |
| Thailand | 32 648 | 0.1 | 36 173 | 0.1 | 10.8 |
| Africa | 158 915 | 0.5 | .. | .. | .. |
| Egypt | 21 569 | 0.1 | 21 605 | 0.1 | 0.2 |
| Kenya | .. | .. | 7 151 | 0.0 | .. |
| Morocco | 9 155 | 0.0 | 726 | 0.0 | -92.1 |
| Nigeria | .. | .. | 1 582 | 0.0 | .. |
| South Africa | 38 199 | 0.1 | 3 300 | 0.0 | -91.4 |
| Origin country undetermined[2] | .. | .. | 10 119 448 | 28.7 | .. |
| | | | | | |
| **Total non-OECD Countries** | 9 056 001 | 28.7 | 10 147 540 | 28.8 | 12.1 |
| | | | | | |
| **TOTAL** | 31 556 890 | 100.0 | 35 249 046 | 100.0 | 11.7 |

1. Latin America includes Central America, Carribean, South America and Mexico.
2. Origin country undetermined includes Middle East only.

# YUGOSLAVIA

### ARRIVALS OF FOREIGN TOURISTS AT HOTELS
#### (by country of nationality)

| | 1988 | Relative share | 1989 | Relative share | % Variation over 1988 |
|---|---|---|---|---|---|
| Austria | 468 188 | 8.6 | 471 277 | 8.6 | 0.7 |
| Belgium | 95 925 | 1.8 | 106 026 | 1.9 | 10.5 |
| Denmark | 59 990 | 1.1 | 34 851 | 0.6 | −41.9 |
| Finland | 21 350 | 0.4 | 19 948 | 0.4 | −6.6 |
| France | 230 629 | 4.2 | 209 226 | 3.8 | −9.3 |
| Germany | 1 406 895 | 25.8 | 1 309 745 | 23.8 | −6.9 |
| Greece | 139 108 | 2.5 | 148 532 | 2.7 | 6.8 |
| Iceland | 1 685 | 0.0 | 1 171 | 0.0 | −30.5 |
| Ireland | 7 572 | 0.1 | 6 072 | 0.1 | −19.8 |
| Italy | 718 446 | 13.2 | 875 132 | 15.9 | 21.8 |
| Luxembourg | .. | .. | .. | .. | .. |
| Netherlands | 242 342 | 4.4 | 252 120 | 4.6 | 4.0 |
| Norway | 24 168 | 0.4 | 23 977 | 0.4 | −0.8 |
| Portugal | 4 487 | 0.1 | 3 913 | 0.1 | −12.8 |
| Spain | 50 600 | 0.9 | 55 133 | 1.0 | 9.0 |
| Sweden | 85 065 | 1.6 | 72 817 | 1.3 | −14.4 |
| Switzerland | 64 442 | 1.2 | 62 594 | 1.1 | −2.9 |
| Turkey | 79 053 | 1.4 | 72 297 | 1.3 | −8.5 |
| United Kingdom | 601 558 | 11.0 | 571 042 | 10.4 | −5.1 |
| Other OECD-Europe | .. | .. | .. | .. | .. |
| **Total Europe** | 4 301 503 | 78.8 | 4 295 873 | 78.2 | −0.1 |
| | | | | | |
| Canada | 39 638 | 0.7 | 35 123 | 0.6 | −11.4 |
| United States | 250 687 | 4.6 | 221 624 | 4.0 | −11.6 |
| **Total North America** | 290 325 | 5.3 | 256 747 | 4.7 | −11.6 |
| | | | | | |
| Australia | 21 610 | 0.4 | 24 541 | 0.4 | 13.6 |
| New Zealand | 4 018 | 0.1 | 4 232 | 0.1 | 5.3 |
| Japan | 14 615 | 0.3 | 15 005 | 0.3 | 2.7 |
| **Total Australasia and Japan** | 40 243 | 0.7 | 43 778 | 0.8 | 8.8 |
| | | | | | |
| **Total OECD Countries** | 4 632 071 | 84.9 | 4 596 398 | 83.7 | −0.8 |
| | | | | | |
| Yugoslavia | .. | .. | .. | .. | .. |
| Other European countries | 653 166 | 12.0 | 725 627 | 13.2 | 11.1 |
| Bulgaria | 12 696 | 0.2 | 21 722 | 0.4 | 71.1 |
| Czechoslovakia | 148 666 | 2.7 | 134 636 | 2.5 | −9.4 |
| Germany (D. R.) | 35 139 | 0.6 | 35 034 | 0.6 | −0.3 |
| Hungary | 101 187 | 1.9 | 95 004 | 1.7 | −6.1 |
| Poland | 46 644 | 0.9 | 42 786 | 0.8 | −8.3 |
| Rumania | 6 949 | 0.1 | 6 651 | 0.1 | −4.3 |
| USSR | 272 056 | 5.0 | 362 198 | 6.6 | 33.1 |
| Origin country undetermined | 171 558 | 3.1 | 170 653 | 3.1 | −0.5 |
| | | | | | |
| **Total non-OECD Countries** | 824 724 | 15.1 | 896 280 | 16.3 | 8.7 |
| | | | | | |
| **TOTAL** | 5 456 795 | 100.0 | 5 492 678 | 100.0 | 0.7 |

# YUGOSLAVIA

## ARRIVALS OF FOREIGN TOURISTS AT REGISTERED TOURIST ACCOMMODATION
### (by country of nationality)

| | 1988 | Relative share | 1989 | Relative share | % Variation over 1988 |
|---|---|---|---|---|---|
| Austria | 804 483 | 8.9 | 745 691 | 8.6 | −7.3 |
| Belgium | 162 404 | 1.8 | 169 590 | 2.0 | 4.4 |
| Denmark | 118 055 | 1.3 | 74 933 | 0.9 | −36.5 |
| Finland | 29 492 | 0.3 | 26 974 | 0.3 | −8.5 |
| France | 371 492 | 4.1 | 315 177 | 3.6 | −15.2 |
| Germany | 2 749 303 | 30.5 | 2 462 455 | 28.5 | −10.4 |
| Greece | 162 082 | 1.8 | 164 292 | 1.9 | 1.4 |
| Iceland | 2 531 | 0.0 | 1 587 | 0.0 | −37.3 |
| Ireland | 17 533 | 0.2 | 16 159 | 0.2 | −7.8 |
| Italy | 1 238 164 | 13.7 | 1 424 021 | 16.5 | 15.0 |
| Luxembourg | .. | .. | .. | .. | .. |
| Netherlands | 523 776 | 5.8 | 490 541 | 5.7 | −6.3 |
| Norway | 45 849 | 0.5 | 38 077 | 0.4 | −17.0 |
| Portugal | 8 121 | 0.1 | 5 973 | 0.1 | −26.4 |
| Spain | 74 510 | 0.8 | 80 186 | 0.9 | 7.6 |
| Sweden | 140 677 | 1.6 | 120 735 | 1.4 | −14.2 |
| Switzerland | 126 348 | 1.4 | 121 143 | 1.4 | −4.1 |
| Turkey | 85 793 | 1.0 | 79 629 | 0.9 | −7.2 |
| United Kingdom | 673 495 | 7.5 | 649 875 | 7.5 | −3.5 |
| Other OECD-Europe | .. | .. | .. | .. | .. |
| **Total Europe** | 7 334 108 | 81.3 | 6 987 038 | 80.8 | −4.7 |
| | | | | | |
| Canada | 47 347 | 0.5 | 41 364 | 0.5 | −12.6 |
| United States | 295 419 | 3.3 | 257 978 | 3.0 | −12.7 |
| **Total North America** | 342 766 | 3.8 | 299 342 | 3.5 | −12.7 |
| | | | | | |
| Australia | 29 675 | 0.3 | 32 273 | 0.4 | 8.8 |
| New Zealand | 8 767 | 0.1 | 8 725 | 0.1 | −0.5 |
| Japan | 15 226 | 0.2 | 15 641 | 0.2 | 2.7 |
| **Total Australasia and Japan** | 53 668 | 0.6 | 56 639 | 0.7 | 5.5 |
| | | | | | |
| **Total OECD Countries** | 7 730 542 | 85.7 | 7 343 019 | 84.9 | −5.0 |
| | | | | | |
| Yugoslavia | .. | .. | .. | .. | .. |
| Other European countries | 1 090 010 | 12.1 | 1 108 076 | 12.8 | 1.7 |
| Bulgaria | 16 396 | 0.2 | 24 166 | 0.3 | 47.4 |
| Czechoslovakia | 271 725 | 3.0 | 245 229 | 2.8 | −9.8 |
| Germany (D. R.) | 59 942 | 0.7 | 54 800 | 0.6 | −8.6 |
| Hungary | 200 373 | 2.2 | 201 680 | 2.3 | 0.7 |
| Poland | 164 160 | 1.8 | 113 176 | 1.3 | −31.1 |
| Rumania | 8 967 | 0.1 | 7 865 | 0.1 | −12.3 |
| USSR | 302 928 | 3.4 | 407 926 | 4.7 | 34.7 |
| Origin country undetermined | 197 259 | 2.2 | 192 985 | 2.2 | −2.2 |
| | | | | | |
| **Total non-OECD Countries** | 1 287 269 | 14.3 | 1 301 061 | 15.1 | 1.1 |
| | | | | | |
| **TOTAL** | 9 017 811 | 100.0 | 8 644 080 | 100.0 | −4.1 |

# YUGOSLAVIA

## NIGHTS SPENT BY FOREIGN TOURISTS IN HOTELS
### (by country of nationality)

| | 1988 | Relative share | 1989 | Relative share | % Variation over 1988 |
|---|---|---|---|---|---|
| Austria | 2 626 120 | 9.3 | 2 510 472 | 9.0 | −4.4 |
| Belgium | 564 124 | 2.0 | 653 376 | 2.3 | 15.8 |
| Denmark | 389 952 | 1.4 | 215 115 | 0.8 | −44.8 |
| Finland | 136 514 | 0.5 | 126 862 | 0.5 | −7.1 |
| France | 806 555 | 2.9 | 808 225 | 2.9 | 0.2 |
| Germany | 9 405 947 | 33.3 | 8 781 176 | 31.4 | −6.6 |
| Greece | 186 130 | 0.7 | 214 158 | 0.8 | 15.1 |
| Iceland | 3 998 | 0.0 | 3 079 | 0.0 | −23.0 |
| Ireland | 53 399 | 0.2 | 39 374 | 0.1 | −26.3 |
| Italy | 2 092 067 | 7.4 | 2 628 237 | 9.4 | 25.6 |
| Luxembourg | .. | .. | .. | .. | .. |
| Netherlands | 1 623 471 | 5.7 | 1 766 036 | 6.3 | 8.8 |
| Norway | 156 596 | 0.6 | 117 445 | 0.4 | −25.0 |
| Portugal | 8 275 | 0.0 | 7 325 | 0.0 | −11.5 |
| Spain | 85 597 | 0.3 | 100 303 | 0.4 | 17.2 |
| Sweden | 475 805 | 1.7 | 393 509 | 1.4 | −17.3 |
| Switzerland | 306 403 | 1.1 | 289 026 | 1.0 | −5.7 |
| Turkey | 97 353 | 0.3 | 90 812 | 0.3 | −6.7 |
| United Kingdom | 5 384 427 | 19.1 | 5 300 494 | 19.0 | −1.6 |
| Other OECD-Europe | .. | .. | .. | .. | .. |
| **Total Europe** | 24 402 733 | 86.4 | 24 045 024 | 86.1 | −1.5 |
| | | | | | |
| Canada | 92 554 | 0.3 | 74 387 | 0.3 | −19.6 |
| United States | 517 103 | 1.8 | 463 586 | 1.7 | −10.3 |
| **Total North America** | 609 657 | 2.2 | 537 973 | 1.9 | −11.8 |
| | | | | | |
| Australia | 38 251 | 0.1 | 42 063 | 0.2 | 10.0 |
| New Zealand | 5 792 | 0.0 | 7 124 | 0.0 | 23.0 |
| Japan | 29 252 | 0.1 | 31 175 | 0.1 | 6.6 |
| **Total Australasia and Japan** | 73 295 | 0.3 | 80 362 | 0.3 | 9.6 |
| | | | | | |
| **Total OECD Countries** | 25 085 685 | 88.8 | 24 663 359 | 88.3 | −1.7 |
| | | | | | |
| Yugoslavia | .. | .. | .. | .. | .. |
| Other European countries | 2 786 338 | 9.9 | 2 889 905 | 10.3 | 3.7 |
| Bulgaria | 26 465 | 0.1 | 49 936 | 0.2 | 88.7 |
| Czechoslovakia | 1 332 160 | 4.7 | 1 231 620 | 4.4 | −7.5 |
| Germany (D. R.) | 183 813 | 0.7 | 161 665 | 0.6 | −12.0 |
| Hungary | 304 827 | 1.1 | 296 402 | 1.1 | −2.8 |
| Poland | 184 154 | 0.7 | 191 955 | 0.7 | 4.2 |
| Rumania | 34 454 | 0.1 | 35 732 | 0.1 | 3.7 |
| USSR | 633 628 | 2.2 | 832 999 | 3.0 | 31.5 |
| Origin country undetermined | 374 676 | 1.3 | 377 703 | 1.4 | 0.8 |
| | | | | | |
| **Total non-OECD Countries** | 3 161 014 | 11.2 | 3 267 608 | 11.7 | 3.4 |
| | | | | | |
| **TOTAL** | 28 246 699 | 100.0 | 27 930 967 | 100.0 | −1.1 |

# YUGOSLAVIA

## NIGHTS SPENT BY FOREIGN TOURISTS IN REGISTERED TOURIST ACCOMMODATION
### (by country of nationality)

| | 1988 | Relative share | 1989 | Relative share | % Variation over 1988 |
|---|---|---|---|---|---|
| Austria | 5 113 842 | 9.8 | 4 515 219 | 9.2 | −11.7 |
| Belgium | 994 398 | 1.9 | 1 082 666 | 2.2 | 8.9 |
| Denmark | 809 491 | 1.5 | 505 461 | 1.0 | −37.6 |
| Finland | 173 466 | 0.3 | 160 671 | 0.3 | −7.4 |
| France | 1 222 230 | 2.3 | 1 122 647 | 2.3 | −8.1 |
| Germany | 19 790 249 | 37.8 | 17 530 275 | 35.6 | −11.4 |
| Greece | 217 018 | 0.4 | 235 603 | 0.5 | 8.6 |
| Iceland | 8 461 | 0.0 | 4 662 | 0.0 | −44.9 |
| Ireland | 113 118 | 0.2 | 95 354 | 0.2 | −15.7 |
| Italy | 5 365 700 | 10.2 | 6 144 277 | 12.5 | 14.5 |
| Luxembourg | .. | .. | .. | .. | .. |
| Netherlands | 3 612 166 | 6.9 | 3 485 615 | 7.1 | −3.5 |
| Norway | 334 973 | 0.6 | 248 578 | 0.5 | −25.8 |
| Portugal | 22 656 | 0.0 | 12 613 | 0.0 | −44.3 |
| Spain | 133 049 | 0.3 | 156 001 | 0.3 | 17.3 |
| Sweden | 827 388 | 1.6 | 710 499 | 1.4 | −14.1 |
| Switzerland | 532 704 | 1.0 | 485 003 | 1.0 | −9.0 |
| Turkey | 108 145 | 0.2 | 103 378 | 0.2 | −4.4 |
| United Kingdom | 5 859 928 | 11.2 | 5 879 335 | 12.0 | 0.3 |
| Other OECD-Europe | .. | .. | .. | .. | |
| **Total Europe** | 45 238 982 | 86.4 | 42 477 857 | 86.4 | −6.1 |
| Canada | 126 321 | 0.2 | 101 857 | 0.2 | −19.4 |
| United States | 720 087 | 1.4 | 633 199 | 1.3 | −12.1 |
| **Total North America** | 846 408 | 1.6 | 735 056 | 1.5 | −13.2 |
| Australia | 59 056 | 0.1 | 65 010 | 0.1 | 10.1 |
| New Zealand | 15 199 | 0.0 | 15 239 | 0.0 | 0.3 |
| Japan | 30 749 | 0.1 | 32 917 | 0.1 | 7.1 |
| **Total Australasia and Japan** | 105 004 | 0.2 | 113 166 | 0.2 | 7.8 |
| **Total OECD Countries** | 46 190 394 | 88.2 | 43 326 079 | 88.1 | −6.2 |
| Yugoslavia | .. | .. | .. | .. | |
| Other European countries | 5 681 666 | 10.9 | 5 381 224 | 10.9 | −5.3 |
| Bulgaria | 40 776 | 0.1 | 57 424 | 0.1 | 40.8 |
| Czechoslovakia | 2 441 517 | 4.7 | 2 239 148 | 4.6 | −8.3 |
| Germany (D. R.) | 400 313 | 0.8 | 347 424 | 0.7 | −13.2 |
| Hungary | 865 852 | 1.7 | 931 175 | 1.9 | 7.5 |
| Poland | 872 979 | 1.7 | 540 503 | 1.1 | −38.1 |
| Rumania | 43 011 | 0.1 | 40 679 | 0.1 | −5.4 |
| USSR | 818 675 | 1.6 | 1 043 925 | 2.1 | 27.5 |
| Origin country undetermined | 478 967 | 0.9 | 468 624 | 1.0 | −2.2 |
| **Total non-OECD Countries** | 6 160 633 | 11.8 | 5 849 848 | 11.9 | −5.0 |
| **TOTAL** | 52 351 027 | 100.0 | 49 175 927 | 100.0 | −6.1 |

# WHERE TO OBTAIN OECD PUBLICATIONS – OÙ OBTENIR LES PUBLICATIONS DE L'OCDE

**Argentina – Argentine**
Carlos Hirsch S.R.L.
Galería Güemes, Florida 165, 4° Piso
1333 Buenos Aires    Tel. 30.7122, 331.1787 y 331.2391
Telegram: Hirsch–Baires
Telex: 21112 UAPE–AR. Ref. s/2901
Telefax:(1)331–1787

**Australia – Australie**
D.A. Book (Aust.) Pty. Ltd.
648 Whitehorse Road, P.O.B 163
Mitcham, Victoria 3132    Tel. (03)873.4411
Telex: AA37911 DA BOOK
Telefax: (03)873.5679

**Austria – Autriche**
OECD Publications and Information Centre
4 Simrockstrasse
5300 Bonn (Germany)    Tel. (0228)21.60.45
Telex: 8 86300 Bonn
Telefax: (0228)26.11.04

Gerold & Co.
Graben 31
Wien I    Tel. (0222)533.50.14

**Belgium – Belgique**
Jean De Lannoy
Avenue du Roi 202
B–1060 Bruxelles    Tel. (02)538.51.69/538.08.41
Telex: 63220    Telefax: (02) 538.08.41

**Canada**
Renouf Publishing Company Ltd.
1294 Algoma Road
Ottawa, ON K1B 3W8    Tel. (613)741.4333
Telex: 053–4783    Telefax: (613)741.5439
Stores:
61 Sparks Street
Ottawa, ON K1P 5R1    Tel. (613)238.8985
211 Yonge Street
Toronto, ON M5B 1M4    Tel. (416)363.3171

Federal Publications
165 University Avenue
Toronto, ON M5H 3B8    Tel. (416)581.1552
Telefax: (416)581.1743

Les Publications Fédérales
1185 rue de l'Université
Montréal, PQ H3B 3A7    Tel.(514)954–1633

Les Éditions La Liberté Inc.
3020 Chemin Sainte–Foy
Sainte–Foy, PQ G1X 3V6    Tel. (418)658.3763
    Telefax: (418)658.3763

**Denmark – Danemark**
Munksgaard Export and Subscription Service
35, Norre Sogade, P.O. Box 2148
DK–1016 Kobenhavn K    Tel. (45 33)12.85.70
Telex: 19431 MUNKS DK    Telefax: (45 33)12.93.87

**Finland – Finlande**
Akateeminen Kirjakauppa
Keskuskatu 1, P.O. Box 128
00100 Helsinki    Tel. (358 0)12141
Telex: 125080    Telefax: (358 0)121.4441

**France**
OECD/OCDE
Mail Orders/Commandes par correspondance:
2 rue André–Pascal
75775 Paris Cedex 16    Tel. (1)45.24.82.00
Bookshop/Librairie:
33, rue Octave–Feuillet
75016 Paris    Tel. (1)45.24.81.67
    (1)45.24.81.81
Telex: 620 160 OCDE
Telefax: (33–1)45.24.85.00

Librairie de l'Université
12a, rue Nazareth
13602 Aix–en–Provence    Tel. 42.26.18.08

**Germany – Allemagne**
OECD Publications and Information Centre
Schedestrasse 7
5300 Bonn 1    Tel. (0228)21.60.45
Telefax: (0228)26.11.04

**Greece – Grèce**
Librairie Kauffmann
28 rue du Stade
105 64 Athens    Tel. 322.21.60
Telex: 218187 LIKA Gr

**Hong Kong**
Swindon Book Co. Ltd.
13 – 15 Lock Road
Kowloon, Hongkong    Tel. 366 80 31
Telex: 50 441 SWIN HX
Telefax: 739 49 75

**Iceland – Islande**
Mál Mog Menning
Laugavegi 18, Pósthólf 392
121 Reykjavik    Tel. 15199/24240

**India – Inde**
Oxford Book and Stationery Co.
Scindia House
New Delhi 110001    Tel. 331.5896/5308
Telex: 31 61990 AM IN
Telex: (11)332.5993
17 Park Street
Calcutta 700016    Tel. 240832

**Indonesia – Indonésie**
Pdii–Lipi
P.O. Box 269/JKSMG/88
Jakarta 12790    Tel. 583467
Telex: 62 875

**Ireland – Irlande**
TDC Publishers – Library Suppliers
12 North Frederick Street
Dublin 1    Tel. 744835/749677
Telex: 33530 TDCP EI   Telefax : 748416

**Italy – Italie**
Libreria Commissionaria Sansoni
Via Benedetto Fortini, 120/10
Casella Post. 552
50125 Firenze    Tel. (055)645415
Telex: 570466    Telefax: (39.55)641257
Via Bartolini 29
20155 Milano    Tel. 365083
La diffusione delle pubblicazioni OCSE viene assicurata dalle
principali librerie ed anche da:
Editrice e Libreria Herder
Piazza Montecitorio 120
00186 Roma    Tel. 679.4628
Telex: NATEL I 621427

Libreria Hoepli
Via Hoepli 5
20121 Milano    Tel. 865446
Telex: 31.33.95  Telefax: (39.2)805.2886

Libreria Scientifica
Dott. Lucio de Biasio "Aeiou"
Via Meravigli 16
20123 Milano    Tel. 807679
Telefax: 800175

**Japan– Japon**
OECD Publications and Information Centre
Landic Akasaka Building
2–3–4 Akasaka, Minato–ku
Tokyo 107    Tel. 586.2016
Telefax: (81.3)584.7929

**Korea – Corée**
Kyobo Book Centre Co. Ltd.
P.O. Box 1658, Kwang Hwa Moon
Seoul    Tel. (REP)730.78.91
Telefax: 735.0030

**Malaysia/Singapore – Malaisie/Singapour**
University of Malaya Co–operative Bookshop Ltd.
P.O. Box 1127, Jalan Pantaí Baru 59100
Kuala Lumpur
Malaysia    Tel. 756.5000/756.5425
Telefax: 757.3661

Information Publications Pte. Ltd.
Pei–Fu Industrial Building
24 New Industrial Road No. 02–06
Singapore 1953    Tel. 283.1786/283.1798
Telefax: 284.8875

**Netherlands – Pays–Bas**
SDU Uitgeverij
Christoffel Plantijnstraat 2
Postbus 20014
2500 EA's–Gravenhage    Tel. (070 3)78.99.11
Voor bestellingen:    Tel. (070 3)78.98.80
Telex: 32486 stdru    Telefax: (070 3)47.63.51

**New Zealand – Nouvelle–Zélande**
Government Printing Office
Customer Services
33 The Esplanade – P.O. Box 38–900
Petone, Wellington
Tel. (04) 685–555    Telefax: (04)685–333

**Norway – Norvège**
Narvesen Info Center – NIC
Bertrand Narvesens vei 2
P.O. Box 6125 Etterstad
0602 Oslo 6    Tel. (02)57.33.00
Telex: 79668 NIC N    Telefax: (02)68.19.01

**Pakistan**
Mirza Book Agency
65 Shahrah Quaid–E–Azam
Lahore 3    Tel. 66839
Telex: 44886 UBL PK. Attn: MIRZA BK

**Portugal**
Livraria Portugal
Rua do Carmo 70–74
Apart. 2681
1117 Lisboa Codex    Tel. 347.49.82/3/4/5
Telefax: 37 02 64

**Singapore/Malaysia – Singapour/Malaisie**
See "Malaysia/Singapore – "Voir "Malaisie/Singapour"

**Spain – Espagne**
Mundi–Prensa Libros S.A.
Castelló 37, Apartado 1223
Madrid 28001    Tel. (91) 431.33.99
Telex: 49370 MPLI    Telefax: 575 39 98
Libreria Internacional AEDOS
Consejo de Ciento 391
08009 –Barcelona    Tel. (93) 301–86–15
Telefax: (93) 317–01–41

**Sweden – Suède**
Fritzes Fackboksföretaget
Box 16356, S 103 27 STH
Regeringsgatan 12
DS Stockholm    Tel. (08)23.89.00
Telex: 12387  Telefax: (08)20.50.21
Subscription Agency/Abonnements:
Wennergren–Williams AB
Box 30004
104 25 Stockholm    Tel. (08)54.12.00
Telex: 19937  Telefax: (08)50.82.86

**Switzerland – Suisse**
OECD Publications and Information Centre
Schedestrasse 7
5300 Bonn 1    Tel. (0228)21.60.45
Telefax: (0228)26.11.04

Librairie Payot
6 rue Grenus
1211 Genève 11    Tel. (022)731.89.50
Telex: 28356
Subscription Agency – Service des Abonnements
4 place Pépinet – BP 3312
1002 Lausanne    Tel. (021)341.33.31
Telefax: (021)341.33.45
Maditec S.A.
Ch. des Palettes 4
1020 Renens/Lausanne    Tel. (021)635.08.65
Telefax: (021)635.07.80
United Nations Bookshop/Librairie des Nations–Unies
Palais des Nations
1211 Genève 10    Tel. (022)734.60.11 (ext. 48.72)
Telex: 289696 (Attn: Sales)
Telefax: (022)733.98.79

**Taiwan – Formose**
Good Faith Worldwide Int'l. Co. Ltd.
9th Floor, No. 118, Sec. 2
Chung Hsiao E. Road
Taipei    Tel. 391.7396/391.7397
Telefax: (02) 394.9176

**Thailand – Thaïlande**
Suksit Siam Co. Ltd.
1715 Rama IV Road, Samyan
Bangkok 5    Tel. 251.1630

**Turkey – Turquie**
Kültur Yayinlari Is–Türk Ltd. Sti.
Atatürk Bulvari No. 191/Kat. 21
Kavaklidere/Ankara    Tel. 25.07.60
Dolmabahce Cad. No. 29
Besiktas/Istanbul    Tel. 160.71.88
Telex: 43482B

**United Kingdom – Royaume–Uni**
HMSO
Gen. enquiries    Tel. (071) 873 0011
Postal orders only:
P.O. Box 276, London SW8 5DT
Personal Callers HMSO Bookshop
49 High Holborn, London WC1V 6HB
Telex: 297138  Telefax: 071 873 8463
Branches at: Belfast, Birmingham, Bristol, Edinburgh, Manchester

**United States – États–Unis**
OECD Publications and Information Centre
2001 L Street N.W., Suite 700
Washington, D.C. 20036–4095    Tel. (202)785.6323
Telefax: (202)785.0350

**Venezuela**
Libreria del Este
Avda F. Miranda 52, Aptdo. 60337
Edificio Galipán
Caracas 106    Tel. 951.1705/951.2307/951.1297
Telegram: Libreste Caracas

**Yugoslavia – Yougoslavie**
Jugoslovenska Knjiga
Knez Mihajlova 2, P.O. Box 36
Beograd    Tel. 621.992
Telex: 12466 jk bgd

Orders and inquiries from countries where Distributors have
not yet been appointed should be sent to: OECD Publications
Service, 2 rue André–Pascal, 75775 Paris Cedex 16, France.
Les commandes provenant de pays où l'OCDE n'a pas encore
désigné de distributeur devraient être adressées à : OCDE,
Service des Publications, 2, rue André–Pascal, 75775 Paris
Cedex 16, France.

OECD PUBLICATIONS, 2, rue André-Pascal, 75775 PARIS CEDEX 16
PRINTED IN FRANCE
(78 90 01 1) ISBN 92-64-13424-7 - No. 45297 1990
ISSN 0256-7598